IRAN'S GRAND STRATEGY

IRAN'S GRAND STRATEGY

A POLITICAL HISTORY

VALI NASR

PRINCETON UNIVERSITY PRESS

PRINCETON & OXFORD

Published by Princeton University Press

41 William Street, Princeton, New Jersey 08540
99 Banbury Road, Oxford OX2 6JX
press.princeton.edu

All Rights Reserved

GPSR Authorized Representative: Easy Access System Europe - Mustamäe tee 50, 10621 Tallinn, Estonia, gpsr.requests@easproject.com

Library of Congress Cataloging-in-Publication Data

Names: Nasr, Seyyed Vali Reza, 1960– author.
Title: Iran's grand strategy : a political history / Vali Nasr.
Description: Princeton : Princeton University Press, [2025] |
    Includes bibliographical references and index.
Identifiers: LCCN 2024036105 (print) | LCCN 2024036106 (ebook) |
    ISBN 9780691268927 | ISBN 9780691268934 (ebook)
Subjects: LCSH: National security—Iran—History—20th century. | National
    security—Iran—History—21st century. | Iran—Foreign relations—1979–1997. |
    Iran—Foreign relations—1997– | Iran—Politics and government—1979–1997. |
    Iran—Politics and government—1997– | BISAC: HISTORY / Middle East / Iran |
    POLITICAL SCIENCE / History & Theory
Classification: LCC DS318.83 .N39 2025 (print) | LCC DS318.83 (ebook) |
    DDC 327.55009/04—dc23/eng/20241216
LC record available at https://lccn.loc.gov/2024036105
LC ebook record available at https://lccn.loc.gov/2024036106

British Library Cataloging-in-Publication Data is available

Editorial: Fred Appel and James Collier
Production Editorial: Jaden Young
Text and Jacket/Cover Design: Karl Spurzem
Production: Erin Suydam
Publicity: Kate Hensley and Kathryn Stevens
Copyeditor: Cindy Milstein

This book has been composed in Arno and Scala Pro

Printed in the United States of America

10 9 8 7 6 5 4 3 2 1

To Iranians, their abundant love for their homeland and their unshakable faith in its destiny. May they find lasting peace and prosperity, and Iran finds its rightful place in the world.

You may not be interested in war, but war is interested in you.

—MICHAEL WALZER, *JUST AND UNJUST WARS:*
A MORAL ARGUMENT WITH HISTORICAL ILLUSTRATIONS

Getting history wrong is part of being a nation.

—ERNEST RENAN, *QU'EST CE QU'UNE NATION*
(*WHAT IS A NATION*)

CONTENTS

A NOTE ABOUT THE BOOK

This book is not a comprehensive political history of the Islamic Republic of Iran, nor does it contend that exploring the role of national security in statecraft and the evolution of its grand strategy should come at the expense of other salient social and political factors that have shaped Iran since 1979. Rather, this book focuses on the origins and development of that strategy over the past four and half decades, shaping Iran's international outlook and foreign policy, and organizing state, society, and economy to realize its national aims.

The use of the terms "national security" or "strategy" in this book do not imply that there has always been a clearly argued set of documents that have meticulously laid out plans of action. That said, there are debates among the ruling class, scholars, and opinion makers, and then sustained decision-making, that have coalesced into discernible plans of action.

This book draws on excellent scholarship in English and Persian on Iran's foreign relations and domestic developments, which have influenced or reflect its national security concerns as defined and debated by Iranians themselves. More so, the narrative relies heavily on conversations with contemporary decision-makers, activists, and opinion leaders as well as published oral histories, memoirs, and interviews—especially political and war memoirs that have been published in Iran—and public debates over foreign affairs in various academic and public forums and mass media in Iran. The aim is to capture the logic, assumptions, and evolution of Iran's strategic thinking as argued by Iranians themselves. The book inevitably renders judgment on the sagacity of that thinking, but I have tried to make sure that does not overshadow the main aim of the book.

For the reader's sake, throughout the text I have transliterated Persian names, place-names, and technical terms in a simplified form reflecting their common pronunciation in Persian in lieu of an academic system that would capture how they are spelled in Persian. When applicable, I have used the common transliteration of names or terms that have gained universal currency in English. The only exception to these rules is Persian names and terms that appear in direct quotations or titles of published works in English. Finally, the titles of primary and secondary Persian sources appear in only their English translation in the notes. Full Persian citations are provided in the bibliography.

August 30, 2024

ACKNOWLEDGMENTS

I have incurred many debts in writing this book. Friends, colleagues, and students as well as current and former government officials, scholars, activists, and thought leaders from Iran as well as in Europe, the Middle East, and the United States listened to my ideas, challenged them, honed them, and shared their own impressions and reminiscences. I am grateful for their friendship and erudition. Some have asked to remain anonymous, and some I have chosen not to name to protect their privacy and security.

I am deeply thankful to Gholam Reza Afkhami, Hasan Ahmadian, Dlawar Ala'Aldeen, Farhad Alaaldin, Abbas Amanat, Mohammad Ataie, Kayhan Barzegar, Hal Brands, Zbigniew Brzezinski, Gholamali Chegenizadeh, Houchang Chehabi, Suzanne DiMaggio, Abdol-Rasool Divsallar, Lukman Faily, Maria Fantappe, Nasser Hadian, Stephen Heintz, Mustafa Al-Kadhimi, Hadi Kahalzadeh, Bijan Khajepour, Stephen Kotkin, Adnan Mazarei, Saad Mohseni, Stephen Mull, Yukio Okamoto, Tom Pickering, Sergei Radchencko, Arash Reisinezhad, Barnett Rubin, Amrallah Saleh, Djavad Salehi-Isfahani, Barham Salih, Muhammad Al-Shummary, Randa Slim, Ali Vaez, Sanam Vakil, Frank Wisner, and Fareed Yasseen for their valuable insights and suggestions.

The Rethinking Iran Initiative at the School of Advanced International Studies of Johns Hopkins University has been an intellectual home and provided me with indispensable administrative support at various stages of this project. I am grateful to Narges Bajoghli and the initiative's dedicated staff for their friendship and help in making this book possible, and a special note of thanks to Francis Najafi for his support of the initiative's work.

Narges Bajoghli, Bilal Baloch, Ali Gheissari, and Kevan Harris read this book in manuscript form and made valuable suggestions. I am deeply grateful for their friendship and erudition. Vahid Abedini was an indispensable fount of knowledge. He pointed me to important sources and helped me navigate the intricacies of contemporary Iranian politics. I am also grateful to the anonymous reviewers who read the manuscript for Princeton University Press. Their recommendations have greatly improved the structure and arguments of the book.

Ben Platt did an excellent job editing the text and improving its structure and flow. The outcome reflects his mastery. A special note of thanks to Cindy Milstein for their excellent copyediting of the final draft, Kathleen Strattan for preparing the index, and David Campbell, James Collier, and Jaden Young and the team members at Princeton University Press for their great work in producing this book. My editor, Fred Appel, adeptly guided this project in its inception. I am grateful for his sage advice, patience, and support as I honed my arguments and worked through various drafts.

Last but by no means least, my deepest gratitude is reserved for my family, for their love, patience, and support as I labored through the research and writing of this book.

IRAN'S GRAND STRATEGY

Introduction

On October 7, 2023, the Palestinian group Hamas launched an audacious attack on Israeli towns and kibbutzim north of the Gaza Strip, killing some twelve hundred Israelis and taking over two hundred hostages. Israel was shocked by the depravity and scale of the attack, and embarrassed by how easily Hamas outwitted its intelligence and breached its defensive wall to force the Palestinian issue back onto center stage. Israel reacted with a ferocious assault on the Gaza Strip. The ravages of the ensuing war and the humanitarian catastrophe that it unleashed, coupled with prospects of, first, war between Israel and Hezbollah, and then Israel and Iran, was a watershed moment for the Middle East. The United States' hope for a lasting Arab-Israeli peace as the foundation for regional economic integration and a trade corridor stretching from the Arabian Sea to the Mediterranean was replaced by worries over imminent regional conflagration.

This was the latest chapter in the decades-long Israeli-Palestinian conflict, but also the bold manifestation of the ascendance of the Axis of Resistance, a regionwide revisionist political and military alliance of like-minded militias stretching from Lebanon through Syria, Palestinian territories, Iraq, and Yemen, formed and backed by Iran, and anchored in the same goal of defying America and defeating Israel.[1] The axis was demonstrating its power and reach along with its ability to upend America's plans for the region. This manifested a strategy that Iran has honed and doggedly pursued for decades to confront the United States and assert its influence in the region.

Hamas was part of the Axis of Resistance and shared Iran's strategic objectives. Iran and its close ally, Lebanon's Hezbollah, had trained and funded Hamas's military wing—and its sister organization, the

Palestinian Islamic Jihad—boosting its intelligence and operational capabilities. Once Israel embarked on its war in Gaza, Iran and other axis members came to Hamas's aid. They mobilized their military, political, and communications networks across the region, launching drone and missile attacks on Israel from Lebanon as well as US forces in Iraq and Syria, and immobilizing maritime trade in the Red Sea from their perch in Yemen. They displayed an uncanny ability to translate their shared strategic objective of combating Israel and the United States into a coordinated but flexible region-wide response. Israel retaliated against Hezbollah, and then in a show of force Israel attacked Iran's consulate in Syria in April 2024. Iran responded with a brazen attack on Israel with hundreds of drones and missiles, which led in turn to an Israeli attack on a military base in Iran. Then in July Israel assassinated the head of Hamas in Tehran and two months later killed Hezbollah's chief in Beirut. Iran again reacted with a barrage of missiles aimed at Israel. These exchanges brought the region to the verge of an all-out war. The axis had thus announced itself as a formidable regional force. That only increased the specter of direct confrontation between Iran and Israel, which would inevitably entangle the United States in broader conflict. Not long after, in October 2024, Israel invaded Lebanon to destroy Hezbollah and thus Iran's footprint in the Levant. Awaiting a conflagration, the Middle East's security once again sat on a knife's edge.

The West was surprised by the capabilities of the axis, and was clearly unaware of its intent and plan of action. Its understanding of Iran's strategic calculations is hopelessly inadequate and dangerously outdated. The West still looks at Iran through the prism of the 1979 Revolution, and the central role that religion and the clergy played in it. It is true that revolutionary ideology defined the character of the Islamic Republic during its formative years, and the values and memory of the revolution remain embedded in Iran's statecraft, but as this book will make apparent, the revolution no longer explains Iran's actions on the world stage. In fact, Iran's policies during the Gaza war should convince us that the time that Iran's actions could be neatly explained by Islamic ideology or intent to export its revolution is in the past. Rather than confirm the caricature image of an archaic theocracy begrudging modernity and seething at the West, the war in Gaza made it clear that Iran today sees itself as the inspiration for a global movement of resistance to the United States—a reinvocation of the familiar anti-imperialism and anticolonialism ideals of the latter part of the twentieth century—and seeks to organize the Middle East around it. To achieve this aim, Iran is acting on assumptions and calculations that reflect historical experiences, security imperatives, and great power ambitions.

The Islamic Republic has long moved past its revolutionary beginnings and evolved into a prototypical nation-state. Islam remains the language of Iran's politics, and an instrument in the hands of its political class and military leaders to realize political and economic interests at home and define national interest abroad, but those aims are now secular in nature. Over the past four and a half decades, Iran has embraced a particular vision of national security that was defined in broad brush by the Islamic Republic's two supreme leaders who have led the country since the revolution, Ayatollahs Ruhollah Khomeini and Ali Khamenei. That vision is inimical to the United States, and seeks Iran's security and greatness in keeping US influence at bay. In practice, this vision has found manifestation in the evolution of the grand strategy that has been guiding Iran's statecraft. This book will tell the story of this grand strategy. It will show that the authoritarian nature of the Islamic Republic notwithstanding, it is strategic considerations rather than managing dissent and domestic stability that is front of mind for Iran's rulers.

Consider that the October 7 attack and the Gaza war came barely a year after popular unrest swept across Iran, seriously challenging the Islamic Republic's hold over the country. In September 2022, thousands of Iranians had taken to the streets to protest the death of a young woman, Mahsa Amini, at the hands of the morality police who enforce observation of the hijab—head covering for women. Almost immediately, the protests evolved into a direct challenge to the core ideological foundations of the Islamic Republic as women across Iran shed their scarves, burned them in public, and symbolically cut their hair to decry the imposition of religious strictures on individuals, society, and politics by law and brute force. The protests soon attracted a broader cross section of political dissent in urban areas, and most intensely in ethnic minority regions of Baluchistan and Kurdistan. These protests were an undeniable revolt against the domination of religious strictures over society and politics, the theocratic underpinnings of the Islamic Republic, and its harsh authoritarianism and mismanagement of the economy. For many Iranians and more so observers in the West, this was, at last, a secular and liberal backlash against Islamic rule in Iran, and the authoritarian imposition of its writ on society.

In the West these two events, spanning 2022 to 2023, were two sides of the same coin. Iran's incessant confrontation with the West and aggressive regional actions were the reason why the Islamic Republic was facing anger at home. Iran's policies, its critics surmised, had isolated it in the region and the world, and subjected its economy to severe sanctions, impoverishing its population, which was no longer willing to assume the cost of the grand strategic schemes that its leaders were pursuing. Was this not obvious to the guardians of the Islamic Republic that their strategy of defiance and confrontation was exacting an exorbitant cost on their population, loosening their hold over power? If the October 7 attack and its aftermath was evidence, that was not the conclusion that Iran's rulers drew from the popular revolt of September 2022.

The country's supreme leader, Ayatollah Khamenei, saw that revolt not as a sign of the failure of Iran's foreign policy but rather its success. The protests were a plot hatched by Iran's enemies exactly because Iran was winning, getting closer to its goals.[2] In dozens of interviews and speeches after the protests started as well as after calm returned, the state's leader chose not to focus on the inviolability of the religious strictures that the protesters had challenged or talk about the country's dire economic situation. In fact, references to Islam and its laws were conspicuously scant in his remarks. Instead, he warned of a concerted attack on Iran's national security. Observers in the West are quick to dismiss such references to foreign intrigue, which are also echoed by leaders such as Russia's Vladimir Putin or Turkey's Recep Erdogan, as cynical ploys to delegitimize dissent. But these turns to protecting the nation against foreign intrigue, especially during crises, reflect the Iranian leadership's deeply held views, and the prism through which they see and react to events.

In his comments, Khamenei carefully analyzed the protests as a conspiracy, meticulously planned and instigated by the United States and its allies to weaken Iran, engineer regime change, and even break up the country. In a tweet in September 2023, on the eve of the first anniversary of the uprising, he accused the United States of forming a "Crisis Group" dedicated to destabilizing other countries, "including Iran." The United States, he tweeted, "wished to create crises in Iran by aggravating ethnic [and] religious differences and using the issue of gender and women. That is [the] US's plan."[3] Looking back at the protests in a 2024 speech, he asserted that resistance to the religious and legally mandated observation of the hijab is a "foreign project" and "imposed crisis."[4] These were clarion calls to the country's security forces, making it clear to them that what they faced on the streets was not a battle between religion and secularism, and dictatorship and democracy, but instead a struggle between Iran and the United States. Stability and order demanded foiling foreign intrigue.

The defense of the hijab, therefore, has become a matter of shoring up state authority, and the harsh measures used to suppress the protests and punish those who participated in them have been justified not to protect Islamic rules but rather to defend the homeland. In fact, the protests achieved a notable victory in that observance of the hijab grew lax after the 2022 protests as throngs of women have since routinely appeared in public without head coverings. But the authorities do not display the same resigned attitude when it came to vigilance against a perceived foreign hand in destabilizing Iran.

Khamenei tells rapt audiences of security officials, politicians, and clerics that Iran is close to achieving its strategic goals, asserting, "It has climbed the foothills and is nearing the mountain peak."[5] It must remain steadfast and not tire of the journey. The closer it gets to the summit, the more America will strive to block its way. He sees the October 7 attacks and the war in Gaza through this lens; the crisis before America and Israel are evidence that Iran is getting closer to the peak. The imbroglio has taken away Israel's aura of invincibility and put America on its heels in the region and more broadly the Global South. It has also cast Iran and its Axis of Resistance as veritable regional power brokers.

But what lies at the peak that Khamenei speaks of? What is the goal that Iran seeks? In 2005, Khamenei charged the National Expediency Council (Majles-e Tashkhis-e Maslahat-e Nezam), consisting of senior state leaders, with producing a strategic vision for the Islamic Republic. The result, "The Vision for Islamic Republic of Iran in the Horizon of 2025" ("Cheshmandaz-e Jomhouri Eslami Iran Dar Ofoq-e 1404"), was an Iranian version of similar multidecade "visions" that have proliferated across the developing South. Iran's Vision 2025 likewise called for industrialization and economic growth, cultural, educational, and technological advancement, and building a modern Islamic state.[6] The goal this vision set before Iran was to become the premier political, economic, scientific, and technological power in West Asia.

Four years later, in March 2009, in a speech to mark the start of the fourth decade of the revolution, Khamenei confirmed the commitment to this vision, stating that the coming decade would be one of "progress, development, and justice." In that speech, he also identified the United States as the main obstacle to realizing those goals.[7]

The vision embedded regional ambitions in national ones, but as Khamenei admitted, it also revealed the fundamental contradiction in pursuing a vision of development in tandem with insisting on confrontation with the West. Faced with this dilemma, Iran's rulers have argued that it is the United States that is at war with Iran, intent on blocking its path to the realization of its goal with economic sanctions and domestic unrest, and by containing its regional influence. Iran must overcome that challenge through resistance—economic, political, and military. Iran has not progressed on the goals of its Vision 2025 as planned, but it has invested considerably more in resisting America. That resistance, it expects, will protect it against US pressure, but also give it leverage, time, and space to continue to pursue its national objectives.

Twenty years on, the goals that Vision 2025 had in mind are moving further from Iran's grasp. Although Iran's rulers do not openly acknowledge the costs inherent in resisting the West, the price that the country is paying for pursuing it is undeniable. So why stay on this course, especially if it is true that behind the veneer of revolutionary legacy and

Islamic ideology, today's Islamic Republic functions as a modern legal-rational nation-state?

States have interests, but it is state leaders who interpret them and act on them.[8] It is a country's leadership that defines what is essential to national security, where it begins and ends, and how to pursue it.[9] That conception then informs their grand visions, guides their quotidian actions, and explains their patterns of behavior.[10] Iran's conception of national security has evolved since 1979 around a distinct and deeply held view of national interest and national security, rooted in both recent and not-so-recent history—legacies of colonialism and national humiliation, loss of territory and foreign intrigue, and then war with Iraq and confrontation with the United States. That conception of national security is now ensconced in the worldview of Iran's leaders, guiding their defiant actions on the world stage. Those actions are not ideological expressions or random acts of violence devoid of direction; rather, they reflect a strategy and plan of action to execute it. It is appropriate to question the wisdom of that strategy, and that has become ubiquitous in public debates within Iran. That does not, however, obviate the fact that there are assumptions, a line of reasoning, and a particular reading of history that account for Iran's worldview and actions.

...

In 2015, a senior Iranian official, on a visit to the United Nations in New York City, met with former US Secretary of State Henry Kissinger. Reflecting on his own firsthand experiences with political transitions in the Soviet Union and China at the end of the Cold War, Kissinger probed his Iranian guest on when it might be that Iran would similarly abandon its revolutionary ideology and embrace pragmatism, as Kissinger had once summed up in an article: when would Iran cease being a cause and act as a nation-state—and when would Iran bury the hatchet with the United States.[11]

That pointed the conversation to philosopher Immanuel Kant and his theory of "perpetual peace," which stipulates that conflict between states ends when the protagonists have exhausted themselves with conflict, and are no longer willing to spend blood and treasure for even an iota more of gain in influence or territory. It is only then, Kant had argued, that states will see greater value in peace than in war. Had Iran reached that point of exhaustion, Kissinger wondered? Could it see Kant's reasoning through the fog of its ideology?

Yet Kissinger was surprised that his Iranian interlocutor had already mastered Kant. (In fact, he had translated the German philosopher into Persian.) When would the *United States* exhaust itself, wondered his Iranian interlocutor? When would *it* see reason and change course in the Middle East? Iran, he emphasized, was not pursuing a religious vision but rather a grand strategy that sought security by exhausting America so that it would quit the Middle East and leave Iran alone. For Iran, greatness would come despite the United States, not by hitching its wagon to its regional agenda. The United States will not accept the Islamic Republic and the revolution that produced it. Rather than either surrender to American demands or abandon its ambitions, Iran has opted to resist the United States as a necessary step to achieving its goals, expecting that its path will be meandering and fraught with conflicts as well as setbacks, but moving forward nevertheless.

On that day in 2015, it was not Islamic ideology but rather Kant that sat between American and Iranian statesmen as they pondered what comes next. According to this Iranian statesman, Iran was *not* a cause, and Iran's actions on the world stage were *not* a matter of ideology. Instead, Iran's foreign policy was calculated and pragmatic, a matter of national security: working to compel the United States to abandon its own cause against Iran and its containment of the country.

That exchange reveals the mindset at play in Tehran, along with its logic, aims, and expectations—as flawed as they may be. It reflects a strategic calculus—one that assumes that by applying sustained pressure, American plans for the Middle East will come to naught, and Washington will tire of containing Iran and shift course.

Fast-forward a decade, and it has been the United States—and not Iran—that is showing signs of exhaustion. After all, three consecutive American presidents starting with President Barack Obama have made clear America's wish to reduce its commitment to the Middle East, whether to pivot to Asia or focus on Russia—although that may well change in the face of recurring crises in the region. Iran has played its part, and its leaders believe a big part, in bringing about the exhaustion that has led America to shift its gaze away from the region. Iran's grand strategy, then—and not its ideological fervor—has yielded this unexpected success.

Why and when did the Islamic Republic come to this grand strategy? How and why has it changed over the course of the past four decades? If the West is to contend with Iran, then it must move past its shibboleths about the country in order to understand what Iran is after and why. Only then can it ponder about how it influences how Iran will evolve in the future.

The following chapters will trace the origins and development of Iran's grand strategy, its core assumptions and allure, and how it has evolved over the past four decades to shape Iran and its relations with the West. Most of all, this book reveals how Iran's strategy—no matter how we may judge it—is an overlooked influence in shaping Iran's own society and politics—the failure of reform, recrudescence of hard-line conservative forces, growing imbalance in civil-military relations, and country's peculiar political economy.

Every state's grand vision could reflect hubris. That is true of Iran also, but to understand its actions abroad as well as its policies at home, we must understand that there is reasoning and calculation behind Iran's choices even when its behavior appears irrational and self-defeating.[12] Its drive to amass power and its strategy to assert its position is directed at securing its homeland against internal chaos and foreign intrigue. It is that concern, be it real or illusory, that shapes the assumptions, logic, and intent of Iran's strategy, and how and why the country has latched onto certain conceptions of national interest and national security.[13]

The Islamic Republic is the product of a revolution inspired by Islamic ideology. Key events since the 1979 Revolution have left a deep impression on the country's leaders, and as such, also account for how state and society have been organized. Between 1979 and 1989, Iran was transformed by the tumultuous upheaval of a great revolution, hostage crisis with the United States, brutal eight-year war with Iraq, and further confrontation with the United States in Lebanon. All of these early experiences combined to shape how the revolution's leadership saw external threats and devised strategies to confront them. It is in interpreting the lessons of those events and addressing the strategic vulnerabilities that they exposed that Iran conceived the strategic objectives of its statecraft. It was in that context that Iran embraced the ideas of "sacred defense" and "resistance," describing the goals of defense and deterrence.

Iran's rulers concluded then that they failed to win their war with Iraq because Western powers, their Arab allies, and international organizations had all sided with Iraq. Still, Iran had pulled itself up by its own bootstraps to survive the war. Undaunted by the outcome, those who led and fought in the war emerged from it with confidence and a belief in their own efficacy. They did not want another costly war and, given that, going forward, Iran must stand on its own two feet to win security and grandeur by resisting and defying the Western-led international order. It must organize state and society around this goal, and build its economy and defense by going around international economic sanctions. This became the bedrock of Iran's grand strategy.

That national security conception also builds on Iran's historical experiences, and how the country's collective memory has internalized them into its anxieties and ambitions—fear of foreign interference, loss of sovereignty, chaos, and disintegration, but also great power status deserving of an ancient civilization—yet its distinct characteristics reflect the imprint of what has come to pass after the 1979 Revolution.

The goal of resistance would in the decades that followed the revolution became the country's grand strategy as Iran focused on the United States as the singular threat to its national security. This became especially true after 9/11, the US invasion of Iraq in 2003, onset of a nuclear standoff between Iran and the West, and regional impact of the Arab Spring. It was during that long decade between 2001 and 2011 that the national security conception formed in the first decade of the revolution was expanded into a grand strategy of resistance. Iran's nuclear program or its regional strategy of "forward defense"—to confront America's superior military power through asymmetrical means and extend Iran's defense parameter inside the Arab world—are all expressions of this broader grand strategy.

These ideas are more than reactions to specific threats and not just military doctrines. They are grand strategic visions, and organizing principles for state and society, that are foundational to the Islamic Republic's conception of itself and its place in the world. They have effectively shaped the Islamic Republic, its politics, economy, and social institutions. This book will trace the evolution of this grand strategy along with its roots, assumptions, and evolution.

Iran's security vulnerabilities as well as experiences with war, occupation, and imperialism are by no means unique. But how every nation reacts to those challenges is unique to it. Geography, culture, and most important, history loom large on those reactions. This is not to suggest that there is a teleology at play or that the past is a prologue to the future but instead that the trajectory that Iran has embarked on has to be understood against the background of the country's historical memory.

Writer Mark Twain famously said, "History does not repeat itself, but it often rhymes." Just as the foreign policy of the young Soviet Union could not help but remember the invasions of Napoleon and the might of Peter the Great, so too has the Islamic Republic's strategic outlook been informed by, and fed on, the collective memory of invasions, near disintegration, and humiliating imperialist interventions throughout the nineteenth and twentieth centuries. Those experiences have formed a broad consensus on the causes and implications of such critical turning points as the Constitutional Revolution of 1905–6 or military coup of 1953. The founder of the Islamic Republic experienced firsthand the First and Second World Wars, occupation of Iran by the Allies, and coup of 1953.

The monarchy that the revolution toppled had sought to strengthen and empower Iran through economic development and social modernization, and by harnessing the benefits of a close alliance with the West. The Islamic Republic that the revolution wrought has looked for strength and grandeur in resistance to the West even at great economic cost to the country. Yet as the following chapters will show, there are similarities and in some areas continuities between these two visions, and unsurprisingly, they are juxtaposed in public debates in Iran today. The history that preceded the Islamic Republic has become the context and foil for how it wants to shape the future.

CHAPTER 1

Loom of History

In his popular book *Iran and Its Loneliness,* first published in 1997, eminent Iranian historian Mohammad Ali Eslami Nodoushan argued that a feeling of singularity (uniqueness) is foundational to Iranian national consciousness. Being distinct by virtue of civilizational qualities, history, religion, language, and culture has also meant that Iran is alone: the sole Persian Shia country in a region dominated by Arab and Turkic Sunni Muslims. Loneliness has been the other side of the coin to uniqueness; grandeur and grand ambitions are thus matched by deep anxieties.[1] That loneliness has cast a continuous shadow on Iran, accounting for both its perception of vulnerability in its region and determination to make its greatness known to the world.[2]

That strategic loneliness goes back to the beginnings of the Iranian state under the Safavids, the monarchy that ruled over Iran between 1501 and 1722. The geographic, cultural, and religious reality of Iran today was in large measure set in place during that era. It was the Safavid shahs (kings) who carved Iranian territory from the ruins of the Abbasid Empire against the backdrop of the rise of the Ottoman Empire to their west and Mughal Empire to their east to create—in the center of the Islamic world—a domain for Persian people and Shia sect. Not all Persian speakers lived in Iran or would embrace Shiism, but enough would for the country to become Shia and forge Iran's identity so as to coalesce around Persian and Shia. Although the boundaries of Persian and Shiism are not coterminous with that of modern Iran, the two are inseparable from the country's identity.[3]

Fearing being overrun by the bourgeoning Ottoman domain to the west led the first Safavid king, Esmaʻil I, to distinguish Iran's religious identity from its neighbor as a matter of strategic choice.[4] He embraced Shiism as a national faith, and then he and his successors imposed it on their subjects by fiat. At the time of Esmaʻil's embrace of Shiism, two-thirds of the population of his capital Tabriz were Sunnis, and the Shia centers of learning all resided in Arab lands. That audacious act of religious conversion was not a reflection of the king's personal piety—for he adhered to a heterodox mix of Shia millenarianism and mysticism, and some of his followers in that creed viewed him as God, and others as the promised messiah—but rather a strategic calculation that changed the course of Iran and marked one of the most important turning points in the history of Islam.[5]

Iran's turn to Shiism anchored state authority in an alliance between the monarchy and the Shia clergy to protect Iran as the home of the "true faith." In this condominium, the kings posed as "guardians" of the Shia domain—a function that legitimated monarchy until the 1979 Revolution replaced the kings with the clergy in performing that function.[6]

The Safavids ruled Iran for over two centuries, during which Iran reached the apogee of its power as an empire and civilizational force. Their denouement in 1722 ushered in a prolonged period of instability, civil wars, invasions, and occupations punctuated by fleeting periods of stability. Iran thus entered the age of imperialism in the nineteenth century weakened and vulnerable. It survived that long century, but was not able to turn its fortunes. The ruling Qajar monarchy (1789–1925) defined Iran, the homeland of Shiism, as the "protected domains" (*mamalek-e mahrouseh*)—protected from threats, internal and external. But its attempts at protection remained stillborn. Efforts to consolidate power as well as restore order and security were undermined by colonial intrigue, urgent threats to its territorial integrity, steady decay, and ubiquitous chaos.[7] Iranians and their rulers continue to grapple with this history in contemporary discussions on foreign policy challenges.

A Weak State in the Age of Imperialism

Early in the nineteenth century, facing an expansionist Russia and avaricious Great Britain, the Qajar kings ceded ever more rights and territory to the imperial powers.[8] Following defeat in two catastrophic wars with Russia between 1804 and 1828, Iran lost around 10 percent of the country's territory, which was home to around 10 percent of its population, and submitted to humiliating concessions.[9] The two treaties that ended those wars, Golestan and Turkmanchay, stand as singular symbols of national humiliation for Iranians to this day.

What saved Iran from disintegration and colonialism was that in the century between the Congress of Vienna and World War I, Britain eyed Russia with suspicion. London and Moscow could not agree on how to divide Iran, and Britain did not want a border with Russia and to bring it closer to India. That negative balance between rival colonial powers gave Iran the de facto ability to play one against the other to at least remain sovereign. Iran ambled through the nineteenth century unable to shore up national power either by asserting monarchical autocracy or instituting fundamental reforms—as were advocated by the fabled stateman of mid-nineteenth century, Mirza Taqi Khan Amir Kabir, celebrated to this day as Iran's first champion of development. As the century progressed, the state atrophied, the country fell into the grip of chaos and insecurity, and its territorial integrity and sovereignty came into question.

By the turn of the century, the depth of that crisis brought together an unorthodox alliance of merchants, secular intellectuals, and clerics to demand a constitution in the hope that curbing the absolutist powers of the monarchy and instituting the rule of law would shore up security and independence.[10] They demanded political representation, individual freedoms, and political accountability. They won themselves a constitution in 1906—the first of its kind in the Middle East—but not respite from chaos.

The shadow of the Constitutional Revolution looms large over Iran's politics as a watershed moment when the people combated autocracy and demanded the rule of law along with individual and political freedoms in the hope of securing and modernizing the country. Echoes of that call continue to resonate in Iranian politics, including as recently as during the 2022 protests. The Constitutional Revolution cannot, however, be reduced to a democracy movement. Its call for political reform was prompted and ultimately judged by the fundamental desire to protect Iran from chaos, subjugation, and disintegration.

The hard-won constitution protected democratic rights, but the country still found itself in a quagmire. Freedom did not produce a strong state. Without that strong state democracy was neither a solution nor tenable. In the words of Daryush Shayegan, an eminent contemporary intellectual, "The constitution was very good, but it was akin to buying furniture without having a house."[11]

The advent of World War I drastically changed the international context in which Iran had found itself for almost a century. With Russia and Great Britain on the same side, there was no obstacle to dividing Iran among them. The 1907 Anglo-Russian agreement drew a line across Iran, giving the north to Russia and south to Great Britain.[12] The two imperial powers then occupied Iran, plunging the country into greater chaos and famine.[13] Iran was saved from that calamity by the October Revolution of 1917. Russia's attention turned inward, and the Red Scare in the West changed Britain's calculus. London's solution was now to turn Iran into a veritable buffer state, a semisovereign protectorate, under the 1919 Anglo-Persian Agreement.[14]

A Grand Strategy of Survival

Pleasing to London, the colonialist intent of the 1919 agreement was a fiasco for Iranians and death blow to its nascent democracy.[15] Iranians understood that winning a constitution by itself was not a guarantor of sovereignty and security. Iran *first* needed a strong state to secure its borders, impose order, develop the country, and transform its society. Echoing the mindset of France's Third Republic, captured by sociologist Eugene Weber as "turning peasants into Frenchmen"—a leading intellectual and statesman of the time, Ali Akbar Davar, said of similar radical change in Iran, "Iranians would not become human beings voluntarily. Salvation must be forced on Iran."[16]

This laid the foundations for many of those who had championed the Constitutional Revolution—merchants, secular intellectuals, and clergy—to rally behind the cause of a strong state. That opportunity presented itself in 1921 when a little-known military officer, Reza Khan, marched his troops on Tehran and staged a coup. Once firmly in the saddle, Reza Khan abrogated the Qajar monarchy and built a new state in its stead. Reza Khan would rule Iran during the interwar period.[17] He was a capable state builder, a self-made man hailing from humble origins, shrewd, hardworking, ruthless, and fiercely nationalistic; "a simple soldier who within the span of 25 years, through competence and effort, rose to be king and put the imperial crown of Iran on his head."[18] He quickly created a national military to force Soviet troops from northern Iran, foiled British plans for carving out spheres of influence in southern Iran, subdued insurgencies, separatist movements, and tribal militias in the country's south and north, and waged a relentless campaign against brigands and local power brokers to concentrate power at the center.[19]

He looked to the secular republic that Kemal Ataturk was standing up in next-door Turkey as a model. The Shia clergy, however, saw a Kemalist republic not as defender of the faith but instead as a detriment to it. They prevailed on Reza Khan to continue the tradition of Shia monarchy and become king: Reza Shah Pahlavi.[20] What he achieved in Iran was nothing short of miraculous, especially in how he mobilized the country's meager resources to realize its strategic aims.[21] He restored Iran's territorial integrity, ended the chaos and decay, and built fundamental institutions for a modern state to propel commerce and industrialization. He pursued state building as the sine qua non for national security in defiance of malign Western influence; his was a grand strategy of national survival. His success in realizing its goals is why there is an Iran today.

Reza Shah addressed the fundamental failure of the Constitutional Revolution—namely, building a strong state, and ending chaos and disintegration. There was, though, a paradox inherent in the forging of a strong and centralizing state. It was what Iran needed to survive, but such a state also set the country on a trajectory to authoritarianism. Economist Daron Acemoglu and political scientist James Robinson write that a strong state is necessary for economic prosperity and progress, but if it is not shackled by sufficiently strong social institutions capable of checking its exercise of power, the country will easily slide into authoritarianism.[22] Such a shackle was not extant, then, and thus the state Reza Shah was building quickly became brutish and autocratic, overshadowing the security and progress that it was engendering, thereby alienating many of his original supporters. The clergy grew alarmed at his secularization policies, change of dress, and abolition of hijab. None other than the future leader of the Islamic Revolution, Ayatollah Khomeini, then a young cleric, rose to the challenge to strongly condemn the assault on religion.[23]

It was not, however, domestic opposition that would undo Reza Shah but rather the calamity of another great war in Europe. World War II made Iran a significant prize for both Nazi Germany and the Allies. As German forces pushed east, Britain saw firm control over Iran as vital to protecting its oil interests in the Persian Gulf and creating "a major supply route to Russia through the Persian Gulf." Shoring up Soviet resistance to the German offensive, explained British statesman Winston Churchill, "became our prime objective."[24]

On August 25, 1941, 150,000 British and Soviet troops attacked Iran.[25] The British captured the oil province of Khuzestan in the southwest and then pushed north into central Iran as Soviet armies moved into the northwest province of Azarbaijan and pushed southeast toward Tehran.[26] Reza Shah was dethroned and sent into exile—replaced by his young son, Mohammad Reza Shah, who would come to be known in the West simply as the Shah. Allied soldiers occupied cities and took control of the country's infrastructure, and commandeered its food to feed themselves and sustain the Soviet Army. The country's economy was pulverized, and its people, denied their neutrality and sovereignty, fell into hunger and destitution. The occupation likely saved the Red Army from defeat. But for Iran, it was a calamity. What Iran had built under Reza Shah had not been sufficient to ensure its sovereignty and security.

Allied Occupation and Specter of Dismemberment

The years of occupation were devastating for Iran. Red Army soldiers and British Indian troops marched in the streets of cities and towns, reminding Iranians daily of humiliation and defeat, but provided little in the form of security. Highway robbery and banditry once again reared its head, the economy faltered, the national currency plummeted, and development projects ground to a halt.[27] Shortages caused both high inflation and unemployment, poverty, and hunger.

With Red Army soldiers in control of large swath of the country, communist activism grew prominent, especially in the form of the Tudeh (Masses) Party of Iran, which quickly became the most significant force on the streets.[28]

Despite its sacrifices and contributions, Iran's fate at the end of the war remained far from certain. The three global powers had agreed in 1942 to restore Iran's full sovereignty at the conclusion of the war. Once the war ended, American and British forces left in accordance with that agreement, but the Soviet Union dragged its feet.[29] Instead, Soviet leader Joseph Stalin demanded economic concessions while throwing his support behind communist parties in Iran's northwest Azarbaijan and Kurdistan Provinces, which were demanding secession. Those provinces became de facto Soviet republics in 1946, and then in March 1947, the Red Army poured armored brigades into those regions to deploy along the Turkish and Iraqi borders.[30] Three days later, Churchill delivered his famous "Iron Curtain" speech in Fulton, Missouri, promising to respond to Soviet expansionist aims. A week later, on March 12, 1947, US president Harry S. Truman issued his terse warning to Stalin that would become the Truman Doctrine. On March 24, Moscow announced that its troops would leave within six weeks. The troops were gone within a month.

Iranian prime minister Ahmad Qavam's dexterous diplomatic maneuvering was credited for buying Iran time and giving Moscow cover for the withdrawal, but in reality it was because of American pressure that Stalin decided to abandon his economic and territorial claims and leave Iran.[31] The young Mohammad Reza Shah along with his ruling elite and military commanders all knew Iran would need the West if it was to survive its menacing neighbor to the north. The Cold War was not just a reality Iran had to live with but instead the reason why Iran had survived and would continue to do so. Iran could not be neutral; it had to align itself with the West and make sure that the West saw Iran's value.

This imperative for close alignment with the West would become an article of faith for Mohammad Reza Shah. His singular focus on "the grand design of Soviet expansionism" and the imperative of the West's willingness to stand up to it was captured years later in a book, where he wrote, "I had lived as neighbor to the masters of the Kremlin my whole adult life. In forty years, I had never seen any wavering of Russia's political objectives: relentless striving towards world domination."[32] In one of his last television interviews before the 1979 Revolution sent him into exile, he said that his principal goal had been for Iran not to become "Iran-istan"—that is, another Muslim Soviet republic.[33]

It is impossible to understand the Shah's outlook and Iranian politics during the remainder of his monarchy without considering the deep influence of 1946, the Cold War, and his fear of the Soviet Union. Many observers have seen him as a modernizing autocrat, whose heavy-handedness and grandiose ambitions alienated his people. Yet both his autocracy and determined drive to modernize Iran were part of a strategy to ensure Iran's security and territorial integrity. It built on his father's grand strategy of survival.

Oil, Nationalism, and the 1953 Coup

It would not be long before fear of the Soviet Union and the memory of 1946 would have to compete with another worry over Iran's sovereignty and security: battling imperialism over the rights to national resources.[34] At issue was the oil concession Iran gave to the British Anglo-Iranian Oil Company at the end of the nineteenth century. Reza Shah had quarreled with Britain over its one-sided terms. Failing a satisfactory resolution, by the 1950s, the concession had turned into a point of contention between Iran and Great Britain three decades in the making. Iran was unhappy with the oil company's practices, and furthermore, demanded a larger share of the oil revenue—especially after the Allied occupation, engineered by Great Britain, devastated the Iranian economy without any compensation.[35] Iranian anger grew with British obduracy, especially since Iranians knew that Mexico and Saudi Arabia had secured better deals from American companies.[36]

The oil concession was symbolic of Britain's rapacious imperialism as well as repeated violations of Iranian rights and sovereignty. Many Iranian politicians were old enough to remember firsthand Britain's agreement with Russia to divide Iran into spheres of influence, promoting separatism in southern Iran, and leading the charge to occupy Iran and change its ruler. Even if many had come to dislike Reza Shah, they nevertheless saw the ease with which Britain toyed with Iran's politics and sovereignty with resentment and worry.

By 1951, demand for change to the oil concession dominated Iranian politics. Many merely hoped for a fairer share of the oil revenue. But veteran politician Mohammad Mossadegh wanted to go further, to nationalize Iranian oil altogether. This would put Iran on a collision course with Great Britain. That worried the Shah, the military, and a segment of the political elite, which continued to see the Soviet Union as the principal threat to Iran and favored a more tempered approach that would protect Iran's ties with the West.

With Britain in no mood for compromise and Iranian nationalist feelings running high, the Shah had no choice but to appoint Mossadegh prime minister. Mossadegh lost no time in nationalizing the Anglo-Iranian Oil Company. Thus began a two-year, convoluted impasse: Iran insisted on its right to its own oil against British intransigence. Mossadegh tried to manage a high-wire act of international diplomacy to maneuver an increasingly anxious Washington as he hoped to compel an obdurate London to accommodate his demands, all the while riding the tiger in a steadily more chaotic political scene at home.

It has become accepted wisdom that the oil crisis pivoted on the question of Iran's sovereign rights to its national resources as well as

Mossadegh's right as prime minister to end colonial control of Iranian oil and reject the Shah dismissing him from that perch—in other words, anti-imperialist nationalism and democracy. Yet it was not those issues that separated Mossadegh and the Shah. It was rather the disagreement over what constituted the principal security threat to Iran, Soviet Communism or British imperialism, and whether Iran could confront one without compromising with the other, that set Mossadegh, the Shah, and his like-minded military and political leaders on a collision course.

In this, the key issue was not Mossadegh's nationalistic goal but rather his game plan. Having identified ending British hold over Iran's oil as a national objective, how was he going to achieve that goal and still protect national security? Mossadegh's principled stance is unassailable; where he failed was in conceiving a viable grand strategy and credible plan of action to realize it. Those failures doomed his premiership as it invited British aggression, lost American sympathy, and increased the communist threat to Iran. That mix put Iran's national security at risk and thus lost the support of a growing number of Iranians.

Mossadegh had come of age during the turbulent end years of the Qajar period, an era of intense foreign interference that almost culminated in Iran's division. He had lived through Britain's removal of Reza Shah from power—and although Mossadegh was no fan of the king, the manner that Britain decided to change Iranian rulers could not have sat well with his nationalist sensibilities—occupation of the country, famine, and the near loss of the Azarbaijan and Kurdistan Provinces to the Soviet Union. Mossadegh's single-mindedness was forged in that crucible.

The Truman administration was initially sympathetic to Iran's grievances and sought to help defuse the crisis.[37] Mossadegh, however, refused to yield to American entreaties for a compromise, rejecting every avenue to a negotiated settlement that the Truman administration put forth—hoping instead that his steadfastness would compel Washington, worried about Communism, to force London into surrender. In March 1953, he told American ambassador Loy Henderson that if Washington really wanted to prevent Iran from falling to Communism, then it should back Iran's position and pressure Britain to end its blockade of Iranian oil. Henderson was unmoved by the threat and told Mossa-degh that the United States would not support Iran's unilateral abroga-tion of its international agreement with the Anglo-Iranian Oil Company, and that Iran had to agree to a negotiated settlement.[38]

Mossadegh's obduracy played into Britain's hand. Washington came to see him as the problem and lost trust in a compromise solution. In June 1953, Henderson wrote to the White House, "It is my opinion that there is no hope of settling the oil problem so long as Mossadegh is in power."[39] Impervious to the consequences of his misguided strategy, Mossadegh was courting economic ruin—Britain had put a blockade on Iran's oil exports—a British invasion of Iran's oil fields, and steady rise in communist agitation and radicalization of Iranian politics.[40]

Mossadegh had left himself little room to maneuver. His political position would not hold if he were to back away from his maximalist demands. He therefore doubled down on railing against British injus-tice and insisting that Iran get in full its rights without compromise. Winning the moral debate did not resolve Iran's quandary. In this fight, Iran would be alone. It could and would not rely on the Soviet Union, and the nationalization had placed Iran on a collision course with the West. Mossadegh hoped that he could maintain a "negative balance" (*movazeneh-e manfi*)—a concept that would decades later echo in the Islamic Republic's foreign policy mantra of "neither East, nor West."[41] Iran would stand between the two poles and use one against the other to achieve Iran's goal.[42]

That was exactly what worried the Cold War–conscious Eisenhower administration as it watched the growing chaos in Iran as its economy neared collapse.[43] The rising specter of communist agitation, growing economic crisis and sense of despair, and increasing chaos in the Parlia-ment and on the streets also worried the Shah, the military, and the seg-ment of Iranian political leadership that had all along warned of the danger that nationalization posed to Iran's national security.[44] They were not alone. Soon senior clerics in Qom, Tehran, and Najaf—worried by the communist threat too—and erstwhile supporters of the National Front in the Parliament joined them. The influential senior-most Shia cleric of the time, Ayatollah Mohammad Hossein Boroujerdi, actively lobbied against Mossadegh and in favor of the Shah.[45]

The Coup of 1953

The crisis came to an end after the military staged a coup on August 19, 1953, to remove Mossadegh from power. It has become accepted wisdom that the coup, the so-called Operation Ajax, was the handiwork of the US Central Intelligence Agency (CIA)—staging street demonstrations, renting a mob, and then directing the Iranian military to step in and remove Mossadegh.[46]

There is little doubt that both the American and British governments wanted Mossadegh gone, and that they hatched a plan to remove him. They did spend money—a paltry sum of $60,000—to precipitate a crisis in Tehran. There is, however, sufficient evidence to cast doubt on the idea that Washington and London acted as puppet masters deftly manipulating the street and maneuvering the military to carry out the perfect coup.[47] The coup plan that the CIA and Britain's MI6 had hatched in fact failed, and it was a second attempt at a coup a few days later, planned and led by General Fazlollah Zahedi and his network in the Iranian military, that won the day, while the US embassy and CIA station in Tehran appeared to be largely in the dark.[48]

By summer 1953, Britain and the United States were not alone in turning on Mossadegh. Many Iranians too had developed ample skepticism about where Mossadegh was leading the country, and plenty of influential actors were convinced he had to be removed from office. To many Iranians, the specter of Communism was real, and the country's deteriorating economic situation and possibility of direct confrontation with Britain was only making it worse.

The oil nationalization saga was a duel between competing nationalisms and how to protect Iran's national interest. The dominant discourse of the time was about sovereignty: sovereignty vis-à-vis colonial powers and remaining sovereign in the face of the Soviet threat. Democracy and authoritarianism were important because the Parliament and monarchy, prime minister's office and military, were stations from where the two nationalist camps waged their respective campaigns. In the fullness of time and what diplomatic correspondences of that period show, it was not so much American and British perfidy or betrayal of his fellow compatriots that undid Mossadegh but rather his own lack of strategic imagination.

The lore about the 1953 coup, though, turned out differently. Iranians came to view the coup in the rearview mirror of history as a trampling on their national rights and crushing of their democracy by Great Britain and the United States. The coup was a traumatic event for the country—a second regime change in as much as a decade. If for the Shah along with the political and military elites in his corner, it was 1946 that had shaped their views on national security, it was 1953 that shaped the outlook of many Iranians in later decades, especially the revolutionary elite that rose to the helm after 1979. Whereas the Shah's grand strategy was to protect Iran from Communism and the Soviet Union, for the revolutionaries who succeeded him, taking their cue from Mossadegh, a grand strategy had to protect Iran from the West and its interference in Iran's politics.

It should not have come as a surprise that the 1953 coup would also become an important historical backdrop to the Islamic Republic's confrontation with the United States over its nuclear program. In later years, ardent anti-American voices among Iran's leadership drew parallels between Iran's right to a nuclear program and Mossadegh's assertion of Iran's rights to its oil. They have built on that reading of 1953 to preach resistance to the West at all costs, courting severe economic sanctions as had Mossadegh in the 1951–53 period. The Islamic Republic's anti-imperialist resistance before the United States and resisting pressure on its nuclear program sought legitimacy in Mossadegh's legacy. Echoes of Mossadegh can be heard loud and clear in Khomeini's anti-Americanism and Khamenei's vision of resistance.

As the logic of today's hard-liners would come under scrutiny, it would also put to question Mossadegh's position decades earlier, especially since the heirs to Mossadegh's legacy in defining Iran's national interests are not democracy-minded reformers but instead the dyed-in-the-wool guardians of the Islamic Republic. Similar echoes of the Shah and Mossadegh's critics can be heard in the arguments of the likes of former Presidents Ali Akbar Hashemi Rafsanjani and Hasan Rouhani in encouraging the Islamic Republic to engage with the West, contending in effect that a tree that does not bend to the wind will break, and Iran's security interests are best served with compromise and relations with the West. After the 2022 protests it became a common refrain, particularly among the dissentient youths, to blame the coup on Mossadegh's own missteps and fault his version of resistance.

The Shah and Forging Great Iran

Like Mossadegh, Mohammad Reza Shah's reign casts a long shadow on Iran's politics today. The travails of his modernizing autocracy ending in revolution has been amply debated.[49] What is less known but more important to the Islamic Republic's foreign policy is the Shah's grand strategy. How did he assess threats and opportunities before Iran, and what was his vision for tackling them?

The Shah came of age as a statesman during the Allied occupation of Iran and turbulent years that followed it. The events of 1946 and 1953 left an indelible mark on him. He was deeply concerned with Iran's vulnerabilities as well as the dangers that its communist neighbor to the north posed to its sovereignty and territorial integrity. Like his father, he sought security in a strong modernizing state. He saw democracy as chaotic and inherently inimical to effective government. It produced paralysis that benefited foreign enemies. That was the lesson that he took away from the rise and fall of Mossadegh.

When he stepped into the breach in the aftermath of the 1953 coup he had three goals in mind: to concentrate power in a strong centralized state, develop the economy and modernize Iran, and keep the United States on Iran's side in the face of the Soviet threat.[50] During the ensuing decade, he eliminated political rivals and power centers while anchoring power in the monarchy.[51] He proved adroit at cultivating close ties with successive American administrations. As Iran's oil and Persian Gulf security grew in importance to US interests in the years that followed,

Washington too became keen to invest in Iran's stability—providing economic aid, and shoring up its military and intelligence agency, popularly known by its acronym as SAVAK—and strengthen the Shah's regime.[52] Those burgeoning ties worried Moscow, and the Kremlin's hostility to the Shah only fueled his determination to remain close to Washington.[53]

Economic development, however, proved more difficult.[54] So much so that for a time, London and Washington started to doubt that the Shah was the right leader to keep Iran out of the clutches of Communism. Ann Lambton, an influential British scholar of Iran, wrote in a 1956 cable to White Hall, "Persia is drifting . . . 'the Shah cannot govern and will not let anyone else do it' either."[55] The Eisenhower administration even considered backing a coup in 1958, and then the Kennedy administration followed suit by pressuring the Shah to clean house and diffuse tensions by opening the political process.[56]

The Shah responded by undertaking an ambitious program of social and economic reforms in 1963, known as the White Revolution—which among other measures, promulgated land reform and gave women the right to vote.[57] It was in opposition to those reforms that the future leader of the Islamic Revolution, Ayatollah Khomeini, first challenged the Shah.[58]

The White Revolution was followed by a period of significant industrialization and economic growth.[59] Between 1963 and 1977, Iran experienced the largest growth in GDP in its history.[60] Its economy grew at the pace of 10.5 percent per year, making Iran one of the fastest-growing economies in the world at that time. The rise in oil prices in 1974 boosted those numbers, but the economic growth was real and predated that windfall. There was, however, a dangerous paradox at play: the good news on the economic front masked the growing popular resentment against authoritarianism, and radicalization of the opposition—the same trap that Reza Shah's modernization fell into—which would bring together the clergy, the middle classes, and the Left into a broad oppositional alliance, set Iran on the road to revolution.

None of this was apparent to the Shah at the time. By the late 1960s, he saw the future as bright. His country was rising, more secure, and prosperous. He set his sight on Iran becoming a leading industrial nation and "great civilization" (*tamaddon-e bozorg*).[61] His goal now was for Iran to become the premier power in the Middle East and a great power on the world stage. His critics saw this as hubris, but to the Shah this was a realizable grand strategy.

Iran's Moment in the Middle East

The changing geopolitical context provided him with an opening. By the late 1960s, Britain was planning to leave the Persian Gulf. Exhausted by the war in Vietnam, the United States was loathe to step into Britain's shoes to protect the Persian Gulf.[62] American thinking was shifting toward what would be dubbed the Nixon Doctrine. Historian John Lewis Gaddis explains the doctrine as an asymmetrical approach whereby the United States would "apply strengths against weaknesses while leaving allies forms of military activity uncongenial to the United States."[63] In thinking of using "strengths against weaknesses" in the Persian Gulf, the United States had to look to Iran as the ally that with the right military support, could defend the interests of the West.[64]

In 1970, Iran signed a deal with Great Britain to accept sovereignty of its colonial holdings in the Persian Gulf, and significantly, recognize the sovereignty of former Iranian territory of Bahrain.[65] This set the stage for a broader deal with the United States in 1972. During a visit to Tehran in that year, Richard Milhous Nixon arrived at an agreement with the Shah for Iran to play the role of the "gendarme" of the Persian Gulf.[66] The Shah told his guest, "The White House should push the regional powers that had the ability to uphold stability to take on a greater role in security matters. It is better for [the] U.S. to have Iran able to defend [it]self than to have . . . another Vietnam."[67] It had always been Iran that had needed the United States to realize its security goals, but now it was America that was in effect saying "protect me."

The Shah then used this agreement with the United States to play a forward role in broader Middle East security. The catastrophic Arab defeat in the 1967 war with Israel had diminished Arab nationalism and opened the region to a greater role for Iran. The first target was the troublesome Baathist government in Baghdad, which backed by the Soviet military had become a menace to Iran.[68] Iran secured Washington's backing to provide arms to Kurdish insurgents in northern Iraq. With Iran's support, the Kurds stepped up their rebellion between 1972 and 1975.[69] Saddam Hussein was compelled to sue for peace with Iran.[70] The Algiers Accords of 1975 settled border disputes between the two countries and normalized relations between them. It would end when Iraq invaded Iran in 1980.

At the same time, Iran invoked the Nixon Doctrine in the newly independent state of Oman, which was facing a formidable Marxist insurgency in its southern Dhofar region. In late 1973, an Iranian expeditionary force landed in southern Oman to push back the rebels.[71] In a 1975 interview, the Shah explained his decision to intervene in Oman, saying, "Just imagine that these savages should seize the other bank of the Ormuz [Hormuz] Straits, at the mouth of the Persian Gulf. Our life depends on that. And those people at war with the Sultan are savages. They may even be worse than communists."[72] In another interview in the same year, he said, "The Strait of Hormuz is Iran's means of access to the Indian Ocean and the world. It is also the passageway for all Iranian oil. . . . Can we allow a hostile force to take over?"[73]

The Iranian intervention would drag on for another two years, during which up to thirty-five hundred Iranian troops at any one time, joined by several hundred Jordanians, Pakistani Baloch tribespeople, and Omani soldiers—alongside British commanders and Israeli advisers— would wage bloody battles.[74] In the end, the insurgency was defeated.[75]

The campaigns in Iraq and Oman would lay the foundation for a more expansive Iranian foray into Arab politics. Iran normalized relations with Syria and built ties with Shia factions in Lebanon.[76] Most important, was the opening to Egypt.[77] After Anwar Sadat signaled his intention to set Egypt on a new course in 1971, the Shah extended a hand of friendship to him. The Shah wanted Sadat's new brand of moderate Arab politics to succeed. The two leaders also shared a strategic outlook and soon developed a personal friendship. The Shah left Iran for the last time for Egypt in February 1979 and died there soon after. Sadat gave the Shah a state funeral, and he was buried in Cairo's al-Rifaie Mosque.

The Shah was a tireless advocate for Sadat in Washington between 1971 and 1973, appealing directly to Nixon and Kissinger to recognize the significance of the opportunity Sadat presented.[78] During the 1973 war between Egypt and Israel, to Washington's shock and annoyance, Iran allowed the Soviet Union to use its airspace to resupply the Egyptian military.[79] When the war ended, the Shah urged Washington to press Israel to forge an agreement with Egypt. In a sign of how much Iran's position had shifted, the Shah openly threatened Washington that failing a deal between Egypt and Israel, war would resume, and "it will be our war this time, and none of us will have any choice. . . . The Shah of Iran was quoted today as saying his heavily armed country would join a war against Israel if the Middle East crisis was not resolved in accord with UN resolutions."[80]

The Shah was keen for Iran to play a "constructive role" in the broader Middle East.[81] This would make Iran more important to the United States as a stabilizing force.[82] It was with that aim in mind that during Kissinger's shuttle diplomacy between Egypt, Syria, and Israel, the Shah repeatedly offered to help with the talks, getting Iran a seat at the table of the most significant diplomatic negotiations of the time over the future of the region.[83]

Iran's fierce support for Egypt in the 1970s also signaled the growing independence of Iranian policy. Iran was acting at the behest of the Nixon Doctrine, but was increasingly seeing itself as more than an agent. It would be Iran that would define when the Nixon Doctrine was necessary and how it would be implemented; the United States need only supply the necessary military hardware. American diplomatic dispatches of the time are replete with reports of the Shah's tutorials on Soviet strategic threats to the Persian Gulf, or to Pakistan and India, and what America must do in the Middle East to manage Arabs and Israelis.[84] The Shah was worried about everyone's stability—Pakistan, Turkey, and Saudi Arabia—except for Iran's own stability.[85]

Looking back through the prism of today's nuclear imbroglio, the development of a nuclear program was perhaps one of the Shah's most consequential initiatives in the 1970s. Although he did not rule out nuclear weapons, telling an interviewer in 1975 that "if 20 or 30 ridiculous little countries are going to develop nuclear weapons, then I may have to revise my policies," at the time the initiative represented his grand ambitions for Iran as a great power and industrial powerhouse.[86]

This was, however, a major strategic initiative. The Shah was determined to mark Iran's arrival as a major power with nuclear capability. It also marked the apogee of Iran's foreign policy confidence and the Shah's deft strategic maneuverings to gain advantage for Iran amid the volatile complexities of the Middle East. Still, despite Iran's moment of greatness, the Shah's strategic victories masked a brewing insecurity of a different kind: the growing alienation of Iranians from the monarchy and gathering winds of the revolution.

• • •

If Mossadegh's failing had been that of strategic vision, the Shah's was to have his people walk with him, so to speak, in pursuit of his. They abandoned him not because of the wisdom of his grand strategy but rather because of the autocracy the Shah insisted on as necessary to get to his strategic goals. On one occasion when he was asked by a reporter when he would reign as a constitutional monarch, he is reported to have said, "When the Iranians learn to behave like the Swedes, I will behave like the King of Sweden."[87]

Iran's experiences under Mossadegh and Mohammad Reza Shah loom large over Iranian historical memory today. Not only was their era the prelude to the 1979 Revolution, but the contemporary reading of that period, along with the goals, achievements, and failures that shaped it, is embedded in intellectual and political debates, and informs the Islamic Republic's grand strategy of resistance to this day.

In the past, when reigning strategies of state building proved too costly, too ineffective, too authoritarian, and too unpopular, there were revolts and then experimentation with alternative ideas. In this vein, the Constitutional Revolution of 1905–6, nationalist interregnum of the 1950s, and 1979 Revolution each put forth their own formulas.

In the case of the first two, the thought experiments fell short in the political arena to set the country on a new course because they failed the fundamental test of securing the country. Today, the path chosen by the Islamic Republic too is facing a popular reckoning. It is a result of the throes of profound debates over how to balance its quest for security with the fundamental needs of the society and economy, individual freedoms, and a desire for greater engagement with the world. Interestingly, contemporary dissentient voices hark back the 1905–6 era in demanding individual rights, and calling for economic growth and better living standards, and to the strategies that informed the authoritarian developmentalism that the Pahlavi monarchy pursued for most of the twentieth century.

PART I

The Crucible
of Revolution and War

CHAPTER 2

Seeking Revolutionary Independence

In October 1978, two leaders of the Iranian opposition met in Paris to plan for the final stages of the revolution that would erupt in Tehran a few months later. One was Karim Sanjabi, the leader of the National Front that was led by Mossadegh before the 1953 coup. The other was Ayatollah Ruhollah Khomeini, who had led an uprising against the monarchy in 1963–64. The two had been prominent opponents of the monarchy since the 1960s, but were unlikely allies given that each represented very different parts of the opposition: Sanjabi represented the secular democracy-seeking liberals, while Khomeini's followers were primarily drawn from the ranks of the religious social strata. But the gravity of the moment, a revolution to end the monarchy, compelled them into an alliance. Sanjabi had arrived in Paris with a draft declaration of the goals of the forthcoming revolution. The document stated that the future national government of Iran would be anchored in only *two* principles: that it be democratic and Islamic. Yet Sanjabi recollects that in their meeting in Paris, Khomeini, in his own handwriting, added a *third* principle to the declaration: "independence" (*esteqlal*).[1]

Iran's politics and society were forever changed by the Islamic Revolution of 1979: it ended a monarchy, erected a theocracy, enshrined Islamic ideology in state and society, and set Iran on a collision course with the West. But within all of these monumental transformations, there was one putative change that was most evident to the participants themselves: geopolitical independence. Before the revolution itself, before the hostage crisis or US sanctions, before the Iran-Iraq War or efforts to export the revolution as well as the sordid legacy of Iran's confrontations with the West, the future supreme religious guide and leader of Iran valued independence from foreign influence as *equal* to the enshrining principles of Islam in the state.

After the revolution won, asked by Pakistani journalist Mushahid Hussain, "What had been the benefit of the Revolution?" Khomeini answered simply, "Now all decisions are made in Tehran."[2] Indeed, what is most often missed in understanding Iran's revolution and its Islamic Republic is this fundamental commitment to protecting national sovereignty and displaying independence on the world stage. Even as the lofty ideals of the revolution have been eroded, and even as observance of Islamic dictums has been diluted or ignored, that third principle of *esteqlal* has endured and even hardened into a steely national determination—and ethos of resistance.

By 1979, Iranians from competing ends of the political spectrum complained that their politics and culture were shaped by foreign influence. It didn't matter that their monarch Mohammad Reza Shah as well as his father and predecessor, Reza Shah, had fought enemies to protect Iranian sovereignty, unified and developed the country, and strived to better its standing in the world. Myths about a foreign hand in bringing both father and son to power, and festering suspicions about nefarious foreign intrigue set on exploiting and dividing the country, had even deeper roots in the nineteenth century. In the revolution's rendering, it was the British that installed Reza Shah on the throne in 1925.[3] Then, in the 1950s, Iranians asserted independence under a democratic government, led by Mossadegh's National Front. But then, in 1953, the Shah returned to power in a military coup that the revolutionaries believed was masterminded by Great Britain and the United States. In this rendering, Iran's brief window of parliamentary democracy, and more important, geopolitical independence, was over.

Twenty-five years later, however, the pressure against this outside imposition had come to a furious boil. The result was competing swathes of Iranian society sharing the goal of revolution above all. In fact, the 1979 Revolution culminated dissent that gained momentum throughout the 1960s and 1970s, bringing together religious *and* secular, Right *and* Left, opposition into a successful alliance against the Shah. The claim that Iran's monarchy was an illegitimate lackey of the West played a central role in shaping this alliance and fueling its rage.

Yet the alliance's successes concealed deep differences. The Left, for example, was composed of competing voices that were alternatively secular, liberal, or prodemocratic. Still, these broadly defined their revolutionary goals with the slogan of "freedom" (*azadi*). Freedom, for the Left, meant liberation from the clutches of imperialism, Europe, and the United States, but it also meant a broader struggle for economic justice. Despite their temporary alliance with the freedom-seeking Left, though, the religious revolutionaries were motivated by a different slogan: the desire for independence.[4]

By the 1970s, the master narrative in the mind of the Shah's opposition was that Iran had lost its independence after the 1953 coup. In fact, even leftist opposition to the Shah shared with the clergy—who were alienated from the monarchy since their support for the Shah in 1953—a commitment to this anti-imperialism. Anti-imperialism and foreign interference were themes frequently discussed by Khomeini. In an interview with the French daily *Le Monde*, he dismissed the Shah's White Revolution of 1963 as merely an effort to open Iran's domestic market to American exploitation. "It is fifteen years that in my declarations and speeches to my people I have asked for economic and social development," explained Khomeini on the eve of the revolution, "but the Shah is only implementing what imperialists want, to keep Iran backward."[5]

Khomeini's earliest political experience had come when as a young seminarian in Najaf Iraq, he witnessed up close the 1920 Shia revolt against the British occupation that followed World War I. Swept into the emotions of that moment, he was deeply impressed by the audacity and bravery of Shia clerics in rejecting imperialism in the face of overwhelming British military power.[6] As such, Khomeini did not see either liberal democracy or Marxist utopia as the alternative to the monarchy—after all, they too were inspired by Western ideas; instead, he wanted an Islamic state, and cultural as well as political independence.

His Islamic state would not only liberate Iranians from despotism but also give them true security and strength. Iran's state secure in Islam would be strong at home and in the world. In the words of Ali Bagheri Kani, Iran's deputy foreign minister in 2023, it was by combining the "national, revolutionary and Islamic identities of Iranian people that [Khomeini] ensured Iran's national security, territorial integrity and national unity."[7] Although the revolution redistributed wealth to the poor and Khomeini posed as a populist, he did not view the revolution as limited to class warfare and economic justice.[8] He dismissed bickering over economic issues with statements such as "economics is for donkeys"—meaning, idiots—or "we did not rise up to get cheaper watermelons."[9] But what, then, was Khomeini's goal?

The promise of the revolution to him was rather that the clergy would deliver what the shahs had failed to: true security and power. In a series of books and treatises published between 1965 and 1978 when he was in exile in Najaf, Khomeini laid out his views on regional and international issues that would become foundational to the Islamic Republic's outlook on the world. The struggle against United States and Western imperialism formed the backbone of every argument, as did his animus toward Israel. He also identified Western cultural aggression as an ongoing threat, and prescribed an authentic Islamic development to protect Muslim societies in a long and vigilant struggle to mitigate the Western threat.[10] In Khomeini's eyes, the Islamic state was necessary to protect Iranians and Muslims from Western aggression. Islam was thus the source of power needed to protect Iran and wage a war of liberation for Muslims everywhere. This was an outcome, Khomeini argued, that only Islam and its guardians could deliver. This new Islamic state would not only ensure security from external threats but also project power abroad. As much as Khomeini's directives shaped the attitude of the Islamic Republic toward the United States, the early experience of the revolution with the hostage crisis would prove consequential in entrenching anti-Americanism, not for ideological reasons, but national security ones.

With the revolution, Iran's posture toward Israel took a radical turn too. Until the late 1970s, the Shah's Iran had viewed Israel as a strategic partner in confronting their common foe: radical Arab nationalism. The revolution, however, saw Israel through the lens of the Palestinian struggle. In his signature book *Islamic Government* (*Hukumat-e Islami*), Khomeini wrote that Israel uniquely challenged Iran and the Islamic world, characterizing it as a colonial threat, and one that demanded of Muslims an anticolonial response.[11] Khomeini's anti-Israeli posture also reflected the views of the young firebrands in his camp who had been active in Lebanon since the late 1960s and trained in Palestinian camps, and who would form the backbone of religious militias after the revolution.[12]

Khomeini's aggressive denunciation of Israel captured the mood of the Arab street and broader Muslim world, and as such, was important to cultivating the kind of influence for the revolution—and later Iran's regional influence—that he coveted, ensconcing it in the Islamic Republic's worldview. As later chapters will elucidate, animus toward Israel would quickly go beyond mere rhetoric to culminate in Iran's active support for the Palestinian forces, Shia militias fighting Israeli occupation in Lebanon, and attacks on Israeli targets in the region and around the world. It did not take long for Israel to see Iran as its principle regional adversary.

■ ■ ■

The aim of this chapter is not to probe into the full causes of the revolution and trace all of its twists and turns. Instead, it is to understand how the revolution reflected—and then changed—Iran's concerns with national security and national interest. To understand Iran today, one first needs to understand how deeply *independence* is woven into the state's understanding of the world and its strategy for meeting it. Beyond Iran's original ideological assumptions and insistence on independence, it was the hostage crisis and confrontation with as well as purge of the Left, grappling with balancing revolution at home or promoting it abroad, and onset of the Iran-Iraq War, all within the first years of the revolution, that combined to shape and then entrench the worldview that has dominated the Islamic Republic's understanding of national interest, and shaped its security priorities and attitude toward the United States.

The United States as a Shared Threat

Independence meant many different things to different people. Yet one adversary that was shared across the political spectrum then was the United States. "The Shah had made Iran subservient to the West to such an extent that it would take years to repair the damage," declared Khomeini soon after his triumph in February 1979, "and if we want true independence then we have to end all manifestations of American influence, be they economic, military, political or cultural."[13]

In the lead-up to the revolution, the opposition to the Shah rallied around the idea that America's original sin in Iran was to "carry out" the 1953 coup, overthrowing Mossadegh for standing for Iran's rights and imposing on the country a "puppet" regime responsible for despotism. Although that view did not faithfully reflect the historical record, it did provide a narrative that thoroughly delegitimated the Shah and cast the United States as the culprit in oppressing Iranians. As such, the revolution had defied America's will and undone its plans for Iran, and the revolution's triumph had to be followed by not only holding America accountable but also vigilantly guarding against a repeat of its "evil designs." Thus the revolution identified the United States as the greatest threat to Iran's national security and the main stumbling block to the realization of its interests. Subsequently, anti-Americanism (*Emirikasetizi*) became early on integral to the identity of the revolution—a form of anti-Western Islamic nationalism—and central to its conception of itself and Iran's security.[14] It has been displayed since 1979 in murals, public demonstration, and symbolic acts like walking on the American flag. The depth of its ferocity, however, captured world attention in the form of the 1979 hostage crisis.[15]

Anti-Americanism was also embedded in the Third Worldist ideologies of the secular revolutionaries. These leftists saw the United States as the quintessential imperialist power, and viewed international affairs and Iran's role in them through the lens of anti-imperialism. The anti-imperialist discourse of the Left had even seeped into the Islamic ideology that Khomeini was foisting on Iran. What was different was that Khomeini used Islamic terminology—such as "Great Satan" (*sheitan-e bozorg*) or "oppression" (*estekbar*)—in lieu of Marxist terminologies (similarly, he appropriated populist and Marxist rhetoric, such as by using *mostazafan* [downtrodden] in place of "the proletariat"). In fact, Khomeini's signature moniker for the United States, the "Great Satan," was lifted from communist propaganda literature of the 1950s.[16]

Such international defiance seemingly became a genuine aspect of Khomeini's thinking, but it was just as important for him to deny a monopoly to the secular Left over anti-imperialism. Consequently, the revolution embraced Mossadegh's 1950s' vision of resistance and anti-imperialism, now identifying America rather than Britain as the main enemy, even as the religious wing disparaged the former prime minister as a secular political icon. Where Mossadegh had failed, Khomeini's faction argued, the Islamic Revolution had succeeded. This view justified the clerics' claim to sole ownership of the revolution and the purge of secular nationalists, leftists, and liberal democrats in short order. After the taking of American diplomats as hostages, mobs—organized by militant clerics—attacked the offices of liberal political forces and shut down their newspapers. Several liberal politicians were arrested. The same would soon happen to leftist forces.

Religious revolutionaries were also set against America for its promotion of secularism and antagonism to Islam. Anti-Americanism was not Khomeini's creation but rather a bedrock of Islamism and extant in its ideological corpus.[17] Indeed, Khomeini had expected that the United States would object to the religious character of the revolution and the Islamic awakening that it would set off in the Muslim world. This too made the United States the principal enemy of Iran.

If the Islamic Revolution along with the Islamic state it produced would give Iran power and security, then opposing Islam meant wanting Iran weak and subservient. Thus America opposed the Islamic Revolution, in Khomeini's mind, because it wanted Iran to be weak. America had valued the Shah for his secularism, after all, and so would not reconcile to an Islamic Iran.

The Hostage Crisis

If the revolution viewed the United States as the singular threat to Iran, then the logical end of this enmity was to extricate its influence from Iran altogether—not as revenge for its support of the Shah, but as necessary for protecting the revolution. The revolution had cast the 1953 coup as a calamity and blown out of proportion America's "nefarious" but "omnipotent" role in masterminding it. Therefore early on, the revolutionaries lived in real fear of an imminent repeat of 1953.[18]

In fact, although the revolutionaries did not know it then, Washington was too worried about Iran's fragility and the potential gains for the Soviet Union to contemplate interfering with the revolution.[19] That would change with the hostage crisis. That crisis made it clear that revolutionary Iran was determined to challenge America head-on and in unconventional ways, and pose as an aggressive and active threat to its interests. Washington decided that it had to react in kind. Pursuant to taking American diplomats hostage, the United States froze Iranian assets abroad and introduced the first wave of economic sanctions on Iran—the start of a policy that has continued unabated since then, locking the two countries in an escalatory cycle.[20] Then in December 1979, President Jimmy Carter would sign a so-called Presidential Finding, authorizing covert measures to undo the revolution.[21]

The first attack on the US embassy—as an expression of objection to the American presence in Iran—came in February 1979, right after the revolution toppled the Pahlavi monarchy. This attack, unlike the later one that would captivate the world, was the work of communist activists. After briefly occupying the embassy grounds and holding US ambassador William Sullivan at knifepoint, revolutionary authorities ordered the attackers to leave.[22] The provisional government then was led by Prime Minister Mehdi Bazargan, who represented the moderate prodemocracy wing of the revolution. His government favored adhering to international legal and diplomatic norms, and his decision to quickly end the attack on the embassy was putatively supported by Khomeini.[23] Put another way, in those early days, Khomeini had perhaps not yet sufficiently consolidated power to risk alienating Bazargan and his faction nor would he support communist action. Nevertheless, the idea of attacking the US embassy was now on the table.

It is also likely that Khomeini and the religious faction of the revolution were not then as focused on making a show of anti-Americanism as was the Left. Ayatollah Mohammad Hossein Beheshti, an influential revolutionary leader at the time, reacted to the appearance that with attack on the embassy, the Left had shown itself to be more anti-American, saying that religious revolutionaries were more concerned with ensuring Iran's "independence" than the liberals and the Left, and therefore did not want to provoke an American reaction.[24] Nevertheless, as the competition for control of the revolution between its religious and leftist wings intensified in summer 1979, each sought to appear the more ardent anti-American force.[25]

Khomeini took the threat of the Left seriously. The Left was well organized and had moved quickly to arm its militias—by raiding military arms depots and capturing arms manufacturing factories around Tehran. The Left had made its intention to take over the state clear. Furthermore, expecting American intervention to topple the revolution, Moscow had resolved to strengthen and arm the Tudeh Party in the advent of a civil war.[26] The threat of the Left was rapidly consuming Khomeini and his coterie—which as will be discussed later, was why he would insist on preserving the Iranian military as a bulwark against the Left.

The Left's vocal and doctrinaire anti-Americanism—and audacity to act on it—alarmed Khomeini and his circle. It threatened to cast the Left as genuine revolutionaries. The Left's base of power was among the intelligentsia and university students. It should not therefore have come as a surprise that the religious faction would look to its own student followers to steal the Left's anti-imperialist thunder by attacking the American embassy in November before the leftist students had a chance to do so again.

The Shah was admitted to the United States in October 1979 for cancer treatment. He had been in exile in Mexico. As his health deteriorated, his friends in the United States—led by Kissinger and David Rockefeller—urged the Carter administration to allow the Shah to receive cancer treatment in America. Whether the White House then appreciated the sensitivity of the issue in Tehran has been debated.[27] Suffice it to say that the United States took a risk to help an old friend. But that was not the whole story.

Liberals forces had thus far avoided making a show of anti-Americanism since they wished to quickly return Iran to the international order. Bazargan wanted to restore relations with the United States and the West based on the principle of mutual respect and noninterference in one another's domestic affairs.[28] He viewed the Soviet Union as a more urgent threat to Iran than the United States—which put him at odds with both the religious and leftist revolutionaries—and also disparaged revolutionary internationalism in favor of seeing to social and political changes at home. In fact, at the time, Bazargan's team was in contact with Washington exploring some form of normalization of relations. Bazargan defined the revolution as a struggle against dictatorship to build an Islamic and democratic state. He did not harp on anti-imperialism. To Khomeini, Bazargan was, at best, naive, and at worst, an American Trojan horse.[29] Khomeini instead amplified the revolution's anti-Americanism, believing that it was necessary to Iran's resilience.

Then on November 1, 1979, Bazargan met Carter's national security adviser, Zbigniew Brzezinski, on the sidelines of a state event in Algiers. This meeting would prove decisive in the unfolding of the hostage crisis. Bazargan was by then on the outs with Khomeini. His brand of moderate Islamic politics and advocacy of liberal democracy stood at odds with the ideological fervor of Khomeini's coterie, and the Islamic state they had in mind for Iran.[30]

Bazargan, and his foreign minister, Ibrahim Yazdi, had explored ties with the United States as a crutch to protect their position in Tehran.[31] The United States too was interested in arriving at a modus vivendi with this more moderate faction of the revolution, especially to regain access to CIA listening stations on the Iran-Soviet border.[32] And in exchange for that access, the CIA was willing to share intelligence with the Bazargan government.[33] So throughout summer 1979, the CIA had made contact with various officials in Bazargan's circle.[34] The Algiers meeting was an opportunity to solidify a strategic consensus, which could serve as the basis for a new relationship.

Such a détente with the United States, however, was anathema to Khomeini and the radical revolutionaries. Khomeini and his key advisers were highly suspicious of the CIA's intentions. So was the Soviet Union, which saw the Bazargan-Brzezinski meeting as preparation for a repeat of the overthrow of Salvador Allende in Chile in 1973.[35] In a letter at that time, Soviet leader Leonid Brezhnev too had urged Khomeini "to show vigilance in the face of any efforts on the part of the imperialist forces to obstruct successful development of good-neighborly Soviet-Iranian relations, to rebuff aspirations by these forces to plant poisonous seeds of mistrust and suspicion between the peoples of the two countries."[36]

News of the meeting leaked and quickly led to condemnations of Bazargan for ignoring Khomeini's warnings against cozying up to the United States; anti-American street demonstrations followed, making any deal with Brzezinski impossible.[37] Religious revolutionaries did not want a modus vivendi with the United States; instead, they wanted to wholly extricate US influence from Iran. Gary Sick, then on the National Security staff, wrote to Brzezinski that after Khomeini's condemnation, Yazdi "has permitted Bruce Laingen [US chargé d'affaires and the senior-most American diplomat in Tehran at the time] to stay at the Foreign Ministry. For most of yesterday, Laingen was physically in Yazdi's office, using Yazdi's telephone on a permanent basis to pass messages back and forth to Washington."[38] Religious revolutionaries saw such cooperation with the United States as a betrayal of the revolution, and worse, a conspiracy to undo it.[39]

Moreover, religious revolutionaries thought the Shah's admission to the United States and the Bazargan-Brzezinski contacts were connected as part of a larger American plot to undo the revolution. There was anger at the United States for admitting the Shah, but that masked a deeper worry that the revolution was in danger of another regime-changing American conspiracy—and the epicenter of operations was the US embassy—which the hostage takers took to calling the Den of Spies.[40] Khomeini was then voicing these very concerns, and that is why he supported the taking of the hostages, if not surreptitiously instigating it.[41] His private and public support for hostage taking quickly shut down all dissent within the ruling circle.[42] Khomeini understood then that this was not about respecting international norms but instead about wresting control of the revolution from the liberals and the Left. An embassy takeover that was initially expected to last a few days to register Iran's strong protest soon became a long ordeal with no easy end.[43]

The demand for the extradition of the Shah had quickly become the rallying cry of a growing number of street demonstrations organized by university students; some of these were associated with the radical Left, but many were affiliated with the religious wing of the revolution.[44] Religious revolutionary students formed an action committee, and as a means to raise the stakes on their demand for the Shah's extradition, asked a cleric close to Khomeini, Mohammad Moussavi Khoeiniha, to ask the ayatollah for permission to attack the American embassy. Clearly, the example of the February 1979 attack resonated with the students. Khoeiniha said it was better that the students did not ask Khomeini for his opinion—that is, they should act on their own. This would leave Khomeini room to decide whether to support such action, and if not, they would still leave the embassy having made their point.[45] The students followed Khoeiniha's advice and proceeded with their plans accordingly.[46] Importantly, they found receptive ears as they discussed their plans with various revolutionary leaders—for instance, senior security and intelligence commanders Mohsen Rafiqdoust and Mohsen Rezaie, who then provided them with logistical support for their attack on US embassy.[47] After the students took over the US embassy on November 4, 1979, Khoeiniha personally conveyed messages on behalf of Khomeini to key revolutionary organs to toe the line in supporting hostage taking, but claimed that the students had acted on their own.[48]

In the same vein, Khomeini sent the students the message that "now that you have taken them, hold them firm!"[49] Khomeini did not claim that he had ordered the takeover but also refused to either condemn it or call on the students to leave the embassy. Thus ensued a dramatic 444-day saga that plunged the United States into a prolonged diplomatic crisis, weakened the Carter presidency, and left an indelible mark on Iran's politics as anti-Americanism crescendoed into frenzied day after day on the streets of Tehran. US-Iran relations have not recovered from that moment of rupture.

Khomeini's tacit backing of the hostage taking and the spectacle of daily anti-American demonstrations in front of the US embassy in Tehran shocked the world as an unorthodox act of defiance against the norms of the international order.[50] President Carter saw it as the irrational behavior of self-absorbed revolutionaries, swept up with power and the fever of the revolution.[51] Others saw it as the inevitable result of the anti-Americanism and religious fervor promoted by clerics who were guided by a premodern ideology, both ignorant and defiant of the norms of the modern international order.

Khomeini was far more calculating than ideological, though. He saw the hostage taking as a useful tool to rally the masses, embed the revolution, consolidate power in the hands of the clergy, and cut America's hands from Iran. In his followers' eyes, the willingness to challenge the United States and "end the myth of the American superpower's invincibility" imbued him with an unparalleled glow of power.[52] Unlike Carter, Brzezinski, who was a scholar of the Soviet Union and Communism, and knew revolutions well, understood the utility of the anti-American spectacle to the revolution.[53]

And what that spectacle did was decisive. The taking of the hostages meant that Iran's foreign policy effectively abandoned any pragmatic considerations that could have involved engaging the United States; instead, it became a battle between good and evil, which foreclosed any contact with the United States.[54] That, in turn, protected the revolution from what it feared from US interference.

The hostages were eventually released at the end of President Carter's tenure and after arduous negotiations through various intermediaries. That prolonged drama, however, wedded Iran's politics to a perpetual distrust of America and incessant drive to extricate its influence from the Middle East.

Exporting the Revolution

The 1979 Revolution was an Iranian affair, the product of the political and social dynamics of the late Pahlavi period, and the historical developments that had shaped modern Iran. Yet revolutions do not *remain* local affairs. The Iranian Revolution's religious framework as well as the persona of Khomeini as a clerical leader promising a utopian Islamic state had made the revolution immediately an Islamic model relevant to vast swaths of the world.[55] The revolution was also the first successful toppling of a pro-American authoritarian regime, which was a central focus of leftist forces at the time in Latin America, Southeast Asia, and of course the Middle East.

Thus Khomeini emerged not just as a successful Islamist leader but also as a veritable successor to Vladimir Lenin, Mao Tse-tung, and Fidel Castro. This automatically cast Khomeini's revolution as a model, which was something the revolution's leadership was keen to tout around the world.[56] Islamist activists from North Africa to Southeast Asia—from the Philippines and Thailand to Eritrea and Western Sahara—took note, acknowledging the prominent role that Iran now played in the Muslim world and its politics.[57] Most of these activists were Sunni Muslims with their own versions of Islamist ideology and organizations, and therefore didn't embrace Khomeini as their spiritual leader. Even so, they were enamored by his example and drawn to his rhetoric, especially his icon-oclastic anti-American and anti-imperialist posturing.[58] The Iranian Revolution was energizing Islamist activism everywhere, raising expectations that Islamic activism could succeed in the Muslim world where Communism had, until then, failed.

Khomeini himself called on Muslims across the world to emulate Iran's Islamic Revolution and topple pro-American authoritarian regimes. The revolutionary order in Iran too sought to actively help Islamist activists who responded to Khomeini's call. Khomeini, however, was ambiguous as to whether he favored other countries emulating Iran's example and leading their own revolutions, or whether he saw Iran as the epicenter of a borderless global revolution. In other words, as was also true of debates during the early years of the Bolshevik Revolution in Russia, was the revolution beholden to Iranian nationalism and a Westphalian view of the world, or should it assume an internationalist posture?

The bulk of Khomeini's coterie associated the revolution with Iran while supporting positing it as a model for others. A small but influential clique led by young firebrand cleric Mohammad Montazeri and his close comrade in arms Mehdi Hashemi actively promoted the idea of internationalism with Iran as the hub for perpetual world revolution.[59] Montazeri's influence drew from his father's (Ayatollah Hossein Ali Montazeri) prominent position as Khomeini's close confidant. Montazeri and Hashemi created organizations to pursue their goal, and Hashemi joined the nascent Sepah-e Pasdaran-e Enqelab-e Eslami (Islamic Revolutionary Guards Corps, or IRGC) with the aim of organizing it around the same agenda. In 1981, Montazeri was killed in a bombing attack, and Hashemi was executed in 1987 for revealing the details of the Iran-Contra affair, which will be discussed in later chapters. Yet it was Khomeini's senior aides Ali Khamenei and Ali Akbar Hashemi Rafsanjani who resolved on ending internationalism as a goal, and disbanded nascent institutions created to support it in 1981.[60] Khamenei, who would later become president and then supreme leader, disparagingly dismissed internationalism as the goal for the new Islamic Republic, quipping that it is enough for Iran to serve as an example to the world as a true Islamic state.[61] A few months after he became president, he closed down the Special Unit for Islamic Liberation Movements (Vahed-e Nehzatha-ye Azadibakhsh-e Eslami) that Hashemi had created in the IRGC pursuant to a coup that the unit had hatched in Bahrain ended in an embarrassing fiasco.

The ties between the goals of the revolution and Iran's national interest were more complex when it came to Shia Muslims, who for reasons of faith were even more moved by Iran's revolution.[62] Now that they had carried out the only successful Islamic Revolution to date, Shias gained new respect as the vanguard in the Muslim's world's resistance to the United States and imperialism.[63] Moreover, Shias looked to Khomeini to protect them against discrimination, and were ready to organize under Khomeini's leadership and follow his directives. Beforehand, there had been important pockets of Shia activism in Iraq, eastern Saudi Arabia, and Lebanon that supported and participated in the revolution. The seminary and regional network of Iraqi Ayatollah Mohammad Shirazi, which was ensconced in Kuwait since the 1970s, was important in facilitating the movement of Iranian religious activists—some of whom rose to senior ranks in the IRGC after the revolution—around the region, and training in Palestinian camps in Lebanon and Syria.[64] Now, after the revolution's success, these same activists mobilized to further spread Shia militancy.

They found a receptive audience among the Shia in the region.[65] This was most notable in Pakistan (home to the largest number of Shias after Iran) and Lebanon (where Shias became a force through the civil war that had raged in that country since 1975). Encouraged by the example of Iran, Shia activism in Pakistan initially won some religious and political rights, but by the 1990s was defeated by the Sunni extremism that it provoked.[66] Pakistani Sunni extremists soon received support from Iraq and Saudi Arabia in the 1980s.[67] Sunni extremism grew into a force beyond Pakistan. It spread to Afghanistan in the form of the Taliban in the 1990s, confronting Iran since then with a hostile Sunni arc on its east—a challenge on that front it had not faced since the Safavid era in the sixteenth to eighteenth centuries.

Lebanon proved a more fertile ground.[68] There, Shia political activism centered around the Amal organization, which quickly laid the foundation for the emergence of the more militant Hezbollah. The Israeli invasion of Lebanon in 1982 would help radicalize Shia politics in that country, providing Tehran with an opportunity to confront Israel and the United States directly.[69] And revolutionary Iran's ties to Shia militancy in Lebanon deepened over the ensuing decade with the 1983 deadly bombing of US Marines and the French military barracks, the 1985 hijacking of an American airliner to Beirut, and Hezbollah's concerted attacks on Israeli troops occupying South Lebanon (discussed in later chapters). Indeed, the 1983 bombing forced the American military to withdraw from Lebanon entirely.

Such successes, perhaps inevitably, further entrenched confrontation with the United States into revolutionary Iran's worldview. Whether in Lebanon, Pakistan, or elsewhere, all of these efforts built on the lessons of the hostage crisis—namely, that the United States will cave before pressure, and Iran can hound it out of the Middle East. The perception of certain victories against the United States only encouraged revolutionary leaders to further embrace anti-Americanism as well as build their security and foreign policies around it. In their eyes, the revolution had allowed Iran to achieve what had thus far eluded the country. Whereas the United States and Britain could dispense with Mossadegh in 1953, Khomeini was standing tall, humiliating the imperialist powers. The early success with Hezbollah in Lebanon would furthermore convince Tehran of the imperative of a ground game in the Arab world to pursue its anti-American strategy.

But the early victories did not pave the way for future triumphs. In fact, there were no wins beyond Hezbollah for a long time, and then none at that scale. And while for Sunnis, the example of the Islamic Revolution in Iran empowered Islamist ideology and turned it into a ubiquitous concern from Morocco to Malaysia, here too no other dominoes fell. Iran embraced Islamist activism wherever it happened and even endorsed Sunni extremist action, including the siege of the American embassy in Islamabad, assassination of Anwar Sadat, and a Muslim Brotherhood revolt in the city of Hama against Hafez Assad's regime in Syria. Yet none of these efforts produced lasting political results or confirmed Iran's leadership of Islamism. Instead, Iran earned the enmity of Arab governments for what was deemed as raw hostility and interference in their domestic affairs. As with the Bolshevik Revolution in Russia, Iran's initial certainty that its revolution would be adopted everywhere collapsed into an urge to actively promote its adoption wherever it could.

Everywhere it could—certainly Pakistan, but in Iraq, Saudi Arabia, Bahrain, and Kuwait too—Iran built on local Shia enthusiasm to try to replicate the example of Hezbollah.[70] These Sunni states, however, proved resilient. They deployed a mix of suppression and sectarian politics—to draw a wedge between Shias and Sunnis in the population—and made common cause with the United States to contain the Iranian Revolution.

One result was growing sectarian divisions across the region, starting in Pakistan in the 1980s and exploding in the Arab world in the 2000s. Sunni powers found in Sunni sectarianism a powerful tool to curb Khomeini's lure and limit Iran's influence. Casting Shias as religious deviants in the predominantly Sunni Muslim world denied Khomeini and his revolution claim to Islamic leadership.[71]

The battle lines drawn in those early years of the revolution deepened over time. Iran's neighbors viewed its regional intentions with alarm, and Iran's push to export its revolution invited an American-backed regional alignment to contain it. That entangled Iran's commitment to anti-Americanism with its desire to export its revolution.

The United States, stung by its experiences with the hostage crisis and Iranian attacks in Lebanon, was determined to keep Iran at bay. Yet that in turn only made Iran doubly committed to extricate US influence from the Middle East—the United States was now not only a threat to Iranian security but also an obstacle to its regional ambitions.[72] This dynamic led Iran to extend its security apparatus deep into the Arab world; since that in turn mobilized its neighbors against Iran, additional security threats against the Islamic Republic have expanded and endured.[73]

It was Iraq that attacked Iran in September 1980. It would take a heroic effort by Iran to later liberate lands occupied by the Iraqi Army. As the tide of war changed, Iran set its sights on Baghdad and toppling the Saddam Hussein regime. Although the stated justification was to remove from power an aggressor who had violated a treaty with Iran and coveted its territory, the war thereafter became a means to export the revolution. War would achieve what support for Shia militant groups had failed to do.

It was for this reason that Persian Gulf monarchies rushed to support Saddam, shoring up his war effort to keep Iran's revolution from spilling over into Iraq. Iraq thus became the most important bulwark in the containment of Iran—at least until the United States decided to remove Saddam from power in 2003.

• • •

The revolution, early on, did not have a clear vision for Iran's foreign relations. But it did have its own foundational ideas, which served as the prism through which to view the international system.[74] Although Khomeini had aligned the revolution's left-leaning anti-imperialism with its religious core, the two did not always sit well together.[75] In the first three years of the revolution, the foreign ministry was overseen by seven

different ministers or interim ministers. Revolutionary Iran's first foreign minister, Karim Sanjabi, was a doyen of liberal forces, but with each
change the ministry lurched further toward the religious and radical
spectrum of the revolution. The discontinuity itself both confused foreign policy thinking and reduced its influence among the revolutionary
leadership and councils through which they ran affairs.[76]

Moreover, although the revolution was committed to Iran's independence, its vision of the world was confounded by an unhappy mix
of revolutionary idealism and necessary pragmatism.[77] The constitution
of the Islamic Republic, for example, is premised on Iran as a nation-
state. Yet the constitution also asserts that since the Quran states that
"all Muslims belong to one *umma* (religious community)," consequently
the Islamic Republic "must premise its overall policy on this principle
and strive to realize the political, economic and cultural unity of the Muslim world."[78] This mix of nationalism and internationalism was early on
made more complex, as the pendulum swung back and forth in turf
battles between ideologues and foreign policy professionals.[79]

Competition with the Left and the longue durée of the hostage crisis,
meanwhile, set Iran on a slippery slope to extremism, enmeshing radical
Islamic ideology with uncompromising anti-Americanism. So pro-
nounced was the impact of the hostage crisis that it would be dubbed
the "Second Revolution"—not merely a manifestation of the February 1979 Revolution, but a momentous event with its own distinctive
and discrete impact. Antagonism to the United States became a revolutionary article of faith, a belief that peppered the Islamic Republic's
political language and caged its view of the world in a straitjacket. Anti-
Americanism thus became a foundation stone of the revolution, and
inseparable from how it would conceive of sovereignty and national
security.[80]

To Moscow's dismay, moreover, the Islamic Republic also proved
antagonistic toward the Soviet Union. Khomeini's most acid remarks
were saved for the United States, but he was intent on checking Soviet
influence in Iran too.[81] He was especially concerned because of the
communist coup in Afghanistan and leftist agitation at home. Standing
up to Moscow was a mark of Iran's confident new independence as well.

Shortly after the fall of the Shah, the new revolutionary government shut down the Soviet hospital and Soviet-Iranian Cultural Cooperation Society. Next, in May 1979, Iran unilaterally suspended two articles of the 1921 Soviet-Iranian Treaty, which allowed each country to deploy troops in another if its neighbor's territory was being used by a hostile third power as a staging ground against its interests—removing any pretext for a Soviet troop deployment in Iran.[82]

Despite prior support from the Soviet Union, the Islamic Republic ultimately saw independence in attaching to neither pole in the Cold War. Instead, it adopted the motto "Neither East nor West," framing these words in ornate tile at the entrance to the Foreign Ministry.[83] Meanwhile, foreign minister Ibrahim Yazdi, called for "positive nonalignment" (bitarafi-e mosbat), which took the form early on of leaving a number of treaty agreements with both the United States and Soviet Union.[84] This seeming balance represented a singular achievement of the revolution. Reflecting the official line, historian Manuchehr Mohammadi writes, "The Islamic Revolution put an end to over a century of influence and domination of foreign powers [over Iran], and the people, relying on the slogans of independence, freedom, Islamic Republic and neither east, nor west, but the Islamic Republic showed their abiding hatred and grudge toward the presence and influence of exploiting foreigners."[85] What Mohammadi describes was more than a goal for Iran's foreign policy; it was a reaffirmation of a foreign policy identity based on the revolution's values, the Islamic Republic's experiences in its first years of existence, and its reading of Iran's historical struggles against foreign influence.[86]

• • •

In the eyes of the Islamic Republic, then, the revolution fulfilled what Mossadegh had fought for and Iranians had hoped for since at least 1953. After a quarter century, Khomeini had delivered.[87]

This belief—this inherent antagonism to the West—has echoed down the decades and only grown louder with time. This is because Iran now seeks to survive Western pressure and is doing so by constructing a resistance economy closely tied to the notion of nonalignment.[88] This has been embedded in popular culture, school and university curricula, political discussions, and government propaganda.

All of this has amalgamated together, forging what scholars of international relations refer to as "strategic culture": a set of shared assumptions, mode of reasoning, and reading of history that constitute a uniformity of outlook and action among decision-makers.[89] That is, Iran's strategic culture is a potent mix of encirclement fears and outsized ambition, combining its history of standing alone with its surprisingly effective means of projecting power.

With such a worldview, the Islamic Republic defies the international system it identifies with "exploitative" powers, and embraces independence by flouting the international normative order in violent and dangerous ways. Taking diplomats hostage, using terrorism as a tool of foreign policy, attacking American and French troops in Lebanon, and assassinating dissidents in Europe—all of this worked to isolate Iran, giving shape to a broad-based axis determined to contain its behavior. The Islamic Republic's wrongheaded pursuit of independence only accentuated the very security concerns that Iran had long worried about.

CHAPTER 3

The Struggle to Win the Revolution

In the annals of revolutions, Iran's is distinguished not only for its scope or aftershocks but also for how rapidly it unfolded. It took a mere eighteen-month period between 1977 and 1979 for the gathering clouds of dissent to turn into the perfect revolutionary storm that swept the Pahlavi monarchy off its moorings.[1]

Many factors coalesced to produce the revolution. The Iranian economy had surged between 1974 and 1977, and then cooled. The government responded to a sudden fall in the price of oil with belt tightening, angering the middle and lower middle classes.[2] The oil boom of the 1970s had caused shortages and inflation, but also rising income inequality, rapid urbanization, and growing corruption. The Shah's rigid authoritarianism, meanwhile, brooked no political space for dissent. In 1975, the Shah further reduced the political space by replacing the multiparty system with a one-party rule. All of this aggravated the dissent that had been stirring since the late 1950s. Iranians, who had nursed their anger for years, now joined the ranks of the opposition, embracing religious and leftist ideologies. At the same time, Iran's youthful population provided throngs of fervent foot soldiers for the brewing revolution.

In the years leading to the revolution, the Shah was focused on realizing his ambition of great power status (perhaps made urgent by the fact that he was suffering from cancer and sensed that he did not have much time). Still, he paid little heed to the warning signs that the chasm between him and his people was widening. For Khomeini, meanwhile, the divide between him and the Iranian people was shrinking. The normalization of relations between Iran and Iraq (where he lived in exile) in 1975 opened the floodgates for Khomeini to receive visitors from Iran: pilgrims, clerics, bazaar merchants, and of course, leaders of the opposition. Those contacts allowed Khomeini to quickly build his political network within Iran, and perhaps more important, effectively communicate inside Iran with a steady flow of his sermons and lectures, circulated as samizdats in the form of cassette tapes.

The election of Carter in the United States coincided with this growing political turmoil. Carter had campaigned on human rights, and the Shah thus believed that the new president would emphasize humanitarian concerns rather than traditional Cold War politics. In response to this perceived change, the Shah sought to get ahead of Washington by relaxing his grip on domestic affairs.[3] That shift allowed the opposition—which had also been heartened by Carter's rhetoric— to quickly organize and take advantage of the thaw.[4] The stage was thus set for a crisis.

The trigger came in November 1977, when security forces clashed with seminarians in Qom who had gathered to commemorate the death of Ayatollah Khomeini's son. The Shah made things worse by sanctioning the publication of an incendiary article attacking Khomeini in a leading newspaper in January 1978.[5] The next day, large protests in Qom led to the death of some of the protesters.[6] Next, the commemoration of those deaths in Tabriz invited fresh clashes and more casualties. Thereafter, every funeral and commemoration resulted in new casualties and hence an occasion for further protests. As crowds at the protests grew larger, the Shah, caught off guard, proved out of ideas how to gain control of the situation. He swung between appeasement and crackdown, but neither worked. The Shah's appeasement was simply too little too late; on the other hand, he was never prepared to resort to the kind of scorched-earth crackdown that successfully contained subsequent revolts in the Arab world. His legitimacy quickly eroded, and the balance of power shifted to the opposition. Eventually the Shah left for exile, and the Pahlavi monarchy collapsed in February 1979.

The Societal Revolution

In the first months of the revolution, the focus was on finishing off the Pahlavi regime. In this endeavor, the Left was a main driver. Revolutionary cadres arrested scores of military and civilian officials, executing many after summary kangaroo trials on flimsy charges, and then purged government bureaucracies of all of those viewed as loyal to the Pahlavi monarchy—which often meant those who had risen through the bureaucratic ranks. The revolution was zealously shattering the edifice of the state that, as will be discussed in subsequent chapters, the Qajar and Pahlavi monarchs had built over a century and a half.

State shattering had the ideological fervor and methodical approach that is the classic revolutionary goal of finishing off the ancien régime. Iran's revolutionaries adopted a style that was "confrontational, anti-establishment, militant, confident in its own moral superiority, disdainful of authority and intensely political . . . [rejecting] prevailing institutions of authority, cultural norms, and social values to express itself through the medium of a counterculture that adopted a new language, dress code, social relations, and political style." This is a specific kind of politics—during the Bolshevik Revolution, it was known as "war Communism"—that historian Ali Gheissari and I refer to as "war fundamentalism."[7] In attacking the American embassy and taking its diplomats hostage, Khomeini's student foot soldiers were displaying the same war fundamentalism disdain for institutions and norms.

The revolution also drastically changed Iranian society by reversing the secular culture of the Pahlavi era: mandating the hijab for women, changing men's dress, and imposing religious strictures on society and popular culture. An Islamic state demanded an Islamic society and molding its citizenry in Islamic values, no longer as a mark of piety, but as a de facto standard for citizenship.[8] This might be called "Kemalism in reverse," referring to the aggressive campaign of secularization adopted by Ataturk in Turkey after the First World War. But in Iran's case, this Islamization of society took the form of social engineering that not only reflected religious edicts but also a vision of social organization that would produce a more resilient state. Religion, as noted in the last chapter, was not just a matter of morality and ethics but the path to realizing secular ends too: geopolitical independence and power projection.

The budding Islamic Republic also eliminated important economic power centers and propertied segments of society as well as redistributed wealth. Initially, this redistribution was guided by a political motive: eliminating all vestiges of the Pahlavi rule. Specifically, the property of those who fell afoul of the revolution's wrath was confiscated. Soon, however, the process would become more methodical. Large number of private businesses were nationalized.[9] Khomeini had a penchant for populism and had been exposed to socialist interpretations of Islam while in exile. Iraq in the 1960s and 1970s was a hotbed of Communism and Arab socialist experiments, and that had influenced Shia circles in Najaf as well, especially the works of the influential Shia cleric Muhammad Baqer al-Sadr, whose book *Our Economics* (*Eqtesaduna*) was a noted populist reading of Islam's views on economics.[10]

At a more fundamental level, however, economic radicalism was inspired by the Left and the economic ideas of the New Left in Europe that Iranian students had imbibed. Moreover, the revolutionary zeal in eliminating the Pahlavi regime and redistributing property to the lower echelons of society had parallels in Russian and Chinese revolutions. Iran, though, added its own antisecularism as well as a penchant for imposing religious observance on society. As the secular component of the revolution was sidelined, religious revolutionaries made fealty to Islamic ideology the litmus test for who would be accepted as part of the new social and political leadership.

The nationalization of businesses and industries, along with the redistribution of wealth to the lower rungs of society and rural areas, expanded the size and reach of the state. During the first decade of the revolution, the public sector grew, and with it, the state's institutional capacity and reach into society. Part of this process created a welfare state, which in turn expanded the size of the state bureaucracy. In addition, many of the nationalized industries were grouped together in foundations with vast financial capabilities and deep reach into society through welfare activities.[11] These foundations would sit astride the formal bureaucracy, but would be controlled by the revolutionary leadership, creating parallel economic institutions.[12]

However not all religious revolutionaries subscribed to Marxist views of the economy. Many were probusiness and reflected the interests of bazaar merchants. This laid the foundation for intense debates within the ranks of religious revolutionaries between those who supported private property and capitalism in principle, and radical religious revolutionaries whose ideas on economics was inspired by Marxism.[13]

As is expected of revolutions, Iranian society changed in important ways. There was a concerted change in the language and style of government, and a clear rejection of Pahlavi era secularism and Westernism, in favor of customs embedded in networks of relationships that ran through mosques and bazaars, small towns, and their petit bourgeoisie.[14] This was a sharp break with the "Kemalism" that had defined the Iranian state and its quest for modernization during the Pahlavi era. Moreover, the revolution empowered the lower and lower middle classes, elevating them in managing the affairs of the state. Khomeini's Islamic state was anchored in these classes, especially after 1980 when the middle-class component of the revolution, represented by the liberals and leftists, was sidelined.

For the Pahlavi monarchy, Iran's stability was rooted in economic development and social modernization, building a modern state that would secure the country against threats to its territorial integrity and sovereignty from within and outside. The Islamic Republic, meanwhile, sought security, stability, and immunity from outside interference in a different manner: by embedding the state in society, mobilizing the lower and lower middle classes, and aligning the state with Islamic values. That is not how the revolution defined itself, but that is how it came to see the sources of power and security.

In the early months of the revolution, the quest for independence and anti-Americanism was not always the same thing, nor did the religious and leftist revolutionaries see eye to eye on how to achieve it. For instance, it was the Shah's last prime minister, the liberal Shapur Bakhtiar, who first canceled an arms procurement deal with the United States months before the revolution succeeded. Khomeini's senior adviser and later Iran's president, Ali Akbar Hashemi Rafsanjani, later referred to this act as "treacherous."[15] Yet Bakhtiar's actions reflected an abiding demand by the liberals and leftists who had all along stood against the Shah's extravagant spending on the military, and after the revolution called for dismantling the military altogether.[16]

According to a 1987 RAND Corporation study, some 12,000 military personnel—mostly officers—had been purged from the ranks by September 1980; that number would rise to 23,000 by 1986—out of a total force of 480,000 in 1978–79.[17] The purge was not as extensive as might have been expected and was most intense in the early months of the revolution. Then it was the Left that led the charge, seeing the military as an American pawn and potential obstacle to its own takeover of power.

But for religious revolutionaries, the military was important to Iran's security. Khomeini's aide and future president Rafsanjani characterized the Left's campaign against the military as a "conspiracy."[18] Khomeini, who had excoriated the military for its close ties to the Shah and combating the revolution, had reversed course by July 1979, issuing a general amnesty for members of the armed forces. Claiming that the "corrupt" elements had been purged, he asserted that it was time to return the military to the nation as well as embrace it as quintessential for the country's stability and security.[19] His retort to those who asked him to dissolve the military, guilty of crimes against the people, was sharp: "Our military is Muslim, do not insult our military."[20] In a speech in November 1980, shortly after the start of the Iran-Iraq War, Khomeini said that the Left had wished to dismantle the Iranian military as a prelude to going after the clergy. Once the military was gone, only the Left would have military capability and then it could force the clergy out of politics.[21]

Ultimately, with Khomeini's intervention, religious revolutionaries preserved the military, even after discovering a serious coup plot in July 1980. That said, these revolutionaries would seek to "Islamize" the military, and in later years, would debate whether to integrate it into the newly founded IRGC, which was built in the early 1980s by merging disparate revolutionary militias and irregular war volunteers.[22] The coup attempt did not seem to worry Khomeini, who dismissed it as fantastic thinking on the part of exile activists. When told of the plot, he apparently laughed, asking how a coup could be feasible given the mood of the Iranian people.[23]

Another divide between the Left and Right was the question of ethnic identity and regional autonomy. In March 1979, separatist uprisings swept across Iran's Kurdish and Turkman regions (in the country's west and northeast, respectively), a mere two months after the revolution.[24] The Left certainly supported these revolts, but religious revolutionaries believed the Left even encouraged them. It was leftist activists with little or no ties to local communities, according to Sanjabi, who demanded ethnic rights and raised the specter of secessionism.[25] This put the religious and leftist revolutionaries at odds in fundamental ways.[26] The Left supported secessionist movements in the name of ideology, at the same time as it pushed to weaken the military. Committed to the territorial integrity of the country, religious revolutionaries understood the importance of a strong military.[27] And so it was Khomeini who, sensing the danger of both separatism and the Left, ordered the military to be deployed in the Kurdish region.[28]

The fight against Kurdish separatists was also the first instance when religious revolutionary cadres that had been active at the outset of the revolution were merged together and then organized into military units in the form of the IRGC, thereby developing its flexible military structure.[29]

The military campaign in the Kurdish region turned into a prolonged and protracted conflict.[30] The revolution had assumed that it would create a unified Islamic nation. It was quickly disabused of that halcyon assumption. That the Left had stirred the trouble did not detract from the fundamental worry that internal challenges to state authority and the territorial integrity of the country remained real.[31] After Iraq invaded Iran, the Kurdish rebellion became an even more urgent threat, which the Islamic Republic was able to surmount only by resorting to brutality, and even then at a great cost.[32] Political scientist Ahsan Butt writes that the violence with which a regime reacts to secessionist threats is a function of its likelihood of success and whether that ties to an external threat.[33] Kurdish separatism was both a serious threat to territorial integrity and integral to Iraq's calculation in invading Iran.

The experience reinforced a worry that had troubled the Pahlavi monarchy for decades: that a confluence of outside forces could use ethnic troubles to break Iran apart.

• • •

Within the twentieth century, Iran's revolution is unique in that it triumphed without an equivalent to the Russian or Chinese Communist Parties. Instead, the Iranian Revolution was a loosely bound coalition of antiShah forces, all under Khomeini's leadership. Within the coalition, the modern middle classes had secular democratic or Marxist aspirations, and looked to liberal or leftist leaders and their forces; the religious activists, meanwhile, wanted an Islamic state and looked to Khomeini. The Shah was never able to exploit the chasm that separated these aspirations, or perhaps Khomeini was particularly adept at postponing ideological disputes to after the Shah's fall.

Either way, the result was the same. Once the Shah was gone, in the absence of a dominant revolutionary party, the factional coalition came apart, with the fate of the revolution up for grabs. It did not take long before intense competition for power broke into the open.[34]

In the lead-up to the revolution, secular opposition to the Shah refused to view Khomeini and his followers as anything but benign fellow travelers, who would either move to the sidelines after the revolution or be easily dispensed with. Secular women activists saw no threat to their rights; prodemocracy supporters thought Khomeini would retire to the holy city of Qom and the Shah's dictatorship would be replaced with a liberal democracy. For these secular voices, the religious dimension of the revolution was a sideshow not to be dwelled on. Barely a month after the Shah's regime fell, historian and leftist intellectual Homa Nateq dismissed all talk of the forcible imposition of the hijab, saying, "In Iran there is no hijab issue. And if the price of getting rid of dictatorship and imperialism is donning the hejab, all Iranian women will do so gladly."[35]

Such bravado would soon melt away in the face of reality. Soon one hundred thousand women took to the streets to protest compulsory hijab. They quickly would be joined by a larger cross section of liberal democrats and then leftists, each seeking to defend eroding rights as the religious forces started to consolidate power. The Left would rue its Pollyannaish appraisal of Khomeini and the looming religious threat to the secular values of middle-class Iranians. Those who made it to the safety of exile—including Nateq herself—would recant their sugar-coating of Khomeini's agenda.

Now, tensions between religious and leftist revolutionaries bubbled to the surface as the Islamic Republic took shape, through public debates, elections, plebiscites, and wranglings over a new constitution in a constituent assembly.[36] In the end, although Khomeini made some concessions to the prodemocracy voices, the final shape of the new constitution was closer to his conception of Islamic government.[37] Iran would have elections and a parliament, but the ultimate authority would rest with an unelected and unaccountable cleric as the head of state and the Shia domain—ruling as once had the mighty Safavid shahs.[38] This supreme leader, *vali-e faqih* (supreme clerical authority), would be simultaneously "Caesar and Pope," uncontested temporal ruler and spiritual guide.[39] Khomeini embodied the idea, and after him, although his successor did not rise to the same religious eminence, Khamenei would nevertheless possess the same Caesaropapist authority and function.

The liberals and the Left resisted. In the process, they influenced both the political discourse and institutional design of the Islamic Republic, but they failed to maintain their standing in the emerging political order, let alone shunt the clergy aside to own the revolution. Revolutionary purges and violence first liquidated the Pahlavi state and what remained of it; now these same techniques were applied to prodemocracy and leftist forces as well.

The Left, however, had been important comrades in arm in overthrowing the Shah. To dispense with them, religious revolutionaries had to appropriate their ideas and agenda. This was because they needed to divide the Left's constituency and deny it monopoly over such political demands as social justice, economic equity, and anti-imperialism. The fight against the Left thus pushed religious revolutionaries toward radicalism, and importantly, ardent anti-Americanism.

The Left eventually took to armed resistance, which unfolded at the height of the hostage crisis and Iran-Iraq War, and was cast as proof of its treachery.[40] In the end, Khomeini vanquished the Left, appropriated its populist agenda, condemned it for its secularism, and defeated it in pitched street battles.

In 1980, religious zealots attacked university campuses, the bastion of the Left, instigating a cultural revolution to silence secular dissent.[41] Scores of leftist activists were executed; even those given prison terms were, in 1989, summarily executed on Khomeini's orders.[42] The conquest of the "university by the mosque" was set in stone with the symbolism of the country's signature Friday prayers being held weekly on the grounds of Tehran University—a tradition that continues to this day.

How the Hostage Crisis Shaped the Revolution

It was within this context of a life-or-death struggle between the secular Left and religious Right that the hostage crisis unfolded.[43] The world focused on the Shah's admission to the United States as the reason for the debacle. Yet as argued above, anti-Americanism was important to the competition between the religious and leftist wings of the revolution. It was the Left that had both championed anti-Americanism most ardently and carried out the first attack on the US embassy. As the competition for controlling the revolution escalated, religious zealots moved to appropriate the cause célèbre of the Left.[44]

The Brzezinski-Bazargan meeting in Algiers accentuated the fervor of anti-Americanism. As such, it created an opportunity for *both* the religious and leftist components of the revolution to eliminate the more moderate prodemocracy faction as collaborators with the United States. Bazargan could not remain in power as the representative of democracy and rule of law when Iran was flouting fundamental international norms in the form of the hostage crisis.[45] His government resigned after Khomeini explicitly rejected Bazargan's plea to order the hostage takers to evacuate the American embassy.[46] That was perhaps exactly what Khomeini had wanted, especially after the hostage takers were quick to make public the damning evidence of Bazargan's contacts with the United States that they stumbled on in the embassy. With Bazargan's departure from the scene, the revolution purged its liberal wing.

The initial goal of taking the hostages—beyond the stated demand for the Shah's extradition—was to force the United States to leave Iran and let religious forces take credit for that retreat. It was a radical action, designed to protect the Islamic faction's leadership of the revolution and disrupt the suspected American conspiracy to undo it.

The crisis, however, provided far more opportunity than what the hostage takers could have imagined at the outset. The taking of the hostages immobilized the Carter administration and provoked a media frenzy in the West. The focus was entirely on Khomeini and his immediate circle, which suited the religious contenders for power.[47] That allowed religious activists to mobilize large numbers of people for daily demonstrations replete with anti-American slogans and flag burnings. The frenzy was orchestrated for world television, but it nevertheless ensconced radicalism and anti-Americanism in domestic Iranian political discourse on a whole new scale.[48]

The popular mobilization suited the revolutionary leadership in that it convinced American leaders and public opinion that Iran was too unwieldy to be brought to heel, and regime change or military action to topple the revolution was out of the question. In the minds of the religious revolutionaries, the hostage crisis immunized Iran against age-old fears of foreign intervention in the country.

Moreover, the hostage crisis had foiled what Brzezinski and Bazargan might have been planning in Algiers. But more important, the crisis decisively averted what America had putatively hoped to gain by "encouraging" first a military coup in July 1980 (led by remnants of the Shah's military, centered at the Nojeh Airbase in western Iran) and then Iraq's invasion of Iran in September 1980.[49] There is no apparent evidence that Washington was behind either the coup or Iraqi invasion—although members of the Shah's regime were involved in both the coup attempt and encouraging Saddam to topple the Islamic Republic.[50] The revolutionary leadership, however, believed that America instigated both. For stoking revolutionary fervor, that belief was enough.

The hostage crisis also had the benefit of mobilizing the masses in support of the religious leadership at a time when the competition with the Left was heating up. Khomeini dubbed the fall of Bazargan and subsequent purge of the Left as the "second revolution," more, if not equally, important than the first that toppled the Shah.[51]

Thus Bazargan's fall was a warning to the Left. Represented in government now by Iran's first elected president, Abol-Hasan Bani Sadr, the Left for the most part revolved around the militarily well-organized Islamic-Marxist Mojahedin-e Khalq (People's Holy Warriors, commonly known as MEK) along with the Marxist Fadaiyan-e Khalq (Those Sacrificing for the People) guerrilla forces and pro-Soviet communist Tudeh Party. As a mark of early Soviet outreach to the new revolutionary order, the Tudeh Party had publicly endorsed the Islamic Revolution and Khomeini's leadership.[52] It also carried out an effective campaign to cast Bazargan and the liberal wing of the revolution as American stooges.[53] This would not buy the Tudeh much goodwill. Suspicious of Communism, and Soviet intentions especially after its invasion of Afghanistan and given Soviet relations with Iraq, Khomeini hounded and humiliated the Tudeh, and uprooted it from the political scene.[54]

Although religious revolutionaries were understandably antagonistic toward the secular Left—whose communist creed was at odds with Khomeini's Islamic ideology—the same could not be said of MEK. The armed urban guerrilla group mixed a militant and cultish brew of Islamic and Marxist ideological radicalism with a penchant for violence. It was close to left-leaning cleric Ayatollah Mahmoud Taleqani, who enjoyed certain prominence in religious circles. In fact, MEK had early on collaborated with religious activists in carrying out purges, but now it was preparing to dethrone Khomeini and the clerical leadership of the revolution.[55] Khomeini would not tolerate either MEK's ambition or its audacity. Even so, what ultimately led him to break with MEK completely—and order the organization's liquidation—was only when he saw it as a national security threat.

On April 26, 1979, a senior member of MEK, Mohammad Reza Saadati, was arrested on charges of spying for the Soviet Union. MEK denied Saadati's involvement with the Soviet State Security Committee; instead, it argued that Saadati had "exchanged" intelligence with the Soviet Union, and those who were accusing him of espionage were themselves agents of Western imperialism. The strategy backfired.

It only convinced Khomeini that MEK was a national security threat. Even the organization's patron, Taleqani, disowned it.[56] Khomeini ordered the destruction of what he saw as a Soviet Trojan horse, which in turn set in motion a bloody confrontation between religious revolutionaries and MEK's armed cadres.[57]

By 1982, MEK had assassinated some twelve hundred religious and political leaders of the Islamic Republic. The government, in turn, had killed or executed some five thousand members of MEK.[58] At that time, MEK relied heavily on child recruits, especially in carrying out its suicide bombings (an example that was perhaps instructive for its religious opponents who would later turn to children in mounting human-wave attacks against Iraq). But that meant that by 1982, many of those killed and executed in the ranks of MEK were children.

It is important to note that although Khomeini and his religious followers were comrades in arms with the Left in the run-up to the revolution, they did not see Iranian nationalism through the same lens. The Left, and communists in particular, had always championed internationalism and displayed tremendous loyalty to its cause, even at the expense of Iranian nationalism. In the 1940s and 1950s, communists were enamored of Stalin's cult of personality and supported Soviet meddling in Iran—including its attempts to take Iran's Azerbaijan and Kurdistan Provinces. The Left was never able to shake off that legacy; what irked the Shah about Communists' loyalty to Moscow also colored Khomeini's view of them. Indeed, as was discussed in an earlier chapter, it was the fear of Communism and its adherence to the wishes of Moscow that had led senior clergy to rally behind the Shah in 1953. Even on the eve of the revolution, most senior clerics in the prominent Shia centers of learning in Iraq remained staunchly anti-communist.[59]

This stigma of the Left's subservience to Soviet interests persisted. As late as the 1970s, Ayatollah Morteza Motahhari, a prominent cleric and close aide to Khomeini during the revolution, rued the attraction of the Left in Iran and the Shah's inability to contain it.[60] Motahhari was also the most prominent opponent of the influential intellectual Ali Shariati's brand of Islamic Marxism among Khomeini's coterie that was increasingly popular on university campuses and cast a leftist opposition to the monarchy in the garb of religion, and had helped fill the ranks of the like-minded MEK, which was from early on his devotee.[61] Animus toward Shariati was, however, broader in scope among conservative clerics. Motahhari was the most vocal adversary of the Left among the senior clergy, but he was not alone. Khomeini saw the Left's internationalism as a betrayal of Iranian nationalism. Saadati's case confirmed that perception, and that perception played its part in his order summary execution of thousands of leftists in jail in 1989, regardless of their sentences.[62]

With the world's attention focused on Iran, the control of the hostages became the most important determinant of which faction would control the revolution. That was one reason why the religious leadership had every incentive to keep the hostages and the ordeal lasted 444 days.

That also convinced the Left that if it wanted power, it had to act. At that moment, popular mobilization by religious activists around the hostage crisis meant that the Left could not mobilize a mass movement against the clergy. So instead, the Left conspired to take power through paramilitary means, using its well-trained armed militias. The world was focused on demonstrations around the embassy as Iranian cities plunged into pitched battles between the armed religious and leftist forces of both MEK and the Fadaiyan (who led an ill-fated uprising in northern Iran too).

The Left was defeated.[63] Bani Sadr was hounded from office into exile. MEK and Fadaiyan's armed forces were decimated, their networks destroyed, and scores of their activists and supporters forced into exile or arrested and executed.

Nevertheless, the liquidation of the Left was a bloody and costly affair. MEK fought back, not only in pitched battles on the streets, but by assassinating numerous religious revolutionary leaders. These killings included a president and prime minister, and in one daring bombing in 1981, dozens of senior figures at a gathering of the nascent Islamic Republic Party, including the most powerful clerical leader of the time next to Khomeini, Ayatollah Beheshti. Iran's current supreme leader, Ayatollah Ali Khamenei, lost the use of his left hand in one such assassination attempt.

That bloody crucible left its mark on the revolution, hardening its religious leaders against domestic dissent. The defeat of the Left also entailed adopting its populist and anti-imperialist slogans, and the myths that it had, in turn, inherited from Mossadegh and the legacy of the 1953 coup.

The hostage crisis transformed the young Islamic Republic. It radicalized the ruling revolutionary order, but it also gave it self-confidence, allowing it to seek greater legitimacy in the eyes of Iranians for securing and empowering the country in ways unimaginable to Iranian historical memory along with the anxieties embedded in it. In the 444 days of the hostage crisis, revolutionary leaders claimed that Iran showed the United States to be "helpless" and Iran capable of exercising the kind of power against "imperialism" that Mossadegh could only have dreamed of.

The American response to the crisis was construed as less than decisive. The Carter administration first settled on patience, hoping that a series of tactical steps—starting with condemnations, then cajoling, and then threats—would end the crisis. That diplomatic approach reflected the influence of Secretary of State Cyrus Vance on the early decision-making process.[64] Although such an approach was in keeping with how America had managed other crises, Iranians saw it as weakness; it fell far short of the massive retaliation that was expected of the "diabolical" and "ruthless" United States of the revolutionaries' imagination.[65] The Carter administration tried to open a back channel to those among Iran's leadership who were skeptical of the wisdom of hostage taking.[66] Those voices, like left-leaning president Bani Sadr, were on their way out, however.[67] In fact, the US outreach only further convinced Khomeini and the radical elements around him that secularists and the Left were American instruments, and if they advocated releasing the hostages, it must be at the behest of Washington.

Carter's initial approach did not work. American diplomats remained hostages in Iran, so the administration decided to up the ante. It tried to rescue the hostages in a daring military operation, code-named Desert One.[68] American military planes carried soldiers and helicopters inside Iran. The helicopters would ferry American soldiers from the desert landing spot into the heart of Tehran. The soldiers would then break into the embassy, and fly the freed hostages back to the desert rendezvous spot and then out of Iran. Yet the operation had to be aborted after three of the eight helicopters could not carry out the mission. Then as the operation was being called off, one of the helicopters crashed into one of the transport planes, killing eight American servicepeople.[69] The fiasco was an embarrassment to the United States and closed the door to any further military operations to rescue the hostages.

That gave Iran even more confidence to dig in its heels. Indeed, it even allowed Khomeini to brag to his followers that God was on Iran's side since He had intervened to doom the American mission.

In the end, it would be prolonged and secret negotiations that released the hostages. By the time they were released, shortly before Ronald Reagan assumed the presidency, the hostage crisis had run its course for Iranians. Khomeini and the religious revolutionaries had got everything they wanted from the crisis: purging rival factions and consolidating power in the hands of radical religious revolutionaries, posing as an unbending anti-imperialist force that withstood American pressure, and even taking credit for wrecking Carter's presidency and deciding the outcome of American presidential elections. Some have even suggested that Iran had cut a deal with Reagan's team to delay the release of the hostages until after the US presidential elections.[70] True or not, these were powerful notions in Tehran, and became an urban myth not just in Iran but across the Middle East too.

By late 1980, Iran also needed to focus on the war with Iraq. Moreover, Iranians understood that how the crisis would unfold now under Reagan would be different from how it played out under Carter.[71] It was time to end the crisis.

Through the hostage crisis, Khomeini emerged as an unbending anti-imperialist leader, one whose steely message of defiance of the United States at all costs resonated around the world. At the height of the crisis, he responded to the threat of American military action boldly, stating that "America cannot do a damn thing"; this was an even stronger put-down in the original Persian, *Emirka hich ghalati nemitavanad bekonad.*[72] Khomeini was proven right in the minds of Iranians and Muslims around the world, as the hostage crisis was followed with bloody attacks by Shia militias on US and French troops in Lebanon, forcing American withdrawal from that country in 1983.

Khomeini emerged from the crisis as the leader who made Islam triumphant against America. Islam had provided a shield against Western intrigue and military designs on the country. The clergy had protected the Shia domain by defiance and doubling down on religion. Khomeini had risen above the security dilemmas that had bedeviled generations of Iranian rulers. A revolution that began as a crusade for social justice and to end the dictatorship now basked in the glory of having solved Iran's security dilemma.

The outsized importance that the hostage crisis played in the life of the revolution early on focused on the imperative of security and survival. Khomeini and his faction of the revolution had seen the 444 days of the crisis as one of, first, an American and then leftist push to undo the revolution. The young Islamic Republic survived, they concluded, because of the power and appeal of its Islamic ideology, but also a determination among the people to defeat both America and the Left. Virulent anti-Americanism was not only an expression of opprobrium for American intentions but necessary for protecting the country against future American assaults on the revolution as well.

This would wed the Islamic Republic to unending anti-Americanism—so much so that it would gradually become the raison d'être of the revolution. Denying the United States a footprint in Iran and pushing it away from the Middle East would become the singular focus of Iran's security in the Islamic Republic. This crusade was a source of power—at least at first—for the Islamic Republic's clerical rulers, allowing them to enmesh Shiism and Iranian nationalism in a new way.

The Islamic Republic therefore drilled the lessons of the hostage crisis along with virulent anti-Americanism into the population. In time, anti-Americanism would become entrenched in state and society. Yet its value would decline—so much so that it would become an albatross around the neck of the Islamic Republic, posing new sets of security challenges that might have not existed had the hostage crisis not happened.

CHAPTER 4

Sacred Defense

How the War Transformed Iran's Strategy

The largest trench warfare since World War I, the largest tank battles since World War II, and the most prolific use of chemical weapons in war since the Geneva Conventions of 1925—all of this was the Iran-Iraq War. From 1980 until 1988, the conflict cost Iran dearly. Between 200,000 and 250,000 Iranians were killed, and another 300,000 to 400,000 were injured, estimates military historian Steven Ward; 16,000 civilians were killed, and some 2 million were displaced.[1]

Iran spent $160 billion to prosecute the war, but the real cost to the country was the far larger sum of $450 billion.[2] More revealing is that by 1988, Iran was spending a staggering two-thirds of its national income on the war.[3] And such waste was increasingly difficult to recover given the ongoing damage done to the country in the conflict. For example, during the war, Iran lost 60 percent of its oil-refining capacity; the port of Khorramshahr was destroyed, and other cities in Iran's southwest Khuzestan Province suffered extensive damage.

Beyond the human catastrophe, the war years had another effect. The experience of invasion, loss, and sacrifice—along with the triumph, against all odds, in the face of adversity and isolation—indelibly marked the people's psyche. The new republic's very survival was threatened, and by a singular, collective security hazard. But perhaps more important than the threat of conquest was *how* the republic responded, in a manner that necessarily redirected its politics and social organization.

"The Iran-Iraq War . . . because of its vast impact and outcomes, according to a chronicle of the war composed by the IRGC [in a series of official histories, firsthand accounts of the war and memoirs of the war compiled by its media outlets], will affect *every* issue of internal and foreign policy of the Islamic Republic of Iran for at least the next several *decades*."[4] In a 2022 speech, Supreme Leader Ayatollah Khamenei echoed this conclusion by positing the lessons Iran learned during the war as guidelines for how the country should approach its national security.[5]

The revolution may have birthed the Islamic Republic, but as these next two chapters show, it was the Iran-Iraq War that decisively shaped it. Less than a year after the revolution enshrined its social, economic, and political ideals in a new Islamic Republic, Iran's leaders suddenly had to focus on a more urgent goal: the security and survival of the state. The threats to the young Islamic Republic, writes historian of the war Seyyed Jalal Dehqani Firouzabadi—in a manner closely reflecting establishment views in Iran—focused national security on three "existential" goals: the survival of the Iranian people and nation-state, survival of the Islamic Republic, and survival of the Islamic Revolution.[6] Crucially, to the revolutionary leadership, these three goals could *only* be achieved together.

In short, the conflict between Iran and Iraq was a war that would make the state. What that means is that the Islamic Republic today is, paradoxically, not solely or largely the product of the ideology and political struggle for the Islamic Revolution that created it in 1979. Instead, the republic is now decisively an outcome of the failures and successes of Iran's near-decade struggle with Iraq and its allies. While the next chapter will consider how the war remade Iran internally, this chapter explores how the war remade Iran's grand strategy abroad.

■ ■ ■

On September 22, 1980, Iraq invaded Iran. Thus began a grueling eight-year war that claimed the lives of hundreds of thousands of Iranians and Iraqis.[7] The war devastated the economies of both countries as well as large swaths of their territories.[8] Iraq had long worried about Iran's rising strength and was now threatened by its brand of revolutionary

Shiism. Iran's clerical rulers, on the other hand, looked down on Saddam Hussein's regime as a weak, secular, Western-backed dictatorship—a ripe fruit for the next step of the Islamic Revolution.

Indeed, Saddam had reason to worry about revolutionary Iran. Although he tracked the domestic turmoil of Iran closely, still, Khomeini's meteoric rise and the Shia clerics takeover of Iran had surprised and rattled him. Saddam was especially concerned about how the might of this new Shia power could disrupt the fragile stability in a Shia-majority Iraq ruled by Sunnis.[9] He was concerned that with Iran's backing, dissident Shia clerics like Ayatollahs Mohammad Baqer Shirazi or Mohammad Baqer al-Sadr, touted then as "Iraq's Khomeini," would rally Iraq's Shia multitude against his regime.[10] Saddam sought to quickly extinguish any possibility of a Shia uprising through a savage crackdown, purging Shias from positions of power, the butchery of Shia activists, and execution of Shia clerics and political leaders—all of which only alienated Iraq's Shias as well as lay bare his fears of and vulnerability to a potential uprising.[11]

Saddam was committed to toppling the Islamic Republic—according to former prime minister Shapur Bakhtiar, who as an exile leader, met Saddam in Baghdad in April 1980—by his "almost irrational fear of Khomeini. He was particularly concerned about what Khomeini might or might not be able to do among the Iraqi Shia."[12] Thus the stick; but the carrot for Saddam was his conclusion that revolutionary purges had significantly weakened the Iranian military.[13] It was also his conviction—after he was persuaded by eager Iranian exiles like Bakhtiar and General Gholam Ali Oveisi, a former commander of the Iranian Army—that a quick victory would topple Khomeini.[14]

It was an ongoing border skirmish, according to Saddam, that necessitated an invasion of Iran.[15] But it was clear to those in and out of Iran that this was merely a pretext for an "imposed war" (*jang-e tahmili*)— proof of Saddam's perfidy and the West's hostility toward the revolution.[16] Now the revolution gave him a historic opening to settle his disputes with Iran once and for all in Iraq's favor.[17]

Saddam had always coveted Iranian territory, and both enmity with Iran and expanding the Arab world's eastern flank were important to his claim to Arab leadership.[18] And Khomeini, who had lived in exile in Iraq, was no stranger to Saddam's ambitions and machination. For example, although Saddam had agreed to settle border disputes with Iran in the Algiers Accords of 1975, the leader of Iraq did not view those disagreements as resolved; Iraq had acceded to the agreement from a position of weakness and under pressure from an Iranian-backed Kurdish uprising.[19] Even the Shah knew that Iraq would only use the accords to build up its capabilities to challenge Iran once again.[20] In fact, revolutionary Iran's first ambassador to Iraq believed that Saddam had been preparing for war with Iran as early as November 1978—that is, three months *before* the revolution's victory.[21] Ultimately, then, it was this combination of factors—fearing the consequences of Khomeini's victory, but also sensing opportunity in the collapse of the Pahlavi state and its military, and ethnic tensions in Iran's Kurdish regions—that led Saddam to pounce.[22]

Although there was ambition in Baghdad, there was also hubris in Tehran. The revolution's leaders, basking in their domestic victory, felt invincible. They had little knowledge of international affairs and even less so of military issues. Even though Iran's leaders received reports of Iraq's hostile intentions, still, they did little to prepare Iran for war. They discounted the Iraqi threat, believing that Saddam would not dare attack Iran.[23] In fact, since the hostage crisis was still underway when the invasion came, the revolutionary leadership thought that the saber-rattling was an American ploy to force Iran to release the hostages.[24]

Perhaps their greatest error was to believe that the region's secular dictators were weak and intimidated by the power of the Islamic Revolution, as they believed the Shah and his military had been. After all, Khomeini had made no secret of his desire to export the revolution; on one occasion, he had even called on the Iraqi military to revolt and "free the honorable people of Iraq from the clutches of" Saddam's anti-Islamic regime.[25]

Yet Khomeini was oblivious to how neighboring governments would receive his incendiary rhetoric, dismissing the concerns of his close aide Ayatollah Hossein Ali Montazeri who thought that Khomeini's bombast could result in a confrontation.[26] On a different occasion, Saddam sent a message through Iran's ambassador to Iraq that he wished to engage in negotiations, but Khomeini said it was a waste of time and that he would not sell the Iraqi people to Saddam.[27] Instead, Khomeini claimed behind closed doors that Saddam would be swept from power by his own people in six months' time.[28] Taking their cue from Khomeini's belief in Iraqi weakness, other senior revolutionary clerical leaders condemned the Iraqi government from the pulpit. Whether genuinely worried or using these verbal attacks as a pretext, Iraq used them as justification for war.[29]

And so when the attack did come, Iran was caught off guard. Even worse, the scale and ferocity of the assault quickly revealed that this was not just a surgical blow to punish Iran and settle border disputes but also a land grab: a concerted effort to defeat and dismember Iran. This fear was confirmed by Saddam's choice to call the Iraqi offensive "Echoes of Qadesiah," referring to the famous battle at the dawn of Islam centuries earlier when Arab forces decisively defeated Iran and conquered it.[30] That symbolism confirmed the deadly extent of Iraq's ambitions.

The Iraqi military moved quickly across a broad front inside Iran's oil-rich southwestern Khuzestan Province. It captured the port city of Khorramshahr with a population of 150,000. Next, the military entered the oil city of Abadan, home to Iran's largest oil refinery, but failed to capture it.

Despite the early successes and grand ambition, the Iraqi military offensive fell short of Saddam's expectations. Only a month after launching its attack, by October 1980, the Iraqi military was no longer advancing. By December, facing unexpectedly stiff resistance from a mix of regular Iranian military and volunteer militia forces, it found itself effectively halted, only some seventy-five miles inside Iran.[31] Just a few months in, the war turned into a stalemate.

Ending the war would not be easy. Khomeini, for his part, blamed Iraqi aggression on the United States and rejected any negotiations while Iraqi forces occupied Iranian territory.[32] But even this early in the conflict, he also articulated a strategic directive that would guide Iran until the end of the war: Saddam was a corrupt aggressor, and Iran would not negotiate with such a person; Iran would fight until it won, declared Khomeini, even if it took twenty years.[33]

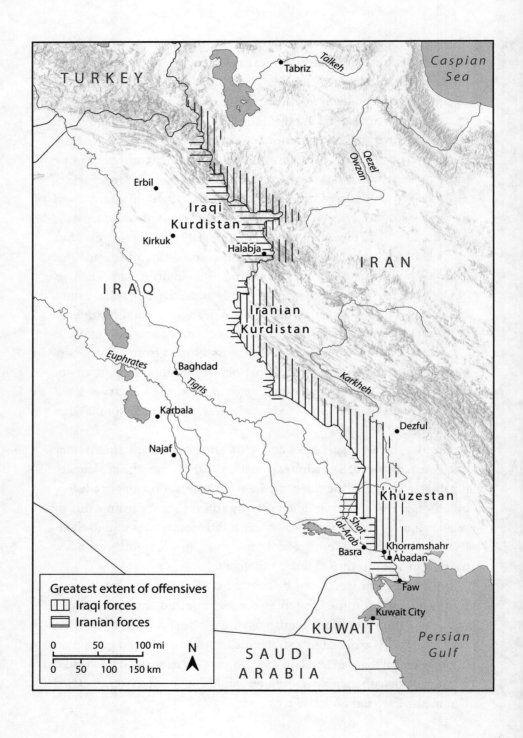

TURKEY

Caspian Sea

Tabriz

Talkeh

Qezel Owzan

IRAN

Erbil

Iraqi Kurdistan

Kirkuk

Halabja

IRAQ

Iranian Kurdistan

Euphrates

Baghdad

Tigris

Karkheh

Karbala

Dezful

Najaf

Khuzestan

Shat al-Arab

Basra

Khorramshahr

Abadan

Faw

Kuwait City

Greatest extent of offensives

▯▯▯ Iraqi forces
▤ Iranian forces

0   50   100 mi
0   50 100 150 km

N

KUWAIT

SAUDI ARABIA

Persian Gulf

In the end, the war took just less than ten years, but that still made it one of the longest wars of the twentieth century. The war unfolded in three clear phases. First—from 1980 until 1982—Iraq invaded and occupied Iranian territory. Next—from 1982 until 1986—Iran recaptured its lost territory and then undertook a campaign to win the war inside Iraqi territory. Finally—from 1986 until the war's conclusion in 1988—the balance of power shifted back in Iraq's favor. It ended after Iraqi forces launched a successful assault to push their way back into Iranian territory, and in the process captured or destroyed a significant portion of Iran's war matériel.

■ ■ ■

For Iran's leaders, the totality of the war (especially filtered through these three phases) rewrote how they thought about national security, domestic politics, and even ruling over Iran. It was these lessons that forged a new strategic outlook, which would dominate the republic going forward. And that outlook would be one of sacred, strategic *defense*.

Fundamentally, the invasion united the country in resisting aggression, and against all the odds, doing so by relying only on its own resources. To wage such a total war, over eight years, the state relied on religious and ideological zeal, and indirectly patriotism. War and resistance had not been a choice, according to Khomeini. Instead, the war was the inevitable path Iran had to follow being attacked:

> We the ever oppressed of history . . . we have no one except God and if we are broken into a thousand pieces, we will not cease in our fight against oppressors. . . . So there is no way, except to fight; thus we must break the hold of the superpowers, especially America. And it is necessary to choose one of two paths: martyrdom or victory, both of which in our belief are victorious.[34]

This was a war imposed on Iran. Even when the battle lines moved inside Iraq's borders, even when Iran called to unseat Saddam or ultimately to liberate Jerusalem itself, the war was not "offensive." It remained throughout the "imposed war." The war effort was cast as a defense or sacred defense (*defa'e moqaddas*).

The war would end in defeat. But the idea of sacred defense would endure; indeed, its promulgation within Iran's society—and especially Iran's strategic thinking—was an unexpected victory for the Islamic Republic. It was a unique inflection point, a break with a history of invasions, defeats, and humiliations, a time when Iran defied overwhelming odds and overcame a concerted campaign by great powers along with their regional clients to defeat Iran.[35]

The lesson of sacred defense started with the belief that to defend itself, Iran had to remain true to its revolutionary ideology. This was because Iran needed ideology to mobilize the population to resist—perhaps the only thing that could allow a country to endure such a total war. Sacred defense relied on popular support for the war campaign. In Supreme Leader Ayatollah Ali Khamenei's words, "During sacred defense the entire country became defensive depth of the war front, every town, village, seminary and university was in the service of defending the country and the revolution."[36] The result was viewed as a triumphant defense of the country before a superior foe backed by the United States and Europe. Consequently, such effective national security *demanded* that the country's politics be organized around ideological commitment. National security and religious ideology would forge a symbiotic relationship, anchored in the alliance between militant religious revolutionaries and the IRGC—led by Khamenei, who was deeply involved in the management of the war at the Ministry of Defense and then as president—a political alliance that would endure as the buttress for the hard-line conservative faction in Iran's politics.

But even the embrace of sacred defense only accentuated Iran's sense of insecurity and vulnerability.[37] After all, at the end of the war Iran had evidently failed in its defense: Iraq remained intact, Saddam firmly in control, and having repelled Iranian offensives, Iraqi forces were back inside Iran. Battered at the denouement of the war, Iran was exhausted and unable to reverse the outcome.[38]

And yet even this defeat was filtered through Tehran's wholehearted embrace of sacred defense. This had surprising consequences. For example, following the end of hostilities, Iranians understandably had a national reckoning with the outcome of the war. But rather than focusing on how Iran had snatched defeat from the jaws of victory—as might be expected—Iran's ruling elite and people fixated on the opposite: the triumph of how Iran had survived the ordeal at all. The war's calamitous end was blamed not on faulty strategic assumptions but instead on international support for Saddam, with foreign powers punishing Iran for its revolution. It was injustice in the world order, Iran's rulers declared, that had denied them victory. But they had, in a way, achieved another victory: managing the war *despite* the array of international forces that had stood in their way; the "Iranian David" had won over the designs of the Goliath of its own making.

Iran's controversial regional policies over the past two decades, the so-called forward defense doctrine that justifies it (which will be discussed in later chapters), had its origins in the blame Iran placed for the outcome of the war on its evident conventional military limitations.[39] The IRGC commanders concluded that Iran failed in its military objectives in Iraq between 1982 and 1988 because it lacked access to the requisite conventional military capabilities. Whereas Iraq received ample advanced weaponry, Iran had to look to the black market for its needs, which fell short on fulfilling them.[40] Whereas conventional military shortcomings had failed Iran in Iraq, perceived success in Lebanon in the 1980s pointed to an alternate strategy: the unconventional use of terrorism, guerrilla warfare, and proxy militias. That strategy would mean ongoing defense through low-level conflict in the Arab world—which would in turn keep Iran's relations with its neighbors and the United States in a state of perpetual conflict. Authors Ariane Tabatabai and Annie Tracy Samuel characterize this strategy as "defensive realism," achieving defense through aggression and unconventional means of warfare.[41] Although Iran has since the 1990s invested in a homegrown military-industrial complex including the manufacturing of a range of sophisticated drones and missiles, its military strategy still favors unconventional methods.

The war also led Iran's rulers to conclude that international norms and agreements provided no protection for Iran. The United Nations had failed to condemn Iraq's invasion.[42] Instead, UN secretary-general Kurt Waldheim impressed on Iran's prime minister that Iran could not expect sympathy and support when it was holding hostage American diplomats in defiance of international law.[43] Even so, Iranian leaders somehow remained convinced that although violating international law, Iran was still entitled to its protections. The United Nations eventually issued a resolution to end the war in July 1982, only after Iraqi troops had withdrawn from Khorramshahr and the battle front was moving inside Iraq, threatening its territorial integrity and the future of the Saddam regime. Calling for an end to the war at that point, Iran concluded, was explicitly to protect Iraq. After all, the international body was not prepared to call for an end to the war when it was Iraq that was threatening Iran's territorial integrity and the future of the Islamic Republic.[44]

In later years, the United Nations remained silent even as Iraq attacked civilian targets in Iranian cities and Saddam used chemical weapons against Iranian troops.[45] During the war, Iraq fired 54,000 chemical artillery shells, launched 27,000 short-range chemical rockets, and dropped 19,500 aerial gas bombs.[46] In the end, international condemnation of such banned weapons only came when there was a chemical attack on the Iraqi Kurdish village of Halabja.[47] Iran's belief in its isolation only became firmer as the war progressed. This was particularly cutting when Tehran concluded—rightly, as it turned out—that it was the United States that helped develop Iraq's chemical weapons capabilities.[48]

Apparently international law did not apply to Iran because of its regime. The international normative order along with the world bodies that represented and advocated it were guided not by their founding principles but rather by the opprobrium for the ideology of the Islamic Republic and its antagonism to the West. And since that regime was not willing to step aside, Iran had to protect itself, assuming an absence of those norms. As the war progressed and in the years that followed, Iran took this lesson to heart. It increasingly flouted international norms of conduct in the name of protecting its security and advancing its interests. In Iraq, Iran pursued the conflict deep into Iraqi territory; in Lebanon, it took hostages and engaged in suicide bombing, and formed Hezbollah as a formidable proxy. Iran's stance became ensconced in a particular view of self-reliant security (the so-called battlefield [*meydan*], a euphemism for the military forces) in lieu of diplomacy in managing Iran's national interest.[49] It extended the IRGC's view of irregular warfare into the conduct of diplomacy and international statecraft.

Emergence of the IRGC

Khomeini's early bravado in the face of an Iraqi attack was backed by the heroic effort mounted by the remnants of the Iranian military and newly formed revolutionary militias to stop Iraqi advances. Battered by revolution and lacking adequate supplies, the military was hard-pressed to repel the Iraqi offensive.[50] As the stalemate set in late 1980, encouraged by revolutionary fighters who were veterans of Palestinian and Shia guerrilla campaigns in Lebanon, Iran turned to guerrilla tactics, deploying irregular militia units consisting of revolutionary fighters and volunteers to harass the occupying Iraqi forces, winning small but important victories. The flexibility of these nascent guerrilla units, along with their ideological zeal and willingness to undertake dangerous missions, led Khomeini to organize them into a formal structure, the IRGC.[51]

Unrest in Iran's Kurdish regions, demanding autonomy and self-rule, started almost immediately after the revolution. Then in spring 1981, taking advantage of the war, Kurdish separatists mounted an insurgency and took control of large parts of Iran's Kurdish region.[52] Although the Iraqi military was not directly involved, Tehran saw the war facilitating the loss of even more territory. Initially the regular military was deployed to quell the uprising, but ultimately it would be the IRGC fighters who would play the most prominent role in suppressing the Kurdish rebellion. It was those campaigns in the Kurdish region that entrenched in the IRGC the imperative of organizing and fighting as a flexible expeditionary force rather a standing army.[53]

In the early years of the war, the military played an important role in checking the Iraqi military's progress in Iran and even rolling back some of its gains. The Iranian military's favored method of warfare was classic military formations and operations—a method captured under its slogan of "fire instead of blood" (*atash beja-ye khoun*). Such traditional tactics sharply contrasted with the new IRGC's popular mobilization strategy to wage unconventional warfare: the so-called people's warfare (*jang-e mardomi*). But the military faced an immense problem on account of the disruptions caused by the revolution and subsequent trade sanctions: the state was simply unable to resupply the military with the money or matériel it required to operate. Without such "fire," the military simply could not continue normal operations against the military-industrial might of Iraq.

Therefore the young IRGC was soon given more say in military planning by Khomeini, relying on its zeal and revolutionary fervor, and irregular guerrilla tactics rather than the professionalism of Iran's military and its classic battlefield planning.[54] That shift would confirm that the Islamic Republic had given up on the idea of protecting and promoting national security with regular military strategy and forces. It had decided to rely on the IRGC's formula of mixing ideology and irregular warfare.[55] That decision would prove decisive in shaping the strategic mindset of the Islamic Republic, not only during the war, but for the decades that have followed. The fateful decision to create and empower the IRGC was, perhaps, to have the most impact on Iran's foreign policy strategy down the decades.

●●●

The occlusion of the military's influence was sudden. And it was hastened not only by battlefield defeats but also by political machinations.

Abol-Hasan Bani Sadr was elected as the Islamic Republic's first president. Although close to Khomeini during the months leading up to the revolution, Bani Sadr was a leftist who was at odds with religious revolutionaries. He rose to the presidency at a time when the Left still wielded significant influence on the streets and religious revolutionaries were not yet able to assert full control over the political process. Bani Sadr soon found himself in the vortex of competition for power between the religious and leftist wings of the revolution.[56]

To challenge Khomeini and the rival religious revolutionaries, Bani Sadr shored up his own authority by foregrounding his role as commander in chief of the military. Bani Sadr's embrace of the military alarmed the religious revolutionaries, who worried that strengthening the regular armed forces could mean losing the revolution to the military domination led by their secular rivals.[57] Moreover, the religious revolutionaries worried that given the military's roots in the secular nationalism of the Pahlavi period, Bani Sadr and his leftist backer could win it over. It was therefore foolhardy to allow the war to empower it.

But the military also lost favor because it lost on the battlefield. In this the regular military was impaired by Bani Sadr's failure to put together a convincing plan for victory.[58] At the start of the offensive to expel the Iraqi forces, Bani Sadr championed the Nasr offensive campaign of January 1981, aimed at liberating Khorramshahr through a direct assault on the Iraqi positions. The offensive failed. Bani Sadr and his military planners had deliberately excluded the IRGC units, which put to question not only planning for the operation but also that any military plan relying on the military and its classic battle plans could succeed. Khomeini intervened, asking Bani Sadr's clerical rivals to take control of the war planning and devise a new strategy centered around the IRGC.[59]

The failure of the Nasr campaign thus doomed Bani Sadr's political fortunes.[60] He had aimed high and come up short; his reliance on the regular military alone had not only proved a folly, but his hapless leadership had weakened the military as well as strengthened the rival political-military alliance of militant clerics and the budding IRGC.[61] The IRGC thus rose on the back of the settlement of a political struggle for power at the center, which consolidated authority fully in the hands of the militant clergy.

Grasping at straws, Bani Sadr next decided to ally himself with MEK. As discussed in the last chapter, MEK had a totally different goal for the revolution, and was already waging a trenchant campaign of assassinations and street battles against the IRGC.[62] Khomeini understood the gravity of MEK's threat and ordered its annihilation, removing perhaps the last alternative power base that might effectively challenge clerical authority.[63] He also removed Bani Sadr from command of the military as a prelude to his dismissal from the presidency. In a parting shot, Khomeini told Bani Sadr, "Put out of your mind the thought that without you the war effort would collapse. I will ably manage this war myself."[64]

• • •

Besides determining *who* led Iran, the war determined *how* they would lead it. The young commanders of the IRGC understood that the war was an opportunity to grow the force.[65] The most prominent of these commanders was Mohsen Rezaie, who served as the IRGC's commander in chief during the war. Rezaie, who would become a towering figure in the IRGC and the security establishment, and would rise to prominent positions in state institutions, would be particularly influential with Khomeini as a strong advocate of continuing the Iran-Iraq War even after the Iraqi forces were driven out of Iran, and he argued for perpetual conflict in the region and with the United States after the war ended.

Rezaie was twenty-seven when he assumed command of the IRGC. Like other IRGC commanders who served then, he had not received formal military training or previously served in the military. What commanders like Rezaie lacked in military experience, they made up for in ideological zeal and self-belief, derived from their role in the revolution, and then combating the Kurdish insurgency and the Left.[66] They were fierce in their commitment to Khomeini and the revolution, and in the belief that their cause was just and victory would belong to them; Islamic ideals and a willingness to be martyred would prevail.

Such views had been drilled into his followers by Khomeini throughout the revolutionary period. After the founding of the Islamic Republic, Khomeini argued that it was championing the cause of justice and being willing to die to realize it that constituted true Islam, and had made the revolution triumphant. The revolution was proof of the superiority of true faith over worldly power; just as they had vanquished the mighty Pahlavi state, they would also defeat Iraq. The IRGC fighters were the true children of the revolution, the ones closest to Khomeini's own thinking. In later years, Rezaie recollected a meeting with Khomeini in which continuing the war into Iraqi territory was discussed.

"We said war will continue until Saddam is punished," Rezaie remembered Khomeini saying, "but that was our minimum demand. If Saddam would not yield, we would have continued the war until we toppled Saddam and captured Israel too."[67] In other words, Khomeini argued for unending war, and by implication, the unending ascendancy of the IRGC—which is why commanders like Rezaie favored continuing the war with Iraq, and why the IRGC today remains inimical to ending hostilities with the West.

•••

The IRGC's war strategy relied on using a large number of volunteers to swarm the battlefield and overwhelm the enemy.[68] The strategy was effective. By summer 1982, Iraq's occupying army had shrunk from 210,000 to 150,000.[69] The IRGC itself was at first a volunteer force, consisting of ideologically committed youths who saw faith as their most important weapon and reason for their victory in battle. It was a deep faith in Shia myths and the "charisma" embedded in Shia piety, according to sociologist Maryam Alemzadeh, that galvanized the IRGC into a viable force—one that could step up to fill Iran's military void in the second year of the war and even lead in turning the war around by liberating Khorramshahr in May 1982.[70]

The IRGC's military strategy reflected its own self-image. It had learned in the first months of the war that Iraqi forces were vulnerable to guerrilla attacks. If such attacks were to be more concentrated and involve larger numbers of "guerrilla" fighters, they could be decisive.[71] Thus the IRGC stumbled on the idea of human wave attacks as an evolution of guerrilla warfare strategy. To mobilize the requisite number of volunteers, all the IRGC needed was to appeal to ideological passion and popular faith (and rely on political instruments to instill such ideology and faith in the population at large). Consequently, Commander in Chief Rezaie and the IRGC frequently argued that the war did not need traditional battlefield strategy because "faith was enough for victory" (*tavakol baraye pirouzi kafi ast*).[72]

Mostafa Chamran, a key founder of the IRGC and Iran's defense minister during the early years of the war, wrote that the success of guerrilla warfare depended on the unity of the military and the political.[73] Since it was guerrilla war that had shaped the IRGC in its infancy, this meant that the IRGC's fighting doctrine required the political anchor of support in both state and society.

But after Khorramshahr, faith only took the IRGC so far. In July 1982, Iran launched the Ramadan offensive, which unleashed three human wave attacks on Iraqi positions in a six-week period.[74] The first human wave was one hundred thousand strong; it included lightly armed IRGC units, but also unarmed and ill-trained volunteers, children as young as twelve, and the infirm and elderly. And it was these volunteers who charged the Iraqi defenses, over battlefields already covered with mines.[75] Such willingness to accept large number of casualties—made possible by the ideological dedication of the volunteers—seemed to give Iran a military advantage. At first, it is true, the Iraqi military was caught off guard by Iran's unconventional methods. But by the third attack, the Iraqi forces had adjusted, and the heavy human toll gained Iran little advantage. In this Iraq was aided by American satellite imagery that alerted the Iraqi troops to the numbers and positions of the Iranian forces and volunteers amassed for attacks, which Iraq likely used to deploy chemical weapons to stop them; in the words of one Iraqi general, "For every harmful insect there is an insecticide capable of annihilating it."[76] Still, even as this strategy grew increasingly ineffective, Iran would continue to use it.[77]

. . .

From 1982 onward, the war settled into a long stalemate. Iran continued to throw enormous resources into its campaigns. The use of volunteers to engage in human wave attacks was blessed by Khomeini, who in January 1982 lauded the "fearless" volunteers willing to sacrifice their lives and famously said, "I wish I too was a *pasdar* [IRGC soldier]."[78] Hundreds of thousands of recruits were sent to the front, where they fought in harrowing battles that claimed many lives, and sent back home many more young people maimed and scarred by the war. Those who died were honored as martyrs, and the vast cemeteries where they were buried became monuments to the war.

The human toll of the war cast a shadow over Iranian society. But the immense loss of life also promoted the celebration of martyrdom, which in turn fed the ideological zeal that the IRGC relied on to continue its campaigns. Iraqi territory changed hands, but Iran did not hold onto any gains. Its push to capture the city of Basra came to naught, most spectacularly in early 1987, when Iran's Karbala-5 offensive was repelled with some fifty thousand Iranian dead.

Every costly military defeat was interpreted by Iran's leaders not as a call to change strategy but instead as a new need to increase the number of fresh volunteers. Iraq's resilience, and even its use of chemical weapons or air raids over Iranian cities, did not prompt Khomeini to reevaluate his support for the IRGC's strategy.[79] Rather, the revolution's leader hoped that "Iranians had not tired of war" and would continue to give to it unquestioningly.[80]

Some in the ruling circles and even within the IRGC's ranks questioned this approach. They hoped that Khomeini would see the folly of relying on faith in lieu of proper military planning.[81] But the IRGC along with its militant backers within the state apparatuses retorted that Iran had no time to build a military from the bottom-up, arm it, and develop appropriate strategies for it. It could not take a break from the war, and it had to devise strategies that would work given the realities it faced. Within such limitations, it was argued, Iran must rely on irregular warfare that depended on ideological vigilance.[82]

Fortunately for the IRGC, Khomeini agreed with them, and whenever dissent grew too loud, he would not hesitate to quell it.[83] For example, in fall 1984, ninety IRGC commanders appealed to Khomeini to rein in Rezaie. In response, Khomeini approved the purge of dissenters, only tightening Rezaie's control. In summer 1985, a committee of Parliament, led by Hasan Rouhani (who would be president between 2013 and 2021), asked to speak with Khomeini about how to end the war. In response, Khomeini immediately ordered the committee disbanded.[84] That, in turn, ended all debate over the cost of the war, rise of the IRGC, and domination of the militant ideology that went with it.[85]

Ultimately, Rezaie was the commander Khomeini wanted to run the IRGC and the war. Perhaps more important, Rezaie's strategy was

Khomeini's strategy, and it fostered the kind of radicalization of domestic politics that Khomeini wanted.

Khomeini's resolve is perhaps most clear in how he handled the dissent of his senior aide and designated successor. Ayatollah Hossein Ali Montazeri opposed the IRGC's military strategy and saw the militancy that supported it as a danger to the revolution. After another failed offensive—Operation Khaybar, in February 1984, which left tens of thousands of Iranians and Iraqis dead—Montazeri derided the IRGC's costly strategy as "a donkey's strategy" (*shive-ye kharaki*)—that is, a stupidly contrived strategy.[86] He warned Khomeini in November 1985 of a concerted campaign to prolong the war—which he thought benefited the IRGC and its militant backers, at the expense of the regular military and institutions of the state—and predicted a creeping coup.[87] But Montazeri's counsel went unheard. Although the chosen successor of the supreme leader, Montazeri was soon openly excoriated within the IRGC and then sidelined by Khomeini altogether.[88]

Khomeini had made it clear he was committed to pursuing the war, but was *also* committed to the political alliances between the militant clerics and the IRGC that was carrying it out. His rejection of Montazeri's dissent, then, presaged clashes between Khamenei and moderates and reformists in the decades that followed.

Khomeini's open embrace of a prolonged war made it more difficult for Iran to separate national security from state building once the war ended, put to rest the strategic culture that dominated the war years, and contain the military and security institutions that had grown on the back of the war.[89] Khomeini not only embraced the IRGC's forever-war outlook but saw expansion of the IRGC as necessary for doing that too. To that end, he ordered the IRGC to develop an air force and navy and pose as Iran's formal military.[90] In effect, he encouraged the IRGC to see its institutional interests in forever war. Added to this was the vast network of hundreds of thousands of war volunteers and IRGC veterans, who would rise through the ranks to dominate politics, society, and the economy through tight-knit personal as well as institutional relations that sustained this strategic culture. That creeping coup that Montazeri had worried about would continue unimpeded during and then after the war. The IRGC and the militant alliance that sustained its strategy foisted on Iran a national security mindset that would define the Islamic Republic going forward, long after the war had ended.

The Writ of the Long War

On May 24, 1982, Iranian military forces—led by the IRGC—took back Khorramshahr.[91] This was a monumental victory for the young revolutionary regime.[92] In defending Iranian sovereignty, the revolution had gained newfound nationalist confidence. Saddam sued for a ceasefire, yet he had already violated the peace of the Algiers Accord when he thought Iran was weak and sought to take Iranian territory. Could Iran trust him?

The revolutionary leadership debated the merits of continuing offensive military operations with preparing for defending Iran's border, albeit through an ongoing war of attrition.[93] Iran's leaders harbored a deep distrust of Saddam, and felt any peace was transient and would leave Iran vulnerable.[94] IRGC leader Rezaie believed that Saddam had wanted only a ceasefire and not a proper peace.[95] Perhaps more important, Rezaie worried that Iran's existing border with Iraq could not be successfully defended; to properly defend Iran, Iranian forces should be on the Iraqi banks of the Arvandroud (Shatt al-Arab) River that sits between the two countries.[96]

Official histories of the war in Iran have unfailingly asserted that Iran continued the war in 1982 not for ideological or expansionist reasons but instead because it viewed a ceasefire or even peace agreement with Saddam as no more a guarantee of peace and security than the Algiers Accords of 1975; Saddam would resume the war, and given what the recapturing of Khorramshahr had demanded of Iran, the country had to go beyond peace with the "aggressor" to ensure genuine stability by removing that aggressor.[97]

Iran's foreign minister at the time, Ali Akbar Velayati, thought that Saddam was not accepting defeat and saw the loss of Khorramshahr as a tactical retreat—a respite to regroup and attack again.[98] Velayati would capture this fear of another war by drawing a comparison between the war with Iraq and the second Russo-Iranian War of the early nineteenth century that ended in defeat and the ignominious Treaty of Turkmanchay.[99] In Velayati's telling, Qajar crown prince Abbas Mirza was at first victorious in battle, capturing the city of Tbilisi and as much territory "as we [Iran] had lost in the first round of the [Iran-Iraq] war." Yet since his troops, much like Iran's forces in the 1980s, were jihadi volunteers, they returned to their villages. This, in turn, opened the door to a Russian offensive that inflicted a costly defeat on Iran. Khomeini, he continued, "was worried about history repeating itself."[100] In other words, as was the case with Abbas Mirza, once Iran demobilized its volunteers it would be vulnerable to an Iraqi attack. Only by toppling Saddam would Iran gain true security. Iran's president at the time and later the supreme leader, Ayatollah Ali Khamenei, said that "had Iran stopped fighting after capturing Khorramshahr, Saddam would have definitely resumed his offensive and [once again] captured Iranian territory."[101]

In later years, with the calamity of continuing the war into Iraq evident to Iranians, there was an attempt to absolve Khomeini of that responsibility. For instance, his son Ahmad claimed that Khomeini had not favored continuing the war into Iraqi territory. At the time when the decision to invade Iraq was made, Khomeini had putatively asserted,

> It was better if the war ended. However, those in charge of the war argued that Iran had to get to Shatt al-Arab (Arvandroud) [push beyond Khorramshahr to the river separating the two countries] and to get war reparations from Iraq. The Imam was opposed. He would say if you were going to continue the war, given your state, you could be unsuccessful, and then the war will become unending. We must end this war at a clear point, and the capture of Khorramshahr is the best opportunity.[102]

It had been Khomeini who had settled the debate over continuing the war, characterizing what became an offense into Iraq in terms of a defense of Iran. His concern had been that unless Iran continued the war, it would be vulnerable to another Iraqi offensive. Khomeini had also been convinced from the outset of the war that leaving Saddam in power would give the United States the opportunity to undo the revolution, saying, "What ails us today and could repeat itself is what will follow our military victory [against Iraq] is that it is not clear that America will give up its greed for this country [Iran] any time soon."[103] This led him to see the removal of Saddam from power as making Iran immune to US pressure. This set the bar very high for national security as requiring regime change in an Arab country. That line of thinking would become embedded in Iran's strategic culture, leading it to seek security in an expansionist presence in the Arab world. Political scientist Christopher Blattman argues that prominent among the reasons why compromise fails to end wars and why they can go on for a long time are leaders not forming a clear understanding of their own strength as well as that of their enemy, and leaders fearing that their adversary will grow stronger in the future.[104] In 1982, these dynamics led Iran to continue the war.

Khomeini thought Saddam could not be trusted.[105] He resolved to continue the war, perhaps sensing that the defeat would unravel the Sunni regime in Iraq and Iran's revolution would win the day in the Arab world's largest Shia country, declaring that it did not matter whether it would take one or many more military operations, but the war would continue while Saddam remained in office, and everyone should be prepared for a long war.[106] He justified his decision in terms of a defensive imperative, however, telling a gathering of clerics that "the people should be told [from the pulpit of mosques] that the war will not end with the capture of Khorramshahr or other cities.[107] The war will continue until the aggressor is punished."[108] Elsewhere he said that if they were going to defend the country, they should do it from a position where their forces did not have to worry daily about the enemy's aggression.[109]

That would come to pass only if Saddam was gone, and the consensus view was that the capture of the Shia city of Basra, Iraq's second largest, sitting at the heart of its rich oil fields and abutting Iran's border, would deal a death blow to Saddam's regime.[110] Although some of Khomeini's advisers, notably Rafsanjani, believed that Iran did not need to capture Basra—or push for Saddam's fall—the country could realize its aims by grabbing a symbolic chunk of Iraqi territory and then dictating its own terms to end the war.[111]

The decision to continue the war was also about political jockeying in Tehran. Various factions of the revolutionary elite as well the IRGC and military, all understood how continuing the war could hurt—or help—their interests.[112] Militant clergy aligned with the IRGC and its corollary volunteer force, the Basij (the Mobilized) had gained prominence during the war.[113] It was the Basij that took credit for the liberation of Khorramshahr after leading an ideologically charged campaign to mobilize support for the war and the fervor of Iranian troops during critical campaigns. Now the IRGC and the Basij wanted to preserve that ideological fervor—but in service of their *own* political interests—by carrying the war into Iraq.[114]

For the next six years of costly and fruitless conflict, the Islamic Republic drilled into its leadership and population a strategic logic rather than an ideological imperative. In retrospect, the decision to continue the war with the aim of removing Saddam from power would prove a consequential strategic mistake.[115] It committed Iran to a maximal goal of capturing Iraq's second-largest city and changing its regime.

This strategic folly was perhaps rooted in Khomeini's persona. He felt vindicated in his dogged determination, which accounted for the victory of his improbable revolution. He saw Saddam as the Shah and the war as a repeat of his successful revolutionary campaign. Khomeini was convinced that he would win the war against all odds and in defiance of all cautionary counsel just as he had won the revolution.

As attaining this strategic objective proved out of reach, Khomeini—but also the IRGC's leadership—increasingly saw abandoning that goal as an admission of defeat, putting to question Khomeini's wisdom, the revolution's reputation, and the IRGC's image and competence. In spiritual terms, Khomeini saw himself above all of his peers; to the multitude, he was a lawgiver with divine qualities.[116] His wisdom was beyond reproach. By hitching his reputation to the outcome of the war, he risked tarnishing his image of infallibility. Persisting on continuing the war only raised the stakes and in due course embedded rigidity into the Islamic Republic's pursuit of its grand strategy.

The second phase of the Iran-Iraq War, between 1982 and 1988, represents the first time since the middle of the Qajar period that Iran

invaded a neighbor, even accounting for the fact that Iraq had started
the war. Furthermore, Iran was seeking to conquer, hold, and shape the
politics of an Arab country. In this, Khomeini underestimated the resilience of Iraqi nationalism and overestimated how much Shia identity
could override that fealty. Khomeini hoped that he could win Iraq's
Shias over by appealing to Islamic and Shia solidarity along with the
promise of an Islamic order that would liberate them from dictatorial
rule. He would thus justify Iran's overreach into Iraq by arguing,

> We have frequently explained to the governments in the region that
> we do not want to fight with you. We are not like that, looking to
> bully and intervene in another country as soon as we have power. . . .
> Our entry into Iraq was to occupy neither Iraq nor Basra. Our home-
> land is not Basra or the Levant, our homeland is Islam. We follow
> Islam. Islam does not allow us to put a Muslim country under our
> rule.[117]

Iran did not want to conquer Iraq but rather to bring it under the umbrella of the Islamic Revolution. Should the revolution take root there
as it did in Iran in 1979, this meant toppling Ṣaddam's secular Baathist
regime.

Nevertheless, just as Iran's Arab minority was cool to Saddam's claim
to be liberating it from Iranian domination, Iraq's Shias resisted Khomeini's violation of Iraqi sovereignty.[118] In January 1987, with Iranian
troops a mere eight miles from Basra, Khomeini called on its population to welcome its Shia brethren. The Iranian offensive was named
Karbala-5 in reference to the martyrdom of the third Shia imam, Hossein. Banking on Iraqi Shia support, Iran had high expectations for the
offensive.[119] But the city's Shia population and the Shia soldiers defending it refused to surrender, and after heavy losses, Iran's siege collapsed. With upward of fifty thousand Iranian dead, Basra became "the
Somme of the Iran-Iraq War."[120] Nationalism in both countries proved
more important than ethnic or religious identity.

A few days later, Rafsanjani noted in his diary that "it has become
clear that it [taking Basra] will not be simple; the enemy fights with
purpose to defend its territory."[121] Rafsanjani was the first to admit it

was time to end the war. In March 1984, soon after he was appointed commander of the war effort, Rafsanjani told Khomeini that Iran should conclude the war after a battlefield victory inside Iraq. Khomeini remained notably silent. Rafsanjani continued to explore a strategy that would give Iran a quick and satisfactory victory, which could then serve as a pretext for ending the war. He argued that if Iraq agreed to cede the oil-rich Majnoun Islands that Iran had captured in battle, Iran should agree to an armistice.[122] That meant setting Iran's goal as consolidating its hold over defendable territory inside Iraq instead of regime change.[123]

Yet Rafsanjani would find both Khomeini and the IRGC uninterested in any goal short of toppling Saddam—in other words, a longer war.[124] Indeed, Rezaie asserted that those—like Rafsanjani—who insisted the IRGC tell Khomeini that it cannot win this war, did not believe that Iran could fight and win *any* war. Rafsanjani had to relent to the IRGC, but hoped that Saddam would fall on his own accord—owing to Iraq's dire domestic situation. Rafsanjani decided to prepare the ground for an endgame, starting with exploring ways to mend fences with Saudi Arabia and open diplomatic channels with Europe—initiatives that would become the hallmark of his presidency in later years.[125]

Repeated offensives did not subdue Basra, and that dimmed the luster of the long war strategy and the belief that Iran could impose its will on Iraq.[126] The regular military maintained that Iran should settle for defending its own borders rather than capturing Iraqi cities. Unable to guarantee success, the IRGC argued that changing tactics or ending the war at that point would lead to settling from a position of weakness. It redoubled its insistence on the same military strategy.[127] And it looked abroad to find another way to break the impasse.

The War Expands: America and Lebanon

Iranian leaders had all along suspected American machinations behind the war.[128] They believed that the United States aspired to use the war to force Iran to release the American hostages, and having been denied a footprint in Iran to repeat the 1953 coup, it was now looking to an Iraqi invasion to bring about regime change to Iran.

These beliefs fed on the deep-seated suspicions of the United States and radical anti-imperialist views that held sway among Iran's leaders at the time; blaming America for the war fit the Iranian leaders' preferred view of the United States. It also drew on intelligence they had gathered on collaboration between Saddam and Iranian political leaders in exile, some of whom were receiving funding and support from both Saddam and the CIA. The United States thus played an outsized role in Iran's view of the reasons for war, and what it meant for Iran and the revolution.[129]

Iran then was not willing to woo the United States, or was capable of it, but was rather determined to defeat America. It was Khomeini who made this goal explicit, and that unyielding posture toward the United States would become embedded in Iran's war strategy and the whole strategic culture woven around sacred defense. The concept was justified for the public in religious terms and was adopted by the Islamic Republic to characterize its stance against Iraq during the war.[130]

To prosecute the war, Iran depended on a societal militancy that simultaneously stoked anti-Americanism. This was because Iran believed that Iraq's resilience in the war could only have been achieved through the backing of the United States, but even more so, because it saw anti-Americanism as necessary for maintaining ideological fervor in support of the war.

For its part, the United States—still bristling from the hostage crisis—was eager to prevent an Iranian victory in Iraq. Such a triumph, it feared, would expand the reach of the Iranian Revolution.[131] In the first years of the war, Washington had not wanted a triumphant Saddam and then grew keen to deny Iran a decisive victory.[132] This mutual hostility would inevitably escalate tensions between the two, which would play out across the Middle East.

In 1983, the war was at a stalemate. Iraq had been pushed back into its own territory, but Iran, although it repeatedly attacked Iraq, could not advance nor achieve a decisive victory. Frustrated with the deadlock, Iraq opened a naval front against Iran. The aim was to disrupt Iran's ability to export oil—Iraq had overland export capability and therefore was less vulnerable to disruption of the flow of oil over the Persian Gulf—forcing Tehran to end the war. At sea, the Iraqi forces attacked Iranian oil facilities and tankers.[133] Iran retaliated with attacks of its own on *all* tanker traffic—including those of nearby countries like Kuwait and Saudi Arabia—signaling that if it could not export oil, then neither could its neighbors.

What followed was the most sustained attack on commercial shipping since World War II.[134] These so-called tanker wars rattled world energy markets and led Persian Gulf oil exporters to pressure the United States to protect the shipping lanes. This aligned with US interests since America was already worried about another cutoff of Middle East oil akin to the one in 1973. But the United States did *not* step in as a neutral referee separating the warring sides; instead, its interventions were directly aimed at Iran. This took the form of the United States providing a military shield so that the Persian Gulf monarchies could retaliate against Iranian attacks. In May 1984, for example, Saudi Arabian fighter jets downed two Iranian fighters, which were targeting tanker ships being loaded with Saudi oil.[135]

Although the United States was careful not to attack Iranian forces on its own, Tehran—according to former Iranian diplomat Hossein Mousavian—interpreted US intervention as an "undeclared war" against Iran.[136] And so when Iran responded, it did so not in the Persian Gulf. Instead, it expanded the conflict into Lebanon.

Since the onset of the Islamic Revolution, Lebanon had been important to Iran.[137] The country had a large Shia population (with close ties to Iran); moreover, Lebanon had a strong Shia militia called Amal, which fought in the country's civil war in the 1970s. In fact, several of Iran's revolutionary leaders, including the first commander of the IRGC, were veterans of Amal.[138] Then in 1982—barely two weeks after Iran took back Khorramshahr from Iraq—Israel invaded Lebanon. Now, suddenly, Lebanon's Shia population entered directly into Tehran's calculations.

Israel's invasion would achieve its goal of eliminating the armed Palestinian presence in Lebanon. But in effectively disarming the Sunni community there, whose power rested on Palestinian firepower, Israel left a vacuum for Shia militias—with whom Iran already had relationships—to fill.

In Lebanon's labyrinthine sectarian politics, however, all was not black and white. The Shia of Lebanon who were resentful of the then heavy-handedness and arrogance of the Palestinian forces during the civil war years, for example, had benefited from the Israeli invasion, and many had been quick to show their gratitude, with villagers in the south of the country even going so far as to greet Israeli troops with rice and flowers. Even more striking, Shias flexed their new muscles by laying siege to unprotected Palestinian refugee camps.

Khomeini was alarmed, both by the welcome that the Israeli forces received and the harsh treatment of Palestinian refugees at the hands of Shia militias. He and the revolutionary leadership saw Israel as an imperialist force, mirroring US attitudes and policies, and in turn, this made Israel inherently inimical to revolutionary Iran's interests and values. Given that the Muslim world then held Israel in contempt, Khomeini had previously sought political capital in casting Iran as a leader in resisting Israel. Now, being seen on the side of Israel and fighting Palestinians was not how Khomeini wanted Shias—or Iran's own Shia-led Islamic Revolution—to be portrayed in the Middle East. The Shias must lead in Arab causes, foremost among them the Palestinian cause; that was how they would gain acceptance among the region's Sunnis. What he charted for the Shias of Lebanon is also true of Iran's own attachment to the Palestinian cause. Moreover, Khomeini worried that the Israeli invasion was a ruse to divert Iran's attention from Iraq, and even worse, create an anti-Iranian Shia beachhead in Lebanon. To counter this narrative—of a fractured, opportunistic Shia community that had *not* been united by the Islamic Revolution—Khomeini focused on Lebanon as integral to the war effort.

Now, three years into the conflict, Khomeini declared that the goal for the war was not the liberation of Iraq but rather Palestine. To win in the Levant, Iran must first win Iraq, and Iraq was a stepping stone to the Levant.[139] A new slogan that became ubiquitous at this time was "the path to Jerusalem ran through Karbala"—that is, through a city in Iraq. Suddenly, the goal before the war was extended further, and Iraq and the Palestinian issue became two sides of the same coin.

And so although bogged down in Iraq, Iran sent fighters to Lebanon.[140] They began organizing new Shia militias that would challenge the Israeli presence there—a task that became easier as Israel decided to prolong its stay in the Shia region of south Lebanon; the liberators quickly became the occupiers. These new Iran-backed militias would soon coalesce to form a new force whose military prowess and political control would dominate in Lebanon's politics for decades to come: the Party of God, or Hezbollah.[141]

Despite the power vacuum created by Israel's routing of Palestinian forces, Lebanon's militant Shia militias did not have free rein. In fact, they faced stiff resistance from the powerful Christian Maronite Phalange forces, which were backed by Israel, France, and the United States. And so to clear the path for Shia militias and put France and the United States on the back heel, Iran upped the ante. In October 1983, Iran orchestrated suicide bombings on the US Marine and French military barracks in Beirut. These deadly attacks claimed the lives of 241 American and 58 French soldiers.

In one sense, the attack was a stunning success for Iran, causing the United States and France to withdraw from Lebanon. (Later, the same tactics would also be used by Hezbollah to force a rare Israeli retreat from an occupied Arab territory without a peace deal. Hezbollah would claim the eventual Israeli withdrawal from south Lebanon in 2000 as a singular Arab military victory against Israel.) But in response, both France and the United States levied economic sanctions on Iran and increased their support for Saddam. In fact, Iraq waged the tanker wars using French missiles and aircraft.[142] The United States turned to economic sanctions. These had originally been imposed on Iran in response to the hostage crisis and then removed in 1981 (as part of the deal that secured the release of those hostages); following the Beirut attacks, however, the United States reinstated them.[143]

These 1983 economic sanctions, designating the Islamic Republic as a sponsor of terrorism, have remained in place now for over four decades. Indeed, they are the foundation for decades of sanctions on Iran. And although self-inflicted, these sanctions nevertheless amplified the Islamic Republic's sense of siege and its fear of ongoing campaigns to overturn the revolution.

Iran responded with a campaign of kidnapping of French and US citizens in Lebanon. This was a tactic that had been employed since 1982. But it now found greater salience for Iran, especially as it saw a growing threat from the United States in the Persian Gulf. The Lebanese hostage crisis would last from 1984 to 1986. The campaign hardened Western attitudes toward Iran; even the eventual release of the hostages, after secret negotiations between Iran and United States in 1985, would not reverse that trend.

Involving itself in Lebanon meant that Iran, in turn, committed itself to confronting Israel. But this also meant this confrontation was now a pillar of its regional strategy, entrenched deeply in the Islamic Republic's security thinking. This dovetailed with other aspects of Iran's emerging security strategy, such as Khomeini's belief that national security required exerting influence across the Arab world and shaping it for Iran's ends. That is, after 1982, Iran pushed to change the regime in Baghdad and exert control over Lebanese politics, but with the stated goal of *only protecting its own security*—in Iraq, against another invasion of Iran, and in Lebanon, against Israel.

The rise of Hezbollah reflected the same approach that also gave rise to the IRGC, as the organization, relying on ideology and religious passion as well as empowering and giving voice and agency to youths who felt marginalized in the dominant social order, recruited local volunteers to conduct daring military operations and suicide bombings against Israeli targets to force Israel to leave South Lebanon, as Iran had forced Iraq leave southern Iran.[144] This approach, as will be discussed in later chapters, would eventually coalesce into the doctrine of forward defense as mantra of the IRGC, which played a dominant role in shaping Iran's ground game in both Iraq and Lebanon.

In Lebanon, Iran successfully forced the United States and France out of the country (and checked Israeli ambitions there). It was a victory achieved by hostage taking and suicide bombing. In Iraq, Iran had fought a neighbor; in Lebanon, it had fought some of the largest imperial powers. In Iraq, Iran did not win; in Lebanon, using a proxy, it saw victory. That conclusion left an indelible impression on Iran. Four decades after Lebanon, Iran's rulers still believe that Iran can win against the West and drive it from the region—if it continues to employ terrorism and guerrilla warfare as a strategic tool.

•••

Despite confrontations in the Persian Gulf and Lebanon, in summer 1985, the United States conceived of an elaborate arms deal to woo Tehran. In the ill-fated Iran-Contra affair, Washington planned to supply Iran with American-made weapons and battlefield intelligence (separately, the proceeds of these sales would be surreptitiously funneled by the United States to right-wing paramilitary forces, the Contras, campaigning against the leftist Sandinista government in Nicaragua).[145] In the Middle East theater, Washington hoped this arms transfer would persuade Tehran to release the US and French hostages in Lebanon.[146] The antitank tow missiles and maps of Iraqi positions were helpful, but not decisive to Iran's war performance.

The elaborate plan was secret. Congress had forbade funding the Contras, and any direct contact between Iran and the United States was taboo in both countries. Still, Iran was then under severe economic pressure and in dire need of arms purchases, so the proposal rose to the highest levels in Tehran.[147] IRGC commander Rezaie was directly involved in the process.[148] Khomeini himself was, at a minimum, apprised of these secret negotiations with United States, and according to Rafsanjani, had even directly approved them.[149]

The transfer of arms paved the way for a secret goodwill trip to Tehran by National Security Adviser Robert McFarlane. But although there were extensive discussions in Tehran, McFarlane never managed to meet key senior Iranian leaders (instead, he met only one senior official), ostensibly because his team included an Israeli.[150] More likely it was because anti-Americanism had become so entrenched by then, especially in the vocabulary and outlook of the militant faction of the revolution that was mobilizing support for the Iraq War. Openly engaging the

United States would be too great a shock to the Iranian body politic and could derail the mobilization effort that Iran's war relied on.

Ultimately, Tehran was not ready to embrace an opening with the United States.[151] Iran was willing to secretly buy military spare parts from the United States, but nothing more. Instead of an opening between the two countries, one Iranian faction leaked news of McFarlane's trip, precipitating a crisis for the Reagan administration and staining its reputation, which in turn hardened its position on Iran.[152] The Hawk and Tow missiles that Iran acquired in the process, however, were important to its war effort.[153] Perhaps if the news of the deal had not leaked, it may have extended further and provided an opening.

The leak had come from Mehdi Hashemi, a close associate of Khomeini's heir apparent, Ayatollah Montazeri, and a leader in the revolutionary organization Liberation Movements Unit, which was dedicated to exporting the revolution. Hashemi was executed for this breach, and his tie to Montazeri was one important reason why Khomeini soured on his heir. Although it did not appear so at the time, Khomeini and his close associates, including Rezaie, were open to engaging the United States; consequently, they rejected the militant revolutionaries' attempt to block that engagement in national security terms.

Rafsanjani would remember in later years that Khomeini understood that Montazeri's demotion and the dismantling of the Liberation Movements Unit were a national security imperative.[154] Montazeri had been an ardent supporter of exporting the revolution while opposing the focus on continuing the war with Iraq.[155] His removal from the line of succession was a signal that Khomeini wanted to concentrate on security issues of more immediate relevance to Iran rather than world revolution.

■ ■ ■

Such was the depth of Iran's preoccupation with the United States—in terms of both real and perceived threat along with the threat that its plotting to undo the revolution through the burgeoning alliance with Arabs posed—that even the Soviet invasion of Afghanistan in 1979 as well as the national security challenge that Moscow's southward push and encirclement of Iran on its eastern flank did not compel Khomeini and his coterie to change course. Khomeini shrugged off the Soviet threat, remaining focused on the United States as the larger threat to the revolution.

The US posture toward Iran took a sharp turn once Iran expelled Iraqi forces. Something of a panic took over the Reagan administration once Iran sets its sights on Basra and toppling Saddam. In July 1982, convinced that Iran could win a decisive victory, President Reagan signed a presidential directive to authorize the United States to do "whatever was necessary and legal" to prevent an Iranian victory.[156] The CIA provided Iraq with battlefield intelligence, including satellite pictures of the Iranian troop buildup on the border that allowed otherwise unaware Iraqi forces to deploy an effective defense of their position.

That "undeclared war" between Iran and the United States would continue to escalate between 1985 and 1989; in Tehran's telling, they came closest to open conflict in summer 1988, exactly when the tide of war had clearly turned in Iraq's favor.[157] In April 1988, as Saddam launched a successful offensive to extricate Iranian forces from Iraq, the United States launched an operation to incapacitate the Iranian Navy, destroying sea platforms and warships.[158] Then in July 1988, the navy vessel USS *Vincennes* shot down an Iranian passenger plane crossing the Persian Gulf. The American warship claimed that it had mistaken the Iranian Airbus plane for an F-14 jet fighter, intending to shoot down an Iranian fighter plane. In Iran's eyes, however, the downing of the plane was deliberate, a part of America's military escalation at the time. The tragedy also served to fuel anti-Americanism among Iranians. It did not help that despite the claim of error, the United States later decorated *Vincennes'* top two commander with "meritorious service" decorations. Error or not, President Rafsanjani interpreted the US military's stepped-up confrontational posture as a signal that America was readying itself to enter the war on Iraq's behalf—especially since the US actions at that juncture could not be justified as relieving pressure on Iraq; Washington had attacked the Iranian Navy when Saddam was on the offensive.[159]

The United States was becoming the most important source of pressure on Iran in the Persian Gulf.[160] That conclusion perhaps contributed to Iran's decision to end the war; as Rafsanjani put it, "I was certain Iran could not prevail in a war against both Iraq *and* the United States, while they have no shame to use chemical weapons and attack civilian planes."[161]

The War's End

Between 1986 and 1988, the Iranian military offensives lost impetus. Now it was Iraq that exerted concerted pressure on Iran with its offensives, air raids on Iranian cities, and use of chemical weapons.[162] Such weapons, although employed by Iraq, escalated tensions between Iran and the United States.

During these two years, Rezaie argued for a continued offensive to keep up the pressure on Iraq. The IRGC had underestimated Iraqi capabilities, though. An all-out Iraqi offensive to push Iranian forces out of the Faw Peninsula in April 1988 left little room for Rezaie's optimism. Iran had captured Faw in 1986 in one of its biggest war victories. Losing Faw was a devastating and clear reversal of fortunes.[163] After Faw, Iran continued to lose the territory it had gained in hard-fought battles with heavy casualties.[164] Adding insult to injury, Iraq used the MEK units that it had sheltered and armed to invade Iranian territory.[165]

All of these setbacks—and the prospect of open confrontation with the United States—led Rafsanjani to more aggressively lobby Khomeini to end the war.[166] Khomeini resisted. Instead, he offered to issue a fatwa to make serving in the war obligatory and told those advising him to end the war, "What are you afraid of? So many young people have been killed, are you afraid that we will call you to be killed?"[167]

Then in July 1988, the Iraqi forces crossed into Iran, capturing the town of Dehloran, a local headquarter of the Iranian Army. This was a major blow; it was the first time the Iraqi military would be sitting inside Iran since 1982.[168] It was only then that it became clear to all and sundry that the "emperor had no clothes"; Rezaie's bravado rang hollow, and he and his fellow commanders and political backers had to admit defeat and embrace a volte-face. Khomeini was thus finally convinced that the long war had failed.

Iran had to sue for peace, but now—unlike in 1982—from a position of weakness. On July 16, 1988, Khomeini wrote a letter to senior state officials that

> The leaders of both Sepah [the IRGC] and military have explicitly confessed that the Islamic Army cannot achieve a military victory in the near future, and that it is the opinion of military and civilian leaders that the war is not in the national interest . . . and with reference to the shocking letter of commanders of Sepah that says given recent defeats, imperialism's support for Saddam, and the enemy's widespread use of chemical weapons, I agree to ceasefire, and to illuminate the reasons for this bitter decision I refer to points raised by the commander of Sepah. . . . [W]e will not be able to secure a victory for another five years . . . [and for that] Sepah must be expanded sevenfold and the military twofold . . . and the country's economy cannot support that . . . and people understand that there will be no quick victory and have lost enthusiasm for going to the front. . . . [T]his decision is as deadly to me as poison . . . and although people will be angry, you must put all your effort to make them understand this decision.[169]

The next day, Iran informed the United Nations that it was accepting Resolution 598 and its conditions for a ceasefire.

In his letter, Khomeini had cited IRGC commanders, placing the responsibility for his decision on their shoulders. It was they who had told Khomeini that they could not win the war for at least five years, and not without significant investment in the military. The combination of resources spent and opportunity cost foregone leaves little doubt that his decision to continue the war after 1982 was a mistake. Iran had failed in its aims in Iraq, and Saddam had emerged from the war stronger and once again holding a sliver of Iranian territory (Iran would win its land back only because by invading Kuwait in 1990, Saddam would need to bury the hatchet with Tehran as he confronted American troops).

Khomeini did not admit it, but many of his civilian advisers knew that it was he who had given the IRGC full support and silenced those who had counseled a different course.[170] Thus for a time, the defeat would check the IRGC's rising influence. But it would not put to bed the strategic culture that Khomeini had foisted on the country and that had dominated during the war, nor the alliance between militant revolutionaries and the IRGC.

■ ■ ■

For eight years, Iran appealed to ideology, and relied on political forces and institutions to mobilize volunteers; some 40 percent of the Iran-Iraq War casualties were from those mobilized by the Basij.[171] Perhaps this is what led the Islamic Republic to believe that the power of ideology was essential to its own survival, the country's national security, and binding the state to society. Just how centrally it is *still* believed that ideology is tied to national security can be found in the curricula of the elite educational institutions (such as Imam Sadeq University in Tehran and the Haqqani Seminary in Qom) that produce many of the country's security, political, and bureaucratic leaders as well as the Imam Hossein University in Tehran that is closely associated with the IRGC.[172]

Behind this security strategy rested a broader worldview that came out of the wartime experience: the power of "resistance," and imperative of inculcating it in state and society as the fulcrum of security.[173] In Khamenei's words, "The lesson of sacred defense is that, national security is ensured by resistance alone."[174] Resistance meant resilience, infusing economy and politics with revolutionary values, and organizing them around the ideal of self-reliance. This was in keeping with Khomeini's insistence on the imperative of independence as the revolution's singular achievement and ongoing goal for Iran. Even as he contemplated agreeing to end the war with Iraq holding the upper hand, Khomeini remained steadfast in his belief.

After all, Iran had overcome its conventional military disadvantage in recapturing its territory and then mounted large offensive campaigns relying on human wave attacks, all thanks to the deep well of ideological and patriotic—at the popular level—fervor as well as the powerful and emotive reservoir of religious passion among its people. As Rafsanjani, who was the speaker of the Parliament at the time, put it, "We depend on ourselves, our faith, and the strength of our people."[175] Prime

Minister Mir Hossein Moussavi, later a dissident leader, would go further, maintaining that "the power of faith can outmaneuver a complicated war machine."[176]

Such belief—in the power of religious passion, ideological fervor, patriotism, and love of the nation as a strategic tool—was what the IRGC had relied on throughout the war. Religious passion and dedication to revolutionary values were not then divorced from nationalism. They were not opposites.

Since the Safavid era, Iranian identity and Shiism have been fused into a single belief to protect Iran. During the war from 1980 to 1989, official propaganda did harp on the religious, but for the people, defense of the nation was equally motivating. The war was cast as a "defense," clearly evoking the example of the third Shia imam Hossein's martyrdom in Karbala in 682 CE.[177] (In this evocation, Saddam was a latter-day Yazid, the Umayyad caliph detested by Shias for killing Imam Hossein.) Iranian offensives to capture Basra were called Karbala. Those who fell in battle were martyrs, and their place was in heaven. The iconography of Karbala would become embedded in the IRGC's public image and the military organization's perception of its own role.[178] The close connection between faith and military might appear in later conceptions of sacred defense, and Iran's security is rooted in this era and ideology.

Sacred defense is a tale of zealotry and sacrifice. The fierce devotion and embrace of martyrdom of the irregular Basij forces, which included thousands of boy soldiers, became legendary during the war. Young boys ran across desert planes and marshlands, often acting as mine sweepers with a fervent belief and bravery that confounded observers.[179] Some thirty-seven thousand children were killed fighting on the front, and large numbers of children would languish for years in Iraqi prisoner of war camps.[180] An ardent belief, and in some cases the macho imagery of soldiers at war that peppered government propaganda, and a belief in the cultural values of chivalry (javanmardi) drove their heroic sacrifices, turning them into battlefield wins.[181]

In this rendering, Iran survived the war thanks to the power of religion and oversight of the clergy. The Iranian state was strong and had withstood the war despite international isolation because it had been fully embedded among the population.

Yet the war had also underscored that Iran's isolation, a Persian Shia state that had embraced revolutionary Islamism, was feared, and the country was shunned by its neighbors, whose own strategies would revolve around containing Iran. The war showed that Iran's power would have to draw on what sets it apart: its ideological fervor.

The strength of ideology had only mattered because the people saw themselves as one with the revolutionary state. Defensive realism would have to be anchored in similar ideological intensity. This would become an important lesson, undergirding a social contract between the revolutionary state and the masses that helped stage the revolution. As will be discussed in later chapters, the memory of the revolution has receded over time and the population identifies increasingly less with its founding ideology, and that is the Achilles' heel of a national security strategy that assumes unchanging ideological commitment.

CHAPTER 5

How the War Made
the Islamic Republic

The war came early in the Islamic Republic's life. Its leaders were new to statecraft, focused still on tearing down the regime they had just replaced. They had yet to master governance, learn about military affairs, and gain a grasp of international relations. Now the war forced them to improvise, build alliances and institutions, organize society and the economy, and fight a war while venerating revolutionary ideals.

Consider the first supreme leader of the Islamic Republic, Ayatollah Ruhollah Khomeini. At the outset of the revolution, Khomeini had fashioned himself as an Islamic leader (perhaps even *the* Islamic leader) and his revolution as *the* Islamic Revolution. The war with Iraq, however, compelled him to abandon such Islamic universalism and focus on the patriotic goal of defending Iran. Even as his rhetoric remained steeped in religious language, Khomeini quickly transformed into a leader of the Iranian *nation* under siege. The main task before him was no longer ensuring the triumph of Islam but instead Iran's very survival. He even personally saw the war in simple nationalistic terms that would have been familiar to every Iranian. "I would rather lose the palm of my hand," Khomeini said to his aides, "than a palm-length of Iranian territory."[1]

Responding to this existential threat, Iran's leaders in a de facto manner embraced patriotism over religion in ways that seem unrecognizable today. Indeed, in the first phase of the war (when Iraq occupied Iranian territory), Khomeini crossed what now seems an unthinkable divide:

he sought to collaborate militarily with Israel, and even did so after securing approval from the United States.[2]

Since neither the United States nor Israel wanted Saddam to emerge from the Iran-Iraq War as an Arab juggernaut, the goal was to have Israel provide parts to resupply Iran's American-made military equipment. The convergence of interests went so far as Iran providing Israel with intelligence that it used in bombing Iraq's nuclear facility at Osirak in June 1981—which Iran too had sought to destroy at the start of the war in September 1980.[3] Even at the time, such collaboration was simply shocking. Mansour Farhang, the Islamic Republic's first ambassador to the United Nations, attended a meeting in which Khomeini approved receiving Israeli aid, provided it remained secret. At this point, mused Farhang, perhaps for Khomeini the Quran was only "holy" because "it was full of loopholes."[4]

In so many surprising ways, then, Khomeini sought balance between revolution and nationalism, Islamic idealism, and the security of the nation. This delicate balance would remain an unresolved tension at the heart of the Islamic Republic for decades to follow. And yet as demonstrated in the introduction, the years of sanctions may have finally tipped the scale away from the revolution's founding ideal and toward the realpolitik of national security.

■ ■ ■

Iranians sacrificed enormously for the war. At that time, revolutionary zeal dominated society, and the government relied on this spirit to resist.[5] Hundreds of thousands of women joined the war effort as fighters, drivers, doctors, nurses, and journalists, and even helped with propaganda and fundraising.[6] The war brought the country together; still, this spirit hardly erased the searing experience of fear, scarcity, and loss.[7] The official tales of heroism and national feelings of coming together to fight the war do not tell the whole story of how Iranians had to cope with the trauma and scars of the war for many years to follow.[8]

It was difficult for any Iranian not to feel the toll of the war close to home. The many dead and wounded came from cities, towns, and villages across the country. The names of these dead—the so-called martyrs (*shohada*)—adorned buildings and streets. The magnitude and gravity of the loss was enshrined in cemeteries across the country, none more prominently than at Tehran's Behesht-e Zahra cemetery, where fountains still flow with red water, and pictures of those fallen in the war stretch as far as the eye can see.[9]

The war terrorized Iranians of all walks of life. During the War of the Cities, starting in early 1984, Iraqi jet fighters and Scud missiles explicitly targeted civilians in urban areas to demoralize the population and hasten the war's end.[10] According to Iranian medical researchers, 414 missiles hit Iranian cities, with the majority falling on Dezful in the southwest and Tehran.[11] The horrendous sound of incoming missiles, especially the thunderous boom of the Scuds, terrorized entire cities. The missiles killed 2,312 civilians and injured 11,625 others.[12]

The missiles were even more horrifying after Iraq used chemical weapons on the battlefield between 1984 and 1988, killing tens of thousands of Iranian soldiers, and leaving many more permanently infirm, and Iraqi propaganda explicitly stated that the missiles could be bearing chemical weapons.[13] Iranians worried that Iraqi missiles could also carry chemical weapons; after all, Iraq had still not been punished for violating international law for using such weapons. Iranians felt vulnerable and alone, forgotten by the international community, which seemed to tolerate the use of illegal weapons against them because of the contempt that the West had for their government. And so as Khamenei put it, Iran felt aggrieved because "every form of support, money, political support, and others were at the discretion of one side of the war. . . . On the other side was the Islamic Republic, alone, truly alone."[14]

War and the Consolidation of the State

Just as the Austria and Prussia's attack on revolutionary France in 1792 empowered the Jacobins and pushed the incipient revolution to its Reign of Terror, Iraq's invasion of Iran too empowered Iran's equivalent of Jacobins. The eight years of war helped the Islamic Republic to consolidate its hold over the country. That consolidation had a particular character—one that would be anchored in the ideological fervor that had sustained Iran's military through the war and the military institutions that had led in battle. For both the clerical leaders of the revolution and the IRGC, use of ideology would be seen as necessary for security.[15] This conclusion would shape the Islamic Republic's development after the war.

A triumphant IRGC became the clergy's Praetorian Guard and the buttress to manage foreign security threats. It evolved from a guerrilla force at the outset of the war to more regimented combat units, laying the foundations for its emergence as a full-fledged military force after the war.[16] The war gave rise to a political class consisting of war veterans who now feel entitled to define Iran's interests and mold its future. They have anchored the country's national security in a "battlefield" (meydan) mentality that continues to privilege those in uniform at the expense of diplomats in shaping the country's foreign policy.[17]

The continuation of the war empowered militant revolutionaries capable of mobilizing popular support for the war, and consolidated an alliance between militant clergy, hard-line revolutionaries, and the IRGC under the banner of Those Who Do Jihad for the Revolution (Mojahedin-e Enqelab)—which continues to shape hard-line factions to this day. Khamenei, who was first deputy defense minister and then president at the time, and was deeply involved with the war, became a linchpin of this alliance, and would rely on it to wield power and shape the Islamic Republic during his decades since as supreme leader. Whereas Montazeri or Rafsanjani were skeptical of the IRGC's strategy, Khamenei stood out among Khomeini's senior aides for his unwavering support of the IRGC and its conduct of the war.

As Iran mobilized more and more of its society and economy in pursuit of total war, this alliance, backed by Khomeini, grew prominent in politics and extended its reach into state institutions. The war in effect radicalized the revolution, as it pushed Khomeini to entrench militancy to win the war, weakening pragmatic revolutionaries favoring rational state building at home and the normalization of foreign relations abroad. Khomeini may have favored such radicalism all along, but the war made it a necessity.

■ ■ ■

The war, combined with the hostage crisis, facilitated the elimination of liberals and the Left, and marginalization of moderate senior clerics, notably Ayatollahs Kazem Shariatmadari, who had been a senior voice in Qom before the revolution, and Hossein Ali Montazeri. The war focused all Iranians against an external enemy—one who coveted Iranian territory. There was little support for leftist agitation. Instead, large numbers of Iranians rallied to the flag to defend the country behind the ideology and military force that would lead the charge.

The elimination of opponents of endless war such as Montazeri favored the ideological fervor that would undergird the war as leftist challenges to Khomeini were easily cast as treason. This was learned the hard way by MEK, which decided to throw its lot in with Saddam in the hope that Iraq would undo Khomeini. The organization would never be able to rise above the accusation of treachery and betraying the country in war.

As early as 1982, after the capture of Khorramshahr, calls to end the war were dismissed by the IRGC and its allies as a futile effort by pro-Bazargan liberal forces to restore their fortunes.[18] It didn't matter whether this characterization was a way to depict opponents of the war as antirevolutionaries or the clerical leadership believed the argument. Either way, the war—and the ideological fervor that it relied on—was a way for the religious hard-liners to consolidate power. The war and the interests of the militant faction at the helm had become enmeshed.

The Left was soundly defeated by 1982. But it was not until the war's end, in 1989, that the Islamic Republic would execute thousands of leftists who were still in prison. Perhaps this is the grimmest, but clearest example of how the war and the elimination of the Left were entwined in the consolidation of the Islamic Republic.

The end of the war came a year before Khomeini died, in June 1989. He had to drink from the "poison chalice" and accept defeat.[19] In February 1989, protests broke out in South Asia and the United Kingdom against the author Salman Rushdie's book *Satanic Verses*. Eager to recapture his aura of power and energize the demoralized country, Khomeini jumped on the bandwagon and issued a controversial fatwa condemning the author for blasphemy—a transgression that according to Islamic law, justified his murder.

The fatwa along with the international furor that followed it placed Khomeini and Iran at the center stage of world attention. It confirmed that the West still saw Iran as the epicenter of Islamic radicalism and Khomeini as a formidable foe to be contended with, even as Iran had suffered defeat in the war. The fatwa was his way of making sure his leadership and the militancy that the war had engendered would endure.

Khomeini never acknowledged the folly of his embrace of the long war. Instead, he celebrated Iran's commitment to ensuring its independence in a struggle that went beyond Iraq. The Rushdie affair had allowed him to shift focus from Iraq to the West, and from military issues to ideology and culture, thus perpetuating resistance and revolution on a whole new front where the legacy of the Iraq War did not resonate.

Just as he had added in his own handwriting the word "independence" to the declaration of the revolution's principles, he would once again harp on the same issue on his deathbed in his last will and testament to the people, asserting that *independence* was the foundation stone of the Islamic Republic, and to remain independent Iranians had to protect and preserve it.[20]

The War's Impact on Political Participation

The military implications of the war for Iranian security and politics cannot be underestimated. The psychological, political, and social impact of the mobilization needed for launching wave after wave of deadly attacks; the investment in ideological radicalism that facilitated and justified that mobilization; the sacrifices that families made across the country for this war; the terror that Iraq's Scud missiles and chemical weapons unleashed on the population; and the economic and social contract that the Islamic Republic would enter into with the population as a result—all had profound effects on the state and society, and how the two would relate to one another going forward. The cost of the war and how Iran fought it utterly transformed the young Islamic Republic.

Unlike the communist revolutions of the twentieth century, Iran's revolution was not led by a party. The Leninist axiom that the revolution must be propelled by an "organizational weapon" did not hold for the

Iranian Revolution.[21] Instead, Iran's revolution relied on the network of mosques and clergy to disseminate its ideology as well as mobilize and coordinate street protests. It was only two weeks after the revolution had succeeded that the clerical leadership tried its hand at creating a party, the Islamic Republic Party.[22] That experiment was quickly abandoned, though. The new party had to compete with the mosque and clerical networks, especially as the mobilization needs of the Iran-Iraq War were better served by the mosque network, and the successful direct contact mobilization campaigns of the Construction Jihad (Jahad-e Sazandegi) and Construction Mobilization (Basij-e Sazandegi).

Unlike a party that works through cadres and members, the Islamic Republic's instruments for war mobilization and distribution of benefits were not encumbered by organizational boundaries. Moreover, they drove popular participation at the mass level. The success of this approach during the war years consolidated a de facto contract between the state and the population that consecrated popular participation in national politics. The state welcomed this participation as both necessary and a return to popular engagement with war mobilization. The social contract may have been formally economic, but it also ensured popular participation in the political process.

The absence of a consolidated revolutionary party, and the ad hoc arrangement between religious, liberal, and leftist factions of the revolution, led to intense debates over the shape of a new constitution in 1979. In the end, the Islamic Republic adopted an eclectic constitution that recognized both the supreme authority of a clerical overhead and popular elections for various offices and consultative bodies. The constitution also recognized the semiautonomous powers of competing consultative bodies, the Guardian Council, and Parliament, for instance, as well as institutions whose functions would rival those of government institutions. This degree of diffusion of power enshrined in the constitution protected and gave real meaning to elections as arbiter in struggles of power that were embedded in the constitutional design of the Islamic Republic.[23] As will be examined in future chapters, the institutional diversity and role of elections would remain core features of the Islamic Republic. The war would further confirm this trend.

The ideological fervor that the state disseminated through its mass contact arms, meanwhile, led Iran's rulers to believe that the masses were deeply supportive of the state, and their participation would not challenge but rather strengthen the Islamic Republic. Years later, Supreme Leader Khamenei would reflect that "in the early years of the revolution political bickering at the helm of the state and sowing discord by small organizations [leftist and liberal groups and activists] had divided the people but the sacred defense firmly unified the people."[24]

The state thus saw its population as de facto loyal "party members," bound to the state by fidelity to a common ideology. As such, national elections were encouraged and remained open as if they were intraparty elections. The state would vet candidates and disqualify anyone it deemed outside the bounds of that common ideology as if they were not party members, but then as with intraparty elections, the vote would remain open and the outcome respected.

This would, in time, entrench national elections in Iran for parliamentary and consultative bodies, and a variety of state offices from president to city councils and mayoralties, albeit these elections were limited in that they were not open to any candidate not given the stamp of "party approval" of the state. Still, the Islamic Republic came to see its version of an "Islamic democracy" (*mardom salari-ye dini* or religious popular sovereignty) as an ideal.[25] Hence it would not evolve into a closed dictatorship and would have real electoral contestations, but the ballot boxes would remain narrowly confined by the boundary lines of official ideology. As will be discussed in later chapters, major political debates unfolded in national elections, which would ensure both ideological continuity and challenges to it.

■ ■ ■

The war also deeply impacted Iran's economy. Continuing the conflict after 1982 required the republic to shape its institutions and societal relations around the war effort, producing a web of entitlements and welfare programs that has since constrained economic growth.[26] This was a total war involving all aspects of Iranian society and the economy.[27]

Its demands thus impoverished Iran. Iran poured enormous resources into the war as its oil revenues dwindled.

Even as the state was depleted of resources, however, the war demanded of the Islamic Republic greater investment in society. For example, the war led Iran's revolutionary leaders to look at rural development as more than spreading social justice or an economic policy goal. According to political scientist Eric Lob, now the Islamic Republic saw rural development as a means of reaching deep into the population quickly to protect the Islamic Republic against internal (the Left) and external (Iraq and the United States) enemies.[28]

Rural development was the channel through which the Islamic Republic would indoctrinate vast areas of the country that had not been part of the revolutionary mobilization of 1977–79. Those channels would also facilitate the recruitment of soldiers and volunteers for the war effort.[29] The same mobilization efforts were extended to educational institutions to recruit 550,000 school-age children and university students to fight at the front.[30]

Organizations affiliated with this effort such as Construction Jihad or Construction Mobilization would soon grow into large economic and political machines, deeply ideological, staffed by war veterans and vigilant hard-liners with footprints across the country as well as vast patronage resources that would bind large numbers of Iranians to the Islamic Republic. They would become important to the stability of the Islamic Republic. But they would also anchor its politics in the ideological fervor and militant politics that were the staple of war mobilization.[31] These organizations have been important in disseminating the ruling order's account of the war long after the guns fell silent in 1989. They have also been important in perpetuating an expanding welfare state and have themselves become notable parastatal economic actors.

The revolution had promised to redistribute wealth, but it did not have a clear conception of a welfare state. This was especially true of its clerical leadership. So as the clerics confronted a challenge by the Left, they felt not only the need to hone their economic message but to quickly close the lower wrung of society to the Left too. Shia clerics and the mosque network had historically served a social welfare function;

with the clergy ruling the state, its institutions could now play that same role. There were differences of opinion between clerical factions; some had ties to the merchant classes and the bazaars—which had historically filled clerical coffers with religious taxes and contributions—and supported private sector activity, and others promoted a far-reaching redistribution of economic resources and dominant role for the state in the economy.[32]

The Iraq War did not settle the debate but instead gave greater impetus to the creation of a welfare state with significant control of the economy. Sociologist Kevan Harris argues that it was through investments in redistributive mechanisms and institutionalizing social support that the Islamic Republic forged a social contract with the population.[33]

The impact of this burgeoning welfare state would go beyond war mobilization, and profoundly impact social development in Iran through building roads and the electrification of rural areas as well as one of the world's most impressive family planning programs and a reduction in population growth after the war ended.[34] Yet the welfare state spawned parastatal institutions, foundations, and social organizations that worked in parallel with government agencies, and would multiply in number over time to produce a Byzantine economic system outside government control, and instead subservient to various power centers as well as vested political and economic interests.[35]

This would make the job of proper economic planning more complex. But it ultimately strengthened the power center that by virtue of its control of welfare institutions, commanded significant political capital and economic resources, and thus could greatly influence politics and policymaking. These vested interests have, since the time of the war, veered to the right of the political spectrum, favoring the kind of ideological politics and resistance security mindset that relies on the mobilization of the lower strata of society.

The war also turned the IRGC and Basij into powerful political institutions.[36] After the liberation of Khorramshahr in 1982, a "great victory" (*pirouzi-e bozorg*) in which the IRGC and the Basij played a prominent role, Khomeini saw them as indispensable military institutions and invested in them as the state's primary Praetorian Guards.[37] "I will not replicate Mossadegh's error," said Khomeini. "His reliance on Zahedi and his armored comrades was misguided. I envision the Basij as a safeguard to uphold Iran's political structure and sovereignty."[38] Whereas the IRGC would remain concerned with protecting Iran's borders, the Basij's domain in national security would be protecting the ruling regime against internal enemies—a tool for social control.[39] The clergy understood that they needed armed forces that were born of revolution and fully committed to its core ideology, and the nascent IRGC and Basij have since their inception seen the clergy as the necessary religious and ideological guardians that they needed to protect the country.

Many of the IRGC and Basij veterans of the war would rise to prominent positions in the government as well as the military and security apparatuses of the Islamic Republic, and would forge close professional and family ties with hard-line clerics. In the process, they evolved from ragtag revolutionary youths into military people with a corporatist identity coupled with a distinct security and political outlook.

Consider Khamenei's second son, Mojtaba, who fought in the war as part of the Habib ibn Mazaher Battalion (named after a companion of the early Shia imams). The Habib ibn Mazaher Battalion of the IRGC was prominent in such fabled battles of the war as Fath Al-Mobin (Manifest Victory). This brutal assault on Iraqi positions in Khorramshahr in March 1982, which combined tank and artillery units with human wave attacks, has been credited with liberating the city.[40] Habib is therefore a celebrated battalion—although Mojtaba served in it in the mid-1980s, but is closely associated with its tight-knit and influential network of war heroes, and volunteers and IRGC veterans.

In later years, many veterans of the Habib ibn Mazaher Battalion would rise in the security services. Mojtaba would follow his military service with seminary education and then become a powerful political player as his father's principal adviser, but also behind the scenes as the nexus between the IRGC and security services and militant clergy, and efforts to perpetuate the strategies of resistance and forward defense born during the war.[41]

...

The close ties between the IRGC and hard-line clerics—embodied in Mojtaba Khamenei's background and current role—has ensured that the security mindset and mantra of sacred defense remain at core of the Iranian state, and the "battlefield" dominates in Iran's foreign relations. In effect, all aspects of politics become gradually but surely securitized as the memory of national defense during the war years becomes extended into a grand strategy of perpetual resistance. This has had a profound impact on the trajectory of the Iranian state's evolution over the past four decades. It has opened the door to the IRGC's steady usurpation of political power. Nowhere has this been more clearly reflected than in Iran's regional policies. The anti-Americanism that Iran has wrapped itself in and persistently used as cudgel against America's allies in the Middle East has manifested itself in the growing domination of the IRGC over regional policymaking, but with the result of drawing a deep wedge between Iran and its Arab neighbors.

Iran's leaders have laid the blame on the Arab world. They argue that their Arab neighbors were hostile to Iran and its revolution from the get-go. They had joined hands with the United States and European countries to support Iraq's war effort. Iran has since held a grudge against its Persian Gulf neighbors, seeing Iraq's aggression as merely the tip of a much larger Arab spear directed at Iran. From Iran's perspective, a Persian and Shia country saw the limit of how welcome it was in the Middle East. The Islamic Republic has coveted acceptance and leadership in the region; this has presented Iran's revolutionary leaders with a challenge—one that they conceptually sidestepped by laying the blame on Arab leaders and American machinations. It also made Iran more eager to exploit the Arab street's anger at Israel, championing the Palestinian cause as a means to rise above the limitations of its Persian and Shia identities that separated it from the Arab world.

Still, the resistance Iran faced has at its core been a security threat, especially because Iraq emerged from the war bullish, and the Arab world more anti-Iran and closer to the United States, and Tehran believed that United States aimed to weaken Iran and topple its regime.[42] Iran's rulers would not deduce from these facts that it was necessary they adopt a new strategy. Instead, they would set their sights on forward defense as the optimal strategy to protect Iran's interests. As will be discussed in later chapters, that strategy would fully blossom after the United States toppled Saddam in Iraq in 2003, but the roots go back to as early as 1982 when Khomeini justified pushing into Iraq as imperative for Iran's security.

Soon after the war ended (and pursuant to America's victory in the first Gulf War), in 1992, Iran would issue its first formal military doctrine. The doctrine was acutely aware of Iran's strategic weaknesses. The country was isolated, it failed to win its long war with Iraq, its economy was depleted and its people exhausted, and it had just watched its nemesis, the United States, shred the Iraqi military to pieces, expelling it from Kuwait. Rather than relying on conventional military tactics and weaponry, Iran had to adopt a flexible military strategy. It had to emphasize defense and deterrence, cyber capabilities, and missiles—and later drones—in lieu of an air force or advanced navy.[43]

Iran needed a military along with a strategy suited for an isolated and vulnerable country. That conclusion also meant investment in nuclear capability, a sizable weapons manufacturing industry along with cyber and missiles capabilities, and proxy militias that could ensure a footprint in the Arab world and later Afghanistan too. That meant anchoring its regional policy in the IRGC, and in the words of former foreign minister Javad Zarif, "favoring meydan (battlefield) over diplomacy."[44]

The IRGC was intent on making its dominance over regional policy clear. General David Petraeus, a former US commander in Iraq, recollects that in 2008, General Qasem Soleimani sent him a message; it read, "General Petraeus, you should be aware that I, Qassem Soleimani, control Iran's policy for Iraq, Syria, Lebanon, Gaza, and Afghanistan," which Petraeus interpreted as Soleimani asserting that it is he who runs Iran's regional policies.[45]

. . .

The majority of Iranians today were born after the war, and do not remember the sacrifices and terror of those years. Soon after the war ended, a divide emerged between those who felt the impact of the war intensely and remained committed to the mantra of sacrifice and resistance, and those who wanted to leave the war years behind.[46] Over time, that chasm has only widened—fueling important political struggles over the future of the Islamic Republic in the decades that have followed the war, as will be explored in later chapters.

For those who have remained true to sacred defense, this chasm challenges how they see the national culture and national interest, and justifies dedicating national resources to Iran's ongoing foreign policy campaigns.[47] Bridging the chasm has therefore been viewed as crucial to sustaining the spirit of resistance and political stability in the country. In Khamenei's words, "The new generation does not know many aspects of sacred defense. We must do something that the new generation learns about sacred defense. That is what I expect of myself and others."[48]

The Islamic Republic has thus sought to propagate broadly the narrative of resistance and sacrifice as well as the imperative of ideological fidelity to the revolution, in school textbooks and university curricula, state media, and institutions affiliated with the war effort dedicated to infusing popular culture with themes of sacrifice and resistance along with the celebration of martyrdom and heroes.[49] A myriad of wall murals across Iran celebrate the martyrs of the war and its signature campaigns from the liberation of Khorramshahr to the siege of Basra.[50] There is a steady stream of media interviews, oral history accounts, and memoirs of the war, many by veterans who rose to high ranks in the IRGC such as Generals Hossein Ala'ie, Hossein Hamdani, Yahya Rahim-Safavi, Mohsen Rezaie, Ali Shamkhani, or Qasem Soleimani, and civilian leaders during the war such as Ayatollah Rafsanjani or Ali Akbar Velayati, wartime speaker of the Parliament and foreign minister, respectively.[51] There are semiofficial histories of the war by academics and journalists, some sponsored by state institutions, such as those by Ja'far Shiralinia, Morteza Sarhangi, Hedayatollah Behboudi, and Mohammad Doroudian.

The interest in documenting the war, recounting its lessons, and capturing the spirit of sacred defense have increased markedly since 2011, in good measure to justify Iran's involvement in Syria. Many of the works on the war are produced by the IRGC and state-sponsored documentation centers, such as the Center for Documents of the Sacred

Defense (Markaz-e Asnad-e Defaʿe Moqaddas) or Center for Documents of the Islamic Republic (Markaz Asnad-e Jomhouri-e Eslami) as well as several publishing houses backed by the IRGC and its affiliates, such as Niloufaran, Howzeh-e Honari (Art Circle), or Soureh-e Mehr (Holy Verse of Light), which also train researchers and authors as well as publish journals, magazines, and popular novels, and film production houses that capture the national mood of the war years through documentaries, television serials, and feature films.[52] All work to inculcate the imperative of resistance in new generations.[53]

The popularity of novels and short stories of authors such as Mahmoud Dolatabadi (a well-known contemporary novelist with no affiliation to the Islamic Republic), Ahmad Dehqan, Habib Ahmadzadeh, and Zahra Hosseini attest to how widely these themes are circulated in society. These books and films are not directed at reinforcing the strategic culture at the top, but as conveyed in Hosseni's novel *Da* (*Mother* in Kurdish), tell the people, "We sacrificed during the war and prevailed, and if it comes to it, we will do it again."[54]

The war is portrayed as a repeat of Karbala, the seventh-century battle in which the grandson of the Prophet and venerated Shia imam Hossein led his seventy-two troops to confront the vastly larger army of the caliph. Hossein and his companions were martyred in the cause of truth and justice, challenging an insidious usurper. In the Islamic Republic's telling, in the war with Iraq, the Iranian nation was like Hossein's besieged troops and family, and just as Hossein's resistance all of those centuries ago in the end had been a moral victory that has been the source of power keeping Shiism alive through the centuries, the Islamic Republic too would embrace the mantra of resistance, not only to mobilize the people, but because its leaders truly believe that it was the power of resistance that sustained Iran through the war.[55] Resistance continues to take inspiration from Hossein's heroics at Karbala, but it is not a mere reenactment of that saga; it fuses that historical memory with the imperative of defending Iran before foreign aggressors.

The war employed religious symbols and mythology, but it is about national security. Those who fought in the war and those who sacrificed for it were inspired by religion and ideology, but they are patriotic

heroes because they provided the country with a public good: its security and sovereignty.[56] As such, the mythology around the Iran-Iraq War
heightens national security consciousness, and depicts ideology and
religion as necessary to achieving it. It puts religion in the service of a
national goal. There is an undeniable nationalist ring to the mythology
that the Islamic Republic and IRGC are weaving around the war.[57]

• • •

The memory of the war is fading. Most Iranians today were born after
the war and do not remember the sacrifices the country made, or the
mood of fear and anxiety that dominated during the war years. The state
they live under, however, is acutely aware of the experiences of that war
and continues to hold onto its legacy. The war gave birth to a strategic
culture that continues to dominate the Islamic Republic's outlook, forging an enduring understanding of the imperative of national security
that continues to dictate Iran's foreign policy, but also organize state and
society.

The revolution gave birth to the Islamic Republic, and the hostage
crisis defined its posture toward America, but true to sociologist Charles
Tilly's famous dictum that "war made the state," it is the Iran-Iraq War
that shaped the state that revolution wrought.

PART II

Khamenei and the Grand Strategy of Resistance

CHAPTER 6

After the War

Reform or Resistance

All wars are followed by reconstruction—winding down the wartime mobilization and returning to normalcy—rebuilding and growing the economy. Iran in 1989 was no exception. Exhausted by the eight-year conflict and deflated by its outcome, the Islamic Republic too had to look past the long war. The shift was accelerated by Khomeini's death in 1989 as well as the rapid pace at which the Iraqi threat dissipated once Saddam invaded Kuwait a year later in 1990. As the United States prepared to invade, Iraq gave back to Iran territory and military matériel it had captured in the last stage of the war, and freed Iranian prisoners of war without any Iranian concessions in return.[1] The two events provided Iran with a new beginning as well as much-needed time and space to attend to social and economic troubles while crafting a strategy for economic development.

Iran's economy had suffered immensely during the war. There had been no investment in infrastructure or industry, and shortages had ravaged the economy and increased poverty.[2] Such troubles had especially effected urban areas, whose populations had swelled with war refugees and higher fertility rates encouraged by the government during the war—to build a so-called army of twenty million to lead Iran's human wave campaign to victory.[3]

The needs of reconstruction and development, however, conflicted with the ideology and institutions that had dominated during the war, and were credited with Iran's resilience through it. Those forces re-mained vested in—as well as *believed in*—the national security mindset of the war years. As such, they resisted relaxing ideological vigilance or compromising institutional structures that had mobilized the country in support of the war.

This was a key reason advocates of development argued that eco-nomic growth too was necessary for national security.[4] Rafsanjani, as will be seen in this chapter, was the most ardent and articulate advocate of this view, believing that the Islamic Republic had to be based on "ra-tional government" (*hukoumat-e aqlani*), and looking to national inter-est rather than ideological zeal to govern and defend the country. To do so, he held, required economic reform and pragmatic foreign policy.[5] He faced resistance from hard-line clerics, parastate institutions, and the IRGC. Nonetheless, Rafsanjani as president was able to lead a liftoff for reconstruction and development—and the IRGC too would soon pres-sure Rafsanjani for a role in development projects.[6]

The years after the war witnessed something of a "Thermidor," to borrow historian Crane Brinton's famous characterization of when a revolutionary state shifts from fervor to normalcy.[7] Yet Iran's Thermidor remained limited, frozen in a struggle between fervor and normalcy. And this struggle was dominated by the argument over national secu-rity. Whether this debate was real or wartime's vested interests used it as a pretext to protect political and economic privileges did not matter. Either way, the Islamic Republic never resolved this struggle.

Indeed, as Iran's economy and population changed in the decade after the war, the chasm between development and ideological vigilance deepened. Finally, the argument itself became a security concern. What had once been the "one Iran," the wartime-united nation when Iranians had stood shoulder to shoulder, now became "two Irans": one devoted to state ideology along with its religious and patronage institutions, and the other advocating economic development, political opening, and engagement with the West.

As in all politics, who gets what, when, and how drove the ebbs and flows of reform and retrenchment. But unique to Iran, such changes were also propelled by the national security argument: how the Islamic

Republic had come to see Iran's enemies, and how it understood its own role in protecting the country.

The Second Islamic Republic

By the time that Khomeini died, it was evident that the institution of *velayat-e faqih* (rule by the *supreme* clerical scholar and jurist) could not continue as Khomeini had defined it. The most senior clerics in the world of Shiism had been aloof from politics, and had no experience, desire, or base of support among the cadres of the Islamic Republic to succeed Khomeini. The clerics who had led the revolution as well as worked in the political and bureaucratic institutions of the Islamic Republic were not religiously accomplished and widely respected; they had spent their years in politics and government rather than in seminary and on scholarship. Khomeini in the end had been a *vali-e faqih* that was impossible to replicate.

He himself understood that. Without his charisma and authority, his successor could not protect the revolution that he had led and the state that he had built. Even the fusion between Islam and politics—that is, the ideological fervor that had toppled the Shah and then carried Iran through the war—could be at risk.

It was thus in a fatwa in January 1988 that he announced a new and hitherto unheard of religious tenet, declaring that velayat-e faqih was a "primary commandment of Islam and has priority over all derivative commandments, even over prayer, fasting and pilgrimage to Mecca."[8] In effect, Khomeini extended his earlier contention on velayat-e faqih (rule by jurisconsult) to *velayat-e motlaqeh faqih* (absolute authority of jurisconsult).[9] The intent was that the authority of his successor would come from his office rather than his persona and religious following. To leave little room for doubt, Khomeini sought to vest absolute obedience in his successor (as a primary commandment of the faith) and give them uncontested authority to control all aspects of government. The main function of the supreme scholar-jurist would thus be to serve as the "guardian" of the Islamic Republic—the state ruling Iran as opposed to leading the Shia religion.

Up until the 1988 fatwa, the Islamic Republic had contained within it two separate theories of government: one velayat-e faqih, which was based on the belief that sovereignty belonged to God, with political authority drawing its legitimacy from the Divine, and the other a different belief, in which it was elected government that vested sovereignty in the people. Under Khomeini, the two had coexisted. Fearing that after him popular sovereignty might grow dominant, he asserted the sanctity of velayat-e faqih by giving it absolute powers and vesting all meaningful state powers in the office of the supreme leader. This argument for theocratic absolutism, what Iranians now call *nezam-e velaie* (a system that sets the vali-e faqih above religion and state), would give Khomeini's successor the means to keep popular sovereignty at bay as well as protect the ideological moorings of the state after defeat in war and the need to rebuild the country.

Khomeini died in June 1989. The Council of Experts briefly debated the choice of his successor.[10] The council was hurried in its task by reports that the Iraqi military was once again mobilizing to take advantage of the political vacuum.[11] It settled on an interim period with a senior cleric fulfilling the role and then appointed Khamenei, a younger clerical lieutenant of Khomeini of moderate scholarly reputation, and who was then president and had played a key role in Iran's war campaign. The sweeping powers that Khomeini had now vested in his successor would compensate for the fact that Khamenei was a jurist (*mojtahed*), but by no stretch of the imagination was he the supreme clerical scholar-jurist at the time—a grand ayatollah. He was rather the Islamic Republic's supreme guardian, a position that would increasingly be referred to not as vali-e faqih but instead as "supreme leader" (*rahbar aliqadr*) of the Islamic Revolution. With this the qualification, the religious stature of the leader of the revolutionary state was diminished; it was now enough that he be recognized as a jurist.

The Constitution was revised to formally augment Khamenei's powers, notably giving him control over Iran's military and security forces.[12] The revised Constitution also created a national security council and set of oversight councils, which all under the control of the supreme leader, would limit government decision-making, legislation, and participation in politics.[13] Thus the ability of the formal state institutions—the executive and legislature—to drift away from the core ideologies of the revolution would be checked.

This institutionalization of absolute authority in the office of supreme leader, however, created a duality of power that ultimately only exacerbated the divide between advocates of change and retrenchment.[14] As such, Khamenei would become the chief guardian of the values and institutions of the revolution, its ideology, and key apparatuses of the state. Khamenei became the representative and defender of Khomeini's theory of velayat-e faqih (namely, that it is religiously mandated that the supreme clerical jurist rules the state), and his deathbed assertion that its hold on Iran had to remain absolute. Those clergy, politicians, and journalists (as well as their respective institutions) that closely identified with an unyielding fidelity to Khomeini's wishes would come to be seen as *vela-ie* or *velayatmadar*, both terms meaning a close affiliation with velayat-e faqih.

Today, Khamenei remains the supreme leader of the Islamic Republic, the literal successor to Khomeini himself. Khamenei is a defender of the revolution, but more important, especially in the first years of his tenure as supreme leader, he was a state builder. He created and organized the state—its political ideas and structures along with its economic and military institutions—to give long-term coherence to the Islamic Republic as a defender of Iran and its security.

Nevertheless, when he ascended to the role of supreme leader, Khamenei vacated the role of president. He was succeeded by another mid-ranking cleric and speaker of the Parliament, Rafsanjani, who emerged as the standard-bearer of pragmatism and development. He did not see his job as keeping faith with Khomeini's vision but rather as managing the state's affairs.

Although there have thus far been six presidents under Khamenei, the tone set by Rafsanjani—as being a counterweight to the velayat-e faqih, although to differing degrees—endures even today. The rivalry between faith and pragmatism, between supreme leader and president, would unfold over the following two decades, symbolizing Iran's tortured grappling with continuity and change.[15] Rafsanjani recollects a long meeting with Khamenei to convince him to agree to talks with the United States:

> We debated for a few hours but didn't get to a resolution. Usually when I disagreed with him, I accepted his views as my guide. He is the Leader, and definitive opinions is his prerogative. But I told him, I cannot say anything more, our issue is between us and God. Eventually on the Day of Judgment you and I will be asked about all these troubles and losses that were inflicted on the state (*nezam*) and Muslims, and if you will take responsibility then I have nothing further to say. He said, yes, I will answer to God.[16]

Khamenei and the Eternal Distrust of the United States

Over the decades that followed Khomeini's death, Khamenei has towered over Iran's politics, economy, and social development. His views on social and political questions have changed over time—as his power grew—and he has even tactically experimented with policies, adapting, adjusting, and even conceding them to changing circumstances.[17] Yet his commitment to protecting the Islamic Republic has remained unwavering. As president, he had overseen Iran's war effort in the 1980s, and was closely tied to the political and institutional arrangements that managed the war effort. Because of this, Khamenei continued to believe that the lessons of the war years were fundamental to national security: resistance, sacred defense, and defending against the United States. And he eagerly protected the alliance between the militant clerics and IRGC that had emerged from the Iran-Iraq War.

Khamenei has always sought consensus among the leading power centers before pursuing a policy. Given his abiding distrust of the United States, though, he has always settled on protecting the state's ideology and power structure; if he ever ceded ground to those favoring greater openness to the West, it was only if he saw the state under threat. In the early years after he assumed the position of supreme leader, his main challenge was to consolidate his own power to be able to perform the role that he believed Khomeini intended for him. He had to articulate the core mission of the state—to make sure that the Islamic Republic was organized around resistance and the national security vision of sacred defense—and bring together the politicians, clerics, and military and civilian institutions that were key to that sacred mission.

Khamenei was not a prominent cleric, nor has he grown into one. He has not gained fame and stature for his scholarship in religious jurisprudence, although he is well-read in a variety of topics from Western philosophy to history, literature, and especially poetry.[18] When in jail in the 1960s, he shared cells with communist activists, whom he befriended.[19] He was impressed by Ali Shariati and had close relations with his family, and had also read anti-imperialist intellectuals such as Franz Fanon and the Third Worldist literature of the 1960s.[20] Khamenei had read and translated anti-Western critiques of Islamic revivalist thinkers like Mohammad Iqbal of India and Pakistan as well as the ideological tracts of Sunni Islamist thinkers, notably the Egyptian Muslim Brotherhood leaders Hasan al-Banna and Sayyid Qutb.

Domestically, Khamenei sees himself as guardian of the revolution's values. He pays homage to its founding ideology, and does so increasingly as the means to cultivate and protect a base of support among the poorer social strata and die-hard revolutionaries. On the international scene, however, Khamenei's worldview is Westphalian, anchored in the idea of Iran as a nation-state. This even extends to how he sees the world of Shiism. For example, in the early days of the revolution, he discouraged Islamic internationalism as a goal for the Islamic Republic.[21] In early 1990s, he ignored warnings from senior clerics to forbid Ayatollah Mohammad Reza Golpayegani to pay stipends to seminarians in Pakistan, and accepted that Najaf's Ayatollah Ali Sistani, as opposed to Khamenei himself or another ayatollah resident in Iran and representing the Islamic Republic, would serve as source of emulation for *all* Shias outside Iran. These actions acknowledged, in effect, that Iran's theocracy did not automatically extend beyond Iran's borders to minister to religious affairs of the Shia faithful everywhere.[22]

His views on the United States were not drawn from religion but rather from his political education. He has harbored a deep suspicion of US intentions, believing that America has only one goal in Iran and that is "regime change": to topple the Islamic Republic. He believes that every American overture is ultimately a ruse to open the way for realizing that goal. To preserve the Islamic Republic and protect Iran's national interests, the United States must be kept away. In this vision, the perceived American role in the 1953 coup, and fear of it planning another venture in Iran after the revolution, made the preservation of the Islamic Republic and Iranian national interest one and the same.

It is important to note that Khamenei does not believe that his legitimacy as supreme leader lies in being a supreme scholar or jurist, as had Khomeini. Instead, he maintains that he is the "perfect" combination of clerical and secular knowledge, given his seminary education and clerical experience, knowledge of Western political ideas and Islamism in the Muslim world (which he gained through reading), and decades of experience in politics as a revolutionary activist, president, wartime commander, and then the titular head of state in Iran. This reflects what Khomeini sought in his successor, saying that his successor should have political wisdom and guile, successful in the "world of wiliness and politics" (*jahan-e neyrang va siyasat*).[23] Khamenei sees that legitimacy in sui generis terms as a combination of religious and secular knowledge coupled with the experience that he possesses, which supports his authority to rule over and protect the Shia domain, with what the monarchy once stood for now summed up in one person and his office.

Khomeini's theory of velayat-e faqih was based on the view that in the absence of the Hidden Imam, who is the Lord of the Age (*Imam-e Zaman*) as well as the true ruler of the world and Iran, it is the clerics who by virtue of their mastery of religion serve as his plenipotentiaries. Under Khamenei, however, this emphasis has subtly shifted to asserting that as a true Islamic state, it is the Islamic Republic that is the plenipotentiary of the Hidden Imam. State propaganda has popularized the idea that Iran's government is the Hidden Imam's government (*hokoumat-e Imam-e Zaman*). Protecting and managing that state requires not just a leader who is steeped in religion but statecraft and military affairs too. That, Khamenei believes, makes him uniquely qualified to lead the Islamic Republic with the implied support of the Hidden Imam.

Unlike Rafsanjani—who saw opening Iran's economy to the world as necessary for development—Khamenei has always seen Western powers as intent on subjugating countries like Iran, keeping them subservient and backward to exploit their resources. Khamenei is well-read in the Islamist ideology, which is replete with anti-imperialism, yet his anti-imperialism shows more the imprint of the methodical anti-imperialism of the New Left thinking of the latter part of the twentieth century. For Khamenei, echoing the ideas of the left-leaning dependency theory in political science, genuine development cannot come from engaging the West but rather only by decoupling from it. To be truly independent, Iran must be developed, and for that it must be self-reliant.[24]

He is driven by the belief that it is his calling and mission to protect Iran and the Islamic Republic. In an interview, he recollected that after he was severely injured in an assassination attempt in June 1981—soon after he became president—on the way to the hospital he came in and out of consciousness, each time thinking he was dying and then being brought back to life. He concluded then that God saved him and did so for a purpose. He implied that purpose was defending the country and preserving the Islamic Republic in the face of all adversity.[25]

Still, Khamenei grew into the role of supreme leader without his predecessor's charisma and religious standing. As such, he had to assert authority at a time when the revolution's fervor was tempering and a new middle class was pushing for reform. Since he could not cultivate support among those demanding change, Khamenei found his constituency in the poor and the growing number of those for whom the economic changes of the postwar period shunted them to the sidelines. Consequently, he positioned himself as the standard-bearer of the revolution's ideology, harping on themes of social justice and empowerment of the dispossessed, and bolstering the welfare state that served them. Whereas Rafsanajni would seek to empower technocrats, Khamenei would look to security forces, the IRGC, and Basij as the prop for his authority.

Khamenei's first government post was as deputy minister of defense, then he served as the head of the Parliament's Defense Committee, and then he served a wartime president for close to a decade. His mindset is shaped by those military experiences, and he feels close to those in uniform—and sees that relationship as more important to his political mission than connecting with his fellow clergy. To him, ideological vigilance is the linchpin of national defense; sacred defense would not have been possible without ideological commitment. It is for this reason that the event that perhaps most profoundly shook Khamenei was the collapse of the Soviet Union. He saw that unraveling as the consequence of the dissipation of ideological vigilance and embrace of Western liberal ideas in its stead. He became determined that Iran's revolution would not end where Russia's did. That has guided his disparaging of reform and insistence on ideological fidelity.

Rafsanjani and Development

From the early days of the revolution, Rafsanjani had been a close confident of Khomeini. A wily politician, Rafsanjani closely followed Khomeini's lead in domestic and foreign policy; during the Iran-Iraq War, he was even identified as somewhat of a hawk. Yet Rafsanjani always approached the war pragmatically. Rather than seeing the conflict as a fountainhead of unending ideological vigilance and a campaign that Iran had to carry forward until absolute victory, Rafsanjani viewed it as merely a phase that Iran had to go through before focusing on a different path.

In 1982, Iran's leaders debated whether to pursue the war into Iraqi territory. At that time, Rafsanjani was one of the extremists counseling Khomeini to capture some Iraqi territory to force Saddam to accept definitive defeat, if not fall from power. Even then, though, Rafsanjani differed from the other hawks by not seeing the goal of the war as capturing Baghdad or Basra.[26] By implication, then, Rafsanjani rejected the wartime mantra that Iran's future state building must be founded on sacred defense.

In 1968, Rafsanjani wrote a biography of the Qajar era reformist prime minister Mirza Taqi Khan Amir Kabir, who first championed fundamental political reform and economic development as the sine qua non for Iran's survival and progress, and during the Pahlavi period was lionized as a national hero for championing progress and modernization.[27] Rafsanjani wrote that book almost a decade before the revolution. It was rare for clerical activists in the 1970s to write about and laud a secular figure. And earlier, Rafsanjani had translated Akram Zu'aytir's account of the emergence of the Palestinian National Movement, which had given him an acute awareness of the evils of imperialism. In the biography of the Qajar minister, Rafsanjani celebrated Amir Kabir for standing up to imperialism, but also underscored the importance of development as the path to free nations.[28] It was this early on admiration for development as key to solving Iran's security problems that would manifest itself when Rafsanjani became president. In applauding Amir Kabir, Rafsanjani was also appealing to secular national symbols and identity—a trend that he would continue during his presidency by celebrating national literary and historical figures.[29] This was a move to go beyond religion and ideology to anchor the Islamic Republic's legitimacy in Iranian nationalism.

In 1989, Rafsanjani played a central role in the transition of power at the helm of the Islamic Republic from Khomeini to Khamenei.[30] At the time of the succession, Khamenei was close to the economically conservative and probusiness side of the revolution, and the left-leaning religious revolutionaries relied on Khomeini's son Ahmad to exercise influence. Rafsanjani was the balance between the two factions, and in that role, he engineered Khamenei's rise and the marginalization of leftist revolutionaries.[31] He understood then that Iran needed economic development and not more Jacobin economic policies. In the process, Rafsanjani moved from speaker of Parliament to become president—a post that he held until 1997.

As president, Rafsanjani proved to be a pragmatist, perhaps because he came from a mercantile family and perhaps because he was unusually well traveled, having journeyed to the West and Japan—a rarity for a member of Khomeini's clerical inner circle.[32] He favored a rational approach to faith, free of superstitions and ideological harangue. He was cautious about how he framed rational religiosity, calling Islam the rational religion (din-e aqalaniyat).[33] He referred to the term often when he sought to persuade an audience of the wisdom of a pragmatic foreign policy measure. He had an appreciation for how economics works and what development had achieved elsewhere.

Rafsanjani was the architect of a new school of thinking in the Islamic Republic that viewed economic development as the bedrock of national security, saying, "We should take advantage of the country's factories as forward bunkers in fighting the enemies of the revolution."[34] In this, Rafsanjani was harking back to the Pahlavi monarchs' vision of economic development making Iran secure and powerful. In effect, he was integrating that earlier vision into the revolutionary discourse, seeing Iran's future as a marriage of Pahlavi era developmentalism with the revolution's ideals and rhetoric. Iranians were quick to understand this and took to referring to him facetiously as "Akbar Shah."

The imperative of economic development, in turn, demanded the normalization of revolutionary politics at home—rational decision-making based on expertise versus ideology by technocrats rather than died-in-the-wool revolutionaries—and a pragmatic foreign policy abroad.[35] That combination of Islam and development should be the revolutionary ideal Iran showcased and exported to the world.[36] He argued that Islam enjoins people to prove the worth of religion by deeds and achievements, and not proclamations.[37]

Rafsanjani wanted to set the revolution on a different course; in short, he wanted a Thermidor: to shift Iran's preoccupation with external threats during the first decade of the revolution to reconstruction at home.[38] He proclaimed that rather than exporting the revolution, Iran should be a model of Islamic development, and pointed out that Khomeini had shared this view.[39] He defined his approach to foreign policy as one of reducing tensions (taneshzodaie) and not creating problems with other countries, and claimed in later years that he had beseeched Khomeini to end Iran's hostility to the United States and Saudi Arabia before he died, and open the door for the normalization of the revolution.[40]

Khomeini may have defined the first decade of the revolution, but Rafsanjani would define the next two. Rafsanjani exerted influence not only during his own term as president but also through those of Mohammad Khatami and Hasan Rouhani.[41] None succeeded in definitively reorienting the Islamic Republic. Still, Rafsanjani's vision for the future of the Islamic Republic has endured in the intellectual and political platform of moderates and reformists, and remains the foil for the state that the resistance forces have built.

■ ■ ■

Once in office as president (1989–97), Rafsanjani set development as his government's goal.[42] At the end of the war, Iran faced an economic crisis, especially in its cities. The population explosion coupled with migration to urban areas had put transportation, housing, and social services under great pressure. There was high unemployment and growing poverty. Tensions erupted in the form of sporadic but persistent protests—with a few turning violent in 1992 and 1993. If Khamenei's presidency had been all about managing the war, Rafsanjani had to be about jump-starting reconstruction.[43] He referred to his first cabinet as a "cabinet of development" (*sazandegi*) and himself as commander of development (*sardar-e sazandegi*)—an intended parallel with the vaunted title of commander of the IRGC.

Rafsanjani increased investment in transportation, education, and health care as well as urban development, and expanded the private sector and job-creating industries.[44] These goals drew heavily on the technocratic practices of the Pahlavi period, such as five-year planning, urban development, and energy and infrastructure investment.[45] The 1989–94 five-year plan forecast an ambitious 8 percent economic growth per annum, creation of two million new jobs, and threefold increase in imports between 1989 and 1993 to $25 billion, with investments in heavy industry and infrastructure along with a significant expansion of the private sector so that it would provide for the majority of the investments of the five-year plan.[46] During the plan, the government built oil refineries, upgraded the electric grid and urban infrastructure, constructed roads and pipelines, and expanded steel, aluminum, and industrial manufacturing. The financing came from redirecting state funds from the war economy to investment, upgrading the taxation system, privatizing the bloated public sector, increasing the export of oil, and borrowing from abroad.[47] In 1995, for example, Iran's foreign debt stood at $30 billion, up from $10 billion in 1989.

Still, oil and foreign borrowing remained limited sources of revenue given Iran's continuing anti-Western posture and the acts of terrorism it carried out in Europe. Moreover, accruing foreign debt was unpopular inside Iran. Although Khamenei backed Rafsanjani, there was protest against the idea because, as Ayatollah Montazeri put it, borrowing from the West and its financial institutions betrayed the ideals and sacrifices of the revolution.[48]

Rafsanjani's reforms were impressive. These gains, though, had to coexist with the remnants of the war economy and ethos of sacred defense. Rafsanjani writes in his memoirs that after

> the acceptance of the [UN] Resolution [598] and the silencing of tanks, artillery and missiles talk of reconstruction started, plans for development, Nowrouz, the Spring, and life. . . . There was no more planning for funerals for martyrs, anxiety for what was happening at the front, sinking of ships and vicious attacks by the enemy on civilian targets. However, there were those who had gone to the front with love for martyrdom; and did not like peace and tranquility. They were attached to ideas of martyrdom and going to heaven. They showed their yearning.[49]

Development demanded clipping the wings of the bureaucracy and shifting resources from the patronage networks that were set in place during the war. It also required setting national development as the focus of the Islamic Republic in lieu of the ideological underpinnings of the state.

Resistance came initially from many war veterans, who coveted the jobs Rafsanjani was shifting from them to the new breed of experts. Moreover, they were deeply attached to the ideals that had sent them to the front—and this conflicted with Rafsanjani's new agenda.[50] Those veterans as well as fellow committed revolutionaries saw Rafsanjani's policies as class war waged against them. Such resentments fueled resistance to reform, which culminated in Rafsanjani losing the presidential race years later in 2005 to the populist Mahmoud Ahmadinejad.

Rafsanjani's opponents may have expected that his lofty plans for development would fail.[51] Yet as the reforms unfolded between 1990 and 1995, resistance grew more dogged and tied to vested interests, which found useful arguments in the lower strata of society's anger with rising inflation, corruption, and growing income inequality. There were state institutions unreconciled to losing ground to development projects or a new private sector, and there was resistance to relaxing ideological vigilance. That vigilance was embedded in the lower classes, which felt disenfranchised by economic change too, and did not identify with Rafsanjani's technocrats and the rising middle class. Rafsanjani was challenging the standing of important clerical power centers and parastatal institutions, but also the idea that ideology had been key to the wartime mobilization and sacrifices necessary for an isolated country to wage it. Moreover, the reliance on international markets for financing development during his first term as president between 1990 and 1995, and pushing Iran's domestic and foreign policy toward legal-rational behavior, rankled the left-leaning Jacobin faction that viewed empowering "capitalist leaches" as a betrayal of the revolution. In addition, privatization increased income inequality as well as gave rise to business conglomerates—crony capitalism that produced new wealthy powerful economic brokers along with larger-scale corruption.[52]

Although Rafsanjani was the president and chief promoter of development, the ultimate authority nonetheless lay with Khamenei. As supreme leader, he was guardian of the core values of the revolution, ideological conformity, and institutional arrangements of the war years.[53] As much as Khamenei may have supported development as necessary to the national interest, he saw his task as preventing the erosion of ideological vigilance and setting limits on pragmatism in government. In this Khamenei held fast to the belief that in the war with Iraq, Iran had been saved not by development but instead by Islamic ideology. In his mind, Iran needed both development *and* ideology, and the latter was more important to the country's interests and survival than the former. Khamenei may have agreed that the ideological excesses of the war era should come to an end, but not so the ideological character of the state.

These differences would coalesce into factional politics.[54] Initially, the struggles were about whether the state should command control over the economy or efforts should be made to resuscitate the private sector. Soon, however, the debates spread into questions of social and foreign policy as well, especially since Rafsanjani's development strategy relied heavily on international borrowing.[55] As a result, Rafsanjani's experiment with normalcy and reorienting Iran remained limited. In the first term of his presidency, he had more room to maneuver, as Khamenei needed time to consolidate his position. But once that happened, and as the early gains of Rafsanjani's economic policies improved conditions, conservative resistance to his development goals grew.

Now a coherent resistance formed, from Khamenei and the IRGC to power centers and state institutions that opposed Rafsanjani's pragmatism as well as normalization of Iranian politics. This deep state used the levers of power in its hands to resist reform. It soon became a veritable stumbling block that forced Rafsanjani to compromise and ultimately retreat.[56] In the end, he would not be able to institute a coherent agenda for development as the national goal and attract foreign investment, or organize state institutions around achieving it.[57] Rather, his tenure would promote development as an expediency to relieve pressure on the Islamic Republic.

The Rafsanjani presidency was caught in perpetual, paradoxical stasis. On the one hand, under Rafsanjani, Iran pursued meaningful economic change as well as the normalization of its politics and international affairs. But at the same time, the deep state that rose to stymie Rafsanjani's presidency harassed and terrorized intellectuals and political activists, brazenly assassinated dissidents at home and in Europe, and was blamed for acts of terror—most notably, bombing the US Marine and French military barracks in Lebanon in 1983, hijacking a TWA passenger jet in 1985, and bombing the Israeli embassy and the Jewish cultural center in Buenos Aires in 1992 and 1994, respectively. These acts would not just invite international opprobrium but also economic sanctions and puzzled the world to ask which "state" was in charge in Iran: the deep state, built on the ideology and institutions of war fundamentalism and the Iran-Iraq War, or Rafsanjani's faction, which thought revolution should end and true development and state building start.

The burgeoning deep state's resort to assassination and bombing in the West was not random; it revealed how the sacred defense mindset was evolving into a broader national security strategy. The assassination of the Shah's last prime minister, Shapur Bakhtiar, an exiled opposition leader, in Paris in 1991, and the assassination of Kurdish dissidents in Berlin in 1992, which came to be known as the Mykonos affair for the restaurant where it happened, were carried out by Iranian intelligence agents to eliminate what was seen as political and separatist threats to the Islamic Republic. The bombings in Argentina were carried out in response to Israeli attacks on Hezbollah camps in Lebanon, and the bombing of the Al-Khobar Towers in Saudi Arabia in 1996 was a retaliation against the tightening of the US containment cordon around Iran. These made it clear that the military, intelligence, and political power structure that had evolved during the war was still managing Iran's national security, independent of the Rafsanjani government's economic and diplomatic agenda. Later, it was even revealed that a senior intelligence official, Saeed Emami, ran an operation out of the Ministry of Intelligence to use acts of terror—including the assassination of several prominent intellectuals and activists in Iran—to undermine Rafsanjani's policies.[58]

The assassinations and bombings in the West made it impossible for the Rafsanjani to contemplate opening up to the United States and normalizing relations with Europe—which his aides and later biographers have claimed that he was eager to do.[59] He had more luck in burying the hatchet with Saudi Arabia. Rafsanjani understood the importance of Iran-Saudi relations to regional stability, negotiating a security agreement that changed the tenor of relations between the two countries.[60]

These attempts to reorient Iran's relations with the rest of the world were also a response immense changes in the region. After all, Rafsanjani's first term as president saw the end of the Cold War and the Soviet Union's de facto withdrawal from the Middle East after 1989, the shifting inter-Arab alignments after the American-led expulsion of Iraq from Kuwait in 1990, and the decision by several Arab states to join a US containment of Iraq.

Consider even just Iraq. Rafsanjani's first year in office was punctuated by exhausting and fruitless negotiations with Iraq on implementation of UN Resolution 598, which had ended the Iran-Iraq War. This diplomatic stalemate would change only after Iraq invaded Kuwait and faced the wrath of the international community.[61] Even then, radical voices, dominant in the Iranian Parliament, argued for Iran joining Iraq in resisting the United States, especially after Saddam tied his invasion of Kuwait to Israel's occupation of Palestinian territories.

But Rafsanjani understood that this was a moment for asserting the primacy of strategy over ideology. He therefore stood firm against such flights of revolutionary fancy, contending that the expansion of Iraqi influence to the southern shores of the Persian Gulf was to Iran's detriment, and by siding with the people of Kuwait and against Saddam's aggression, Iran would win Arab goodwill and international recognition.[62] By insisting on Iran's neutrality in the war and defeating arguments from militant revolutionaries to join Iraq in an Islamic fight against America, Rafsanjani won an important victory for pragmatic geostrategic thinking over ideological posturing. (Even so, once Saddam was pushed out of Kuwait, Iran increased its criticism of the United States and demanded it leave the Persian Gulf.)[63] Rafsanjani used this policy to find a new balance in Arab-Iran relations in this changing regional picture through the normalization of ties and accommodation wherever possible.[64] He maintained that the more threatening Iran was to its neighbors, the more they would rely on the United States and invite it into the Persian Gulf. It was in Iran's interest to prevent that.[65] Neutrality during the heady months of the crisis also allowed Iran, as a frontline state on Iraq's border, to expand its diplomatic engagements in the region and with Europe; still, there was no support at home for turning this into a strategic realignment that would fundamentally change relations with the West.[66]

United States

Although Rafsanjani was firmly in support of building Iran's indigenous military production capacity to defend itself, he was keen that Iran did not appear menacing to its neighbors.[67] Rafsanjani understood that Iran's development required moving away from ideological posturing to engage with the West—and given the Islamic Republic's sordid history with the United States and the supreme leader's sensitivity to the issue, perhaps first, the "West without the United States."[68]

Soon after he assumed the presidency, Rafsanjani decided to pick up on President George Herbert Walker Bush's statement in a 1989 speech that "goodwill begets goodwill" to test the waters with the United States. In 1990, he ignored Khamenei's counsel and started a negotiation with the United States through the aegis of the United Nations, offering to free American hostages in Lebanon in exchange for the unfreezing of Iranian assets.[69] This, he thought, would both pave the way to improving ties with Washington and give Iran's strapped economy a much-needed financial boost. But by the time Iran released the American hostages in 1992, Washington was no longer ready to release Iran's frozen assets as promised.[70] The supreme leader chided Rafsanjani for his naivete.[71] Tehran saw this rebuff as double dealing, and responded with renewed hostility to the United States, intensification of its activities in Lebanon, and resumption of terrorist acts in Europe.

Tehran also saw a different motivation at play in Washington. The US invasion of Iraq had weakened the Arab world, and that had shifted Israel's focus to Iran. It was Israel, Tehran believed, that was goading Washington to get tougher with Tehran. Iran saw a new push to isolate it in the region and cut its access to the world economy, and package it as the new urgent security threat that the United States had to deal with.[72] In fact, Tehran was convinced that since the 1990s, Israel had undermined every opportunity for a breakthrough between Tehran and Washington—all the instances that Khamenei would recount as evidence of American insincerity and double dealing. This meant that the enmity between United States and Iran was no longer limited to mutual grievances but instead reflected Israel's national security thinking. Washington's primary goal was to prevent Iran from reaching parity with Israel and even weaken it to Israel's benefit. This line of thinking turned Israel into a national security threat, and that made Iran's commitment to Hezbollah and determination to assert its presence in the Arab world vital to protecting itself against what it saw as an American and Israeli plan to cage Iran. That laid the foundations for an increasingly direct shadow war between Iran and Israel that has escalated precipitously since the Gaza war of 2023–24.

· · ·

In 1994, the United States deployed new economic sanctions to ratchet up the pressure on Iran. The new sanctions barred American companies from trading with Iran or investing in the country as well as governments and companies in third countries from trading in US goods with Iran. Even in the face of these hard tactics, Rafsanjani tried to build a bridge to the United States. A year later, in 1995, Iran awarded a major oil contract to the American oil conglomerate Conoco.[73] Rafsanjani had hoped that a business deal of that magnitude could keep new sanctions at bay while sidestepping the fraught political and security issues that stood between the two countries. Yet the promise of an oil deal neither assuaged America nor undid the long shadow that Iran's anti-American and anti-Israel regional posture cast in the United States. And so facing congressional pressure, the Clinton administration scuttled the deal.[74]

This was crucial in terms of how Iran's leadership would view the world going forward. Here was Rafsanjani, a relatively moderate president, decisively snubbed in his determination to build ties with the United States. His setback was orchestrated by a Democratic president, and one who imposed the most significant and lasting set of sanctions to date on Iran.[75] Moreover, Clinton's sanctions (combined with the Iran and Libya Sanctions Act of 1996 passed by the US Congress) firmly focused Iran's leadership on sanctions as a national security issue for Iran.

It was true that Rafsanjani had underestimated the depth of Iran's image problem in the West. But in fact, the heart of the problem was his own inability to resolve Iran's untenable duality: on the one side, the ideological and security mindset of the deep state; on the other, the needs of development.

Rafsanjani was the first in a series of pragmatic Iranian leaders who hoped that Washington would shore up its position by looking beyond the activities of the deep state and reward moderates with engagement. Washington, however, would only engage with Rafsanjani and his fellow travelers if they could show that they have brought to heel the supreme leader and deep state. This became a pattern in US-Iran relations: those Iranian leaders in favor of engagement with the West would feel let down by the United States, which would only prove right the supreme leader's deep suspicions of America.

Khamenei and the deep state were not in favor of the normalization of Iran's foreign policy and lost no opportunity to excoriate Rafsanjani for his pragmatism.[76] Many still held to Khomeini's view that the United States was the "Great Satan," and that "this is not a confrontation between Iran and America, but between Islam and *kufr* (blasphemy)."[77] Khamenei believed that America was not to be trusted and engaging it would prove futile—only weakening the Islamic Republic or opening the door for US infiltration into Iran to undermine the Islamic Republic.[78] He would reiterate this view in the following decades and every time a president would push for engaging the West.

Before he died, Khomeini had further stoked the fires of revolutionary disdain for pragmatism and normalcy in relations with the world by issuing the highly controversial and inflammatory fatwa against Salman Rushdie.[79] The jurisprudential justification for such a fatwa was far from straightforward, but for a leader of a country to engage in such unconventional behavior was a deliberate insistence on flouting the norms of international relations: a return to where the Islamic Republic stood when holding American diplomats as hostages. The Rushdie affair also purported to cast Iran as a central player in a clash between Islam and the West, a standoff in which Iran's national interest was subsumed under a larger ideological cause.[80] Little surprise, then, that to stymie Rafsanjani, a hard-line foundation renewed the fatwa and placed a bounty on Rushdie, promising a reward for killing him, all with the support of economic forces opposed to Rafsanjani's privatization plans.

The End of the Cold War

The Rafsanjani period coincided with the aftermath of the fall of the Berlin Wall, collapse of the Soviet Union, and opening of China and its turn toward the West. The demise of two states built on great revolutions was disconcerting to Iran's revolutionary elite. The example of Mikhail Gorbachev along with the impact of glasnost and perestroika on breaking the Soviet Empire and humbling Russia aroused deep suspicions of where Rafsanjani's pragmatism could lead. Khamenei was not keen on presiding over the end of the Islamic Republic, and saw unending reform and normalization with the West as exactly that. In many respects his determination to constrain Rafsanjani was a strategy of regime survival and preventing Iran from being the next revolutionary domino to fall. It was after the collapse of the Soviet Union that Khamenei first spoke with worry about the threat that Western cultural penetration and the specter of a "velvet revolution" posed to the Islamic Republic. To thwart that outcome, he charged a network of state institutions—and later, government agencies and the Parliament—to limit Western cultural influences. He repeated warnings about the corrosive influence of Western culture in speeches in the years that followed, and redoubled investment in combating this perceived threat after the 1997 and 2009 elections when reformism looked ascendant, and again after the 2022 protests rejecting mandatory hijab that rocked the Islamic Republic.

The collapse of the Soviet Union was significant in another regard. In one sweep it removed a singular strategic menace that had hounded Iran for over a century.[81] Communism as an ideological threat was gone. Even more important, Russia moved far back from Iran's borders, leaving behind a vast buffer area of new states in the Caucasus region and Central Asia—many former Iranian territories. These new states had ethnic and cultural affinity with Iran, opening new economic and strategic possibilities.[82] But these posed new challenges too, as in the case of talk of unification of Iran's Azarbaijan and the new independent Republic of Azerbaijan. This, for example, compelled Rafsanjani to cooperate with Ankara and Moscow to protect Iran's interests.[83]

Crucially, the Soviet threat had previously been an important pressure on Iran to mend fences with the West. After all, it was the Soviet military threat that brought China and the United States closer in 1971, and it was the Chinese invasion of Vietnam in 1979 that persuaded Hanoi to make peace with Washington. But now with the collapse of the Soviet Union, this pressure on Iran was removed. Conversely, the collapse of the Soviet Union meant there was no need to think of better ties with the West as pivotal to a strategic balancing act. The historic changes of the post-1989 period provided no impetus for a strategic shift in Tehran, even as it embarked on a pragmatic development strategy at home.

Iraq's threat to Iran while Saddam remained in power, or the rise of the Taliban and Pakistan's nuclear weapons test, all in the 1990s, did not rise to a level that would compel Iran to reorient its geostrategy. In fact, the United States would continue to hold Iran's gaze.

The Struggle at Home

Still, the Rafsanjani years brought greater rationality to the state. His government placed greater emphasis on expertise rather than ideological orientation in the choice of technocrats, and gave coherence to the judiciary, Central Bank, and economic decision-making bodies. The cultural revolution was formally ended, and higher education was strengthened.[84]

These changes were consequential. For instance, in 1977, the number of university students stood at just 154,000 (although there was at least an equal number also studying abroad). But by 1997, the last year of Rafsanjani's presidency, that number had risen to 1.25 million—a significant increase even after accounting for population growth.[85] Those graduates would swell the ranks of the middle class and improve the managerial capacity of state institutions. Most important, they gave Iran scientific and technological capacity that sustained Iran's nuclear, high technology, manufacturing, services, and health care capacities as well as cultural achievements in future decades.[86]

On the economic front, the Rafsanjani years were a turning point. The first decade of the revolution had witnessed economic stagnation. The revolution had been a shock to the economy, and the total war had skewed imbalances between economic sectors, increased shortages, and accelerated poverty. And in the first decade of the revolution— remarkably, even despite the war—Iran's population had grown by

45 percent, while oil income had declined along with production and exports. The country had become more dependent, and the growth of patronage and welfare had bloated the public sector while increasing economic inefficiency. The economy needed investment and jobs, structural reforms, and real growth. Ideological politics was a stumbling block. Nonetheless, under Rafsanjani, aggressive monetary policy, infrastructure development projects, financed with increased government debt, and the rise of a new private sector—including attracting the return of expatriate businesspeople and technocrats—breathed new life into the economy.[87] Moreover, Rafsanjani's government implemented one of the most successful population control programs to date in the developing world. While birth rate stood at seven children per household at the end of the 1970s, that number had dropped to two per household by the end of the 1990s.[88]

Economic changes also opened the door to inequality, corruption, and a shadow economy.[89] The new private sector and emerging middle class—and their corresponding consumerist culture—enjoyed higher standards of living than the poorer strata, which remained dependent on entitlement and welfare programs. High-rises shot up across Tehran, changing the face of the city, many through deals that benefited speculators and were open to corrupt influences. Crony capitalism wove businesspeople, bureaucrats, and connected politicians into lucrative financial networks. The inequality and corruption contradicted the values of the revolution as well as the language of sacrifice and dedication that had characterized the war years. Even Rafsanjani himself would build a formidable business empire that expanded further after he left office to include banks, manufacturing, Iran's second-largest airline, oil and gas, and foreign holdings.

The Politics of Social Change

These changes may not have transformed how the Islamic Republic was governed, but their social and hence political impact was nevertheless monumental.[90] Although Rafsanjani and his government continued to espouse fidelity to the core values of the revolution, those who benefited from their policies were no longer lured by strict and austere ideology, or talk of resilience and the ethos of sacred defense. Instead, they gravitated to those interpretations of Islamic ideology and views of the Islamic Republic that would accommodate their social as well as economic aspirations.[91] Furthermore, it soon became apparent that as much as the war years had unified the country and integrated its population, the secular middle class of the Pahlavi era had remained intact. The Islamic Republic had dominated but not eradicated it. With the opening of the Rafsanjani years, it once again spread its wings to play an important part in the private sector, but especially in the social and cultural arenas.

This social transformation confronted increasing ideological stubbornness from conservative clerics and the deep state. They opposed the social and political changes wrought by development, but also used the cudgel of ideology to resist economic reforms that impacted vested interests. This seeming impasse between fidelity to revolutionary ideology and the imperative of pragmatic change prompted serious debates over religious reform. A new breed of religious intellectuals (*rowshanfekran-e dini*), some laypeople and some from the ranks of younger clergy, emerged to argue for an interpretative reading of Islamic law and Islamic ideology to facilitate pragmatic change.

The most prominent of these thinkers was Abdol-Karim Soroush. An ardent revolutionary in the early 1980s, Soroush became a vocal advocate of an interpretative reading of Shia law free of clerical control. Soroush and his like-minded intellectuals provided religious cover for the kind of social and cultural changes that were prompted by development as well as were needed for it to continue. To many, this seemed the beginnings of a reformation of Shiism.[92]

These ideas were appealing to middle-class people and the younger technocrats in the government, who were looking for a new formula that would allow an Islamic state to accommodate economic and social change. Conservative clerics, however, were in no mood to countenance a challenge to their monopoly over the interpretation of religion by lay intellectuals and younger clergy. Nor were they willing to compromise on the ideological underpinnings of the revolution.[93] The consumerist habits of the new middle class and cultural openings that it demanded were minor challenges to the rigid ideological position of the guardians of the Islamic Republic. But talk of religious reform posed a more fundamental challenge since it was attractive to the new elites (in this case, pious technocrats and state managers). As such, it posed a serious threat from within.[94]

All of this convinced the conservative elite that they could not easily coexist with this new ideological and political compact, which had emerged from the war, alongside the cultural opening that development and postwar reconstruction demanded. They responded forcefully. Soroush soon beat a hasty retreat into exile. Young clerics who had espoused similar ideas were defrocked and marginalized. And the conservative clerics began cultivating their own breed of intellectuals and technocrats, some with ties to powerful seminaries in Qom, and they mounted a strong defense of the core values of the revolution. They started propagating a new conservative agenda, which would unfold in domestic politics and foreign policy over the next two decades.

The Rafsanjani years thus caused a clear fissure in Iranian society and politics. On the one side were the forces for reform born of shifting demography and social changes wrought by economic development. On the other side were guardians of the state who held fast to the ideological vigilance of the war years that had united the country behind the state. It was such vigilance, in their minds, that accounted for Iran surviving the challenges of the 1980s at all.

Khatami and the Challenge of Political Opening

In the end, the Rafsanjani era was an experiment in grafting pragmatism to the militant revolutionary body politic of the Islamic Republic (at least as it had been forged during the first decade of the revolution). As such, it did make significant changes to the economy, society, and even foreign policy. But its gains remained limited and vulnerable to reversals. Those who benefited from and championed the changes felt frustrated, and were eager to push for more. At the same time, though, hard-liners sought to end the experimentation with pragmatism. In their eyes, enough development had happened to stabilize the country's economy and address the dire problems that war had inflicted on the Iranian economy and society. Now they could consolidate their hold on state and society, retaining some of Rafsanjani's wins, but firmly caged under their own ideological and political control.

By the last year of Rafsanjani's presidency, the conservative press ratcheted up attacks on advocates of reform. Meanwhile, security forces openly intimidated writers, artists, and social activists.

Conservative leaders now were also happy to pursue the kind of militancy abroad that had isolated Iran during the first decade of the revolution. By the last year of Rafsanjani's presidency, most European ambassadors had left Iran, and the US Congress had passed the Iran and Libya Sanctions Act, which further restricted Iran's access to the global economy. Instead of opening to the United States, Iran found itself the object of the Clinton administration's "dual containment" policy aimed at caging both Iran and Iraq.[95] More alarming was the US display of decisive force in expelling Iraq from Kuwait, placing the northern part of the country under a no-fly zone and rallying the Arab world to isolate Iraq. All of these US actions convinced Khamenei and the IRGC that it was imperative to remain strategically vigilant, and organize the state and society around national security. This meant rejecting the pragmatism exemplified by Rafsanjani, and instead doubling down on resistance, sacred defense, and the ideological vigilance of the war years.

It was then that Khamenei and advocates of resistance decided to retake control of the presidency. Since becoming supreme leader, Khamenei had sought to consolidate his powers, but even though he had achieved much, he felt that Rafsanjani's stature and policies had prevented him from fully consolidating his position. Now Khamenei's preferred candidate for president was the conservative cleric Ali Akbar Nateq Nouri. Yet he could not run uncontested. The Guardian Council decided on the slate of candidates, which included—as a token concession to the forces channeled by Rafsanjani—a little-known cleric who did not seem an obvious reformist contender: Mohammad Khatami.

Khatami had not been a revolutionary activist in the 1970s, and was not part of either Khomeini's or Khamenei's inner circles. A debonair intellectual, he had served as the head of the national library and minister of culture. In both of those positions, however, he had engaged intellectuals and writers, gaining a reputation for his tolerance and pragmatism. Conservatives did not take Khatami seriously and believed that the election of their candidate was a foregone conclusion. Yet the outcome would be nothing short of an earthquake in Iran's politics. Khamenei and his allies could control who ran, but uunbeknownst to them, they had lost control of who voted and how.

During the Rafsanjani years, the idea had been confirmed that elections were integral to the Islamic Republic, and a mechanism to engage and rally its citizenry. Elections, it was believed, would not challenge the state but rather *confirm* the Islamic Republic and its ethos, *renewing* the bond between the leadership and its people. Indeed, Rafsanjani's polices had even brought new social classes into the electoral process. But by 1997, Iran had undergone profound changes.[96] The country had moved past the war and the sacrifices it demanded. The population was forward-looking, largely seeking to put the memory of war behind as it sought a different future. The population was more literate and engaged. Women now constituted a larger part of the workforce and were also more literate. The country's intellectual climate too had grown more sophisticated during the postwar decade. The conservative elite did not realize how much Iranian society yearned for normalcy and engaging the world.

Moreover, Khatami hit a chord during the electoral campaign. His religious garb looked impeccably tailored and made of fine cloth, his smiling face stood in sharp contrast to the dour visage of his rivals and the revolutionary leaders, who saw seriousness as a mark of ideological vigilance. Khatami's own writings on Islam and the revolution spoke of humanism and tolerance.[97] Technocrats and pragmatic managers who had supported Rafsanjani's developmentalist policies saw continuity in Khatami, and secular intellectuals whom Khatami had supported made his case to the middle classes. Many revolutionary activists of the early days of the revolution—who had been sidelined by the brand of revolutionary conservatism now dominant in Iran, such as the future presidential hopeful and opposition leader Mir Hossein

Moussavi—all flocked to Khatami and helped run his campaign. State managers who were in positions of power, and especially the pro-Rafsanjani mayor of Tehran, Gholam Hossein Karbaschi, used the capital city's political machine and popular newspaper to help Khatami. Conservatives had also underestimated this degree of institutional mobilization to support Khatami.

Most observers had come to expect that Khatami would do better than expected, but no one was predicting he would win.[98] Yet his victory was as decisive as it was humiliating to the conservative establishment; even a significant number of the IRGC's rank and file along with an estimated 70 percent of the Iranian Armed Forces voted for Khatami.[99] In a high-turnout election, wherein some 80 percent of the eligible voters cast their ballots, Khatami won a thumping 69 percent of the vote, overshadowing Nateq Nouri's share of the vote by a margin of 44 percent. On the eve of the election, Khamenei had publicly called on Iranians to vote for his favored candidate. The outcome was an embarrassing rebuff.

Iranians quickly dubbed the election a "second revolution." The popular vote had soundly defeated the fundamental ideological and institutional alliance between militant clerics and the IRGC that had emerged from the war. Indeed, the population seemed to have moved past all the assumptions of that alliance, especially the primacy of the values of the revolution and imperative of adhering to them to defend Iran. The population was looking for more than modest concessions; instead, it sought a clear break with the social and cultural norms that had shaped the Islamic Republic.

The outcome was a challenge for both Khamenei and Khatami. Khamenei had to use all the levers of power—and quickly—to rally his allies to block radical changes. The Soviet Union had collapsed a mere eight years before, and Gorbachev's precedent was very much on everyone's mind. The popular enthusiasm that the election had generated made the task of containing change difficult, as did the fact that so many among the rank and file of the state and even IRGC had voted for Khatami. Consequently, one of the first steps Khamenei took was to remove the long-serving IRGC commander Mohsen Rezaie, and purge the force's ranks of the less than ideologically vigilant officers and soldiers. He also instituted a commissariat within the force to vet officers and ensure that the IRGC would remain bound by the ethos of the state.

Khatami believed that Iran's national security needs would be best served by increasing popular support for the state by expanding participation in politics combined with greater engagement with the world community by extending a hand of friendship to all countries around the world (except Israel).[100] Khatami, however, had the challenge of instituting the popular support into a meaningful political force, and delivering on the expectations he had generated in the face of what he understood would be fierce resistance from Khamenei and his allies.

During the campaign, Khatami had referred to "democracy" and "civil society" (*jame'eh madani*), rejected state enforcement of religious observance, and talked of the rule of law and cultural freedoms.[101] Achieving all of this would be a tall order. It demanded the cooperation of the legislature and bureaucracy. While under Rafsanjani the impetus for change came from the government, now it was the enthusiastic voters who took the lead in realizing Khatami's promises. Debates over the nature and extent of reform moved from inside the halls of power to salons and publications on the outside, facilitated by an explosion in the number and diversity of newspapers, magazines, and books.[102] The intellectual effervescence quickly moved beyond Islamic reform to liberal democracy and political openness.

Khatami's election also empowered a new breed of political operatives who set their sights on expanding the scope of civil society activism and push for democratization. For them, Khatami's election was only the first step in fundamental political change in Iran. They developed plans for an ambitious effort at decentralizing power by handing over governance to local bodies through elections. In February 1999, one thousand Iranian towns and cities elected municipal authorities and mayors. This effort at broadening the scope of democracy was important in instituting political change, and for a time, constraining the conservative guardians of the state.[103]

Khatami spoke of the "dialogue of civilizations" too—a nebulous concept that he used as a euphemism for dialogue and engagement as well as a counterpoint to Samuel Huntington's popular "Clash of Civilizations" thesis that then dominated in the West. He improved ties with Saudi Arabia and the European Union, which led the United States to expect an imminent breakthrough in its relations with Iran as well.[104] Even this outreach to the world hit a chord with Iranians, who yearned to end their country's isolation. This desire became glaringly obvious when in November 1997, Tehran erupted into impromptu street celebrations after Iran's national soccer team qualified for the 1998 World Cup, the first time after two decades of absence from the competition. Jubilant crowds took over the streets as people danced and celebrated— some women without their headscarves. Security forces in effect lost control of the streets for two days, unable to enforce order or religious strictures. The country's rulers saw firsthand the popular enthusiasm for openness and international engagement, and that directly challenged the deep state's conceptions of Iran's national interest.

Yet Khatami had not anticipated his own success. He was torn between those who believed he must compromise and serve as a bridge between the forces he had unleashed and the powerful institutions of the Islamic Republic, and those who were rejecting compromise and encouraging him to forge full steam ahead toward political opening. The intellectual activism and popular enthusiasm had certainly sped far ahead of him, and quickly, and some of what it would produce would be out of his control.

Encouraged by Khatami's victory, Ayatollah Montazeri—Khomeini's onetime heir—wrote a statement criticizing Khamenei and questioning his religious credentials, asking for limits on the powers of the supreme leader.[105] Lay and clerical followers of the Islamic reform movement resurfaced, now arguing for democracy and secular society.[106]

Soon Khatami came under intense pressure from conservatives. The new commander of the IRGC, General Yahya Rahim-Safavi, publicly excoriated Khatami for the "national security threat" that his cultural opening had put before the state. "Can we withstand American threats and [the United States'] domineering attitude with a policy of détente?" he asked in a speech. "Can we foil dangers coming from [America] through 'dialogue between civilizations'?"[107]

The most serious national security threat at this time, however, did came not from the United States but rather from the Taliban's ascendance in Afghanistan. In 1998, the Taliban forces sweeping over northern Afghanistan made a show of their fierce sectarianism by attacking the Iranian consulate in the city of Mazar Sharif, killing eleven diplomats and journalists. Iranians were shocked and angered.[108] Iran mobilized 270,000 troops along Afghanistan's border, but ultimately decided against war. Khamenei argued that Afghanistan could be a quicksand from which Iran would not be able to extricate itself, and the Taliban attack was likely a trap to get Iran into war on its east side while America and its allies pursued their policies in the Middle East.[109] Yet the IRGC actively supported the Northern Alliance, playing an important role in sustaining its military resistance to the Taliban.

The deep state went beyond public criticism to contain the enthusiasm for change Khatami had unleashed. Conservatives in Parliament and the judiciary as well as on the Guardian Council blocked legislation and government initiatives. Security forces shut down newspapers and put journalists in prison, and took to violently intimidating intellectuals and reformist dissidents. A special clerical tribunal in 1997 tried reformist clerics, defrocking and imprisoning them. In 1998, veteran democracy activists Daryoush Forouhar and his wife, Parvaneh Eskandari Forouhar, were murdered by security forces. Former Tehran mayor Karbaschi, who had helped Khatami's election, was put on public trial on television for corruption. And an attempt was made on the life of Khatami's adviser, Sa'id Hajjarian, leading to public demonstrations.

Khatami was reluctant to take a stand, and his vacillation only emboldened the deep state. When in July 1999 students protested the closure of a reformist newspaper, IRGC and Basij forces stormed university dormitories. The brutal show of force marked the first crackdown of its kind in the Islamic Republic. Security forces saw student protests as a serious threat, not only to the authoritarian nature of the state, but to their conception of the ideological and security arrangement that provided national security. Students were rejecting theocracy, and demanding liberal democracy and engagement with the West—exactly what Rahim-Safavi had told his audience would defang the

Islamic Republic's national security. Twenty-four IRGC commanders wrote Khatami menacing letters, saying that their patience had reached its limits.[110]

Khatami quickly caved; he chastised the students for providing the IRGC with an excuse to clampdown and then stood by as security forces brutally suppressed student protests. That was a watershed moment. The deep state succeeded in forcibly suppressing reformists to protect the ideological and institutional backbone of the Islamic Republic.

They nevertheless understood that blocking reformists was only the first step. To truly manage Iran, they needed a viable conservative alternative that could hold its own in the political arena. The decision to reverse the openings of the Rafsanjani-Khatami era came from above, but was soon followed with investments in programs that inculcated ideological values and hard-line political views in government and society. Conservatives invested in their own media outlets, replicating the appealing style of reformist media. Self-styled conservative intellectuals posited a new approach to relations between the clerical leadership and society, which adopted the Rafsanjani-Khatami developmentalism, but grafted it to the theocratic structure of the state. Universities such as Imam Sadeq and Imam Hossein (affiliated with the IRGC) dedicated their curriculum to inculcating in the next generation of mandarins of the Islamic Republic with values of the revolution and the worldview of sacred defense.

Similarly, seminaries in Qom, especially the Haqqani seminary associated with the hard-line Ayatollah Mohammad-Taqi Mesbah-Yazdi—a doctrinaire advocate of shedding Iran of all Western influence to achieve true greatness—trained cadres of turbaned political operatives and security officials to protect the same worldview in the halls of power, especially in the intelligence agencies and key ministries. Mesbah had been prominent in the Mojahedin-e Enqelab (a faction of militant clergy that in the 1980s, supported the IRGC's emerging strategy for conducting the war). He was known as the IRGC's ideologue, and his close lieutenants had led education and political bureaus in the force.[111] His coterie constituted the core of the political coalition,

Jebhe-ye Paidari (the Resilience Front), the rejectionist front that is today the most ardent opponent to engagement with the United States and accepting a nuclear deal.[112] The defining doctrinal anchor of this front is the ideal of resistance. Its discourse on politics and national security employs the language of Islam, but at its core it is secular— achieving power and security that obviates engagement with the United States.

The rise of this new breed of conservatives in security agencies and government institutions dovetailed with the supreme leader's own consolidation of power.[113] Khamenei had risen to the apex of the Islamic Republic without deep support among the mandarin class that ran the state. He spent the next decade working to gain political stature; build his own base of power in the IRGC, Basij, judiciary, and powerful parastatal institutions; and create a powerful secretariat, the so-called Household of the Leader (*Beyt-e Rahbari*) that has allowed him to oversee the government. By the end of the 1990s, Khamenei became what reformist journalist Akbar Ganji, borrowing from Max Weber, referred to as a "latter-day sultan": an omnipotent, unelected, and unaccountable leader, whose exercise of power defied the republican intent of the Islamic Republic in the interest of serving a conservative agenda.[114]

The conservative guardians of the state were not opposed to economic development, but now promised to implement it more effectively while remaining close to the values and goals of the Islamic Republic.[115] The IRGC and parastatal institutions, meanwhile, co-opted the burgeoning private sector in a bargain that promised prosperity and a certain tolerance for cultural openness in lieu of calls for fundamental reforms.[116] Under Rafsanjani, the IRGC had started to enter the economic sphere. Now, though, it began to play a much more prominent role in the economy, further extending the political responsibility it had assumed in containing and then rolling back reformism.[117] The IRGC laid claim to large economic projects in key sectors such as construction, telecommunications, and energy, forming behemoth conglomerates like Khatam al-Anbia that today own interests across the gamut of economic sectors. From that perch, the IRGC co-opted private sector companies along with the middle classes attached to them through subcontracting and business deals, fostering a crony capitalist system, which would both empower the IRGC and allow it to manage politics.[118]

This approach co-opted enough of the middle class to stabilize theocratic rule and its national security state. Within a few short years of Khatami's explosive victory, the Islamic Republic had shown itself able to adapt without conceding on the sacred defense mindset. Ultimately, the years between 1989 and 2005 were a period of intense struggle between three elements of Iranian society: ideological fervor, technocratic management, and democratization. For a time, it looked that an alliance between technocrats and democrats could isolate the ideologues gathered around the supreme leader. But by 2005, it was the ideological faction that was co-opting technocracy to marginalize calls for democracy.[119]

Ahmadinejad and the Denouement to Reformism

By 2001, reformism had lost its momentum. The conservative forces had secured firm control over Parliament and the judiciary, and by the end of Khatami's second term in 2005, they had decisively expanded their footprint in the economy. In so doing, the IRCG made sure there would be no glasnost in Iran. And this conservative agenda would unfold amid the dramatic geopolitical changes that followed Al-Qaeda's attacks on the United States in September 2001.

By the time of the presidential elections for 2005, reformists were in disarray. With no credible standard-bearer, they endorsed Rafsanjani as their candidate. He appealed to the middle class, promising to continue to push for economic growth and political reform. Reformists expected Rafsanjani to be a more formidable advocate of change than Khatami— more difficult to intimidate than the outgoing president. But his conservative rivals looked to the poorer classes, left behind by the economic growth of the 1990s, and built their comeback on populism and the promise of economic justice. Khamenei and his allies turned to the little-known former mayor of Tehran, Mahmoud Ahmadinejad, to lead the charge.

Ahmadinejad hailed from a humble background and made much of his plebian lifestyle. He lived in a modest house in a lower middle-class area of Tehran, dressed shabbily, and spoke to the poor in the "us versus them" language of populists the world over. In folksy rhetoric, he promised to combat income inequality and corruption as well as give a greater share of national income to the poor.[120] He capitalized on the unfulfilled economic expectations of the poorer masses and resentments that had grown toward the newly rich as well as the wealthy stalwarts of the Islamic Republic.[121] Class division had returned to Iran, and reform had become the cause of the well-to-do; the poorer and conservative Iranians wanted economic benefits and equity. Indeed, the poor were still looking to the egalitarian values of the revolution for economic relief. The yawning economic gap was coupled with the cultural chasm between those who wanted a liberalization of politics and religious strictures, and those who remained closely tethered to piety and revolutionary ideals.

These struggles energized the rising middle class and advocates of change, but also the deep state. The presidential campaign was hard-fought, but to the surprise and chagrin of reformists, populism carried the day.

Ahmadinejad had long been affiliated with the IRGC and Basij, and now he expanded their economic footprint.[122] In fact, it was during Ahmadinejad's presidency that the IRGC became both the largest recipient of government contracts and largest source of contracts to the private sector. Ahmadinejad's government gave the IRGC preferential bank loans, and opened the door for the IRGC to buy all or parts of large numbers of state-owned enterprises along with private sector companies through the Tehran Stock Exchange.[123]

At the same time, even though Ahmadinejad was championed by hard-liners and security forces, he was not a perfect fit with their views. For example, he continuously hinted that he was in contact with the Shia messiah, the Twelfth Imam. This fit well with his populism, but irked the clergy, who saw his claims as heterodox and an unwelcome intrusion into their domain. Moreover, he asserted his powers to challenge those of the supreme leader, ultimately driving a wedge between him and Khamenei.[124]

Nevertheless, Ahmadinejad's presidency saw the consolidation of power in the hands of ardent conservatives and the IRGC, and the entrenchment of the mantra of sacred defense in the state's vision for Iran's future. By opening the economy to the IRGC as well as the bureaucracy to hard-line conservative clergy and politicians, the Ahmadinejad era enabled the deep state to solidify a network of control across government, economy, and important state and social institutions. Khamenei and his conservative allies saw Ahmadinejad as useful in rallying public support—at least for a time—behind their agenda, restoring the unity between people and the state around ideology and the goals of sacred defense.

The same mantra that had guided Iran through the war in the 1980s—believed the supreme leader, IRGC, and their allies in the political arena—would now see the country through the next phase of state building and geopolitical strategy. This deep state saw that Ahmadinejad's government made it possible to embed the values of sacred defense within government institutions. Over the past decade, these institutions had been the vehicle for economic growth, political reform, and the aspirations of the rising middle class. Now they could be the vehicle of ideological retrenchment. And this would be achieved by means of a new conservative technocratic class—one that had ties to the increasingly captive private sector, but also to the IRGC along with its web of political and religious affiliates.[125] Thus the Ahmadinejad presidency was not a throwback to the pristine ideological fervor of the 1980s but instead a systematic application of the 1980s to the 2000s.

To those outside Iran, it was Ahmadinejad's crude bombast—in particular, his denial of the Holocaust and declaration that Israel would be wiped off the face of the map—that was both most noticeable and disconcerting. After the limited hopes of Khatami, and after it was revealed that Iran's nuclear program was thriving, the arrival of this populist demagogue aroused the worst fears about the Islamic Republic in the West. Yet in the Middle East and larger Muslim world, Ahmadinejad found instant popularity because what dominated perceptions was anger at the Bush administration's Islamophobia and invasion of Iraq.

This political capital was welcomed by the Islamic Republic. It was this, perhaps, that deluded Khamenei and the IRGC into thinking that anti-Americanism and hostility to Israel was winning Iran reliable strategic support on the Arab street.

Ahmadinejad tried to turn populism at home into a foreign policy platform, harking back to a time when anti-imperialism and nonalignment bound developing countries into a common front.[126] He found kindred spirit in Venezuela's Hugo Chávez and Bolivia's Evo Morales, who were also riding on the crest of populism and anti-Americanism. This quaint axis of populists was neither large enough nor geographically concentrated to be taken seriously. The theatrics surrounding the idea, however, allowed Ahmadinejad to claim that he was advancing the revolution's anti-imperialist mission, echoing Khamenei's belief in the promise of an Axis of Resistance against the West.

These maneuvers underscored how much of Ahmadinejad's rule broke with the preceding decade and a half of pragmatism and reform. Yet he was merely the face of the change instigated by the supreme leader and the alliance of the IRGC and hard-line conservatives. To Khamenei and the IRGC's leadership, the radical changes to regional security stemming from 9/11 and the American invasion of Iraq urgently demanded a response. It was in this context that they worked to restore the mantra of sacred defense and close the book on the decade of economic as well as political reform.

Thereafter, Iran's foreign policy seemed to bend toward radicalism and even the export of revolution. Yet this new direction was motivated not by ideology but rather by deterrence and Tehran's pursuit of national interest.[127]

CHAPTER 7

Forward Defense

Seeking Strategic Depth for Resistance

Al-Qaeda's attack on the United States in September 2001 shifted the American focus for a time away from Iran. Tehran may have assumed then that the United States would now see Sunni extremism rather than Iran's Shia theocracy as the principal threat against which it had to defend. After all, what had struck America was Sunni militancy. Al-Qaeda was born of the Afghan jihad that the United States had backed in collaboration with Pakistan and Saudi Arabia. Its rank and file hailed from Arab countries, most notably Saudi Arabia, America's principal regional ally and a pillar of containment of Iran. Even the extremist ideology that Al-Qaeda espoused, and the network of seminaries and religious institutions across South Asia that disseminated it, were soon blamed on funding from the oil-rich Arab states.

The attacks also put the Taliban, which had hosted Al-Qaeda, in America's crosshairs. Iran had viewed the Taliban as an enemy since the attack on the Iranian consulate in 1998, and as a result, the IRGC's Qods Force had been supporting the anti-Taliban Northern Alliance in Afghanistan's ongoing civil war.[1] The military campaign to topple the Taliban and the diplomatic effort to set up a new state in Afghanistan were highwater marks in US-Iran cooperation—a rare opening built on the convergence of interests between the two over Afghanistan.[2]

American diplomat Ryan Crocker recollects that immediately after the 9/11 attacks, he met with an emissary of the IRGC's Qods Force's commander, General Qasem Soleimani, in Geneva. The Iranian envoy gave Crocker detailed maps of Taliban locations as well as advice on what targets the US Air Force should focus on.[3] Iran supported the American military campaign against the Taliban, giving the United States access to Iranian airspace for search-and-rescue missions in Afghanistan. Even the IRGC coordinated with US military in organizing the Northern Alliance forces to defeat the Taliban. Soleimani, who later gained notoriety in the West for leading his Qods Force in campaigns against US forces in Iraq and Syria, was instrumental in persuading the supreme leader to cooperate with the United States to get rid of the Taliban. His deputy (and later his successor at the helm of the Qods Force), General Esma'il Qa'ani, was put in charge of working directly with the US military at the operational level.[4] Iranian diplomats then joined their US counterparts at the Bonn conference in 2002 to draft a new constitution for Afghanistan and put in place a new government for the country. Iran's ambassador to the United Nations at the time and later foreign minister, Mohammad Javad Zarif, worked closely with his US counterpart, ambassador James Dobbins, to bring the Bonn conference to a successful conclusion.[5] Iran too wanted the Taliban gone and saw danger in Al-Qaeda. According to Zarif, the conference would not have succeeded without Soleimani's active support.[6]

The cooperation, however, did not transform relations between the two. Soon after the Bonn conference, Israel accused Iran of supplying arms to Palestinian groups, and with that United States and Iran quickly returned to their default antagonistic positions. The events of 9/11 and their aftermath could have reduced tensions between Iran and the United States. Instead, President Bush included Iran in his infamous "Axis of Evil" speech. It was this defamation—even after cooperating in Afghanistan—that signaled to Iran that the United States remained a threat—especially since the speech also called for preemptive military action against hostile states that were developing nuclear weapons and could disseminate them to terrorists. Iran's incipient nuclear program at the time was not known to the world; its rulers understood the implications of Bush's threat: that his new doctrine would soon apply to Iran.

Khamenei concluded from this experience, then, that any signal of reconciliation would be interpreted by Washington as weakness and only invite further American pressure.[7] And so the Axis of Evil insult justified and reinforced the national security mindset of the deep state, helping to place the nail in the coffin of reform.[8]

Then came the US invasion of Iraq. The 2003 Iraq War was different from 1991. This time, the United States was not enforcing international norms by reversing a specific Iraqi violation; instead, it was going to war to remove Saddam from power, and replace him with a democracy that would spread from Iraq to end authoritarianism and Islamic radicalism across the Middle East. Within this troublesome region, war was the scalpel with which the United States would remove all malignancies. And within America's grand project, Iran saw itself squarely in the crosshairs.[9]

After all, the Iranian Revolution was the fountainhead of Islamist re-surgence in the region. If democracy were to sweep the Islamic Republic from power, then the rest of the region and the Muslim world would follow suit. American rhetoric on the eve of the war was menacing. US officials spoke of Najaf becoming the beacon for moderate Shiism and a competition for Qom, or Iranians being inspired by Iraqi democracy would revolt. The Bush administration's bravado was captured by a popular refrain of the time: "Everyone wants to go to Baghdad. Real men want to go to Tehran."[10] In essence, the war on Iraq would be just the beginning; Iran would be next.[11]

Iranians took note. As Iran's first ambassador to Iraq after the inva-sion, former IRGC commander Hasan Kazemi Qomi, put it, "After Iraq it was Iran's turn."[12] That suspicion was also stoked by the timing of the revelation of Iran's nuclear program, only months before the US inva-sion of Iraq began; "at that juncture in 2002 that America was getting ready to invade Iraq, the American invasion and Iran's nuclear program were put before the international community as a single special security case. America knew about Iran's program, what it was after at that point in time was to build the case against Iran," as it had used the fear of a nuclear program to invade Iraq.[13] Khamenei set the tone for this way of thinking, arguing in speeches that the West fully well knows Iran does not want a nuclear bomb, but chooses to keep sounding the alarm because it wants to play mind games with Iran's leaders. If Iran gave up its nuclear program, the West would find another issue to continue its pressure.[14] Tehran quickly concluded that the United States would follow the same playbook as Iraq, tightening sanctions on Iran, waging a psychological war against the country, and building a case for international legal, public, and military support for war with Iran.[15] The ease with which the United States dismantled Saddam's military and toppled his regime was a worry for Tehran, and not only because its own military was equally vulnerable. In addition, going forward the United States was likely to be more confident and aggressive in asserting its policies in the Middle East.

Khatami sought to head off American aggression. On May 3, 2003, merely a month after US troops arrived in Baghdad, his office gave a two-page letter to the Swiss ambassador in Iran—whose embassy oversees the Interest Section for the United States in Iran—to relay to Washington. The letter offered broad-based talks on the key outstanding issues between the United States and Iran—even on the future of Hezbollah.[16] It was a road map for the de-escalation of tensions and putting relations on a new trajectory.[17] The Bush administration ignored the letter. Perhaps it assumed that Iran was desperate, and rather than negotiate with it, the United States should seek to overthrow it.[18]

Khatami had shared his letter with Khamenei. The supreme leader was not supportive. His reaction was, "You are the president and can decide to write this letter, but my recommendation is that you not do it. Mark my words, America will let you down and will construe the letter as weakness." When Washington rejected Khatami's overture, Khamenei felt vindicated. Khatami rued the fact that "America had proved the supreme leader correct."[19]

As we have seen, Khamenei was convinced that the United States viewed any outreach from Iran as a sign of weakness. He would later also chide Ahmadinejad—who wrote letters to President Bush and offered talks—for merely inviting American pressure. At one meeting of the Supreme Council of National Security, Khamenei said that "America is like a dog, if you back off it will lunge at you; but if you lunge at it, it will recoil and back off."[20] Even as he gave the green light for Iran to negotiate a nuclear deal with the United States in later years, he advised Foreign Minister Mohammad Javad Zarif to adopt an emphatic and harsh tone when speaking to his American counterpart. He told Zarif that "America's approach is one of hiding a hammer of steel in a velvet glove. Be careful how you engage with them, beware of their pretense of friendship hiding their true enmity." America wants to get Iran to surrender. We will negotiate as equals to achieve gains for Iran but we will not surrender.[21] General Soleimani captured Khamenei's mood, saying, "The Superpowers' friendship with us is like the friendship of a wolf and a sheep."[22] The Islamic Republic would be eaten up if it trusted the United States. Former IRGC commander Mohammad Baqer Zolqadr told a gathering of the force, that "US enmity with Iran has a long history, but it has failed because of [the] Iranian people's doggedness."[23]

What Iran needed, argued these voices, was not a conciliatory tone with the United States. Instead, the Islamic Republic could only deter the United States by doubling down on intransigence. Moreover, Iran would build up its regional and military capacity to make sure America's project in Iraq fails, and in turn, this would make Iran appear to the United States as a far more difficult military target than Saddam's Iraq.[24]

The Strategic Promise of Shia Iraq

Ultimately, however, the Iraq War was a strategic win for Iran. The United States had removed Iran's nemesis from power; after all, toppling Saddam was Iran's justification for continuing its war with Iraq after 1982. Iraq had been the most menacing military threat to Iran and the Arab bulwark in its campaign to contain Iran. Moreover, the United States did not replace the Baathist state with a viable order. Rather than state building, as promised, the war's main achievement was state shattering. This chaotic vacuum presented Iran with a unique strategic opportunity to expand its influence in Iraq. At first, Iranian influence spread into southern Iraq quickly and organically. Tens of thousands of Iranian pilgrims, long denied access to the shrine cities of southern Iraq, poured across the open border. Religious and commercial ties followed suit. Clerics and seminarians started going back and forth between Najaf and Qom, and Iraq's widely popular senior Shia cleric, the Iranian-born Ayatollah Ali Sistani, found a wide following in Iran as well.

Americans were right to suspect that freeing Iraq of the clutches of Saddam's dictatorship would open the borders between the two countries. But they were wrong in assuming that the transfer would only move in one direction and it would be Iraq immediately influencing Iran to change, and not the other way around. In fact, what emerged was a broader Shia religious and cultural sphere that emanated from Iran but embraced both countries: a "Shia crescent," according to Jordan's King Abdullah, stretching from Lebanon to the Persian Gulf.[25] This decisively changed the regional dynamics in Iran's favor.[26] The king captured the angst in the Sunni Arab world, which was quick to realize the strategic implications of what had unfolded in Iraq: far from pressuring Iran, now the Islamic Republic had greater room to maneuver.[27] The opening of Iraq empowered Shias in that country, and that in turn favored Iran. Now Iraq would become the first Shia Arab state, providing Iran with an important Shia ally in the Sunni-dominated Middle East. Referring to the new governments in both Afghanistan and Iraq, Khatami explained to this author at the time that "regardless of where the United States changes regimes, it is our friends who come to power."[28]

Within Iranian society as well, the opening of Iraq had an important impact. New access for Iranian pilgrims to the shrine cities of Iraq energized popular piety around a passionate commitment to Shia saints. The personal attachment to the saints had been used by the Islamic activists during the revolution and afterward in entrenching the Islamic Republic as well as pursuing the war with Iraq in the 1980s. This time, however, the surge in the popular veneration of the saints was not promoted by the state. In fact, at some level, such popular feeling reflected a defiance of the rigid Islamic dictums promoted by the state in favor of individual piety. It appeared that Iranians, across various social classes, were wresting control of Shia symbols from the monopoly of the state.

Still, the doyens of the Islamic Republic understood the political value of energized religious passions, even if they had little to do with them. The IRGC found this trend useful in lionizing its own history and its commitment to protecting Shia shrine cities in Iraq—and later Syria. It encouraged this popular piety by investing heavily in facilitating pilgrimages to Iraq and encouraging Iranians to participate in major Shia commemorations there, such as Arbaeen, the anniversary of the fortieth day after the martyrdom of the third Shia imam, Hossein. During Arbaeen, Shia devotees walk between the shrine cities Najaf and Karbala over a two-week period, share food and lodging, and forge bonds of piety and community.

Since 2003—that is, since Iraq's borders crumbled, and Iran encouraged participation—Arbaeen has grown into a mega event. Millions of Shias from across the world participate each year. In fact, Arbaeen has evolved into the core of a community consciousness for Shias that transcends Iran or Iraq, reflecting the very idea of a region-wide sense of a Shia community and domain that, as will be discussed below, Iran's forward defense has envisioned. Indeed, it is this transnational community that supports the Shia militias Iran has created and supports.[29] This is an example of how Iran's regional reach has been effective because Tehran is so closely bound to its clients and proxies by a shared view of threats that face Shias, in a region that has historically been dominated by Sunni Islam. Iran has done much to forge this common worldview, which speaks to not only Iran's interests but the interests of all Shias too.

The IRGC has also funded a growing music industry around popular "raves," wherein large numbers of young men gather and are swept up by the passion and energy of the elegies for the imams put to music.[30] Putting Shia passion to popular music had its roots in the 1980s, when the songs of the well-known *maddah* (performers who sing *madh*, or dedicated religious elegies and songs) Gholam Ali Kuwaitipour, which put religious elegies to pop music, were ubiquitous as a sort of soundtrack of the war years. In the 2000s, these songs were performed at concerts and raves, and a bevy of maddahs gained popular fame. The opening of Iraq's shrine cities only boosted the popularity of this musical genre.

In this instance of popular Shia piety, the IRGC again saw a bridge between different social strata and political opinions. Yet its greatest usefulness was in generating support for Iran's regional foreign policy in the name of securing Iran's access to Iraq and defending its shrine cities. This broader Shia community helped portray Iran as a defender of Shiism beyond its borders. After all, saints that matter to Iranians are buried not just in Iraq but also as far away as Syria (which would grow in significance after 2011). In addition, such popular piety helped persuade the Iranian populace itself that Iran has interests beyond its physical boundaries.

The Battle for Iraq

Iraq's Sunnis had long been in the minority, but for at least a century, had constituted the ruling elites of the country. Following America's invasion, the Shia majority—who shared popular culture and religion with Iranian Shias—seemed fated to rule, which engendered a Sunni resistance. Since Sunnis were opposed to the transfer of power to Shias, their insurgency aimed to reverse that. The Islamic extremist faction of the insurgency, led by Abu Musab Zarqawi, targeted Shia civilians in heinous bombing attacks on mosques and markets, killing hundreds.[31] The attacks were deliberately designed to make clear Sunni resistance to Shia ascendancy, but also to provoke a sectarian civil war—plunging Iraq into violence that would confound and defeat American occupation. This they achieved in February 2006, when the Sunni insurgency carried out a deadly bomb attack on the Shia Askariyah Shrine in the city of Samarra, where two Shia imams are buried.[32] As planned, sectarian bloodletting followed.

Faced with Sunni hostility in Iraq and across the region, Iraq's nascent Shia political order had only Iran as its crutch. This allowed Iran to build political and military ties with Iraq's Shia. Iranians were quick to organize the maverick Iraqi Shia leader Moqtada Sadr's Mahdi Army into a fighting force.[33] Both Iran and Iraq's Shias felt the need for Iraq's Shias to have their own means of defense, but also to use it against the United States to make sure that Washington did not take the Shias for granted. The fear was that facing a tough Sunni insurgency, the United States might cut a deal with the Sunnis at the Shias' expense. And so as the United States got bogged down in a bloody insurgency, Iran's influence expanded among Iraq's nascent Shia political forces.[34] That influence has proved resilient.

Later, in 2014, the Shia control of Iraq was threatened by the rise of the Islamic State for Iraq and Syria (ISIS), which took over large parts of Iraq, including its second-largest city, Mosul. Even this tragedy hardly dented Iran's rise. By 2019, as an official study by the US Army stated, Iran was the de facto winner of the Iraq War.[35]

Forward Defense

President Bashar Assad of Syria traveled to Iran on the eve of US invasion of Iraq in March 2003. Assad was deeply worried about the coming war's implications for Syria.[36] In Tehran, Assad met first with Khatami and then Khamenei. His vice president at the time, Abdul-Halim Khaddam, recollects that Khatami told Assad that France's President Jacques Chirac had told him in a phone conversation the previous day, "I am afraid Iraq is only the first step." Khatami then added, "If America wins quickly then we will have a problem." Assad agreed, adding that "the only solution is resistance."

Later the same day, Assad and Khatami met with Khamenei. The supreme leader concurred that an American invasion of Iraq was an imminent danger: "The American plan is much broader than Iraq. It was developed after September 11 to change the geopolitics of the whole region"—meaning that its aim was to also change the regimes in Iran and Syria. Khamenei agreed with Assad's proposed remedy: "If the war happens then we must follow the general policy of preventing this crocodile from swallowing the bite easily. . . . The only option is to resist, and this resistance will be as long as Vietnam."[37]

Khaddam's notes from those meetings suggest that the seeds of resisting the United States in Iraq to frustrate its plans for Iran and Syria were sown on that day in March in Tehran: Syria would encourage and support a Sunni insurgency, and Iran would mobilize the Shia resistance around what would soon evolve into a broader strategy of combating the United States in the Middle East.

■ ■ ■

In 2003, Iran formally embraced the strategic doctrine of forward defense (*defa' pisehrou* or *defa'-e roubejelo*): the imperative of defending Iran by being present inside the Arab world, providing it with a minimum of "relative security" (*amniyat-e nesbi*).[38] Foreign policy debates in Iran have viewed forward defense as a reflection of the reality of Iran's strategic vulnerability: a Persian Shia country in the midst of Arab and Sunni rivals, without any reliable alliances and facing containment imposed by the world's principal superpower.[39]

If sacred defense has been about organizing state and society in support of national security, forward defense is the narrower military strategy, necessitated by deterrence but made possible by opportunity, to pursue that security in the region. Forward defense needs and feeds on sacred defense as the war with Iraq did two decades earlier. It is a strategy that both protects against threats emanating from the Arab world, and fills vacuums left by collapse of state and regular militaries there: Lebanon after Israel's 1982 invasion, Iraq after America's 2003 invasion, and as will be discussed in the next chapter, Syria and Yemen after the collapse of the state during Arab Spring 2011, and Iraq again after ISIS's 2014 rampage.

Forward defense sounds like a throwback to the enthusiasm for extending Iran's regional influence in the early 1980s; Iran's Arab rivals have certainly thought so. Yet forward defense more accurately echoes the Shah's regional policies in the 1970s. Then the Shah conceived of a so-called Green Plan (*Tarh-e Sabz*) to augment Iran's influence in the Arab world by cultivating ties with nonstate actors in Iraq and Lebanon—the Shias in the case of the latter. The plan's roots went back to 1958 when an Arab nationalist coup toppled the Iraqi monarchy and Lebanon fell into civil war. Back then, Colonel Mojtaba Pashaie, who was the Middle East's point man in Iran's intelligence services, described Iran's regional posture in an increasingly hostile Arab world in terms that eerily parallel depictions of forward defense today: "We should combat and contain the threat in the east coast of the Mediterranean to prevent shedding blood on Iranian soil."[40]

This leaning into the Arab world in the name of defense found clearer expression during the Iran-Iraq War, when Khomeini argued that to defend Iran, the Islamic Republic had to topple Saddam. And this, in turn, meant pursuing a long war into Iraq. In 1982, the decision to continue the war into Iraq had rested on the contention that given geography and Iran's international isolation, the country would be hard-pressed to defend itself against Iraqi aggression. Iran's prime minister at the time, Mir Hossein Moussavi, had said, "We will continue our advancement [into Iraq] for as far as it is necessary for our own national defense."[41]

In the end, Iran failed to address that strategic vulnerability through the war, although was spared renewed Iraqi aggression thanks to America's containment of Iraq after its expulsion from Kuwait. The collapse of the Iraqi state coupled with the political and security vacuum that followed the American invasion of Iraq in 2003 gave Iran the opportunity to achieve what it had hoped it would through war between 1982 and 1988.

For decades, then, Iran wanted to assert control in Iraq. But in 2003, unlike 1982, it did not countenance invading it. This is why the IRGC floated the new strategic concept of forward defense. The physical border between Iran and Iraq would remain intact, according to the strategy. But Iran would defend itself from inside Iraq using its newfound political influence along with the proxy militias that it would set up—based on the model of Hezbollah in Lebanon in the 1980s—on the back of the security vacuum and sectarian threats.[42]

In military terms, forward defense drew on the IRGC's own experience in the early years of the Iran-Iraq War, when it operated effectively as a loosely organized militia force. Furthermore, the IRGC had learned in the Iran-Iraq War that local populations would resist overt Iranian military presence. Forward defense would therefore not rely on large Iranian troop deployments but rather militias staffed by the local population. Their command, training, and operations would be closely managed by the IRGC, and they would be bound together by the ideals of sacred defense and resistance that had shaped the IRGC and resistance forces inside Iran.[43] Khamenei would call this chain link of the IRGC and its militias the Axis of Resistance (Mehvar Moqavemat) or Resistance Front (Jebheh-e Moqavemat), and credited Soleimani with creating it.[44] Resistance and how it worked in the Iran-Iraq War is the bedrock of the strategic culture that sustains today's forward defense. Indeed, one reason the IRGC was adamant about documenting the lessons of the Iran-Iraq War was to learn from it and teach it to the next generation of its military leaders.[45]

The idea of forward defense became even more compelling as the US presence in Iraq emerged as a vital threat. To defend against it, Iran need not wait until the threat reached its own borders; instead, it could begin its defense inside Iraq by making the US presence there untenable or at least sufficiently difficult so that it would be dissuaded from threatening Iran.[46] In effect, forward defense was a strategy for confronting and defeating a superior military threat. Iran could not and would not engage the United States (or Israel for that matter) in a conventional war. Saddam's humiliating military defeats in 1991 and 2003 had driven that point home in Tehran. Iran instead adopted an asymmetrical strategy to inflict as much pain as possible on the United States in an undefined and protean field of battle, which has since extended in size beyond Iraq into Syria and Yemen. Forward defense, at the outset at least, was not driven by expansionist aspirations but rather pragmatic security needs.[47] It in effect sought victory in deterrence; its aim was "reducing the likelihood of a war on Iran" and not the "likelihood of losing that war [once it started]."[48]

This strategy of "defensive realism" embraces the limitations of Iran's conventional military capability in the face of ongoing worry about US intentions, distrust of neighbors, and international norms and organizations that are charged with enforcing those norms.[49] It deploys Iran's ideological assets to cultivate relations with Shia allies to enhance Iran's security.[50]

In conceiving of forward defense, Iran was deeply influenced by the example of Hezbollah.[51] In Lebanon, the long civil war and sectarian violence had opened the Shia community to Iranian influence. The militia that Iran built in Lebanon had played a direct role in forcing the United States and France out of Lebanon, keeping the Israeli threat against Iran at bay, and provided Iran with significant influence in the Levant. Hezbollah's ability and willingness to serve as Iran's deterrence tool against Israel as well as the organization's steadfast commitment to Iran's defense were particularly significant in broadening the Lebanon strategy into a regional one.[52] Should the West attack Iran, Hezbollah—according to its leader, Hasan Nasrallah—would do "whatever velayat-e faqih [i.e., Khamenei] orders. We would follow it without question and to the best of our abilities. Defending the Islamic Republic is a religious duty."[53] In Iraq as in Lebanon, the vulnerabilities the Shia community felt pushed it in Iran's direction, and the absence of a strong central state allowed Iran to raise up militias that it could control.

Also important was the example of the Sunni insurgency against the US occupation of Iraq. The insurgency showed Iran that even though a regular military force was no match for US firepower, America's military machine was ill prepared for waging an effective counterinsurgency war. Thus if Iran were to protect itself from the might of the US military, it had to build up its irregular war-making capacity. Waging an asymmetrical war against the United States inside Iraq was both deterrence against an American attack on Iran and an amplification of the Sunni insurgency to persuade the United States to leave Iraq altogether.

Therefore soon after 2003, extending Iran's security parameters into Iraq became the focus of Iran's strategic objectives.[54] Realizing that goal fell on the IRGC's Qods Force and its commander, General Qasem Soleimani. The importance of the IRGC to Iran's Iraq strategy was captured in the unprecedented decision to send a former IRGC commander, Hasan Kazemi Qomi, as Iran's first envoy to Baghdad.[55]

Soleimani was a shadowy but towering figure, a battle-seasoned commander and shrewd planner who transformed the Qods Force into a formidable part of the IRGC. He had joined the IRGC in his teenage years and led his unit in the harrowing offensive that liberated Khorramshahr in 1982. Soleimani had risen through the ranks over the years, and gained notoriety as a wily and capable operator, adept at planning, charismatic, popular with his troops, and respected by Khamenei and his fellow commanders in the IRGC. This respect came from his battlefront heroics during the Iran-Iraq War, but also his tactical savvy as the mastermind behind Iran's regional policy in the 1990s, through diplomacy, military and intelligence operations, commanding proxy armies from Lebanon to Afghanistan, and waging successful military campaigns in Syria and Iraq.[56] He soon became the face of the Qods Force and Iran's regional posture. In the West's imagination, he gained a mythical stature, a latter-day incarnation of author John Le Carré's master spy, Karla.[57]

The Qods Force is one the IRGC's four core divisions. It is an expeditionary force dedicated to operations outside Iran.[58] During the Iran-Iraq War, the IRGC formed a special command, Ramadan Camp (Qarargah-e Ramazan), that was charged with expeditionary operations inside Iraq. It trained Shia Iraqi war captives into the Badr Brigade (which decades later after the US invasion, became a major pro-Iran force in Iraq) to carry out guerrilla operations in northern and western Iraq. At the conclusion of the Iran-Iraq War in 1990, Khamenei revamped and expanded the Ramadan Camp into the Qods Force and charged it with managing Iran's regional operations as well as giving coherence to the sundry activities that were run by different radical groups and intelligence units. The force found its footing and gained prominence under its second commander, Soleimani, who assumed his position in 1997.

Soleimani would reorganize the force with the objective of enabling Iran to project power from a position of relative weakness. Faced with the superior conventional military capabilities of its regional rivals, Soleimani adopted a strategy of creating highly competent and effective militias, which could compensate for their fewer numbers and inferior weaponry with tactical expertise and battlefield effectiveness.[59] It would quickly take over operations in Lebanon, and then Iran's military ties with Afghanistan's Northern Alliance and Iran's support for Bosnian resistance during the civil war in Yugoslavia.

With Iran keen to build its security line of defense in Iraq and counter the US influence there in 2003, the Qods Force now emerged from the shadows to shape Iran's regional strategy. It quickly grew to dominate Iran's diplomatic and military presence in Iraq, linking operations there with those in Syria and Lebanon. As such, it was the Qods Force that anchored Iran's regional policy in forward defense.

It was true that the interests of the United States and Iran often converged when it came to forming Iraqi governments and shoring up the authority of the nascent postwar state. But regardless, the Qods Force and Iran's Shia proxies continued to attack US forces. Roadside bombs, improvised explosive devices, the ambush of American troops, and attacks on US embassy and American military bases claimed many

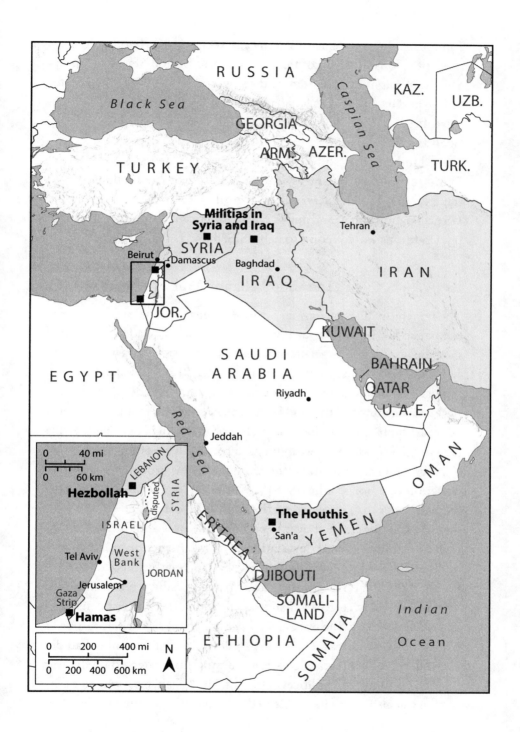

RUSSIA

Black Sea

GEORGIA

ARM. AZER.

Caspian Sea

KAZ.

UZB.

TURK.

TURKEY

Militias in Syria and Iraq ■

SYRIA

Beirut
Damascus

Baghdad

IRAQ

Tehran ●

IRAN

JOR.

KUWAIT

BAHRAIN

QATAR

U.A.E.

EGYPT

SAUDI
ARABIA

Riyadh ●

Red Sea

Jeddah ●

OMAN

0 40 mi
0 60 km

LEBANON

Hezbollah ■

SYRIA

disputed

ISRAEL

Tel Aviv ●

West
Bank

JORDAN

Jerusalem ●

Gaza
Strip

Hamas ■

ERITREA

The Houthis ■

San'a ●

YEMEN

DJIBOUTI

SOMALI-
LAND

ETHIOPIA

SOMALIA

Indian

Ocean

0   200   400 mi
0 200 400 600 km

N
▲

American lives and casualties. Iran's aim seemed to be twofold: first, to prevent a consolidation of ties between the United States and Iraq's Shias that might exclude Iran, and second, to defeat the United States in Iraq and ensure that as had happened in Lebanon in 1980s, it would leave. In so doing, Soleimani and the Qods Force quickly became identified as a singular menace for US forces in Iraq.[60]

And indeed, the United States eventually made its peace with the Sunni insurgency, but not with Shia militias or the Qods Force. In the end, Iran got what it was after. In 2011, President Obama ended the US occupation of Iraq and pulled out all American troops from the country. US troops would return to fight ISIS, but in far smaller numbers.

The 2006 Lebanon War

The imperative and promise of forward defense also became evident in the Israeli-Hezbollah war of 2006. In July of that year, a Hezbollah raid over the border into Israel prompted a full-scale Israeli invasion of south Lebanon. For over a month, Israeli forces attacked Hezbollah positions, imposed an air and naval blockade on the country, and devastated Lebanese civilian infrastructure and Hezbollah strongholds in southern Beirut in aerial bombings. With Iran's help, Hezbollah fought back using guerrilla tactics but also advanced weaponry against Israeli tanks and ships.

After a month of fighting, the United Nations brokered a ceasefire. Lebanon had borne a heavy cost. Nonetheless, Hezbollah had performed better than expected on the battlefield and denied Israel a clear victory. The war claimed over 1,200 Lebanese lives and those of 165 Israelis. Lebanon suffered devastation of its infrastructure and displacement of around 1.5 million people. Hezbollah, however, looked to have repelled the Israeli invasion, and displayed resilience and imposed enough cost on Israel to deter another invasion. And that was construed as a worthy victory. The war allowed Hezbollah to consolidate its power over south Lebanon as it reconstructed what Israeli bombing had destroyed, thereby integrating various communities effected by the war into its economic and political networks. Hezbollah's performance during the war also raised its profile in the Arab world at a time when anger at the United States and its allies over its invasion of Iraq was at a fever pitch.

Iran had not anticipated the war, and putatively, was not happy with Hezbollah for provoking it, but the outcome was a pleasant surprise. Tehran also understood this as the United States encouraging Israel to take the fight to Iran in Lebanon to compel Iran to loosen its grip on Iraq and relieve pressure on the American forces there. If that had been the intent, concluded Tehran, Washington came up short. Hezbollah held its ground, attesting to the depth and effectiveness of forward defense. Iran's strategy of projecting power in the Arab world, and defending security interests from within the Arab world and far from Iran's own borders, had proved to be both viable and effective. So decisive had been Iran's support for Hezbollah during the 2006 war that some in Israel viewed it as the first war between Israel and Iran rather than a continuation of the Arab-Israeli conflict.[61]

Soleimani took credit for Hezbollah's success.[62] He captured the significance of the war for Iran's aims and resistance mindset, saying, "In the wake of Hizbollah's victory in Lebanon, a new Middle East is being formed, not an American [Middle East], but an Islamic one. . . . The Shiite Hizbollah has succeeded in exporting and marketing to Palestine its model of a way of life of faith in God."[63] These words may well have presaged the role of the Axis of Resistance during the Gaza war of 2023–24.

It was also in the Lebanon war that forward defense looked to be crossing the thin line that separates defense and deterrence from offense. The war itself could be viewed as defense against Israel's invasion, but its outcome underscored the potential of forward defense to project Iranian power at a regional level. The war alerted the Arab world to Iran's growing capacity to operate deep inside the Arab world too. Arabs do not accept Iran's deterrence argument and see forward defense as expansionist in its intent, designed to secure regional hegemony. Arab resistance to forward defense after 2006 has showed that the strategy is far from cost free for Iran.

Yet between 2003 and 2006, forward defense looked to have resolved Iran's immediate vulnerabilities in the post-9/11 era. The strategy allowed the Islamic Republic to bolster its security vis-à-vis the United

States and Israel, and confirm its hold on Iraq and Lebanon. Iran's immediate fears from the fallout of the Iraq War were replaced by confidence and even bullishness. That ensconced forward defense in Iran's regional strategy, turned the Qods Force into a regional behemoth, and and reinforced the commitment to sacred defense.

The 2009 Green Movement: Reformists' Last Stand

The apparent success of forward defense had come on the back of Ahmadinejad's electoral victory in 2005 and what looked then as a definitive halt to the reformist agenda. The Ahmadinejad presidency had empowered the IRGC and the constituency for sacred defense.

Still, Ahmadinejad's shock victory in 2005 did not give the supreme leader, IRGC, and their conservative allies the political security they were after. Ahmadinejad's populism had proved an effective bulwark against the reformist challenge, but his presidency had not vanquished reformism. In fact, reformists had been quick to regroup to mount a counteroffensive through the media.[64] They continued to appeal to the values that Khatami and Rafsanjani had floated during the 2005 election, derided Ahmadinejad for his foibles and missteps, appealed to middle-class aspirations, and warned of the dangers of Ahmadinejad's ill-conceived economic and foreign policies along with the growing influence of the IRGC under his watch.

This laid the foundation for the presidential election of 2009.[65] In the run-up to the vote, reformists rallied behind Mir Hossein Moussavi, who had served as Iran's prime minister during the Iran-Iraq War in the 1980s. At that time, Moussavi held leftist views of the economy and society. Since then, however, he moderated his views, becoming an advocate of reform as well as a supporter of Rafsanjani's and Khatami's platforms.[66] Relying on his experience as prime minister and willing to challenge accepted shibboleths, Moussavi was soon embraced by reformists as their flag bearer. To underscore his lineage as a descendant of the Prophet, Moussavi adopted green as his campaign's signature color. The reformist electoral campaign proved effective, and Moussavi looked to be surging ahead of the vote.

The electoral campaign had already made clear the staying power of reformism and that Ahmadinejad's first term in office had not dented the popularity of reformists. In fact, Ahmadinejad was weaker in 2009 than he had been in 2005. His record in office was far from a winning trump card, his populism was not as compelling this time, and he was running against a strong reformist candidate who could not be tarred with the charges of corruption that had hindered Rafsanjani in 2005.

Within hours of what was believed to be a tightly contested election, Ahmadinejad was declared the winner. That result flew in the face of Moussavi surge; that and many aspects of how the votes were tallied left many Iranians incredulous.[67] The stench of a rigged election drew vast crowds into the streets, chanting, "Where is my vote?" At one point there were over two million people on the streets in Tehran.

The Green Movement, as the protests were quickly dubbed for the color of Moussavi campaign, was the most serious protest that the Islamic Republic had ever confronted. It was a testament to the power of the reformists and the middle class's desire for a fundamental change in the direction of the Islamic Republic. The protests also challenged the legitimacy of the Islamic Republic, which had been anchored in its claim of popular participation through elections.

Equally important, the Green Movement made it clear that sacred defense did not have widespread support among Iranians. Far from being committed to resistance and liberation, a majority wanted political freedoms, economic liberalization, and engagement with the world. In other words, the Islamic Republic's strategy for managing the country and its foreign policy lacked broad-based popular support.

The country's leaders were comfortable in the assumption that they had fully entrenched sacred defense in the management of affairs of the state, but the population was far from committed to that course. Moussavi and the Green Movement stood for a very different trajectory of state building—one that was popular enough to sustain a mass movement that could be suppressed only by brute force and considerable cost to the reputation of the Islamic Republic.[68] A state built on the ideal of sacred defense and pursuing forward defense had to govern *despite* popular will—and that was the Achilles' heel of the course on which Khamenei had set the Iranian state.

The protests were against a rigged election, but Khamenei and his coterie saw them as antiregime.[69] The size and scope of the protests were daunting. And so faced with a potentially regime-threatening revolt, the resistance forces cracked down brutally. The IRGC and Basij joined police on the streets. Moussavi along with dozens of reformist politicians were arrested, thousands were killed, and tens of thousands were incarcerated. The suppression broke up the protests.

Still, the Green Movement showed that the middle class was no longer vested in Islamic ideals and revolutionary values. To steady its rule over Iran, the Islamic Republic had to adopt the mantra of nationalism to a greater extent in complement to or at times lieu of Islamic idealism. The political implications of the Green Movement were serious enough to compel the supreme leader to countenance bridging the divide that the protests had exposed. At the end of the Ahmadinejad presidency in 2013, conservatives would back away from another total victory at the polls and leave the door open for a more moderate candidate, Hasan Rouhani—who favored engaging the West in nuclear talks as well as greater trade with Europe and the United States—to be elected president with a comfortable majority.

Having served in national security, Rouhani was not a reformist and did not identify with the Green Movement. But he was a pragmatic politician, and his vision for the state and economy harked back to the Rafsanjani era. He saw a strong economy as vital for Iran and its national security. In what was a clear nod to the Rafsanjani government's approach, on the eve of assuming the presidency he published a book titled *National Security and the Economic System*.[70] The book made the case that Iran would be more secure if its economy was strong, and that would require reforming its sclerotic economic system as well as changing the foreign policy posture that was responsible for it.

Rouhani's election was clearly a concession to popular sentiment by the supreme leader. Allowing a moderate pragmatist to win the popular vote was not, however, a surrender to moderates. Rouhani's election served to reconcile Iranians and bridge the divide that was opened by the Green Movement. Hard-liners around the supreme leader would contain and control Rouhani to ensure that the prerogatives of sacred defense would remain unchallenged. Iran's government was now more moderate, but its control did not extend to overseeing forward defense abroad or propagation of sacred defense at home, or the IRGC's economic and political powers.

Indeed, the IRGC understood that it could not rely on old messages and forms of communication to contain as well as convince the new generation of tech-savvy reformists and youths, whose cultural mores contradicted the ideological moorings of the state. If it was to retain its position, it had to adapt this vision. Anthropologist Narges Bajoghli shows how the Green Movement served as a turning point in the thinking within the IRGC and security state, which used new mediums of communication and propaganda to imbue their military and political programs with nationalism. The IRGC, Bajoghli writes, had to underscore the "national" in its national security agenda and communicate that effectively with the all-important middle class.[71] To that end, it adopted new media strategies, including books, films, and popular music.

There was an urgency in this effort. Unbeknownst to most Iranians at the time, the Green Movement happened when the United States and Israel launched a concerted cyberattack against Iran's nuclear program. Stuxnet, a highly sophisticated malware, inflicted significant damage and slowed Iran's nuclear program.[72] The massive cyberattack soon coupled with additional economic sanctions to jolt the Islamic Republic, making it clear that it had to act quickly and decisively if it was to ward off the heightened threat that it was confronting. As will be discussed in chapter 10, one clear response was to embrace nuclear negotiations. That was not abandoning resistance, which would continue unabated in the form of forward defense, but instead ceding ground to pragmatism on the nuclear issue.

●●●

The war with Iraq in the 1980s shaped the IRGC; Iran's second foray into that country after 2003 then shaped the Qods Force, giving its expeditionary mission an outsized influence in Iran's grand strategy. By

2011, the United States had given up on its presence in Iraq and President Obama decided to remove US troops from that country. That was a victory for Iran, and by implication it should have meant reassessing Iran's regional strategy and unwinding its military engagement in Iraq. That did not come to pass, however, not only because the Qods Force would resist such strategic recalibration, but because regional developments favored continuation of its strategy. The Arab Spring and its aftermath would in turn consolidate the Qods Force's forward defense assets into a regimented regional axis: the Axis of Resistance.

CHAPTER 8

The Rise of the Axis of Resistance

In December 2010, the self-immolation of a fruit seller decrying corruption and injustice ignited massive popular demonstrations in Tunisia that quickly exploded into a tidal wave of street protests across the Arab world. Within a matter of weeks, authoritarian rulers in Tunisia, Egypt, and Libya fell from power, and Arab masses elsewhere, watching the unfolding events in North Africa, took to their own streets to demand similar change.

In the arc stretching from Syria in the Levant to Bahrain in the Persian Gulf, where authoritarian states had enforced the distribution of power along sectarian lines, the specter of political change invoked memories of Iraq 2003: regime change promising to disenfranchise the ruling sectarian minorities and empower the sectarian majorities. The reaction in turn invoked memories of Iraq 2006: sectarian clashes and even civil wars. In Bahrain and Yemen, it was Sunni minority regimes that feared a Shia takeover (Zaidis who are an offshoot of Shiism in Yemen's case), and in Syria it was the Alawite minority tied to Shiism that stood to lose to the Sunni majority. Status quo powers did much to stoke sectarian fears in the hope that it would galvanize the minority community into resistance and increase the regime's chances of survival. In Bahrain, Yemen, and Saudi Arabia—which has had a restive Shia minority—regime overhaul was depicted as serving Iranian aggrandizement, and in Syria the ruling regime pointed to the plight of Iraq's Sunnis after 2003 as the fate that would be awaiting the ruling Alawites.[1]

In Bahrain, quick Saudi intervention quelled the uprising, closing the door to any Iranian gains there.[2] In Yemen, however, the Arab Spring opened the door to a civil war between the Houthis and Saudi-backed Yemeni government. The civil war, as will be discussed later, was important to Iran's regional objectives. But the greatest stake in the post–Arab Spring melee would be Syria.[3]

Going back to the 1970s, Iran had close ties with Syria. Given its rivalry with Iraq, Syria was a natural ally since the late 1970s; thereafter, Iran's stake in Lebanon was to provide a basis for cooperation.[4] After the fall of Iraq in 2003, Iran increased its security and economic ties with Syria, and invested in boosting the Shia presence in the country. Syria has a small Shia population, close to its border with Lebanon. The larger Alawite community that rules the country traces its origins back to Shiism and seeks religious legitimacy through the Shia sect. Also important is that Damascus is home to a major Shia shrine, the resting place of Imam Hossein's sister, Zaynab, whose bravery and oratory after the martyrdom of her brother in 682 is credited with keeping his line—and hence the Shia faith—alive. With the opening of Shia shrines in Iraq after 2003, the many Iranian pilgrims who traveled to Iraq also visited Syria, and similar popular Shia cultural and religious ties began to bind Iran and Syria as well.[5]

Syria also mattered to Iran as a vital link to Lebanon and Hezbollah. With the fall of Saddam in 2003, Iran envisioned an uninterrupted land corridor connecting Iran to Lebanon. But such a greater Iranian sphere of influence would be threatened if the Assad regime fell. Indeed, as was quickly touted in the West once the Arab Spring protests started in Syria, it would be a major setback for Iran, jeopardize the future of Hezbollah, and roll back Iran's regional influence.[6] Iran saw Sunni Arab states as quick to back the opposition to Assad, which Iran was convinced was dominated by extremists, and as the experience of Iraq showed, were bound to be hostile to Iran and Shiism. It was not just the loss of Syria that was a threat but also what would replace Assad at the helm that worried Iran.[7] Iran saw the Syria uprising in 2011 as a project directed at defeating Iran's forward defense and putting the country on its back heel.

Thus Iran was keen to protect that relationship, and convince other clients and allies that Iran would stand by its friends.[8] Furthermore, if the Assad regime fell, then a triumphant Sunni government in Damascus—along with its backers in the Sunni Arab world—would set its eyes on Iraq. There, the Sunni minority that had begrudgingly accepted the political formulation that ended the civil war of 2006 was likely to resume its insurgency era demands, and with the United States gone, Iran would face a full assault on the Shia political order in Iraq.

Iran, then, was better off defending against the Sunni challenge in Syria rather than fight a larger conflict to prevent Sunni restoration in Iraq closer to its own border. To protect Iran's vital interests in Iraq and Lebanon, it was critical that Iran defend Syria as if it was defending Iraq or Iran itself. This proved to be a costly strategy, but one that was unavoidable under the logic of forward defense.[9]

In 2009, President Rouhani and his foreign minister, Zarif, were engaged in nuclear talks with the United States. Both believed ties with Europe and the United States would further Iran's national interests—and a nuclear deal would serve as an anchor for that opening with the West. Both were therefore wary of muddying the waters with the West at a critical juncture by pursuing forward defense in Syria. They understood that Iran had vital interests at play there, but were mindful of the risks of backing a brutal regime in the face of Arab and international outrage.[10] The supreme leader, however, was willing to try Iran's hand at a nuclear deal, but not at the cost of abandoning its position in the region. Khamenei believed that Iran's regional footprint was vital to its national power, especially as it entered in critical talks with the West. To him Iran's power and standing would not come from ties with the West but rather from what it achieved in the region on its own. Furthermore, he believed that the dangers to Iran of losing Syria outweighed the risks incumbent in supporting the Assad regime. Indeed, Khamenei saw Syria as Iran's "strategic depth."[11] As Hezbollah's Hasan Nasrallah put it, "The cost of not intervening in Syria was higher than that of intervening."[12]

The deep state favoring intervention in Syria argued that Iran was not in Syria to save Assad but instead to defeat the American project for the region, which aimed to break up Syria and then turn its gaze on Iran;

just as the United States had created an autonomous Kurdish region in Iraq, it wanted do the same in Syria, Turkey, and Iran.[13] Senior IRGC leader General Hossein Hamedani, who was in charge of standing up militias in Syria and was killed in an Israeli strike there, said of the logic of the war, "Our goal in Syria was strategic. . . . America's goal in Syria was to weaken Hezbollah and force Iran to fight the enemy back into its own borders [avoiding what had been the motivation for forward defense]. Syria is the key to the region; what we lose in losing Syria exceeds what we have at stake in Iraq, Lebanon, and Yemen."[14]

Consequently, the same deterrence argument that had launched forward defense in Iraq now extended it to Syria.[15] That has also found its way into Hezbollah's thinking. Before his death in October 2024, the organization's leader, Hasan Nasrallah, spoke of developments in Lebanon, Iran, Iraq, Palestinian territories, Syria, and Yemen being interconnected—a single zone of concern and operations (*vahdat al-saahaat* or united spheres).

Shoring up the Assad regime was no easy task. The Qods Force had to quickly establish a structure for close collaboration with the Syrian military, intelligence, and political leadership. At first, the role of the Qods Force was to advise and train Syrian forces. But as the Assad regime lost ground to the surging opposition, the Qods Force became more directly involved in the war: sending in elite troops, deploying Hezbollah fighters, and forming Shia militias outside the command and control of the Syrian military and intelligence.

As the war progressed, Iran's rulers saw new opportunities in Syria. With the Assad regime dependent on Iran and vast areas of country without government, the Qods Force envisioned entrenching its presence in the country, with a cordon of militias and military bases to encircle Israel, extending the hot border that it shared with Lebanon into western Syria. This would in time relieve Israeli pressure on the Lebanese border, but also tax Israel's resources, forcing it to defend itself along a longer arc across the Levant.[16] Syria, moreover, would provide Iran with potential naval bases on the Mediterranean, which would give Iran a new kind of regional expanse.[17] In the words of the former IRGC commander General Rahim-Safavi, Iran's defensive parameter was no longer Shalamcheh (the famed battlefield of the Iran-Iraq War in southern Iraq) but the

Mediterranean.[18] He further elaborated that Iran's strategic depth "ought to be 5,000 kilometers (3,100 miles), extending to the Mediterranean and the Red Sea—with air and naval bases."[19]

Iran along with its regional allies, Hezbollah, and Hamas found a new level of capability and sophistication, unity of purpose, and operational integration in Syria. That integration would be at display during the October 2023 attack on Israel as well as Israel's decision to attack Iran's consulate in Damascus in April 2024, killing the IRGC's commander in charge of managing the Axis of Resistance.[20] As will be discussed later in this chapter, the war would prove a turning point for forward defense and its entrenchment in the Levant, and as such would place Syria at the center of an escalating conflict between Iran and Israel.

• • •

Khamenei had ordered the Qods Force to save Assad, but this was easier said than done.[21] Soleimani is reputed to have complained that "we put the pill in Assad's mouth, but as soon as we turn our face, he spits out the pill."[22] General Hamedani recollected, "We told the Syrians 'we have come to transfer our experiences to you,' but the Syrian military was proud. Once we even decided to return [abandon the mission] but [the supreme leader] said, Syria is like a patient who does not know he is sick. He must be told he is sick. He doesn't want to go to the doctor, you must take him to the doctor. If the doctor gives him medicine, he will not take it. You must get him the medicine and give it to him."[23] If the Qods Force was going to keep Assad in power, it had to do so despite the Assad regime.

The war in Syria thus became the remit of the Qods Force. Zarif would in later years complain at length in an interview that diplomats were completely sidelined in favor of generals in managing Iran's Syria policy.[24] It would be IRGC commanders like Soleimani and Hamedani, and later Qa'ani (Soleimani's successor at the helm of the Qods Force), who would manage Iran's Syria policy.[25]

• • •

Soon after opposition to Assad erupted in Syria in 2011, the Qods Force was embedded in Syria's security structure to shore up Assad's defenses.[26]

The Qods Force deployed Basij units to organize militia forces consisting of Lebanese, Iraqi, Afghan, Pakistani, and Shia volunteers from across the region to fight along Assad's besieged army.[27] On the battlefield, these militias were trained and led by Hezbollah and Qods Force units. A militia of around forty thousand fighters consisting mainly of Afghan Hazara Shias, recruited in Iran and Afghanistan, and named the Fatemiyoun Brigade, soon became a critical fighting force in Syria.[28] A sister militia consisting of Pakistani Shias, named Zeynabiyoun, soon joined the fray. Eventually there would be some fifteen militias fighting in Iraq and Syria under the IRGC's command.[29] These forces were effective in combating various anti-Assad fighting forces, providing protection to Shia and Alawite towns and villages, and protecting the land route between Damascus and the Lebanese border.

While the logic of defending Assad may have been self-evident to Khamenei and Soleimani, public support for getting involved in a civil war far removed from Iran's borders could not be taken for granted. Justifying the growing cost of forward defense in terms of blood and treasure to the Iranian public, and the sullying of Iran's image in the Arab world, was a dilemma. A bevy of books, articles, and interviews sought to explain the importance of Syria as well as defending the Assad government before American intervention and the insurgency. These books depicted the anti-Assad opposition as Sunni extremists backed by Israel and the United States, and the Syrian uprising as a sinister American and Israeli plot to weaken Iran—a continuation of the ongoing containment effort against Iran, except that the boundary of the conflict had shifted west, from Iraq to Syria.[30] Iran would resist a second American effort at regime change in the region (the first having been in Iraq in 2003) with the same determination as it had fought against Saddam in the 1980s.[31]

By 2011, the supreme leader and foreign policy decision-makers had come to see the consequences of American intervention as the proliferation of new threats: broken states and ungoverned territories engulfed in insurgencies and civil wars fueling Sunni anger all around Iran from Afghanistan to Iraq and Syria.[32] This unfolding scenario could destabilize Iran, rousing its religious and ethnic minorities, and condemning Iran to the same fate as Afghanistan, Iraq, or Syria.[33] This worry led Iran to view a more direct military presence in the Arab world as necessary to realizing its security needs, which IRGC strategists saw as a justification of defense sliding into offense.[34]

That was why the start of the Syria campaign led the IRGC to invest heavily in retelling the story of the Iraq War, with a view to rekindling the spirit of sacred defense of the 1980s. This history, it imagined, might mobilize support for the Syrian War. There was also the hope that Syria would produce a new generation of devoted young revolutionaries as had the Iraq War.

Involvement in Syria, however, faced skepticism. Early on during the Arab Spring, Iranian reformists associated themselves with popular demands for change.[35] Yet when it came to Syria, these voices saw the case for intervention as weak, and Iran's meddling in domestic affairs of an Arab country to save a brutal regime to be unacceptable and self-defeating.[36] They worried that an emphasis on religious justifications for Iran's intervention—under the banner of defending the major Shia shrine of Damascus—would commit Iran to a problematic sectarian foreign policy. The former reformist mayor of Tehran, Gholam Hossein Karbaschi, received a jail sentence for airing these views.[37]

Even some conservative voices thought the Islamic Republic should take the consequences of intervention in the form of additional US sanctions and the Arab world's censure more seriously. The Islamic Republic had always considered Syria as a pillar for its presence in the Arab world and balancing Saudi Arabia's regional influence. The war in Syria nevertheless was having the effect of putting Iran on its heel in the Arab world to Riyadh's advantage.[38] Risking popular approval among the Arab public clearly conflicted with Iran's long-standing claim that it stood with the Arab masses in their pursuit of justice.

The depth and breadth of these debates marked the first time forward defense was being taken to task.[39] Even so, these cautions and criticisms were no match for the power of the Qods Force and Soleimani's outsized influence on decision-making circles.

■ ■ ■

For many Iranians, the most important gain after 2003 was not strategic—that is, Iraq's neutrality and Iran's forward defense—but instead their access to the shrine cities of Iraq that bound them to their revered imams. Iranians had supported the IRGC's campaign to protect Iraq's Shia shrines from Sunni extremist attacks between 2003 and 2006.

Building on that earlier support, the IRGC quickly cast its military role in Syria as the protection of another important shrine: Zeynab in Damascus. The Fatemiyoun Brigade was created ostensibly for this purpose. It built on new religious fervor inside Iran to fight and even be martyred defending the holy shrines.[40] Defending Shia shrines as a justification for forward defense suggested that defending Iran's interests in the Arab world be extended to protecting religious sites and the honor of the family of the Prophet. As the Qods Force's role in the Syrian War expanded, it invested heavily in covering the war in the Iranian media.[41] Its outlets placed great stress on the militias and volunteers that the IRGC deployed in Syria, dubbed the Defenders of the Shrine (modafe'an-e haram).[42] This juxtaposition of Shiism and Iranian national interest in pursuit of forward defense required reinforcing popular Iranian attachment to Shiism, and especially to the family of the Prophet.[43] This was not the same thing as enforcing Islamic piety. It meant encouraging Shia identity as a religious value, even in competition with Islamic piety. The IRGC-backed cultural outputs that emphasized visiting Shia shrines and participating in such Shia ceremonies as Arbaeen in Iraq as above pilgrimage to Mecca. The Islamic Republic put more effort in facilitating the former than it did the latter. The IRGC literature underscored the importance of Imam Hossein, not only because Islamic revolutionaries venerated his martyrdom and his resistance to oppression is a mantra for the Islamic Republic, but because Zeynab was his sister. This meant that the two siblings connected Iran's missions in Iraq and Syria into one campaign.

It was the effectiveness of this approach that wove a cult of personality around Soleimani and would draw millions into the street when he was killed in January 2020. The IRGC's propaganda efforts did not achieve the kind of popular support for war in Syria that Iraq had garnered a decade earlier, but it did for a time gain broad acceptance for

Iran's intervention in Syria, and notably, energized the resistance forces' base of support to embrace the war.

The Syrian War served as the fulcrum for emergence of a new generation of sacred defense warriors, vested in protecting Shia interests at a regional level and the goals of forward defense. Importantly, those who fought in Syria would become the next generation of leaders in the IRGC and Hezbollah.

•••

Iran's support for Assad proved important but did not end the insurgency against his regime. It further encouraged Turkey and the Persian Gulf monarchies to increase their support for various anti-Assad insurgent groups. Syria soon plunged into civil war—one in which Assad's success was far from assured, but that laid the responsibility for the Assad regime's excesses and cruelties on Iran's shoulders. As the violence escalated, it was Sunni extremist forces that proved to be most effective on the battlefield. Khamenei and the IRGC dug in, believing that Assad's fall now would be a significant blow to Iran. The specter of extremism meanwhile further worried both Iran and Hezbollah. Triumphant extremism in Syria would inevitably spread to Lebanon and Iraq, and threaten Iranian and Shia interests there too.[44] They saw the hands of Turkey and Arab monarchies behind the growing power of extremist forces, and resolved that the campaign against Iran had to be defeated in Syria.

Confronting the Islamic State

Iran construed the rise of ISIS in summer 2014 as an imminent and urgent peril.[45] It posed a larger threat to the Assad regime, and an even greater one to Iraq, and if ensconced there, then it would be a direct threat to Iran on its own borders. The rise of Shia to power in Iraq in 2003 and dejection of Syria's Sunnis in the face of Assad regime's brutality with the onset of the civil war in 2011 created a vast contiguous region of disenfranchised and alienated Sunnis, shut out from power in Baghdad and Damascus. ISIS straddled the boundaries of Iraq and Syria to fuse these unhappy and restless Sunni regions into one revisionist political entity. ISIS's venom was directed toward West, but its expansion threatened Iran's positions in Syria and Iraq, and more broadly everything the forward defense had been set up to defend against. ISIS represented the worst Iran had to fear from the Arab world. Tehran quickly resolved to combat and defeat it.

In summer 2014, ISIS emerged on the scene sweeping over Mosul, Iraq's second-largest city. The Iraqi military melted away as ISIS beheaded Shia captives, and rapidly advanced on Iraq's autonomous Kurdish region in the north, and Baghdad and the Shia heartland in the south. The whole country could have fallen to ISIS or its hold over the Sunni regions of the country could have broken Iraq. Any of these outcomes was perilous for Tehran.[46] Soleimani quickly mobilized the Qods Force to defend Erbil in the Kurdish north from the advancing ISIS fighters. In the south, Soleimani appealed to Iraq's senior-most Shia cleric, Ayatollah Sistani, to command Shia volunteers to form a militia force, the Popular Mobilization Forces (PMF or Hashd al-Sha'bi), which would be trained and led by the IRGC to defend Shia communities as well as combat ISIS in Sunni areas. Soleimani would then extend the fight against ISIS to Syria too.

ISIS's vicious tactics and its vehement anti-Shiism were also beneficial in making the case for Iran's role in Syria back home. It became a common refrain in Iran to say, "If we are not in Syria, then ISIS will be here." ISIS proclaimed a caliphate that enveloped large parts of Iraq and Syria, and its ambitions were regional. In the words of Foreign Minister Zarif, "The West is not quite cognizant of how important Iran's role was in preventing ISIS from becoming a true catastrophe. If ISIS had taken the seats of old Islamic empires in Damascus or Baghdad, then the whole Muslim world would have been at risk."[47] It was ISIS that convinced Iran's rulers that threats emanating from the Arab world were ongoing. And it proved that unless Iran remained vigilant and present in the Arab world, both it and its Shia sphere of influence would be in danger.

Added to this was the belief in the ruling circles that the policies of the United States and its regional allies were responsible for ISIS. In

Zarif's words, "ISIS is the product of two things. First is the U.S. invasion of Iraq, and the foreign presence that creates a dynamic of resistance. Second is the feeling of disequilibrium, which has prevailed in some countries in the region since the fall of Saddam. They are trying to change the status quo."[48] Khamenei would be blunter, asserting that the West had created ISIS, and "Iraq and Syria were only a prelude to creating a quagmire for Iran."[49] This assault on Iran, he would repeat, was a different kind of war, a "hybrid war" (jang-e tarkibi), in which Iran's enemies were using Iran's own tool, asymmetrical warfare through proxies, against it.[50] This war, the supreme leader concluded, demanded of Iran to increase its regional efforts. The same logic that had justified mounting forward defense in 2003 was firmly at play in Syria after 2011.[51] Khamenei credited Soleimani with devising a regional security strategy and expanding the number of proxies that would protect Iran's interests—the Fatemiyoun and Zeynabiyoun in Syria, and the PMF in Iraq—to protect Iran from the "American use of Sunni extremists to weaken Iran."[52]

From 2014 to 2016, the Qods Force and its PMF troops would battle ISIS across Iraq, often supported by American airpower—with the Iraqi military serving as the go-between. There would be no open cooperation as in Afghanistan in 2001, but Iran and the United States both wanted ISIS defeated and Iraq to remain intact.[53] Although Iran accused the United States of setting up ISIS, in practice, they were facing the same enemy and thus coordinated operations in key battles.

The image of American air cover protecting ground operations led by Soleimani and the Qods Force should have improved relations between the protagonists. But the legacy of 2001—collaboration, followed by labeling Iran as part of the so-called Axis of Evil—still loomed large.

The Qods Force had a visible role in the war. Soleimani was often photographed on the battlefield alongside Iraqi PMF fighters. The images conveyed not just that of an Iranian helping hand but also that the security of Iran and Iraq were one, and the forces doing the battle, the IRGC and PMF, were one as well. Moreover, the overt role of Soleimani and the Qods Force in the coverage of the war lionized them for a time inside Iran, and highlighted the logic of forward defense. Khamenei made a big show of awarding Soleimani and the top Qods Force generals with medals, and numerous murals across Iran celebrated their heroics.

Fighting in both Iraq and Syria, however, Iran found it increasingly difficult to sustain Assad in power. It was after ISIS swept across Iraq that the IRGC turned to Russia for help. Ostensibly, Soleimani personally persuaded Russian president Vladimir Putin to intervene in Syria in a meeting at the Kremlin.[54] Both Iran and Russia saw threats in the weakening of the Assad regime as well as the prospect of an ISIS victory in Syria.[55] Russia may have had other reasons of its own for wanting Assad to remain in power, but Iran's role in bringing Russia into the war cannot be underestimated. The Russian intervention in September 2015 proved important to the outcome in Syria. The war dragged on, but Russia's air campaign, special forces, and diplomatic muscle in both the region and on the world stage all helped reduce pressure on the Assad regime.

ISIS was finally pushed out of Mosul and then all northern Iraq in fall 2016. This was a major victory for the Qods Force. It had successfully stood up a new militia in Iraq that had proven effective in withstanding and ultimately defeating the most serious threat to Shia control of the country and its shrine cities since 2003. The campaign had validated forward defense for the IRGC and security establishment in Iran. Iranians had seen a different kind of threat coming from the Arab world—underscored further by ISIS attacks inside Iran. Iraqi Shias were reminded of the ever-present dangers facing their communities, underscoring the importance of their close ties with Iran. Even after ISIS was gone, the PMF remained intact. Iran did not dismantle a battle-seasoned militia that could thenceforth serve its interests as had Hezbollah. In fact, the PMF, parts of which now sit within Iraqi security forces, and the rest divided between some fifty militias, continues to occupy and subdue Sunni regions of Iraq—to prevent the rise of another ISIS-like force there—and has a choke hold on Shia politics as well. Iraqis are unhappy with the PMF's brutish ways. Still, most Iraqi Shias fear that the Iraqi military could melt away once again if Sunni extremism returned. As of this writing, Ayatollah Sistani has not issued a fatwa demobilizing the PMF. Iran has thus gained even firmer control over Iraq after the fall of ISIS.

In the Syrian War, by comparison, Iran's role remained more limited. There were Shia militias such as the Fatemiyoun and Hezbollah fighting against ISIS, but the Qods Force more often led from behind. Still, by 2016 there were some ninety-two hundred IRGC officers, advisers, and soldiers in Syria.[56] Most were engaged in protecting the Assad regime, but some were also busy building an infrastructure for the IRGC and Hezbollah to operate from Syria against Israel. Now the battlefield in Syria had become a test of wills between Iran and Israel. Therefore both Israel and the United States were keen to disrupt the link between Iran and Lebanon through Iraq and Syria. Iran believes that this is the only reason why US troops remained in Syria. Iran has thus deployed Iraqi and Syrian militias to target US troops in Syria to encourage Washington to withdraw them. Iran saw an opportunity in the Gaza war that started in 2023 to escalate this pressure, using the cover of the war to break America's choke hold on Iran's bridge from Iraq to Lebanon.

After the United States defended Israel by shooting down Iranian drones and missiles heading toward Israel in April 2024, Iran became even more convinced that the US presence in Iraq and Syria was for the sole purpose of containing Iran and protecting Israel, and that would give Iran greater incentive to increase pressure on American presence in those countries.

• • •

Iran's role in the war in Syria and the campaign to defeat ISIS further entrenched the IRGC's hold over Iran's foreign policy—the domination of the "battlefield" (meydan) over professional diplomats.[57] Put another way, tactical concerns in Syria then trumped the strategic concerns of the nuclear deal. In effect, Iran's foreign policy fell squarely into the IRGC's hands. The force's outlook was shaped by the demands of the immediate wars it was engaged in. Those demands went beyond military hardware to include an array of resources of the state. Meydan was not just the physical field of battle but rather the broader foreign and domestic arena in which Iran confronted its near and far enemies in a hybrid war, deploying a mix of hard and soft power in economic, cyber, and social domains.

The Axis with Russia

The Russian intervention in Syria forged a strategic partnership between Tehran and Moscow—one that would prove exceptionally important later in Afghanistan, Caucasus, and Ukraine.[58] The two countries already cooperated on defense, including links between security think tanks, and their economies had grown increasingly interdependent—a trend that would accelerate once Russia found itself under sanctions after it invaded Ukraine.[59] But while this new partnership built on these existing relationships, it was managing a delicate war in Syria that deepened their engagement. In Iran, it was the IRGC and Qods Force that were the main drivers in forging and expanding this alliance.[60] From the outset, this was an intelligence and military alliance, complemented by economic deals, all of which were embedded in the deep state in the two countries.[61] The tilt toward Russia was necessitated by forward defense along with Iran's insistence on its resistance posture and anti-Westernism. It also reflected the greater prominence of hard-liners in managing state affairs. Perhaps most important, this new level of cooperation built on the "battlefield" mindset taking hold in Tehran. And once the cooperation began, this mindset only became more entrenched.

In addition to all of these material interests, the new partnership after 2015 fed on a shared worldview. Both Iran and Russia, that is, considered themselves to be aggrieved great powers that saw America as the stumbling block before the realization of their ambitions. Khamenei himself saw the benefit in a close alliance with Russia. He had met Putin on several occasions, and the two had a meeting of the minds on resisting an American-led global order and asserting the historic rights of their respective great nations. Khamenei understood Russia as a partner in a broader global Axis of Resistance to US hegemony and necessary strategic depth (*omq-e rahbordi*) for Iran in confronting the West.

Still, within Iran, the new alliance was not an easy sell. After all, the revolution had idealized Iran's place in the world as "neither East, nor West," and now certain Iranian leaders wanted to collaborate with an old imperialist foe that had even occupied and dismembered Iran in the not-too-distant past. Those who embraced Russia were drawn from the IRGC and security forces, while many diplomats, opinion makers, intellectuals, and politicians criticized the alliance with Russia, and worried about Russian motivations.

But the Syrian War naturally tilted Iran toward the alliance with Russia, as did the greater confrontation between Iran and the United States with Donald Trump's presidency.[62] It was this deepening strategic partnership that led Iran to support Russia's war in Ukraine. Just as the Kremlin had come to Iran's aid in Syria, Tehran reciprocated by throwing its lot with Russia in Ukraine. Iran provided Russia with drones and missiles, which would prove highly effective in damaging Ukraine's civilian infrastructure as Russia escalated its pressure on Ukrainian cities throughout the war. Supplying Russia with sophisticated weaponry raised the ire of Europe and the United States, invited widespread condemnation and further sanctions, and made it more difficult to see a way forward with nuclear negotiations. And yet all of this only deepened the needs of both partners for the alliance and further entrenched the battlefield mindset within Iran's leadership.

Khamenei and the IRGC are calculating that with the war on Ukraine going badly, Russia has vested interest in the resilience of the Islamic Republic. The more Putin's back is to the wall, the more likely Russia will flout Western sanctions to boost Iran's military capabilities. Thus the Kremlin would supply Iran with vital military hardware and technology. In fact, Russians have told their Iranian counterparts often, "No nuclear deal will provide you with the kind of military hardware Russia will."[63] The IRGC sees Russian desperation as a unique strategic opportunity to transform Iran's military capabilities, including acquiring advance jet fighters and missile defense systems that would significantly boost Iran's military capability in the region. That level of Russian support would also give Tehran the confidence to absorb Western and Israeli pressure and plan for a potential military attack in response to an expansion of its nuclear activities. It would also firmly entrench forward defense.

Nor was the burgeoning relationship limited to military cooperation. Increasingly alienated from the United States and Europe, Iran and

Russia resolved in 2022 to expand economic relations.[64] Beyond trade and cooperation on energy issues, the two are now investing in developing transcontinental trade routes. Consisting of roads, railway lines, canals, ports, and shipping lanes on the Caspian Sea and Russian rivers, this new route between Iran and Russia will allow the passage of cargo from the Black Sea through Iran to the Arabian Sea. Crucially, this passage will be free from any foreign intervention.[65] Crucially for Iran, a trade corridor with Russia will run through Azerbaijan and Armenia. Iran has long-standing good relations with Yerevan, and now on Russia's insistence, and after it quietly facilitated Azerbaijan's takeover of the contested Nagorno-Karabakh region, ties between Tehran and Baku are improving.[66] That, Iran anticipates, will help shrink Israel's presence on Iran's northern border.

Of course, such an investment in carving out a trade route will inevitably enmesh the economies of Iran and Russia even further, deepening their strategic relations and commitment to the Axis of Resistance.

This makes good sense from the perspective of Iran's leadership. After all, for Khamenei and the IRGC, the Russia-Ukraine War proved that they were right to see the United States as aggressor and resist it.[67] Russia had gone to war to keep the North Atlantic Treaty Organization (NATO) away from its borders, as Iran had been fighting to keep the United States' presence in the Middle East at bay. Both Russia and Iran did not want to be encircled by the US military. Just as the United States had broken its agreement and left the Joint Comprehensive Plan of Action, the United States, claimed Putin, had broken its promise and expanded NATO eastward. Iran and Russia needed each other, and had to help each other. If Iran helped Russia in Ukraine, then it could count on Russia's help in its own struggle against the United States. The deep-state-to-deep-state relationship that was forged in Syria would be strengthened in Ukraine. Iran now sees a firm ally in its strategic objective of "de-Americanizing" the Middle East. Yet this line of argument was not convincing to all power brokers in Tehran.[68] There was resistance to the tilt toward Russia, revealing a serious disagreement over the strategic shift in Iran's foreign policy.

Forward Defense in Yemen

Syria was the most important expansion of forward defense, but not the only one during this period. In September 2014, Yemen collapsed into civil war, and Iran again found reason to seek security far beyond its own borders.

The origin of the civil war goes back to the early 2000s, when Houthi tribespeople of northern Yemen revolted against the government in Sanaa.[69] The Houthis are Zaydi Shias, with religious beliefs and institutions that differ from those of the Twelver Shias of Iran or Iraq. Their homeland sits on Yemen's border with Saudi Arabia. Saudi Arabia supported the government in Sanaa and viewed the Houthis as a menace whose faith made them a natural client of Iran.

The insurgency gained strength after the Arab Spring roiled Yemen, culminating in Houthis capturing Sanaa in 2014. That alarmed Saudi Arabia. To Riyadh, it looked like Iran was making a bid for Yemen, forging yet another local Shia community into a Hezbollah-like proxy and gaining a foothold on the Arabian Peninsula on Saudi Arabia's southern borders. Saudis attached the adjectives "Shia" and "Iran-backed" to the Houthis at every turn. This was meant to cast the crisis in Yemen as Iran's doing, and the Houthis—far from having any legitimate grievances or claims to power—as mere instruments of Iran's nefarious meddling.[70] Conversely, Iran claimed that Saudi policies had pushed the Houthis to look to Tehran for support.[71]

There is little doubt, however, that the Qods Force was only too happy to arm and train the Houthis.[72] This gave forward defense yet another base in the Arab world. But this one enabled Iran to pressure Saudi Arabia at a time when Riyadh was pressuring Tehran on Syria.

In March 2015, Saudi Arabia led a coalition of Persian Gulf monarchies to invade Yemen with the goal of defeating the Houthis and restoring the Yemeni government's full control. Saudi crown prince Muhammad Bin Salman saw the war as vital to Saudi security. The kingdom had to thwart Iran's presence on the Arabian Peninsula, and by quickly vanquishing the Houthis—as they had the popular revolt in Bahrain during the Arab Spring—teach Iran a lesson. There was, though, no quick victory. Yemen plunged into a bloody civil war that claimed the lives of tens of thousands and produced one of the world's worst humanitarian crises. The Houthis held on, surviving the worst of the attacks by the Saudi-led coalition, and in the process, drew closer to Iran. Moreover, they gained lethal missile capabilities, which threatened Persian Gulf monarchies and the global supply of oil.[73]

All said and done, by the end of the decade in 2020, Iran had achieved its aims in the region. The Houthis remained in control of Sanaa, poised to inflict damage on Saudi Arabia and the United Arab Emirates (UAE). Saudi Arabia now faced a crescent of threats from Iran itself, Iranian proxies in Iraq, and the Houthis in Yemen. In addition, the Houthi missile capabilities not only threatened large parts of Persian Gulf countries and their oil facilities but also the Israeli port city of Eilat—and during the war in Gaza, commercial shipping in the Red Sea. The war in Yemen, much as the war in Syria, had provided forward defense with an opportunity to further extend Iran's security parameter and sphere of influence. It made the Iran-Saudi rivalry center stage to Middle East politics as well.[74] Yet the Houthis' resilience would in the end compel Saudi Arabia to mend fences with Iran as the only way to end the war. The Houthis would thus remain entrenched in Yemen and even grow into a regional power broker during the Gaza war. Their attacks on commercial shipping in the Red Sea in defense of Palestinians would gain them popularity on the Arab street and prominence as a regional force to be reckoned with.

• • •

In Syria, meanwhile, ISIS was defeated by 2016. Now there was no serious insurgent group threatening to capture Damascus. Assad had survived. Iran, with Russia's help, had defied the concerted will of the United States, Europe, Turkey, Israel, and the Sunni Arab states to remove Assad from power. In the process, Tehran had forged a strategic relationship with Moscow, created new proxies, and gained a foothold in new territories, extending its security parameter deep into the Levant.[75] Furthermore, it had done all of that on the cheap, showing that its forward defense was highly effective, even at a fraction of the cost of the militaries with which Iran competed.[76]

So impressive was Iran's achievement at the time that Israel's Prime Minister Bibi Netanyahu raised the alarm before US Congress, claiming that Iran "dominates four Middle Eastern capitals": Baghdad, Beirut, Damascus, and Sanaa.[77] Netanyahu was embellishing to underscore the danger Iran posed. But he was particularly keen to drive the point home to Arab states that forward defense had crossed over into an Iranian regional hegemony. Tehran, for its part, saw Netanyahu's exaggeration as a point of pride.[78]

To understand Netanyahu's fears of regional hegemony, one must not only see the chain link of proxy militias that Iran had successfully planted in Lebanon, Syria, the Gaza Strip, Iraq, and Yemen. More important, these widespread forces enjoyed the protection of Iran's missile umbrella and could soon even be protected by its nuclear capability. Finally, as the cases of Hezbollah, Hamas, and the Houthis showed, all of these groups were more lethal for their access to Iranian missiles.

It was for this reason that Israel responded to Hamas' October 7, 2023 attack with a determined campaign to destroy Hamas and Hezbollah and curtail Iran's regional influence. However, Israel's success in decimating Hamas and Hezbollah will not unravel forward defense but rather lead Iran to better protect it with enhanced missile and nuclear capabilities.

The Missile Component

Iran's interest in missiles goes back to the first year of the Rafsanjani presidency, when Iran was still reeling from its defeat in war and looking for ways to shore up its military capabilities.[79] Indeed, Rafsanjani takes credit for building the program, saying that he was "the father of Iran's missile program."[80] The program was singled out in the 1992 military doctrine as vital to addressing Iran's conventional military limitations and captured the IRGC's drive for military self-sufficiency in the face of isolation.[81] Zarif once referred to the missile program as a substitute for the kind of air force that Iran cannot acquire.[82] Iran's long-range missiles pose a threat to Iran's regional rivals, especially since they have become more sophisticated and accurate even as their range has increased.

Moreover, Iran's ability to retaliate with missiles deters attacks on its proxy forces. Iran has also armed its proxies with short- and medium-range missiles—and more recently, drones—which gives it lethal capabilities. And it has transferred missile-building technology to its proxies. These weapons have not only been used against Israeli and American forces in Iraq; their mere presence constitutes a new kind of regional deterrence.

In Yemen, where the Houthis used missile attacks effectively against Saudi Arabia and the UAE. That missile capability deterred Saudi and Emirati attacks as well as gave the Houthis greater latitude in pursuing their military offensive on the ground. And these, in turn, provided Iran with important leverage in dealing with Saudi Arabia and the UAE. The combination of proxy militia and missiles has, in Tehran's view, defeated the Saudi-led coalition. The war in Yemen dragged far longer than Riyadh and its allies had anticipated, and although it devastated Yemen, it failed to dislodge the Houthis from Sanaa. Instead, the war solidified Houthi ties with Iran—which extended to Hezbollah and Shia militias as well—and turned Yemen into a veritable threat to the Persian Gulf monarchies, Israel, and the global economy. The Houthis have been protected by Iran's missiles, and their control extends the range and scope of the threat Iran's missiles pose to its adversaries.

In 2023, Iran and Saudi Arabia arrived at a détente. The agreement demanded of Iran to cease its military support for the Houthis. Iran, though, would give up that leverage only at the price of the normalization of ties that it had been seeking. In short, forward defense in Yemen proved useful in compelling Saudi Arabia to change course with Iran.

Iran's reliance on missiles for deterrence and asserting its regional position was on full display first in January 2020 when Iran responded to the killing of General Soleimani by launching dozens of missiles aimed at the Ain al-Asad base in Iraq that housed fifteen hundred American soldiers. The barrage was the largest missile attack US troops have ever faced. Surprisingly, there were no US casualties.[83] Then came the daring attack on Israel in April 2024 with some three hundred cruise and ballistic missiles in retaliation for the Israeli bombing of the Iranian consulate in Damascus. The volley of missiles was more disconcerting in terms of their capabilities in October when Iran retaliated for the killings of Hamas and Hezbollah chiefs. In each case, Iran used missiles to send a signal of massive retaliation if attacked, but the message of deterrence also increased the risk of confrontation as the number of missiles it used have been disproportionately high and increased with each reiteration of the message, and in both cases were reckless in risking mass casualties. It also gave Saudi Arabia even more reason to seek protection in a defense pact with the United States, which Iran had hoped to avert. Yet in Iran's eyes, such a display of force had protected and strengthened forward defense—which had been the reason for both the United States' and Israel's attacks.

The Axis of Resistance and War in Gaza

The war in Gaza proved to be a turning point for forward defense—a display of its reach and effectiveness in propelling Iran's regional influence. The October 7 attack on Israel was the handiwork of Hamas' military wing, the Ezzeddin al-Qassam Brigade. The brigade, more so than the main body of Hamas, had grown close to Hezbollah and the Qods Force over the preceding decade.

Hamas' audacious attack took Israeli intelligence by surprise. Its sophistication showed a significant upgrade in the intelligence and military capabilities of Hamas as well as Iran's successful integration of radical Palestinian military forces into its network of proxies in the Levant. This process had been anchored in a shared vision of resistance. Iran's investment in consolidating its allies and proxies into an Axis of Resistance had been both facilitated by and accelerated during the Syrian War—which gave Iran greater reason to see its presence in the Levant as a key policy objective. Hamas, meanwhile, decided that to survive the Israeli blockade of Gaza and even to change the balance of power, it had to build "a society of resistance, an economy of resistance, and an ideology of resistance."[84] In "rearming resistance," Hamas deepened its political and military ties to Iran and Hezbollah.[85] The Levant, as

Hasan Nasrallah had put it, was becoming one single integrated battle-front for resistance. The strategic objective was to focus Israel on con-flicts in and around its borders, and thus thwart its ability to concentrate its shadow war on Iran in and around Iran's borders—to fight Israel in the Levant rather than in Iraq and Caucasus, or inside Iran.

Tehran saw Hamas' attack and Israel's subsequent war on Gaza as a strategic victory for Iran. The war resurrected the Palestinian issue, set aside sectarian divisions along with memories of Iran and Hezbollah's support for Assad, focused regional attention once again on the Levant, and upended efforts to normalize ties between Israel and Saudi Ara-bia.[86] The attack dented Israel's aura of invincibility, and put to question the effectiveness of its deterrence and claim to protect its visibly rattled, angry public. As the war dragged on, demonstrating Israel's willingness and ability to deploy advanced weaponry to destroy large swaths of Gaza—notwithstanding killing tens of thousands of Palestinian civil-ians and turning millions into refugees—it proved unable to easily achieve its aims. Months into the war, Israel had not secured the release of its hostages, nor destroyed the lion's share of the tunnels that lay below Gaza, nor liquidated the bulk of Hamas' leadership or fighters. Its war on Gaza had restored neither deterrence vis-à-vis its enemies nor a sense of security to its own population.

The images of the horrors of war in Gaza, large number of Palestinian civilians killed and made homeless, and entire cities turned into rubble, however, changed the world's perception of the Israel-Palestine conflict. The war isolated the United States in the Middle East along with Israel and its cause across the Global South and even in some quarters in the West. In speeches during the war, both Khamenei and Hasan Nasrallah would claim this global support for resistance as a significant strate-gic win.[87] The war in Gaza also brought into sharp relief the evolution of forward defense. As mentioned earlier, Nasrallah had spoken of "united spheres." The Gaza war revealed what that meant: a full and si-multaneous mobilization of all elements of forward defense to attain a common strategic objective across the region. The concatenation of militias that forward defense had set up now identified itself as the Axis of Resistance. The axis reflected the goals of forward defense, but it was not just Iran's command and control that maneuvered the axis; its cohesion was now assured by a common opposition to American and Israeli "colonialism" in the Middle East. It had evolved into a robust and dynamic network that looked to Iran for guidance and support, yet was versatile in that it followed the same strategy of resistance, but adapted and deployed in accordance with its own local needs. This flexibility allows for more effective power projection by forward defense, but without demanding of the IRGC expansion of its management of axis operations. The axis wanted to prevent Israel from quickly destroying Hamas, but saw parallels between Hamas' fight in Gaza with its own struggles against Israel, the United States, and Saudi Arabia in Lebanon, Iraq, Syria, and Yemen. The Palestinian issue was not just a regional cause; it epitomized resistance to America's role in the Middle East, and as the war in Gaza galvanized the region in support of the Palestinians, the axis saw its cause as the region's cause and thus emerged as a regional force. The millions of disgruntled and angry Palestinians living in and around Israel now see Iran and the Axis of Resistance as their only support in confronting Israel. In this population, forward defense is finding a new base of support and territories to expand into: the West Bank and even Jordan.

Hezbollah was quick to attack Israel with missiles—bogging down a significant number of Israeli forces that otherwise would have been dispatched to Gaza. Shia militias targeted US forces in Iraq and Syria, and the Houthis attacked commercial shipping on the Red Sea. All of this was to pressure the United States to force Israel to abandon its war in Gaza, but by mobilizing a variety of networks across the Middle East to also demonstrate the power and reach of the Axis of Resistance. It presented the United States with an entirely new threat level, not just confronting Iranian-backed militias in Iraq or Syria, but a conflict with Iran and the axis across multiple theaters, all at once. Israel had not managed to vanquish Hamas despite its military might—and rather, had incurred significant cost to its security and reputation. That would deter the United States from contemplating conflicts beyond Gaza. Deterring the United States had been forward defense's original aim.

Iran had showed that it can change the direction of Middle East politics, escalating and de-escalating regional conflicts at will. State-run media and propaganda outlets in Iran basked in the shift in the regional dynamic, claiming that Iran now enjoyed "absolute regional domination" (*qodrat-e motlaq-e mantaqe-ie*). However, in October 2024 Israel turned the tables on Hezbollah and Iran. In a series of intelligence and military attacks Israel killed the bulk of Hezbollah's commanders and senior leadership, including Nasrallah. It also destroyed large parts of south Lebanon and Beirut's Shia strongholds. It was a devastating blow to the Axis of Resistance, one that put to question its deterrence value and brought Iran closer to open war with Israel and the United States. Iran however sees its confrontation with Israel and the United States as a long war. The blow to Hezbollah was a major set back, but it does not alter Iran's grand strategy.

Two decades after its full launch, the contours of forward defense's game plan are coming into focus, exhausting the United States using the strategy of guerrilla warfare. It worked in Iraq after 2003, and Iran expects it to succeed at a larger region level. Henry Kissinger once explained the dilemma facing the United States in Vietnam: "the guerrilla wins if he does not lose. The conventional army loses if it does not win."[88] Iran does not need to defeat the United States or Israel in war—in fact, it does not seek to fight America in battle—just not lose. It was all laid out in that 2015 conversation between Kissinger and his Iranian visitor described in the introduction. It is easy to see why forward defense holds a grip on the resistance-minded Iranian leadership.

It is also a strategy that fits the reality of Iran today. Not only is Iran lacking the wealth and technology to compete with America's superior military might, but it lacks the most fundamental resource needed for sustained large-scale military campaigns: a deep well of soldiers.[89] The last time Iran fought in a conventional war, in the 1980s, the average age in the country was eighteen; it was easy then for Khomeini to say, "A country that has 20 million youth to have 20 million-strong army."[90] In 2003, when Iran launched forward defense, the average age was twenty-three; today it is thirty-three, and by 2030, it will be thirty-seven. Iran simply does not have enough young people to fight large, sustained, conventional wars. That is why it has invested in missiles and drones, and will likely need a nuclear deterrence. Iran is aging, but in the region's

Shia (and Palestinian) communities around it, youths predominate. For instance, the average age in Yemen is nineteen and in Iraq it is twenty—in Gaza it is eighteen and the West Bank twenty-one.

It is for this reason that in Syria, Iran looked to Afghan and Arab Shia volunteers to form the Fatimiyoun Brigade, and in Iraq, relied on Shia youths to fill the ranks of the PMF to fight against ISIS. Between 2014 and 2018, the PMF numbered between 80,000 and 100,000. There are now 120,000 to 150,000 militia fighters. It is through them that Iran controls Iraq. A strategy that will have to rely on non-Iranian Shias for foot soldiers must be wrapped in a broader vision for security of a Shia domain with Iran at its center. It is for this reason that Shia identity cultivated around Arbaeen or defense of the shrines is so important to the viability of forward defense. That vision will be broadened as Iran extends its influence among Palestinians.

■ ■ ■

The IRGC is a military force; it controls vast parts of Iran's economy and is deeply influential in its politics. Yet it cannot prosecute forward defense without the imprimatur of the clergy. Forward defense, in effect, extends the notion of national security beyond Iran's borders to include the protection of shrine cities in Iraq and Syria as well. Those extraterritorial relations rest on religious ties that need the clergy.

Even so, the IRGC does not need the clergy to rule. It now has a ubiquitous presence in the economy, state institutions, and political alliances, and enjoys firm control over the military, intelligence, internal security, and foreign policy. Consequently, the IRGC has grown into much more than the Praetorian Guard of the clerical leadership. Now it has become the state itself.

CHAPTER 9

The Cost of Success

It is easy to see why the IRGC and its hard-line political allies bask in the success of forward defense, believe it to be effective deterrence and a genuine force projection that gives Iran a strong hand in the region, and are so reluctant to scale back the Qods Force's regional activities. Iran's security establishment has concluded that the threats that were posed during the Iran-Iraq War never ended. The designation of Iran as a member of the Axis of Evil, US invasion of Iraq and clamor to extend the war to Iran, war in Syria, rise of ISIS, and Israel's shadow war with Iran are all seen as evidence of an ongoing attempt to defeat and break up the Islamic Republic, which in the eyes of Iran's leadership, is not just a threat to the regime but also to Iran itself.[1]

The strategic success of forward defense has led Khamenei and the IRGC to resolve on protecting and pursuing it at all costs. It gives Iran a flexible and cost-effective means to gain leverage against the United States and better-armed regional rivals—in particular, Israel after the two rivals exchanged missiles in 2024. The ability and willingness to inflict pain on adversaries through irregular warfare serves Iran's defense, but also gives it considerable regional capabilities. As such, it has become embedded in Iran's strategic thinking.[2] The endgame for Iran's leaders is not just Iranian security. Instead, they seek Iranian hegemony: forcing the United States to leave the region and Iran to dominate its Arab neighbors. Put another way, they seek achieve what the Shah already had in the 1970s.

Yet the pursuit of forward defense has come at immense economic, political, and even strategic costs. It is a strategy with no clear end point.

Like nesting dolls, every defense parameter must be enveloped by another one to defend it. It is an expensive strategy—a forever gambit that must continuously expand. The more Iran persists in forward defense as the means to push back against the American containment cordon, the more it brings American attention to Iran. In Zarif's telling, forward defense is not making foreign policymaking easier for Iran but to the contrary, adding burdens to it.[3]

The Windfalls and Pitfalls of Forward Defense

Iran's intervention in Syria raised the ire of the Arab world in ways that had not been the case in Iraq earlier. The Arab street, and Turkey, was then enthralled with the promise of the Arab Spring. There was broad support for the opposition to Assad and the Sunni cause in Syria. If the fall of the dictatorship had led to the empowerment of the majority Shias in Iraq, why should the same not happen in Syria? In this scenario, Iran was the spoiler, supporting a Shia agenda in both Iraq and Syria. A non-Arab state was interfering in the domestic affairs of an Arab state to frustrate a cause popular on the Arab street and enjoying the backing of the region's main Sunni powers.

The Assad regime's shocking brutality against its own people—including the use of aerial bombing, barrel bombs, and chemical weapons—sullied Iran's reputation as well. The strategic logic of supporting Assad came at the cost of a tarnished reputation and widespread contempt in the region. The popularity that Hezbollah's heroics in the 2006 war had garnered, by 2015, by and large evaporated.

This was a hard pill to swallow for the Islamic Republic, which had cultivated its image as being on the side of the people and fighting for justice. It showed that forward defense would ultimately deepen sectarian divisions in the region and provoke Sunni Arab resistance to Iran. Hezbollah especially felt the impact of this backlash both in Lebanon and the broader region. Its defense of the Palestinian cause did not absolve it of defending Assad's butchery.

Equally important, the successes of forward defense in Syria and Yemen led Iran's Arab rivals—Saudi Arabia and the UAE—to mount a concerted campaign to undo the 2015 nuclear deal. That deal, as will be discussed in the next chapter, was negotiated as Iran's forward defense was unfolding in Syria and Yemen. To the Arab states, the deal was less about containing Iran's nuclear program and more about the United States relaxing its containment of Iran in the region. The deal would allow the United States to turn its attention to Asia, but also relieve both diplomatic and economic pressure on Iran, allowing it to pursue its forward defense with greater freedom. This was a strategic calamity for Persian Gulf monarchies and the pathway for Iranian hegemony.

While it was Iranian politicians and diplomats keen on the normalization of relations with the West who negotiated the deal, forward defense was the domain of the IRGC. Iran was thus following two foreign policies: one harking to the Rafsanjani era and the building of relations with the West to promote development, and the other committed to forward defense, resistance, and continuation of sacred defense. The latter would ultimately undermine the former. Resistance to forward defense proved strong enough to prevail on the United States to scuttle the nuclear deal and impose maximum pressure sanctions on Iran, which were in part aimed at hobbling forward defense.

Even after President Trump withdrew from the nuclear deal in 2018, Arab and Israeli worry over forward defense continued unabated. They feared that Iran continued to hold to its positions in Lebanon, Syria, Iraq, and Yemen, but also to advance its missile and drone capabilities. This made forward defense both more resilient and dangerous. For instance, the 2019 Iranian drone and missile attacks on Saudi oil facilities in Abqaiq were launched from Iraq and Yemen.

These worries brought together Israel and the Persian Gulf monarchies of Bahrain, Saudi Arabia, and the UAE. There was a convergence of interests during the 2006 Lebanon War, when both Israel and the Persian Gulf monarchies had rued Hezbollah's power play.[4] It was conflicts in Syria and Yemen, however, that led the Arab states to rise above their concerns for the Palestinians to cooperate with Israel on intelligence and security issues, forging a regional axis to contain Iran. This proved to be a major strategic victory for Israel, which then shunned peace talks with the Palestinians and instead expanded settlements in the West Bank, while also openly courting Arab states to join hands with Israel against Iran. This Arab-Israeli nexus ultimately evolved into the Abraham Accords of 2020, and subsequently a path to the potential normalization of ties between Israel and Saudi Arabia in 2023.[5] Although Iran's rulers would not acknowledge it, this new consensus between Israel and the Persian Gulf monarchies was a strategic blow. That proved costly enough that in 2023, Iran decided it had to find a way to end its hostilities with Saudi Arabia and abate its forward defense push into Yemen to achieve that.[6] Riyadh would soon intimate that Iran must go further, asserting that its "forward-defense must change in long term to create space to work constructively."[7]

Forward defense had unfolded successfully, but precisely because there was no regional axis organized against it. That would no longer be the case. Furthermore, forward defense had opened the door for Israel to expand its diplomatic, economic, and geographic reach into the Arab world, and thus be accepted as a regional actor and even an ally of some Arab countries. If the goal of the Axis of Resistance was to marginalize and weaken Israel, it seemed to have achieved the opposite. This trend also complicated Iran's stance against the United States. The United States no longer had to temper its policies in favor of Arabs or Israel to appease one or the other: both wanted the United States to stand firm against forward defense. The fact that forward defense had been so successful between 2003 and 2022 did not mean that it was a viable strategy going forward, nor that it could be sustained at the same pace and cost as before. The ultimate cost could be war.

This became blatantly evident in January 2020 when the United States killed Soleimani along with his chief Iraqi lieutenant and the senior-most Shia militia commander, Mahdi al-Muhandis, in a drone attack in Baghdad.[8] Weeks earlier, in December 2019, a missile attack by a pro-Iran Shia militia in Iraq killed an American contractor. The United States retaliated with an attack on that militia's base. That led to massive protests in Baghdad, which besieged the American embassy and raised fears of a repeat of the hostage crisis of 1979. It was then that the Trump administration decided to go after the mastermind of forward defense.

The killing of Soleimani was a blow to Iran. Tehran saw it as a frontal American attack designed to weaken Iran.[9] There was a popular outpouring of anger and sorrow in Iran. Millions came to the streets to decry Soleimani's killing. Many were regime supporters, deeply entrenched in the language and psychology of sacred defense, but there were those who wanted to tell the United States they would not support a war on Iran. There were also those who saw Soleimani—for a moment in time at least—as separate from the IRGC, and the man who had defended Iran's interests and protected Shia shrines from ISIS. The reaction in Iran was a uniquely nationalist moment, bringing together disparate groups and usually divergent political opinions.[10]

Forward defense had brought Iran to this point. Nevertheless, the IRGC's inclination was not to back off but rather double down on deterrence—both to dissuade America from going any further and protect its regional equities. There was a tense forty-eight hours when Iran and the United States could have found themselves at war.

Despite that risk, Iran decided to assert deterrence by launching a barrage of missiles on a military base in Iraq that housed tens of American military personnel. None were killed, but it was the largest missile attack that US troops had ever encountered. The retaliation demonstrated what Airiane Tabatabai and Annie Tracy Samuel have written: just how much Iran's strategic outlook depends on deterrence. Iran's attack sought to restore that deterrence, not only against the United States, but against other regional actors, who may have decided to take on Iran's regional proxies after the killing of Soleimani.

The United States decided not to escalate any further, but this incident had also underscored the dangers that forward defense ran for Iran: a larger war on its homeland that it could not wage with proxies. Forward defense was an alternative to conventional military formation, yet it would be a problem if it led to a conflict that needed exactly such a military.

The risks that forward defense poses to Iran were again evident after Hamas' attack on Israel in October 2023. This was clear in October 2024 when Israel's successful assault on Hezbollah led to an audacious Iranian missile attack on Israel. That show of force won accolades for Iran across the Arab and Muslim world, but that provides Iran little tangible protection in the event of a war with Israel and the United States.

At first glance, the war seemed to have done away with the costs of forward defense. Arab-Israeli normalization was put on hold, and gone was the memory of Iran and Hezbollah's support for Assad on the Arab street, replaced with regional fury over US support for Israel. Yet the Arab anger over the war and sympathy for Palestinians is balanced with concerns over the power and reach of the Axis of Resistance along with its capabilities. Iran's assumption may be that the Gaza war will strengthen the Axis of Resistance and further entrench the idea of resistance in the region.

The opening that the war has provided Iran, however, may prove to be transient. Especially once the war is at its end and the Palestinian issue is not as urgent, Iran and the Axis of Resistance will look more ominous, and that could once again serve as the basis for an American-backed Arab-Israeli normalization initiative.

Furthermore, the October 7 attack brought into sharp relief the extent of Iran's ties with militant Palestinian factions, and the military capabilities of the network of proxies Iran had woven together from Lebanon to Syria and the Palestinian territories. Israel pointed to the threat that this development posed to Israel in justifying its attack on Iran's consulate in Damascus in April 2024. That attack killed IRGC commander Mohammad Reza Zahedi, the Qods Force's point person in managing Iran's relations with Hezbollah and the Axis of Resistance. Israel also signaled that it was ready to attack Iran at the highest level regardless of the location to disrupt the Axis of Resistance. Iran interpreted the attack as a significant escalation, and to deter Israel and protect the axis, retaliated with a massive assault on Israel from Iranian soil with hundreds of drones as well as cruise and ballistic missiles. It invoked a new deterrence doctrine, or in the words of the commander of the IRGC, Salami, a new formula: "If you hit us, we will hit back from our own soil."[11] The shadow war between Iran and Israel thus burst into the open, putting the two regional rivals on course to a larger conflict.

The April exchange of missiles did not deter Israel. After a Hezbollah missile killed a dozen Druze kids in the Golan Heights, Israel killed first a senior Hezbollah leader in Beirut and then the political head of Hamas in Tehran. Then came Israel's assault on Hezbollah and its senior leadership. Iran responded with another barrage of missiles. The escalation raised the specter of a larger war in the Middle East, underscoring the fact that every success of forward defense has come at a cost, and as the successes have become bigger, so have the costs—an escalatory ladder that points to a dangerous denouement.

• • •

Today, even if the Islamic Republic chose to abandon forward defense, it would not be easy to do so. The strategy depends on several different militias and hundreds of thousands of foot soldiers, who cannot be easily or quickly demobilized. Most, as with Hezbollah in Lebanon, the Houthis in Yemen, or the Shia militias in Iraq, have developed their own local interests and remain committed to their strategy even without Tehran's leadership. For instance, the Lebanon War of 2006 was instigated by Hezbollah, and the Shia militias are now locked in a power struggle for control of Iraq. Hezbollah has developed its own network of influence in Tehran that can be deployed to constrain the Iranian leadership's room to maneuver. Proxy militias are not weapon systems that can be easily decommissioned.

Moreover, Iran's investment in these militias has fit well with building cultural ties with Shia communities and political ties with non-Shia ones around common goals. This "soft power" exercise embeds support for Iran among Shia and Palestinian populations in the Middle East. It also cultivates enduring political and social ties between the proxy militias and communities they operate in, which in turn provide Iran and its proxies with strategic depth and resilience.[12] Forward defense's success relies on people, local communities, and military organizations. These cultural and social ties add political dimensions to forward defense, which could make it difficult for Iran to easily back away from the strategy.

Since 2003, forward defense has, in effect, changed the Islamic Republic's conception of national security in a fundamental fashion. At first, forward defense implied that protecting national security required maintaining a presence in the Arab world and even controlling its politics.

Through the crucible of the war in Syria, this conception changed. Then Iran's strategy demanded defending the entire Shia domain in the region—in Lebanon, Syria, Iraq, and Afghanistan—as Iran's strategic depth in Khamenei's telling.[13] Viewing those Shia domains sitting outside Iran's borders as integral to the defense of the homeland, and protection of the shrine cities of Iraq and Syria as part of the defense of Iran itself, constitutes a significant expansion of the definition of national security.

Its advocates have justified this conception of national security in strategic terms—defending against the Sunni Arab threat to Iran—but increasingly in cultural terms too. The latter meant conceiving of a Shia domain—and a Shia transnational community—that extends beyond Iran and Iranian nationalism. The ties binding Shia communities around the world to Iran's centers of religious learning—seminaries and the hybrid seminary-university Al-Mustafa International University, which is headquartered in Qom, but has educational outfits around the world—go back to the 1980s. The scope of those educational ties has expanded in recent years in tandem with Iran's interest in defining the contours of the Shia domain. Still, that community is defined not in Islamic terms per se but more so in popular Shia attachment to shrines, the legacy and popular devotion to Imam Hossein, and the legacy of his martyrdom in Karbala. It is not clerics and their expositions on Islamic strictures that drive this effort but rather the elegists (maddahs) and impact on popular culture, and a host of multilingual media programs, publications, and cultural productions around the shrines along with the stories of the saints buried there that travel across Shia communities worldwide. These efforts are designed to also create a common understanding between Shias across the expanse from the Mediterranean to the Indian Ocean, with Iran serving as the center of this Shia domain.

The conception of a Shia domain provides Iran with a strategic depth that failed to materialize from the Shah's Green Plan or even Khomeini's view of Iran as an ideological pivot of an Islamic resistance to injustice and American hegemony—which is once again boldly on display in the Axis of Resistance's role in the Gaza war. In the past, Iran's Persian and Shia identities distinguished it from the Arab- and Sunni-dominated Middle East. Its Persian identity still sets Iran apart. But with the collapse of Sunni domination in the Arab heartland after 2003, Iran could envision strategic depth in pockets of Shia power in the Arab world. Forward defense seeks to cultivate and strengthen this depth.

The new conception of national security reflects the growing control of the IRGC over the Islamic Republic. It also further entrenches that control, confirming the militarization of the state. The Qods Force served as the fulcrum and main promoter of the new conception of national security. Its power is reflected in and dependent on the idea of a larger Shia domain. After 2003, the Qods Force, under Soleimani leadership, played an increasingly important role in shaping the IRGC's overall strategic outlook and how the hard-line conservatives too looked on foreign policy issues. The expansion of the Qods Force's operations and influence has continued under Soleimani's successor, General Esma'il Qa'ani. Soleimani's death did not alter the force's trajectory.

Forward defense has both justified and propelled the consolidation of power inside Iran under the hard-liners. Khamenei and the IRGC have come to believe that to manage the strategy of forward defense demands their exclusive control of power: marginalizing moderates and even conservatives who favor a more nuanced foreign policy. Furthermore, to carry the country through the isolation and international pressure created by that strategy—as well as the nuclear program—demands such political control.

Yet the new Shia consciousness that undergirded forward defense conflicts with how many Iranians understand nationalism and national security. It divides Iranians around national security rather than uniting them (as had been the case during the Iran-Iraq War and even in the post 9/11 period, culminating in fighting against ISIS). Many Iranians continue to question the cost of forward defense and the foreign policy alliance with Russia that it has engendered, especially after ISIS was no more.

This presents forward defense with a fundamental challenge. It also exposes the limits to the viability of sacred defense as a national organizing principle, even one that has shaped the Islamic Republic since the Iran-Iraq War. For their part, the IRGC and the hard-liners imagined that they were unifying the nation with their strategy. And they imagined that this would be decisively accomplished by their

control of all institutions of the state and establishing cultural hegemony over Iranian society. This has proved to be an overreach.

Losing the People: The Domestic Cost of Forward Defense

A sustainable strategy requires popular support, especially if it asks great
sacrifice of people. That was the lesson of the Iran-Iraq War: that popular
support for the effort was critical to prosecuting that war.[14] During that
war, Iranians understood the nature of Iraqi aggression and threat, and
embraced their rulers' mantra of resistance and sacred defense.

Today, the memory of that war is fading. Not only that, but Iranians
are further away from the heady days of revolutionary zeal and resistance,
even while threats have moved further away from Iran's borders. Still,
Iran's strategy remains anchored in the assumptions of the war years, and
is built on the spirit of resistance and sacred defense that guided it. Iran's
rulers see the threats that the country encountered in 1980s as ongoing.
The IRGC and the militantly conservative segment of the political class
also believe that resistance and forward defense have finally solved the
security problems that have dogged Iran for over a century.

They are in effect arguing that forward defense (and as will be contended in the next chapter, Iran's stance on the nuclear issue) is not only
defending Iran against ongoing threats but fulfilling the country's age-
old desire for security, independence, and regional great power status
too.[15] In this endeavor, the focus is on the United States. As former Basij
Forces commander Mohammad Reza Naqdi put it, "The slogan of
death to America continues [because] Iran does not trust America,"
and according to the former commander in chief of the IRGC, General Mohammad Ali Ja'fari, Iran will not accept the US-led "hege-
monic system . . . unless the United States' arrogant nature would
change, in which case there would remain no reason for enmity."[16] Anti-
Americanism has thus become so embedded in the Islamic Republic
that fighting the United States has at times been read back as *the* original
aim of the revolution.[17] These ideas are based on Iran's experiences, but
also reflect the values of the revolution that have been embedded in its

strategic culture, which include resistance against aggression and outside control (including that of oppressed peoples against imperialism), independence, justice, and standing up for Islam.[18] These are all values that Khomeini had spelled out at length in his speeches, interviews, and writings, and Khamenei is committed to enforcing them.[19]

But average Iranians are increasingly removed from these values and unreceptive to the strategy built on them. The hostage crisis and war with Iraq, though, are no longer part of the collective experience of a large part of the population. Sacred defense was premised on ideological vigilance and revolutionary zeal. As elections in the 1990s and 2000s showed, Iranians have largely passed that phase of their history. They are not seeking a future in ideology but instead in the normalization of politics and international affairs.

More important, the cost of forward defense and Iran's nuclear posture have been growing meteorically since 2018, as has the country's isolation. To many Iranians, it looks like many of the threats that forward defense is guarding against are consequences of the strategy's expansionist drive and the methods that it employs in building bases of support in the Arab world. This has raised questions about the wisdom of Khamenei's grand strategy. The country's means are hardly adequate for sustaining its strategic ends—especially as those ends have invited ever more biting sanctions that shrink those means.

The Islamic Republic has touted that it has achieved genuine development. Iran has been under sanctions since 1979. The scale of these sanctions has increased markedly over time in waves in response to Iran's support for terrorism and aggressive polices in the Middle East, and in tandem with tightening the US cordon of containment around Iran.[20] Decades of sanctions have impacted every facet of Iranian state and society, but also constituted an entrenchment of the security architecture that Iran views as a threat to its interests and security.[21] Rather than compelling Iran's leaders to change course, the threat posed by sanctions has only led it to further circle the wagons around the strategies of resistance that first took shape in the 1980s.

Building a resistance economy (*eqtesad-e moqavemati*) has been core to Iran's response. Khamenei wants less carping about economic sanctions and instead to make Iran's economy immune to US economic pressure. Autarky and investment in home industries has built a certain degree of resiliency, helping Iran to absorb the shock of sanctions while maintaining a certain degree of technological advancement.[22] This, however, does not account for the opportunity cost of economic isolation, and many hardships in the form of economic inefficiencies, shortages, high inflation and high unemployment, and proliferation of corruption that Iranians have been facing.

Another long-term cost to Iran is that resistance has anchored Iran's economy in a black market of trade for access to critical imports and exports. This black market is only viable because it is protected by the IRGC. That has in turn opened the private sector, and more broadly large sectors of the economy, to the ever-increasing influence of the IRGC and deep state. In the process, state and social institutions as well as national politics have been formatted in ways that reflect the reality of Iran's economy and the relationships that keep it afloat.[23] An economy that operates outside the bounds of international trade and global financial markets, and must defy and go around the normative order that governs them, will inevitably succumb to structural inefficiencies and endemic corruption. Iran's economy is today in the grip of large conglomerates—some directly controlled by the state or IRGC, and some semiprivate—and powerful business networks that operate as conglomerates. Sanctions have impoverished the people and given rise to a billionaire class with vested interest in the current flawed political economy. As these economic inefficiencies shape political relationships, they ensure the state's authoritarian control of society, but also perpetuate the conflicts and threat perceptions that had produced the sanctions dilemma in the first place.

Persisting on this course has put at risk the social contract that the Islamic Republic forged with its population in the 1980s and many of the economic wins that the middle class has achieved since the Rafsanjani period. The combination of soaring inflation, corruption, and income inequality is tearing Iran's social fabric apart. As a result, Iranians have come to question the wisdom of resistance and sacred defense, and increasingly voice their opposition to forward defense.

During the economic protests that broke out in 2018, for example, demonstrators chanted political slogans against the ruling order, but against forward defense too, saying, "No to Gaza, no to Lebanon," and "Leave Syria and think of us." The protesters did not see any reason why Iran should invest in military operations in the Levant while its own economy was facing a crisis. Reformist dissident politician Mostafa Tajzadeh called Khamenei's "absolute defense" of Assad, whom he depicted as responsible for chaos and violence in Syria, as the "gravest mistake" of Iran's leaders.[24]

One year later, in 2019, reformist criticisms manifested themselves in slogans chanted during nationwide protests. Fueled by economic grievances, these protests shocked the Islamic Republic's leadership, to the delight of its detractors, by expressing disenchantment with forward defense. Slogans such as "From Tehran to Baghdad, poverty, brutality, and dictatorship," or "Neither Gaza nor Lebanon, my life be sacrificed for Iran," showed the population was blaming IRGC expenditures on regional activities for the country's economic ills and believed priority should be the home front, not the Levant. This dissent divided the Iranian public's response at the outset of the Gaza war in fall 2023, when many remained cool toward the Palestinian cause, which they identified with forward defense—those attitudes changed in time after the scale of the devastation of Gaza became evident.

In August 2022, Mir Hossein Moussavi captured the growing criticism of forward defense in a statement he issued from house arrest. He raised alarm about plans for Khamenei's son, Mojataba—a linchpin of the alliance between the IRGC and hard-liners, promoting sacred defense and forward defense—to succeed his father. Moussavi also attacked forward defense directly, arguing that Iran's involvement in Syria had been carried out in the name of protection of the shrine of Zaynab. But he continued,

> The true protection is that of the heart of the believer from an oppressor, but it has been interpreted to support bloodletting in a foreign land to defend a child-killing regime. . . . millions of refugees and hundreds of thousands of dead in Syria, tarnishing Hezbollah's name,

emergence of ISIS, sectarian and ethnic wars in Yemen, the willingness of Arab states to join hands with Israel to confront the "Shia crescent" are all evidence of the wickedness of this wrong path.

He also called General Hamedani, who was killed in Syria, "a general without honor" whose bloody fate on the battlefield was the bookend to his central role in suppressing the Green Movement.[25] Finally, he asked, had Iran not intervened in Syria, would the situation there not have ended peacefully, with a just and democratic outcome?

Moussavi's criticism was biting as well as more thoroughgoing than the chants on the street. His argument was not economic. Instead, it challenged the wisdom forward defense on its own strategic terms, and questioned the cost it imposed on national values and Iran's reputation. Most important, Moussavi exposed the secret hiding in plain view: the political alliance that sustained sacred defense and forward defense was anchored in the household of the supreme leader and would be perpetuated if his son succeeded him. Sacred defense needed the continuation of Khamenei's rule, and IRGC and hard-liners would see to that by suppressing popular political will. This is why Moussavi made sure to mention General Hamedani by name because his role in suppressing the Green Movement dovetailed with his military role in Syria.[26] Iranians—Moussavi was saying—were denied their vote in 2009, so that the ruling order could continue with forward defense.

One month later, in September 2022, Moussavi's argument would define the popular demand of protesters, when protests swept across the nation. Protesters chanted "our enemy is not America; our enemy is here," or "Basiji, Sepahi [the IRGC], you are our Daesh [ISIS]." The latter is a direct retort to the IRGC's assertion that it is protecting Iran from imminent threats like ISIS—and the taunt that if it was not for the IRGC, the women who are protesting for their freedoms would have had the same fate as Yezidi women under ISIS. A university student confronted the city's conservative mayor, saying that "the Islamic Republic is supporting the brutal Taliban regime, and has for long supported Lebanon's Hezbollah, which is also a dictatorship like Mr. Khamenei." These chants and questions effectively maintained that the foundational logic of forward defense was not acceptable, and Iran's regional policy should be based on the values of freedom and democracy—the very values for which Iranians were protesting on the streets. Although such sentiments have somewhat dissipated considering the devastations of the Gaza war, they are still extant in the public discourse.

The leaders of the Islamic Republic continue to see national interests in terms of national liberation, which was the battle cry of the 1979 Revolution. But their critics at home want the national interest to reflect individual freedoms, which was in fact also the battle cry of the 1905–6 Constitutional Revolution.

Moussavi and the protesters on the streets have made this dichotomy clear. Former reformist president Mohammad Khatami too acknowledged the divide that separates these worldviews and said that it would be untenable. It does not serve the Islamic Republic, Khatami argued, to compel Iranians to face a Faustian choice, adding, "Freedom and Security must not be put against each other."[27] But a new vision of national security that embraces both is easier said than done, so long as the IRGC and its allies in the political sphere remain committed to sacred defense.

Today, a considerable segment of the Iranian population does not accept the logic or cost of forward defense, and does not buy into sacred defense's ongoing resistance to the West. The IRGC argues that "what today exists as security, freedom, independence, honor, and pride is indebted to the great epics of the eternal men [who fought in] the Holy [Sacred] Defense."[28] But even if true, contend the dissenters, such history must not be the future. In effect, Iranians are asserting that national interest is not a given. This is the essence of what political scientist Peter Katzenstein sees as the construction of state interests: they are not fixed, nor are they evident certitudes to be defended.[29]

Forward defense was built on the worldview of sacred defense and conceived of as its continuation beyond the Iran-Iraq War. It embodies the fears and anxieties of the war years, but also the commitments to resistance and independence that were the hallmarks of Khomeini's politics. Moreover, forward defense encompasses nationalist aspirations that are deeply embedded in Iranian history and were on full display in the Shah's statecraft. The Islamic Republic seeks legitimacy in what forward defense has accomplished. Ultimately, the state promises, the doctrine of forward defense has defended Iran against external threats, empowered the country as a regional force from the Mediterranean to the Red Sea to the Persian Gulf and Hindu Kush mountains, resolved the country's security, and fulfilled its aspirations of grandeur and independence.

Iran's rulers often point to the Reza Shah era or Mossadeq's stance to underscore these points. The Pahlavis were weak and under the clutch of foreigners—Reza Shah was brought to power and then dethroned by Britain, and the Shah was a servant of America—and Mossadeq's cause was just, but he failed where the Islamic Republic has succeeded. These are the ingredients of state propaganda. But importantly, they also reveal that the legitimacy that the Islamic Republic seeks is deeply embedded in genuine security dilemmas that have loomed large in Iranian political consciousness. Anthropologist Narges Bajoghli writes of a vast museum built by the IRGC:

> One wing of the museum features a large map of the ancient Persian Empire, ruling stretches of Asia. As the visitor continues through the exhibition, Iran's territory shrinks; the country's contemporary size appears small in comparison to the glorified empire painted on the wall. The message is clear: Leaders of previous Iranian kingdoms had recklessly given away territory, thinking more about filling their own pockets than about the well-being of the nation. When the Islamic Republic was attacked by the Iraqi army, backed by the West, it fought to maintain Iran's borders, and, by extension, the nation's dignity as an ancient civilization.[30]

Forward defense is in debate with Iran's past. And therefore it seeks justification in juxtaposition with that past.

Forward defense is also a strategic culture, a way of thinking about interests and security that dominates among a core elite as well as the key institutions associated with national security and running the state. Among the up-and-coming security and political managers, it is a culture perpetuated through the production of information and education curricula. Yet this effort has fallen short of embedding this strategic culture beyond the militantly conservative political spectrum and its core constituency.

Today, the strategic and economic costs of forward defense continue to mount. And political resistance to it has continued to grow. It is only when forward defense begins to truly destabilize the Islamic Republic at home, however, that its wisdom and viability will be questioned. For now, Khamenei and the IRGC remain wedded to it, and the force's growing prominence in national politics ensures that forward defense remains at the heart of Iran's national security thinking and grand strategy of resistance.

It is important to note that forward defense is no longer a strategy for addressing regional threats but also a means of gaining leverage against the United States—now eager to focus on China and Russia—as Tehran and Washington tussle over the future of Iran's nuclear program, and Iran's rivalry with Israel. By summer 2023, as Iran and the United States found themselves at an impasse over nuclear talks, and although the war in Syria was close to its end, new lethal militias surfaced targeting American bases and personnel. Iran's goal was to compel the United States to soften its position at the nuclear diplomatic table. The same pattern of events happened during the Gaza war, this time to compel the United States to force a ceasefire on Israel. Yet the more menacing forward defense has become, and the more its sharp end is pointed at Israel, the more likely it is that the United States will become ensconced in the region.

CHAPTER 10

The Nuclear Gambit

No issue has held as much promise to break through sacred defense—and posed as much threat to Iran's foreign policy—as its nuclear program. Since 2003, the nuclear issue has come to dominate Iran's relations with the West and shape its domestic politics. In the process, it led to a significant escalation of tensions between Iran and the United States, and imposition of a series of new sanctions on Iran's economy, and then opened the door to the first diplomatic engagement between the two countries since 1979—promising to fundamentally change Iran's foreign policy. Next, the rejection of this diplomacy by the United States became the rallying cry for Iran's hardliners.[1] Finally, it was worry over Iran's nuclear program that became the reason for the West to challenge the Islamic Republic's foreign policy at a whole new level.

The roots of Iran's nuclear program, as was discussed in chapter 1, go back to the Pahlavi period. The program then was intended for civilian purposes, although the Shah imagined that could change. He told the chief of the nuclear program, "If small Middle Eastern countries embarked on a nuclearization path, no matter how primitive or crude, then Iran's 'national interest' would dictate that it followed suit."[2]

The nuclear issue resurfaced in senior-level discussions in Tehran toward the end of the Iran-Iraq War.[3] Iraq had used chemical weapons against Iran with impunity, the international community had failed to condemn those actions, and if the war were ever to have resumed, Iran expected Saddam to use weapons of mass destruction. That specific threat dissipated after the first Gulf War. Nevertheless, Iran decided to restart its nuclear program as a civilian endeavor.[4] The national security argument was bolstered by Iran's desire for respect and recognition that would come with nuclear status.[5]

Thus in the 1990s, Iran examined Libya's and Pakistan's paths to nuclear capability. IRGC commanders visited Pakistan to discuss the acquisition of nuclear technology.[6] Rafsanjani, according to his memoirs, discussed building Iran's nuclear program with Pakistan's Prime Minister Benazir Bhutto when she visited Tehran.[7] Hasan Rouhani, who became president in 2013, credits Rafsanjani with establishing a civilian nuclear infrastructure.[8]

Iran's efforts came to light in 2002, shortly before the United States toppled Saddam Hussein. The international community's reaction to the revelations threatened the Islamic Republic. The United States and its European allies were alarmed that an anti-Western theocracy had circumvented the US containment cordon to hinder a nuclear program. If allowed to grow unchecked, Iran's program would, at best, weaken the containment strategy that had maintained regional stability. At worst, the program would give Iran a devastating offensive capability with which to threaten US interests and those of its close allies in the region—Israel in particular.[9] An Iranian nuclear umbrella would constrict Israel's ability to respond to the kind of attack Hamas launched against its territory in October 2023, and the assault Israel launched on Hezbollah in 2024, especially in Iranian territory.

The security conscious supreme leader and his close allies saw the timing of the revelations as a deliberate ploy to take advantage of the international frenzy over the imminent war with Iraq to further sanction Iran at the United Nations, and even include it as a target in the war.[10]

Iran was then in a bind. The nuclear program was not advanced enough so that Iran's leadership could count on it as a deterrent. And yet the very existence of the program was inviting international pressure and the threat of war. Furthermore, there had been no serious discussion of the program inside Iran and hence there was no consensus among the ruling elite as how to respond.[11] President Khatami and his reformist followers favored resolving the issue through negotiations. The IRGC favored dispensing with accommodating the West and building a full-fledged program with military potential—in particular given Iran's inclusion in the Axis of Evil and impending US invasion of Iraq. The supreme leader resisted the argument for negotiations, saying repeatedly that Iran could not trust the United States.

The nuclear issue soon dominated national security debates in Iran. There were extensive deliberations and public debate on whether pursuing a nuclear program would relieve American pressure or invite more of it: Would it serve resistance, or was resistance now necessary just to protect the program? Did the program provide Iran with deterrence, and if so, how? The answer to these questions depended on whether the nuclear program was merely leverage in confronting America, or if Iran was pursuing it for other strategic and military reasons—in other words, would Iran give it up at the right price and in the right circumstances, or was it determined to be a nuclear state.

All of this was fiercely debated among the political class as it pondered how to respond to outside pressure—and the lines of argument did not always neatly fit the reformist-conservative divide. That debate would ultimately draw a clear line between those advocating resistance and no engagement or concessions on the nuclear issue—sticking closely to the mantra of sacred defense—and those who advocated engaging the West in nuclear diplomacy to mitigate threats against the Islamic Republic. The two positions harked back to Rafsanjani's and Khatami's arguments for moving away from revolutionary posturing in favor of a more balanced foreign policy as well as the IRGC and hard-liner's insistence on resistance and sacred defense. The supreme leader did not forbid diplomacy but instead cautioned that Iran had to be tough and protect its interests. Over the past two decades, this divide has shaped domestic Iranian politics and forged Iran's foreign policy posture.[12]

Iran ultimately followed both resistance *and* engagement. At times, this double tactic was a deliberate strategy, and at other times, it reflected confusion borne of unresolved domestic political debates. Iran engaged in nuclear diplomacy first with the European powers in 2003, then Turkey and Brazil in 2010, and ultimately with the permanent members of the UN Security Council and Germany (the so-called P5 + 1) in 2013.[13] At the same time, however, Iran would embark on forward defense, made more urgent by the growing international reaction to Iran's nuclear program.

In fact, at first Iran sought to defuse the crisis immediately. It struck a deal with Britain, France, and Germany in 2003.[14] That agreement would halt Iran's nuclear program in exchange for sanctions relief. Washington, though, vetoed the deal in October 2003.

This came soon after Khatami's May 2003 overture, which only confirmed again for Khamenei that the United States did not want a deal but instead regime change in Iran. Khamenei's instinct would have been to forswear talks with the West, but the nuclear issue was putting Iran in America's crosshairs in a dangerous way, and Iran was then ill prepared to easily rebuff US pressure. It had to remain open to a diplomatic resolution. Ultimately, Iran's rulers concluded that a resolution did not happen in October 2003 because Iran's program was too small to be taken seriously by Washington. The United States could afford to veto a deal—and demand that Iran dismantle its program without any concessions in return—because Washington did not see the program as a real threat. If Iran was going to negotiate successfully, then it had to have a larger program. Yet that could provoke a terse US response.

Iran therefore adopted a particular approach: remaining open to talks (although with no evident progress), while steadily expanding the program—all along continuing to claim that the program was for civilian purposes.[15] To this end, Khamenei even issued a fatwa in 2003 (and reiterated it in 2010) banning the development and use of nuclear weapons.[16] Iran, however, neither trusted the Bush administration nor did it think that its program was large enough to have real leverage at the negotiating table. The United States, for its part, having vetoed the European deal, remained open to a diplomatic resolution. It hoped that what would produce a breakthrough was what political scientist Kenneth Pollock has called "bigger carrots, and bigger sticks": threatening more sanctions, regime change, or war, while offering sanctions relief and civilian nuclear technology.[17]

As the US campaign in Iraq ran into trouble, a rift opened between the Bush administration and its European allies. Now Iran felt greater room to maneuver and drag its feet on a diplomatic resolution even while expanding the program.

The Bush administration was unable to threaten Iran into submission. In the meantime, Israel grew more worried and threatened to go to war on its own to stop Iran's nuclear program.[18] With the Iraq War debacle dominating Western public opinion, Washington found Israel's threats useful: it warned Iran against war, without implicating the United States in threatening another Middle East war. Iran did not flinch.

That all changed with the election of President Obama. Unlike Bush, Obama enjoyed the support of the European powers and was able to quickly translate that into new economic sanctions against Iran.[19] In tandem, Obama made it clear to Iranian leaders—through a series of public messages (for instance, referring to Iran by its official name, "the Islamic Republic of Iran") as well as private letters to Khamenei—that he was not pursuing regime change and was not interested in war with Iran. He was, however, determined to stop Iran's nuclear program—for no better reason than it was the most immediate reason why the United States could be dragged into another war in the Middle East. The sanctions pressure was designed to drive that point home, as was the incapacitating Stuxnet cyberattack that the United States and Israel carried out on Iran's nuclear program.

Tehran could not ignore the combined security threat of an increase in cyberattacks, Israeli saber-rattling, and more sanctions. The containment cordon around Iran was getting tighter. Former president Rafsanjani, who still wielded influence on Khamenei, argued that America was pursuing the same sanctions and isolation strategy against Iran that it had against Iraq between 1990 and 2003. If that was true, then Iran would be allowed to sell a minimal amount of oil to pay for food and medicine, but that the country would ultimately be driven into poverty. Once it was weakened and its institutions degraded, then the West could do what it did in Iraq in 2003.[20] This belief led Rafsanjani to become a strong advocate of nuclear talks and firm backer of the 2015 nuclear deal that would follow.

The message to Khamenei was clear: Iran had to change tactics to gain immunity from the consequences of the new sets of pressures being deployed against it. Obama was serious about a deal, but also had the means to pressure Iran beyond what Bush could. If Iran was serious about a deal, Obama was as trustworthy an American president as the Islamic Republic could hope for.

Yet it was not Obama's messaging but rather the 2009 Green Movement that drove home both the imperative of a nuclear deal and taking advantage of Obama's presidency. The large-scale protests had rattled the Islamic Republic. The depth of popular anger, support for reformists, and distaste among a significant portion of Iranians for Ahmadinejad and what he stood for—all challenged the halcyon view at the top that reformism had been put to bed with Ahmadinejad's election in 2005, and the IRGC and hard-liners' formula for ruling Iran was secure. The leadership felt vulnerable and understood that the Islamic Republic needed stability in foreign relations while it addressed the fallout from the Green Movement. That meant reducing tensions with the United States.

In the meantime, Obama had assiduously avoided intervening in protests in Iran. As would also be true with the Arab Spring a year later, Obama did not believe Iran was on the verge of regime change and democracy, and the United States could not alter the outcome. If it acted too forcefully, though, it could hamper potential nuclear talks, which was what he thought was United States' main interest and objective. Obama would be severely criticized at home for this display of foreign policy "realism." And yet unbeknownst to him, his indifference in the face of protests did not go unnoticed in Tehran and was one reason Khamenei decided to test the waters with a deal with Obama.

Khamenei stipulated that the talks must remain focused only on the nuclear matters, aim for concrete and immediate results, and concentrate on limiting—but not altogether ending—Iran's nuclear program.[21] When Iran first negotiated a nuclear deal with the European powers, Khamenei had told Hasan Rouhani, who led Iran's team, "I would never abandon the rights of the country as long as I am alive. I would resign if for any reason Iran is deprived of its right to enrichment; otherwise, this may happen after my death."[22] Despite sanctions and Western pressure, his views had not changed over the ensuing decade. In other words, these would be limited "arms control talks" and not engagement aimed at the normalization of relations. He also wanted quick results that would improve national security and help stabilize the domestic situation; "centrifuges must turn," he would say, "but so should people's livelihoods."[23]

This approach was fine with President Obama. In the words of his national security adviser, Susan Rice, "The Iran deal was never primarily about trying to open a new era of relations between the U.S. and Iran. It was far more pragmatic and minimalist. The aim was very simply to make a dangerous country substantially less dangerous."[24]

Khamenei asked Oman's Sultan Qabous to invite the United States to secret talks in Muscat. In March 2013, senior American and Iranian officials met in secret in Muscat to discuss a framework for nuclear talks.[25]

Enter Rouhani

Those talks laid the foundation for formal negotiations, which would be helped along with the election of Hasan Rouhani as president in June 2013. Rouhani was a moderate and a protégé of Rafsanjani. He had been Iran's chief nuclear negotiator when Iran conducted talks with the European powers in 2003. He had long advocated diplomacy to resolve the standoff with great powers on the nuclear program and that this was necessary for national security. He had even written a book making that case.[26]

Rouhani's main opponent was, ironically, another nuclear negotiator. Between 2007 and 2013, Saeed Jalili, a hard-line conservative, had led Iran's nuclear negotiating team. Jalili was a celebrated war veteran who had lost a leg in battle. He was firmly opposed to nuclear diplomacy, believing that Iran should pursue its nuclear ambitions unimpeded, and if need be, leave the international Treaty on the Non-Proliferation of Nuclear Weapons to do so. His unbending obduracy would turn him into a pillar of the hard-liner faction as well as a fervent advocate of resistance and autarky.

Rouhani's election may have been made possible by the fact that the Guardian Council took the controversial step of preventing Rafsanjani from running again—trying to avoid a repeat of 2009—which then forced the supreme leader to accept Rouhani as a less contentious moderate in the race. It is also possible with the Muscat talks in mind that Khamenei understood that another hard-line president in the mold of Ahmadinejad would not achieve a breakthrough.[27] After all, despite Khamenei's support, Ahmadinejad and his chief nuclear negotiator, Jalili, had not been able to advance a diplomatic solution.[28] They had held nuclear talks with the United States and European powers only to make a display of obduracy and determination not to reach an agreement, which led the Obama administration to convince Europe to put more sanctions on Iran.

In the end, Rouhani won the presidency comfortably, defeating Jalili, who campaigned on a platform of unending resistance to the United States and no nuclear talks. Rouhani's election showed again that most Iranians then did not support hard-liners and their call to resistance unwaveringly; instead, they favored engagement with the West. The election results thus again entwined domestic and foreign policies. For now, however, the supreme leader had decided to keep sacred defense at a distance to negotiate a nuclear deal.

Nuclear Talks

The negotiations process unfolded over a two-year period between 2013 and 2015. It was true to its original mandate in that it encompassed only Iran's nuclear program, and assiduously stayed away from Iran's missile program or forward defense. It limited but did not eliminate Iran's nuclear program. Iran agreed to conduct enrichment at only a small research level, do away with all enriched fissile material beyond the amount and level stipulated in the deal, dismantle its plutonium reactor and a large number of its centrifuge cascades, and submit to an intrusive international inspection of its nuclear facilities.[29] In exchange, the United States and its European allies would lift sanctions on trade and financial transactions with Iran that were imposed in response to its nuclear activity. The UN sanctions would be removed, and Iran could sell more oil, benefit from more international trade, and gain more access to international financial networks.[30]

The limitations the deal imposed on Iran's nuclear activity would remain in effect for a period of ten years, and limits on the production and stockpile of enriched uranium would extend to fifteen years. The deal would end an Iranian nuclear threat for a decade with the expectation that the removal of the immediate threat would provide time and opportunity for follow-on deals along with an extension of what was negotiated in the 2015 deal that was given the incongruous name the Joint Comprehensive Plan of Action (JCPOA).[31]

The deal was important not only in that it engaged with the immediate crisis that loomed over the Iran nuclear program but also served as the first time Iran and the United States had met at a high level and signed onto an agreement. Photographs of Secretary of State John Kerry and Iran's Foreign Minister Zarif bantering in Geneva had the quality of shock and awe in Tehran. They broke a taboo, and Iranians were elated at the promise of opening the economy to the West and aghast at the prospect of the walls of resistance crumbling.

Rouhani's election to the presidency had buoyed the middle class and those who had supported the Green Movement.[32] Nuclear talks raised expectations of an end to Iran's isolation, economic engagement with the West, and even a gradual moderation of the Islamic Republic. While the negotiations went on, and soon after there was a deal, this enthusiasm translated into public adulation for Rouhani and Zarif.

This startled the advocates of resistance. What they had planned—namely, a narrow arms control deal that would relieve diplomatic and economic pressure to stabilize the Islamic Republic as well as make resistance viable, not to replace it—was increasingly looking to many Iranians as the beginning of fundamental change to the country's politics. The Rouhani government never said that it sought a normalization of ties with the United States or that a nuclear deal could pave the way for other deals on the thorny issues that stood between the two countries.

Nevertheless, many Iranians concluded that beyond the immediate economic wins of a nuclear deal, it would lead to exactly what the Rouhani government would not admit to: normalizations of relations between Iran and the West.

The implications of the JCPOA and its reception with street celebrations by Iranians flew in the face of sacred defense as well as what the IRGC and its allies had long argued: that not only could Iran not trust the United States but that it could not trust any international agreement either. A nuclear deal with the international community was not only anathema to the core belief of the hard-liners but they also viewed it as a risky leap of faith, trusting the West in the face of learned experience.[33] The JCPOA demanded a relaxing of Iran's revolutionary vigilance and the dismantling of its infrastructure of resistance, which its backers had seen as necessary to the survival of the Islamic Republic.[34]

From the outset, the supreme leader had walked a thin line between supporting Rouhani and the negotiations, and reassuring the hard-liners that the talks would not amount to fundamental change. This was not a workable formula. Soon it became apparent to the West that Rouhani and Khamenei along with the advocates of resistance were not on the same page. Progress on the nuclear front was increasingly coupled with an aggressive IRGC show of force in the region and incarceration of many dual national Iranian Americans—who served as the canaries in the coal mine for Iran's receptivity to open up. These exercises were designed to stymie Rouhani, and signal to Western powers not to interpret Rouhani and Zarif's diplomacy as a fundamental shift in Iran and beginning of the normalization of relations.

At home, Rouhani and Zarif were subjected to an almost daily barrage of attacks in the conservative press and on the floor of Parliament. Khamenei stood back, letting the hard-liners vent and cast doubt on the wisdom as well as viability of a nuclear deal, and in the process, put Rouhani on his heels. Advocates of resistance were certainly worried about the deal. But they worried more that it would energize popular enthusiasm and unravel their hold over power. Attacks and intimidation were designed to deter that outcome. Their vehemence forced Khamenei to increasingly distance himself from the JCPOA.

As time went on, he grew angry at the slow pace of sanctions relief. Iran had done its part after signing on to the JCPOA, but the United States was dragging its feet. He accused the United States of perfidy and double dealing: "Sanctions will not be lifted through [nuclear] negotiations. The aim of sanctions is something different. Their aim is to exhaust the people of Iran and cause a rift between them and the Islamic state."[35] And again, "We did say: Gentlemen, they [the United States] will not keep their word, they are devious, they renege on their promises, they do not fulfill their promises."[36] His frustration only grew with Trump's election as did his criticism of the JCPOA. He asserted that Iran had to understand that "diplomacy is not substitute for national defense"—implying that if diplomacy failed, Iran would not be bound by it.[37] Shortly before the United States withdrew from the deal, Khamenei said, "If they [United States] want[s] to use the Security Council as an instrument to deny Iran its rights and what it has gained under international law [the nonproliferation treaty and JCPOA], if they want to act lawlessly, then we too can and will act lawlessly."[38]

There was also opposition to the nuclear deal from powerful interests that had benefited from economic sanctions. Behind the wall of sanctions, institutions and networks that controlled the black economy had amassed great wealth as well as secured commanding positions in various economic sectors. Black market forces were tightly entwined with the IRGC and saw their interests aligned with advocates of resistance in lieu of dealmaking. There was a political economy in opposition to the nuclear deal. The lifting of sanctions on Iran would open new transparent channels of trade, enable direct foreign investment, facilitate financial flows in and out of the country, and entail reforms to the legal and banking systems.[39]

Any degree of normalization of Iran's economy would threaten the lucrative monopoly that the black marketeers and their allies in the IRGC enjoyed. Yet even this opposition was voiced in the language of sacred defense: accusing the government of trusting America as it hatched "sinister" plans to undermine the Islamic Republic through a nuclear deal.

The JCPOA's Aftermath

For the United State and international community, the deal was an important accomplishment. The United States avoided an imminent crisis and potential war in the Middle East, and protected the international nonproliferation regime. In fact, Iran would be the first country to come out of the UN Chapter 7 sanctions without war. The European powers, having championed nuclear talks since 2003, saw the deal as a triumph of diplomacy over military confrontation, which after all, had recently led the United States into a fruitless war when the international community had sought to deal with a nuclear crisis in Iraq. Europeans also saw the deal as the means to moderate Iran through economic engagement.

The regional adversaries of Iran, however, saw the deal differently. Israel thought the deal fell short of addressing its worries over the potential of Iran's nuclear program, particularly at a time when forward defense was getting closer to Israel's borders through Syria. Saudi Arabia and other Persian Gulf monarchies saw the deal as a strategic defeat. The deal seemed to confirm Iran's regional status. As discussed in the last chapter, nuclear negotiations unfolded in tandem with Iran's ascendancy in the Syrian War and onset of the war in Yemen. In both of those conflicts, Iran had prevailed over forces backed by its regional Arab rivals. The anti-Assad coalition backed by the Arab states and Turkey, and even ISIS, had failed to defeat Iran in Syria; the Saudi assault to eliminate the Houthis had instead produced a quagmire in Yemen that was favoring Iran. The Arabs felt more vulnerable to Iran than before. Forward defense had broken apart the containment wall that had blocked Iran's path, and now coupled with a deal with the United States, it presented a considerable challenge. They blamed the United States for opening the door to Iran by removing Saddam from power and then refusing to get involved in Syria to remove Assad from power. America's most recent strategic pronouncements spoke not of its commitment to containing Iran but rather a "pivot to Asia." Without steadfast American containment, these Arab states would not be able to stand up to Iran. Instead, America had opened the path for forward defense to expand Iran's influence and confirm its hegemony over the region.

And in fact, the United States had not properly understood the strategic implications of the nuclear deal for its close regional allies. The deal did not address the threats, real or imagined, that worried them. Rather, it had remained satisfied with addressing the only Iranian threat that might demand of the United States another costly war in the Middle East.

Faced with Arab and Israeli criticism, Washington offered them over $100 billion in new weapons sales. What would assuage the Arabs was not weapons but instead ironclad American guarantees for their security: defense pacts that would confirm a US commitment to containing Iran. President Obama, though, was not prepared to do that. After all, for him, an important win in the nuclear deal was to free the United States from military entanglement in the Middle East to focus on Asia. In a contentious meeting with Arab leaders at Camp David in May 2015, President Obama dismissed their call for American security guarantees and even retorted to one Arab leader's complaint about Hezbollah by saying that "they [Arab leaders] should form their own Hezbollahs."[40] In other words, America will give Arabs all the weapons they need, but they must take charge of their own security. Obama would say as much publicly in an interview: that the path to stability and security in the Middle East was not more American military commitment but rather the region taking responsibility for its own security. "The competition between the Saudis and the Iranians, which has helped to feed proxy wars and chaos in Syria and Iraq and Yemen," said Obama, "requires us to say to our friends, as well as to the Iranians, that they need to find an effective way to share the neighborhood and institute some sort of cold peace."[41]

It was the nuclear deal that had allowed the White House to imagine Middle East stability through a "cold peace" as opposed to rolling back Iran's forward defense with more containment. Therefore it made sense to aggrieved Arabs and Israel to want to undo the deal that founded this leap of strategic imagination in Washington. Now, Arab states joined Israel in launching a blistering criticism of the nuclear deal and ultimately undermining it in the United States.[42]

Ironically, advocates of resistance in Iran did not see the deal as a win either.[43] They did not share the Arab view that the JCPOA would remove American containment to Iran's benefit. Rather, they worried that the deal would weaken anti-American vigilance at home, boost expansion of the reformist-minded middle class, and empower it through burgeoning ties with Western businesses. This would, in turn, blow new life into political moderates, who if allowed back into power, would challenge the sacred defense that the IRGC and its strategic posture was based on. Years earlier, as discussed in chapter 6, Khamenei had identified exactly this process of reform and change as the undoing of the Soviet Union.

Then the deep state would have to spend considerable resources and political capital as well as risk a repeat of the 2009 protests to keep the moderates at bay—a task that would be far more daunting once the effects of the JCPOA took hold. Furthermore, once fully implemented, the JCPOA would once again give the United States a perch inside Iran through businesses or eventually even an embassy. That would reverse Khomeini's insistence that the United States could have no footprint in Iran through which to repeat the 1953 coup. The opponents would excoriate the deal repeatedly for giving up too much for too little, compromising Iran's independence and sovereignty by restricting its nuclear rights, and putting its security in danger by allowing the United States to use the deal as a cudgel to continue pressuring Iran.[44] They compared it to the ignominy of accepting UN Resolution 598 to end the war with Iraq or the infamy of submitting to the nineteenth-century Turkmanchay Treaty with Russia.

That Iran signed the JCPOA flew in the face of its distrust of the United States and the core tenets of sacred defense. In fact, it suggested a degree of pragmatism in service of protecting the Islamic Republic. No less surprising was Iran's quick implementation of the deal as well as the dozen clean bills of health it got from the UN nuclear watchdog agency between 2015 and 2018.

The IRGC also successfully argued that after the deal, the United States had not changed its posture toward containing Iran. Washington quickly supplied billions of dollars in weapons to Israel and the Persian Gulf monarchies, and increased its support for Saudi Arabia's war in Yemen. For the IRGC, focused on protecting forward defense, these steps were notable. It maintained that the nuclear deal was coupled with a strategy of arming Iran's rivals in the region to roll back Iran's regional footprint. Iran had agreed to limit its nuclear program, yet now the conventional military gap with its rivals was expanding.[45] According to the Swedish think tank SIPRI, in 2022, Saudi Arabia's military budget spending was ten times that of Iran, and Israel's was three times, $75 billion and $23.4 billion, respectively, as compared to $6.8 billion.[46] In response, the IRGC sought to boost Iran's missile program and entrench forward defense.

In other words, the nuclear deal, far from a "cold peace," fueled a regional arms race. That escalated pressure on the JCPOA in Europe and the United States, leading them to virtually halt the lifting of sanctions as mandated by the deal. This, in turn, increased pressure on Rouhani and the JCPOA inside Iran.

●●●

Iran's economy got a boost from the deal. Between $50 and $56 billion of Iran's foreign reserves were released; the economy grew by 17 percent over three years, creating 3.5 million jobs.[47] Yet the deal's promised sanctions relief came haltingly, which made it difficult for Rouhani to sustain enough popular enthusiasm to push back against opponents of the deal. Under the barrage of criticism from hard-liners at home and the slow pace of sanctions removal as well as fresh demands on Iran curbing its regional activities and missile program, the exuberance that had followed the signing of the nuclear deal started to dissipate. Even some moderate voices who had supported Rouhani took to criticizing the deal because—unlike arms control deals, where the signatories take near-simultaneous reciprocal steps—the JCPOA demanded that Iran rapidly implement its side of the bargain, but the lifting of sanctions was not bound by the same schedule.

But the deal also had other gains for Iran. President Rouhani wrote that the goals before Iran in negotiating the JCPOA were to preserve Iran's nuclear program while ending the country's "securitization"—that is, prevent a concerted American-Israeli push to tighten the containment of Iran through cyber, economic, and psychological warfare.[48]

Zarif explained repeatedly that under the JCPOA, the United States abandoned the goal of zero enrichment of fissile material in Iran and had agreed that Iran would keep intact the core of its nuclear infrastructure, while also agreeing to abrogate UN resolutions that placed Iran under Chapter 7 status—the same status that Iraq had found itself and had paved the way for a UN-backed war to remove Saddam.[49] Whatever the merits of the deal, in the end it lacked resilience and proved too easily reversible.

US Withdrawal from the JCPOA and Maximum Pressure

During the presidential campaign of 2016, President Trump capitalized on the growing domestic criticism of the JCPOA—especially among Republicans who had long excoriated the deal—promising to undo it in favor of a stronger agreement. In May 2018, Trump fulfilled that promise, formally withdrawing from the JCPOA. He then proceeded to impose a plethora of draconian sanctions on Iran—the so-called maximum pressure strategy. During the following two years, the number of sanctions on Iran went from around 370 to over 1,500.[50] Iran quickly became the most economically sanctioned country in the world.[51] These actions were a serious threat to the Islamic Republic. Moreover, they posed such important strategic challenges that they remade how resistance and sacred defense was understood within Iran's politics.

Maximum pressure, the United States believed, would force Iran to negotiate a new nuclear deal; after all, Washington had concluded that it had been an escalation of sanctions by the Obama administration that had brought Iran to the table in 2013. But the United States also believed that this time it would force Iran to roll back forward defense and put its missile program on hold. In addition, the Trump administration had expected that Iran would quickly cave in. When skeptical European allies warned Washington about the consequences of scuttling the hard-fought 2015 deal, Washington's answer was that "it would be a matter of a few months before Iran would be crawling on its knees beg-ging for another deal."[52] Having witnessed economic protests sweep Iran in late 2017 and early 2018, Washington had concluded that the Islamic Republic was teetering on the verge of collapse, and scuttling the nuclear deal and adding economic pressure would hasten that end. The United States would then get more than a new deal; it would get a new regime.

The Islamic Republic, however, proved more resilient than Washing-ton had expected.[53] Iran's rulers quickly resolved to disabuse Washington of the expectation that just because sanctions had brought Iran to the table in 2013, more sanctions would not achieve the same result and more in 2018. Otherwise, American economic pressure would be un-ending, demanding more and more concessions through more and more sanctions.

For his part, Khamenei did not see maximum pressure as about a new nuclear deal but instead correctly as a strategy of regime change, and Secretary of State Mike Pompeo had signaled just that when he de-manded Iran fulfill twelve American demands, which extended far be-yond Iran's nuclear program.[54] When economic protests would erupt in Iran in 2019 and 2020, Iran's rulers would suspect an American hand. Pompeo fed this fear with statements such as, "[Iran's] leadership must make a decision that they want their people to eat. . . . I'm very confident the Iranian people will take a response that tries to fix that themselves as well."[55]

Given the threats inherent in what Khamenei identified as an "im-posed economic war" (*jang-e eqtesadi tahmili*), Iran realized it needed time to stabilize its economy and build leverage for future talks.[56] It could achieve those aims better if it stayed inside the JCPOA. This was an unexpected maneuver that immediately disrupted the Trump strat-egy. By staying inside the deal, Tehran denied Washington the argument that Iran was in violation of the nuclear deal and thus rally international support to roll back Iran's nuclear program, perhaps by military means.

Maximum pressure was a severe blow to Iran's economy, but it did not collapse.[57] The economy absorbed the shock.[58] Iran adopted strate-gies to circumvent sanctions. It continued to export oil, natural gas, and electricity to neighboring countries and for a time India. Most important, it continued to sell oil to China, managed enough access to trade, and shifted from imports to local production to keep the economy afloat.[59] Oil exports rose from 400,000 barrels a day at the outset of maximum pressure to 700,000 barrels a day in 2020.[60] This was still far lower than the 2.5 million barrels a day before maximum pressure was put in place, but was enough to sustain the economy. Iran cooperated with China, Russia, and other willing trade partners to go around financial sanctions, using currency swaps and even barter trade. Manufacturers who had relied on European capital and intermediary goods replaced trade ties with Europe with new ones with China.[61] That helped local manufacturers expand production to supplant some of the Western imports, but more important for the long run, it tied Iran's economy to a greater extent to China.[62] Scarcities abounded in the economy, causing more inflation and unemployment. Yet the economy did not go into a free fall, as maximum pressure had intended.

The turning point came in April 2019 when President Trump, frustrated that maximum pressure had not yet brought Iran to its knees, decided to further tighten sanctions on Iran. He announced that the United States was going to reduce Iran's exports to zero; this meant ending the waivers the United States had given a few countries to continue to buy Iranian oil while they looked for alternatives. Washington would also pressure China to end its purchase of Iranian oil. With this announcement, Iran decided to change strategy. Pressure would have to be met with pressure.

Iran reacted by declaring that it would resume high-level enrichment activity using advanced centrifuges to produce stockpiles of enriched uranium proscribed by the JCPOA—but it would remain in the deal. Tehran was also sending a signal to Washington that its economic pressure risked a major crisis. Trump might have thought that he could increase economic pressure on Iran without risking war. Iran was now determined to disabuse him of that halcyon assumption.

Meanwhile, Iran responded to what it construed as American economic warfare, backed by a shadow war waged by the United States and Israel—consisting of cyberattacks, sabotage, and assassinations as well as stoking popular unrest through media outlets targeting Iranians from the West—by strengthening the IRGC and extending its reach into society and the economy. The fingerprints of the Qods Force and IRGC's intelligence wing in decision-making manifested itself in more aggressive Iranian behavior in the region along with greater securitization of the public sphere.[63] To protect Iran from unending US pressure, the Islamic Republic decided to unleash forward defense.

In May 2019, four tankers were attacked off the coast of the UAE port of Fujairah in the Gulf of Oman.[64] Instability in the Persian Gulf would threaten the stability of energy markets and the global economy. The UAE and Saudi Arabia had supported US withdrawal from the JCPOA and sanctions on Iran. Iran also intended to warn its neighbors of the cost of supporting maximum pressure. The UAE's main urban centers are a mere hundred kilometers from the Iranian shores. They are in easy reach of Iranian missiles and drones, and that made the UAE's energy and tourism sectors vulnerable to Iran.

The Fujairah incident was followed by additional attacks on tankers in the Persian Gulf and an audacious downing of a US surveillance drone.[65] That act brought the United States close to military retaliation. According to President Trump, US fighter jets and missiles were ready to commence attacks on Iranian targets when he changed his mind.[66] The downing of the American drone showed both Iran's willingness and capability to escalate the crisis in ways that the United States had neither anticipated nor wished to see unfold.

With these attacks, Iran showed that it had crossed a Rubicon too. It had become more aggressive, risk taking, and dangerous, and willing to directly challenge US containment. The American response to Iranian aggression was further sanctions on Iran, to which Iran responded with further aggression. In September, Iranian drones and missiles carried out a sophisticated attack on oil facilities in Abqaiq and Khurais in eastern Saudi Arabia. The audacity of the attack, and Iran's technological prowess as well as ability to go around Saudi and American radars and air defense systems, caught Washington by surprise. Iran was again signaling that it was not going to passively endure sanctions but was also showcasing military capabilities that could prove deadly and that the United States may have not been aware of. In short, maximum pressure could lead to a war that could be more difficult and costly than the United States might have assumed.

In the impasse over the nuclear issue, Iran had embraced forward defense as a vital and primary means of protecting itself, adding a whole new dimension to the strategy. It was now put to the task of defending against American maximum pressure, using not just proxies on land but also naval attacks, employing sophisticated missiles and drones. Furthermore, these attacks were a direct challenge to the credibility of American containment as well as the spirit and letter of the Carter doctrine—which had committed the United States to the military defense of the Persian Gulf against urgent threats to global energy security and US interests there—and Trump's strategy of managing Iran's nuclear program.

Iran's decision to escalate regional tensions ultimately led to Trump's decision to have General Soleimani killed in January 2020. Trump's goal was to degrade Iran's regional military capacity, but also reestablish deterrence and restore containment's credibility.

Iran was shocked. The American escalation was unusual and audacious. It also showed a degree of risk taking on Trump's part that Tehran had not anticipated. Iran did not want to go to war, but it could not let Trump conclude that such an act would be cost free. Khamenei demanded maximum revenge, but not immediately. Iran would retaliate at a time of its choosing—and later identified several American officials responsible for the decision to kill Soleimani as targets for retribution. Khamenei, however, would seek to temper expectations, especially within the ranks of the IRGC, declaring that true revenge for Soleimani's killing—and a true guarantee for Iran's security—would be America's departure from the region.[67] Whereas Khomeini had sought to extricate the American presence in Iran, Khamenei was in effect expanding that goal to ending the US presence in the region.

Khamenei was nevertheless raising the bar for the country's national security too. Forward defense now had a larger goal before it: expelling the United States from the Middle East. The opening salvo, to show resolve, assuage domestic public opinion, and deter further US assassination attempts, was a ballistic missile attack on the Al-Asad base in Iraq.

■ ■ ■

Trump's withdrawal from the JCPOA, maximum pressure, and killing of Soleimani had a profound impact on Khamenei; it was a "paradigm shift in his thinking," to paraphrase observers who know him. Khamenei's distrust of the United States deepened, and his rhetoric become more strident and hard-hitting. His dark view of America and renewed determination to resist marks another pivotal formative experience in the Islamic Republic's understanding of security threats along with how to address them. He ushered the hard-line Paidari faction to the helm of power, reflecting his hardened resistance and rejection to engaging the United States. The faction quickly dominated key positions in the executive, legislature, and security forces.

In Rafsanjani's view, Khamenei's distrust had already been growing with experience since the 1990s.[68] In 2013, at the start of the nuclear negotiations, he told a gathering of senior officials the story of the Prophet standing alone to defend the young Muslim community before the second wave of enemy attack during the fabled Battle of Uhud in 625 AD. What he conveyed to his audience is that if there is a "second wave of attack" against Iran after the JCPOA, if need be, like the Prophet, Khamenei will stand before the enemy.[69] That second Western attack came in the form of Trump's withdrawal from the JCPOA and the imposition of maximum pressure on Iran. Khamenei then told a gathering of students, "As regards direct negotiations with the United States, it was my naivete, I should not have allowed it then, and I will not allow it now."[70] Here, he replicated the example of the Prophet at Uhud in standing up to the United States.

In 2003, when Libya agreed to dismantle its nuclear program in exchange for normalization of relations with the West, Khamenei had told a gathering of senior security officials that the decision was "foolish" and would be Mu'ammar Gaddhafi's "undoing."[71] That prediction, thought Khamenei, proved correct when the West intervened in Libya to topple his regime in 2011. Still, he set aside his instinct to approve nuclear negotiations with the West in 2013. After Trump left the nuclear deal, Khamenei concluded that he had been right all along. He would not repeat Gaddhafi's mistake. He has repeatedly lauded a 2020 law passed by hard-liners in the Parliament that mandates the government to match noncompliance by Western powers with the JCPOA with noncompliance on Iran's part—locking Iran into escalation.

The scale of Iran's confrontation with the United States since 2018 harked back to the dark days of the Iran-Iraq War when the Islamic Republic had to fight to the teeth for its survival. To survive this latest challenge, concluded Khamenei, Iran needed to rely on sacred defense along with its mindset, ideology, and those institutions that embodied its spirit. In that vein, Iran did not need Rouhani or Zarif but instead committed "revolutionaries" who see the world through the prism of sacred defense. Maximum pressure convinced hard-liners that there was no positive path forward with the United States; the Islamic Republic had to continue to rely on resistance and sacred defense, and it had to build its defense and deterrence capabilities in the form of a serious nuclear program, sophisticated missiles and drones, and entrenchment of forward defense.

Sanctions now posed an even graver national security threat to Iran as the United States' principal instrument of coercion against Iran. The US withdrawal from the JCPOA had proved to Khamenei that engagement would never remove this threat to Iran; the West would not remove sanctions after signing deals with Iran. It was pointless to expect that economic engagement with the West would provide for Iran's development needs. To the contrary, Iran had to develop and survive despite economic ties with the United States and Europe. It was then that he resolved on a "look East" policy, relying to a greater extent on China and Russia. He also redoubled his commitment to resistance, giving it clearer meaning as a national development strategy, touting the resistance economy as viable and necessary to national security.[72] If Iran had to choose between economic development and national security, it would choose national security. Talk of a resistance economy signaled that Iran was going to stand firm on its political position and was preparing itself for crushing economic pressure.

For Khamenei, the idea of a resistance economy went back to the Iran-Iraq War.[73] Khamenei had referred to the concept more frequently and with greater detail after Rouhani's election to the presidency.[74] It was a foil for Rouhani's argument that national security needed economic engagement with the West.[75] Toward the end of his presidency, in June 2020, Rouhani told a gathering at the Central Bank that "Iran's economic problems could not be solved without engaging the global economy," which justified his drive to negotiate the JCPOA. The same day, twenty-four economists—representing Khamenei's position—countered that "it is only by self-reliance and without sanctions relief that Iran's economy could be saved."[76]

It was little surprise, then, that Khamenei characterized maximum pressure as a blessing in disguise, forcing Iran to develop the means to survive independent of the international economic system. Sanctions have led Iran to produce an impressive array of consumer and advanced industrial goods at home. Iran even makes its own oil tankers. This degree of autarky is inefficient, especially since it has unfolded in tandem with corruption, mismanagement, and debilitating government control of the economy. Still, the United States had shown that being integrated into the global economy would make a country vulnerable to American pressure. Therefore surviving that pressure required surviving outside the global economy. And for a time, the strategy of a resistance economy even proved successful: the economy exceeded the goal of surviving to grow at the rate of 4.3 percent in 2020 and 3 percent in 2021.[77]

All of this showed a fundamental shift in Iran's position. Even if Iran agreed to fresh negotiations—as it did eventually in 2021—diplomacy would become more difficult. Iran would now try to calibrate what it gave up and how quickly to account for the US ability to reimpose sanctions.[78]

That would shift control over talks decidedly into the hands of those who had opposed the JCPOA and ties with the West.[79] The US withdrawal from the JCPOA was a nail in the coffin of Rafsanjani and his school of national security thinking in Iran. It weakened those who had favored diplomacy with the West among opinion makers, the business community, and the broader public. The driving force in Iranian society for change, opening the country and turning toward the West, had been the middle class.[80] Between 1990 and 2010, the size of the middle class had risen from 40 percent to half the population, and the size of the poorer classes had shrank from half the population to 20 percent.[81] Maximum pressure shrunk the Iranian middle class, reducing its economic importance and political influence.[82] The result was a hardening of the country's politics. The supreme leader—who had tacitly supported nuclear talks and endorsed the JCPOA—now distanced himself from Rouhani and the deal, saying that he had warned Rouhani all along.[83] Rouhani was increasingly seen as naive, and that it was a mistake for him to have trusted the United States. This would make it difficult for him to govern.

If in 2013 the supreme leader had concluded that moderates would do better in negotiating with the United States, he now resolved on the opposite. The moderates, he thought, had signed a weak deal with no enforceable safeguards and shown Iran to be weak before the West. That had led Trump to conclude that he could simply renegotiate the nuclear deal. Iran's goal now, Khamenei concluded, was to show the United States that Iran was not weak. It would not negotiate another deal; it would withstand American pressure and take steps to deter further American escalation. Intractable and antagonistic hard-liners would be better placed to achieve these goals. Furthermore, a cohesive control of all institutions of the state in the hands of proponents of resistance was necessary for the seamless implementation of the resistance economy.

Popular perception then was that the Rouhani government had failed. The JCPOA had come to naught, and his government had presided over an economic downturn—aggravated by the onset of the COVID-19 epidemic, which claimed Iran as one of its worst expressions early on and led to much popular disgruntlement with the Rouhani government—and increases in the debilitating environmental problems of pollution and water scarcity further weakened the moderates' position.[84]

It was in that context that in 2020, hard-line advocates of resistance took over Parliament, and then in June 2021, in a low turnout presidential election, Ebrahim Raisi won the presidency. Raisi was the hand-picked candidate of Khamenei and the supporters of resistance. A mid-ranking cleric and former judge, he rose through the ranks of the judicial bureaucracy thanks to his powerful father-in-law, who served as Friday prayer leader of Mashhad, and his ties to militant conservatives. All through his career, he had been an unknown with no political experience. The one notable item on his résumé was serving as one of the judges in 1989 who had ordered thousands of leftists to be executed, without due process, on Khomeini's orders. Ahead of the elections, Khamenei appointed Raisi as head of the judiciary—an important perch from which he could contest the elections. Hard-liners waged a propaganda war through the media, popular television shows, and harangues on the floor of Parliament. Throughout, they argued that Rouhani and the JCPOA were responsible for maximum pressure; diplomacy with the United States had been treasonous, only worsening sanctions and encouraging American assertiveness in the region; and that persisting in this path would only invite more American pressure.[85]

Rouhani had come to power in 2013 on the crest of popular optimism and now faced the brunt of popular dissatisfaction. With the outcome of the 2021 election, the marginalization of the moderates was complete. Even moderate and pragmatic conservatives found themselves on the outside.

Until his death in a helicopter crash in summer 2024, Raisi's administration—coupled with firm control of the hard-liners and advocates of resistance over the Parliament, judiciary, and Guardian Council—produced the uniformly hard-liner control of all branches of government that Khamenei wanted.[86] Raisi formed a cabinet of dedicated hard-liners; indeed, many in his inside coterie were close associates of Ahmadinejad and Jalili. These hard-liners replaced experts and technocrats in the bureaucracy in a throwback to the 1980s, when ideological commitment trumped expertise. In addition, a large number of cabinet posts and governorships of provinces as well as the management of state-owned enterprises went to former commanders of the IRGC, deepening its control over the state.

The American withdrawal from the JCPOA created a crisis of national security for Iran that favored expansion of the IRGC's control over the economy and politics.[87] Raisi's election and the shape of his government in effect indicated that Iran, for all practical purposes, was now in the grip of the IRGC serving the grand strategy of resistance.

Back to Nuclear Diplomacy

During the campaign for the 2020 presidential elections, President Biden indicated that he wished to restore the nuclear deal that his Democratic predecessor had signed. Once in office, however, Biden dithered. There were strong bipartisan headwinds in the Congress against restoring the deal. Key provisions of the deal would expire in 2023 while Biden was in office; the Trump years had squandered the time that the signatories of the deal had expected would provide opportunities for trust building and lay the foundation for follow-on deals. The criticisms of the JCPOA early on—that it did not deal with regional issues and Iran's missiles—were still haunting the deal.

Biden decided that the United States would countenance returning to the JCPOA only if Iran would agree to additional nuclear restrictions as well as the curtailment of its missile program and regional activities. In the words of Secretary of State Anthony Blinken, the United States was after "a longer and stronger deal." And then the United States would want to see full Iranian compliance with the JCPOA before it would rejoin. To solve this conundrum and get Iran to agree to additional restrictions, the Biden administration decided to keep maximum pressure in place.

Tehran concluded that Biden, much like Trump, thought that Iran was weak, and having cashiered its nuclear program in 2015, it had little leverage to resist American demands. Hard-liners argued that the United States was not interested in a deal, and it was pointless to negotiate; Iran should simply build up its nuclear program, and if need be, exit from the Treaty on the Non-Proliferation of Nuclear Weapons. It had been a mistake to negotiate in the first place, and it would be a mistake to negotiate again.

Others contended that while Iran had made mistakes in negotiating the JCPOA, Iran had to persevere. The lesson of the past was that a deal had been possible only after Iran built up its nuclear program between the failed 2003 deal with Europeans and start of the 2013 negotiations with P5 + 1. Iran had made a mistake going to the table too early and then implementing the JCPOA too fast. Its strategy should now be to build its program and then demand a "stronger and longer deal" of its own—one that lifted more sanctions and guaranteed there would be no repeat of the withdrawal of 2018.

This approach prevailed with Khamenei. Iran started to mount its own maximum pressure. Through spring 2021, Iran accelerated its enrichment activity at an alarming scale. It suspended the International Atomic Energy Agency's monitoring of nuclear sites and commenced enriching uranium, first up to 60 percent, saying it could push that limit to 90 percent.

Under the JCPOA, Iran was allowed only 202.8 kilograms of low-enriched uranium at 3.67 percent until 2031. By 2021, when the Biden administration assumed office, Iran had enriched around 2.5 tons of uranium, of which 114 kilograms were enriched to 20 percent and 18 kilograms to 60 percent.[88] By December 2023, Iran had over 5 tons of enriched uranium and was producing 9 kilograms of 60 percent enriched uranium per month.[89] Tehran had deployed advanced centrifuges in contravention to the JCPOA stipulations and hinted that it might leave the JCPOA altogether to pursue a more secretive nuclear program. Under the JCPOA, Iran was permitted to operate a limited cascade of first-generation centrifuges. By 2021, it was operating over 2,100, including more advanced second-generation centrifuges.[90] By 2023, that number had risen to 13,000, of which 5,800 were advanced centrifuges.[91]

The United States and Israel sought to slow the program through acts of sabotage at Iran's nuclear enrichment and centrifuge production facilities in Natanz and Karaj.[92] Israel also assassinated Iran's top nuclear scientist (and later other military officials and scientists), and carried out debilitating cyberattacks against industrial facilities as well as Iran's energy and electricity grids.[93] These were all done to warn the Islamic Republic and foment public discontent.[94]

These operations, however, did little to deter Tehran. In fact, the effect was the opposite. Iran rebuilt damaged facilities quickly and further accelerated its program.[95] Iran's breakout capacity—the time required to produce enough enriched fissile material for one bomb—started to shrink rapidly. It would soon get down to two weeks. And given the know-how Iranian scientists had gained and the infrastructure they had built in the process, the JCPOA restrictions would no longer be adequate to ensure that Iran remained two years away from breakout.[96]

It was after Iran flexed its muscles that the United States changed its position and agreed to engage in indirect talks in Vienna in 2021 to fully restore the JCPOA. It now faced an even more distrustful and adamant Iran—one that had now fully subscribed to the idea that only an aggressive posture with the United States would yield results and the Islamic Republic's interests lay in doubling down on resistance.

After months of negotiations, Iran decided not to sign a new deal with the United States. The issue was not the terms that were on the table in August 2022 but instead Iran's worry that the United States would not implement what it signed. To get these guarantees, Iran needed to persuade Washington with an even larger nuclear program to negotiate with.

Maximum Pressure's New Allies

Maximum pressure widened the gulf between Iran and the West, and that in turn accelerated Iran's reliance on Russia and China.[97] Iran saw Russia and China as larger powers than they were. The impression of China's unending meteoric economic growth, ultimately supplanting the United States as the world's largest economy, gave Iran's rulers the impression that they were betting on the right horse.[98] Iran needed China and Russia to fend off Western pressure in international organizations, but also to compensate for the loss of trade with the West and drop in its oil exports.

Iran now saw that its strategic interests rested with China and Russia, great powers that were also at odds with the American-led international liberal order.[99] China and Russia too saw themselves as historic nations deserving of global standing and influence in their own regions, which ran counter to what they construed as American hegemony.[100] The three countries saw advantage in banding together. In Tehran's rendering, Beijing and Moscow had backed Iran at critical junctures at the United Nations, within the JCPOA, through trade circumventing economic sanctions. While China's ties with Iran were economic, Iran's ties with Russia were anchored in a security relationship that was forged during the Syrian War. After 2018, a growing number of think tanks and media outlets, associated with proresistance politicians, the IRGC and supreme leader's office promoted the idea of "turning East" and imagining an "Axis of Resistance"—this one between the three Eurasian powers—as the preferred strategic option for Iran. The belief in the viability of such an axis, and that Iran needed a strategic depth in the East to confront the West, influenced how Iran reacted first to maximum pressure and then to nuclear talks in Vienna.[101]

The belief that China and Russia too shared Iran's antagonism toward the West allowed advocates of resistance to imagine that Iran was not alone, and that its vision of resistance could triumph. Tehran saw China expand its reach into the South China Sea, tighten its control over Hong Kong, and reassert its claim to Taiwan, viewing the United States as the obstacle to the realization of its goals. Russia saw America and its European allies encroaching on Russia's sphere of influence, seeking to free Ukraine, Belarus, and Caucasus from Russian influence, integrating them into the European Union and bringing NATO to Russia's borders.

Antagonism toward the United States did create a convergence of interests. Particularly in Central Asia, all three banded together to keep the American influence in the region to a minimum, and to that end, Iran started the accession process to join the China and Russian-led Shanghai Cooperation Organization in 2021. There were also joint naval maneuvers between China, Iran, and Russia starting in January 2021 in a signal of closer strategic ties.[102] These steps toward greater coordination and cooperation between the three powers were notable.[103]

Iran, however, read more into this convergence than did China and Russia, and especially that there was a three-sum Axis of Resistance. Russia and Iran did forge deeper strategic ties. But although relations with China remained deep, these did not reflect a mutual understanding of the world order and how to resist the United States.[104] As such, despite Iran's insistence to the contrary, relations with China remained largely economic and transactional.

Still, China saw Iran as an important actor. As China's own relations with the United States grew fraught, Iran's independence from American influence was a notable advantage. Iran's geography alone made it important to China's Belt and Road Initiative, interest in West Asia, and the hope to create a Eurasian sphere of economic influence for China.[105] Iran was also a large market as a country rich in energy and mineral resources, and free of Western economic ties. China had long taken advantage of the sanctions regime on Iran to buy cheap Iranian oil and build trade ties with Iran's beleaguered industries. It built railways as well as managed oil and gas fields and petrochemical facilities. Chinese companies provided Iranian businesses with capital and intermediary goods, and a circuitous access to world markets.

It was to build on these ties that the two countries at one point contemplated forging a strategic partnership that would entail upward of $450 billion in Chinese investment in Iran.[106] Khamenei even charged Ali Larijani, a senior foreign policy hand and former speaker of Parliament, to lead this effort, coordinating between various government institutions to come up with an assessment of Iran's infrastructure and development needs and projects that should form the core of the partnership.[107]

The partnership was not signed as expected. Despite its interest in deeper ties with China, Iran was still wary of being controlled by Beijing once it owed China for its investments in Iran. The Rouhani government along with dissenting voices in the foreign policy establishment and the press argued that it was premature to throw Iran's economic lot in with China when Iran was negotiating to restore the JCPOA. The survival of that deal needed the United States and Europe to build economic ties with Iran, and not see its economy as a Chinese sphere of influence.

For China, too, there were reasons to pause. The escalation of tensions between Iran and the United States meant that a sizable deal with Iran would further complicate US-China relations. Unless the JCPOA was restored and some sanctions were lifted on Iran, most Chinese companies could not operate in Iran. As hopes for restoration of the JCPOA faded, China warned Iran that so long as Iran's economy remained closed to the world and its banks remained outside the global financial network, China could not see economic benefit in a strategic partnership.[108]

For China, there was also the problem of balancing its burgeoning ties with Iran with its deepening economic interest in Saudi Arabia and the UAE. Saudi Arabia is China's largest energy supplier. Chinese companies are keenly interested in business and investment opportunities in the Persian Gulf's wealthy Arab monarchies, and those countries have in turn heavily invested in China. Their influence with Beijing has tempered its enthusiasm for moving ahead with a deeper partnership with Iran. This became clear during the Arab-China States Summit in Saudi Arabia in December 2022 when President Xi Jinping shocked and irritated Tehran by joining his hosts in statements that demanded Iran cooperate with the International Atomic Agency, desist from interfering in the region, and even resolve the status of the three Iranian islands the Shah took back from the UAE in the 1970s through diplomacy. To Iran's dismay, Russia too would soon issue a similar statement.

Iran had clearly read too much into its relations with China's, and Beijing's, commitment to an axis with Russia and Iran. The Chinese were showing unhappiness with the unchecked application of forward defense. In March 2023, they would use their leverage with hard-liners in Tehran to broker a détente between Iran and Saudi Arabia. Iran agreed to help bring the war in Yemen to an end—in effect, reining in one of forward defense's projects—in exchange for sustaining ties with China and reducing Arab animus.

Forward defense had forged Iran's strategic ties with Russia, but it was a point of contention in its strategic partnership with China. It has always been viewed as a threat by Iran's Arab rivals. Maximum pressure and Iran's determination to resist American pressure had only underscored that threat, and now China was pushing back against forward defense. Whereas ties with China had been favored by a broader spectrum of foreign policy and economic power centers in Iran, relations with Russia had been the focus of the IRGC.

Russia's assault on Ukraine in 2022 put to question its viability as a strategic depth for Iran in the long run. Although Iranian-Russian military cooperation deepened during the war, it was clear that the war would greatly diminish Russia's strategic and economic capacity. Sanctions on the Russian economy, and the poor performance of its military on the battlefield—to the extent that it needed Iranian weapons supplies—had weakened Russia's international standing and diplomatic clout on the world stage. Collaboration with Russia would not bring lasting relief but rather invite greater Western pressure. This was a serious challenge for Khamenei's assumption that Iran could easily seek strategic depth in an Axis of Resistance. Instead of an axis, relations with Russia and China were proving a balancing act, which extended to managing different opinions and interests inside Iran.

Nuclear Conclusions

Iran and the United States negotiated indirectly—along with other member of P5 + 1—for several months in Vienna. In August 2022, they arrived at a final agreement on the steps Iran would take to fully comply with the JCPOA and the sanctions the United States would lift in return. In the final hour, Iran dithered.

The country's leadership remained deeply suspicious of US intentions—that Washington might sign but not implement the agreement, which would politically damage the Raisi government. The hardliners who now ran the country did not want to restore a deal they had characterized as treason when Rouhani had concluded it. They had decided that the JCPOA had been a way in which the United States would compel Iran to live under containment in exchange for modest sanctions relief, and that going back to the JCPOA would only entrench the containment of Iran. If Iran did not want containment—and as Khamenei had said, wished the United States to leave the region—then Iran should not seek to revive the JCPOA or abide with any regional conversation that seeks to rein in forward defense. Iran would instead look to limited transactional agreements to barter narrow concessions on its nuclear program for commensurate but concrete sanctions relief. A comprehensive international deal like the JCPOA will be both difficult and risky—it could be once again reversed, yielding little benefit to Iran.

By 2022, Iran had moved further into the fold of resistance and sacred defense.[109] Maximum pressure had battered its economy, transformed its society, and hardened its politics. Just as eight years of the Iran-Iraq

War shaped the strategic culture of the Islamic Republic, so did the four years of maximum pressure reinforce the lessons of that war: that Iran could not trust international agreements, and it was alone in facing threats. Survival, as in the 1980s, demanded self-reliance, ideological vigilance, and sacred defense.

The Gaza war along with the escalation of tensions between Iran and Israel during that war, and the prospect of direct confrontation between the two, reinforced this outlook. Israel's role in undoing the JCPOA, the growing audacity of its acts of sabotage, assassination of Iranian scientists and security officials—as well as Iran's regional allies—and support for regime change and separatism has elevated Israel into Iran's main regional adversary. Iran's enmity toward Israel is no longer limited to the Palestinian issue but reflects a fundamental shift in outlook: the principal threat to Iran from the region comes no longer from the Arab world but from Israel, and it stems from Israel's desire to be the sole power in the Middle East. Having defanged the Arab world, and enjoying iron-clad American diplomatic and military support, Israel has now set its sights on Iran. Their rivalry is now a great power competition for regional supremacy—which both cofirms and complicates Iran's regional posture against the United States. Iran sees Israel as an instrument of US Middle East policy, and believes the Israeli position in the region and against Iran is only possible with America's backing. The rivalry against Israel is a new stage in Iran's decades-long resistance to the United States. The escalation of tensions between Iran and Israel thus gives forward defense and the nuclear program greater strategic significance.

Iran has therefore responded to the increased American and Israeli threats, especially after Israel's concerted attacks against Hezbollah in October 2024 and threatening Iran's own territory militarily, by signaling that it was prepared to change its stated position—and set aside Khamenei's fatwa—to build nuclear weapons.[110] That shift would also protect what Iran has perceived as the shift in the balance of power in the region in its favor against American and Israeli efforts to reverse it. Nuclear capability will not be a substitute for forward defense but rather protect and augment its strategic utility to Iran.

CHAPTER 11

The Price of Resistance

The impact of maximum pressure on Iranian society and the economy cannot be overstated.[1] Over a five-year period, between 2018 and 2022, Iran's economy contracted by 7.3 percent and its per capita income by 14 percent, poverty rose by 11 percent, and the average living standards fell by 13 percent (although between 2021 and 2023, this number improved).[2] The rial collapsed in value as inflation ravaged the economy. Food prices rose by 186 percent and health care by 125 percent.[3] As disposable income shrank, Iranians spent 30 percent less on education and 32 percent less on entertainment. In 2017, 45 percent of Iranians could be considered middle class; by 2020, that number had fallen to 30 percent— where it remains.[4] With sanctions in place, the economic downturn became ongoing and continues to impact all aspects of Iranian society today.[5] In tandem, the size of the black market economy expanded, and networks of businesspeople, influential politicians, and institutions dominated by current and former IRGC commanders proliferated, aggravating corruption and income inequality on an unprecedented scale.[6]

These trends gave hard-line political and intellectual leaders along with the constellation of institutions that support sacred defense and resistance broad leeway to engineer a takeover of the country. In the populace's mind, however, dire economic conditions and spiraling corruption sparked questions about the national security outlook that had brought Iran to this point.

Hard-liners have blamed the country's isolation on American aggression. They have argued that Iranians must resist that pressure valiantly, and in the name of justice and the national interest. Many Iranians have been shocked by Israel's brutal war in Gaza and sympathize with the leadership's argument that Iran must protect itself against a similar assault. Yet more and more Iranians are unhappy with the high cost they must pay for valiant resistance. They think more compromise rather than unbending resistance and obduracy ought to guide the national interest.

Until August 2022, many Iranians still faulted Trump for wrecking the JCPOA. But after Iran failed to sign a new deal, they started to question the wisdom of the die-hard supporters of resistance. The culprit behind their hardship was no longer just Trump but also the Islamic Republic's national security outlook.

In summer 2022, Raisi was reluctant to sign a deal with the United States, only to be embarrassed by yet another American withdrawal down the line or American failure to implement the deal; he would then stand accused of the same naivete as Rouhani. His coterie of hard-liners who had all along opposed nuclear talks with the United States did not want to be the ones who ushered Iran into the deal, which they had not long before characterized as treasonous. Iran needed the benefits of a restored deal, but Raisi's government saw the political cost as more than the economic benefit. Moreover, these leaders remained firmly attached to the idea that the national interest rested with the resistance economy, and a restored deal would divert attention from that imperative.

For most Iranians, the lofty idea of a resistance economy fell far short of its goals in practice. Western sanctions were too effective for Iran to contend with over time. They had "hollowed the bones of Iranians," in Rafsanjani's words.[7] Forward defense had certainly succeeded in deterring an American war on Iran and neutralizing Iraq. But its continued application incurred costs in the form of economic retrenchment and poverty, public apathy, and anger, which the Islamic Republic cannot easily ignore.

Over the decades, the imperative of resistance has augmented the IRGC's reach into the economy and state institutions. Heightened security has given its guardians broad scope to interpret what it means and what is needed to realize it. During the Ahmadinejad presidency, the IRGC increasingly looked to use its perch in the economy to extract resources in support of its various projects. This trend accelerated apace with the growing impact of sanctions on the national budget, especially after the United States imposed maximum pressure on Iran in 2018. The Raisi government increased the number of IRGC seats in the cabinet and appointed over a dozen governors to lead provinces with direct access to their budgets. The result has been to aggravate corruption and economic mismanagement, and worst of all, decisively put Iran's economy in the grip of extraction.

Development may still be the espoused goal. In practice, though, resistance is condemning the economy to the opposite. The 2020s are not the 1980s. Far from rallying to support resistance, a growing segment of the Iranian public has become angry, tired of resistance, dubious about its logic, and disenchanted with those who have advocated it. Ascenting to hard-liners takeover of government under Raisi proved to be a costly overreach. It no longer matters whether the theory behind resistance is flawed or hard-liners also proved incompetent in implementing it.[8] Their failure despite uniform control of all levers of power could simply become an inflection point.

The fundamental national security logic of the Islamic Republic and dominant strategic culture of its ruling elite has reached its apogee, and now it is losing the population. Iranians understand only too well the impact on their lives of the trade-off between resistance and economic prosperity. Khamenei believes that Iran will weather what his accolytes have termed a "hard winter" of economic hardship, and will soon be triumphant in defying the United States and then development will flow without hinderance. "The peak is near," he advises, "we must not tire at this last push to the top."[9] For many Iranians, however, the emperor has no clothes; the Islamic Republic is losing its public. Its insistence on resistance and confrontation with the United States has reached its limit of popular support. The population has grown apathetic. Participation in national elections, always hailed as a symbol of legitimacy and popular support for the Islamic Republic, has declined precipitously in tandem with the consolidation of power in the hard-liners' hands. Only 48 percent of eligible voters cast their ballots in the 2021 presidential elections that brought Raisi to power. That was a record-low turnout in presidential elections going back to 1979—then the 2024 parliamentary elections registered the lowest turnout of any national election since the revolution, 40.6 percent (and as low as 11 percent in the capital city of Tehran).

The Islamic Republic would face its most serious public rebuke to date in fall 2022, when an uprising revolted against the political and economic structures that have evolved in the shadow of sacred defense and resistance—the state that national security has built.

The 2022 Protests

One issue the Raisi government was vigilant about soon after it took office was reinforcing morality rules, women's dress, and observance of the hijab, to be specific. With conservative voices firmly in charge, during Raisi's first year in office, morality police roamed the streets, mostly in small towns and less affluent parts of major cities, looking for women with lax head coverings.[10] Those rounded up were fined and forced to attend morality classes. Iran was reeling from economic pain, and disappointed in Raisi's election as well as the dimming prospect for a nuclear deal and sanctions relief. Many Iranians with access to satellite TV and social media had been imbibing exile outlets' searing criticisms of the Islamic Republic, especially while sheltering in place during the COVID-19 pandemic. The enforcement of morality rules at a time of anger and despondency was like throwing a lit match onto dry hay.[11]

That was exactly what happened when Mahsa Amini, a twenty-two-year-old woman, died of head injuries that she had incurred during her arrest by the morality police. The brutality of the police—which exemplified how the security forces dealt with the population as a whole—and the circumstances and reason for her death—her observance of the hijab—incensed Iranians and exploded in widespread protests across the country.

Moreover, Amini hailed from Iran's Kurdish region, and her kinfolk were on the forefront of the protests. This added Kurdish grievances to the broader issues of enforcement of morality and police brutality that surrounded her death.

The protests were initially led by women, mostly in their teenage years—the so-called Generation Z (*daheh-e hashtadiha*), or those born between 2000 and 2010. The youths on the streets were not protesting a specific political grievance (as in 2009) or economic hardships (as in 2018 or 2020). This time, the protesters were demanding individual freedoms, flouting the Islamic Republic's policing of what they wear and what they do. In other words, they were defying the enforcement of the foundation of the state's ideology, which was integral to its vision of sacred defense.[12]

The protesters adopted the slogan "woman, life, freedom" (*zan, zendegi, azadi*), demanding individual freedoms and rights. The simple and yet all-encompassing call for women's rights, better lives, and freedoms challenged how hard-liners had imagined organizing the economy and politics to confront security threats as well as realize the Islamic Republic's ambitions. As Raisi's father-in-law, Ayatollah Ahmad Alamolhoda, the Friday prayer leader of Mashhad, put it, "If flaunting the hijab becomes ubiquitous, leading to degeneration of morality and sexual freedoms, then the youths who ought to become religious warriors [as in, those who fought in the Iran-Iraq War] will become libertines."[13]

The rage and fearlessness of the protests caught the leaders of the Islamic Republic by surprise. It was clear that the Islamic Republic, despite all of its investment in promoting sacred defense and the imperative of resistance to outside aggression in service of protecting national security, had lost its youths. The young did not want any of what the Islamic Republic peddled. They wanted individual and social freedoms, anchored in secular Western norms. There was broad sympathy for the fearless youths on the streets. Most Iranians did not see the point of enforcing morality and brutalizing young people in the process. They also wanted better economic conditions, which meant flexibility in nuclear negotiations and greater integration into the world economy in lieu of perpetual resistance.

Even those who counted themselves in the ambit of the Islamic Republic joined the chorus of criticism. Women who observed the hijab, whose families were loyal to the Islamic Republic, privately decried the excesses of the morality police and opposed any forceful crackdown on teenagers on the streets. They also echoed the underlying feminist demands of the protesters, arguing that the problem in the Islamic Republic was not just hijab but rather the entire patriarchal social and legal structures that governed family law, labor relations, and the access of women to jobs and services.[14]

Iran's women are highly educated, constituting most university students, including in science, technology, engineering, and mathematics at elite technical universities. They have adopted modern values, whether they observe hijab or not, such as contraception, gender equality, and women's rights. This has its roots in the Pahlavi period's women's emancipation and investment in their literacy and upward mobility as well as in the family planning and social welfare programs of the Islamic Republic after the Iran-Iraq War. Still, despite the social revolution that has unfolded in Iran over several decades, women are grossly underrepresented in leadership roles in politics and management of the public sector in Iran, and the country's laws openly discriminate against them.

Women who wear the hijab, young and old, saw their own desire for an end to the entire patriarchal system reflected in the protesters call for "woman, life, freedom." The Islamic Republic was not only facing the anger of Generation Z but also the political awakening of a much larger segment of its population, including those who counted themselves as religious and accepting of the Islamic Republic. They did not join the protests, but the shift in their attitudes was important. Dissent toward social strictures and foreign policy became pervasive in media and social media.

The images of young women standing up to the Islamic Republic, rejecting the hijab, and demanding rights quickly captured the imagination of public opinion around the globe, turning the protests into a referendum on the Islamic Republic to the outside world. Calls for women's freedoms evolved into chants of "death to dictator [Khamenei]" and calls for democracy in Iran. The daily spectacle of Iranian people rejecting the underlying values of the Islamic Republic along with its insistence on ideological vigilance in the name of resistance and security was deeply embarrassing and disturbing to state leaders. It worried them that their adversaries would see their hold on power slipping and seek to take advantage of their moment of weakness to pressure Iran to compromise on its nuclear program as well as shrink its footprint in the Middle East.

Although protests erupted in many parts of Iran, however, they ultimately remained small and limited to Generation Z. They were ongoing on almost a daily basis, and drew sympathy and support across social classes, but the political consciousness they fostered did not translate into the kind of mass mobilization and crowd size that had rattled the Islamic Republic in 2009. This owed to several factors. The message of the protests was powerful, but they lacked leadership and a clear plan for what they would achieve if they were to succeed. Iranians were unhappy with their lot, yet did not see how young protesters would change that for the better. The Islamic Republic was quick to plant seeds of doubt through its propaganda outlets, arguing that whatever the gripe of the population, people should worry that Iran could be heading toward Syria's fate.[15] One IRGC commander taunted the protesters, saying, "Those who take off their scarves in the street should know that 'four' people taking off their scarves does not endanger the Islamic Republic. They saw how Christian and Yezidi women were sold in Iraq [by ISIS]. If there is no security for Iran, you will be sold as well."[16] He was drawing a parallel between what the protesters were doing in Tehran and the Arab Spring in the Levant: the end would be Syria and ISIS.

Yet it is illuminating that even this commander did not defend hijab on religious grounds. Instead, he denounced the protests on national security grounds, suggesting that the IRGC's priority was security. A former IRGC commander and a hero of the Iran-Iraq War went further, telling a Friday prayer leader of Tehran, "We will not sell our honor for your survival," again suggesting that the IRGC was not keen on defending ideology for ideology's sake.[17] Rather, the IRGC's mission and vision was security, and ideology mattered only if it supported that cause.

The protesters were unimpressed by what they saw as the ruling elite's security fearmongering. In response to the government's assertion that the IRGC had protected Iran from ISIS and that danger still threatened Iran's interests, protesters chanted, "You [Khamenei] are our Daesh [ISIS]." Still, fear of chaos and a fate like that of Syria, the Islamic Republic concluded, would hold back the older generation from joining its children on the streets, as would fear of the economic consequences of prolonged protests for a population already struggling to make ends meet.

This was a consequence of the sanctions. Maximum pressure had dissipated the ranks of the middle class, sapped many Iranians of their disposable income and savings, made businesses more dependent on the IRGC for access to goods, services, and finances, and made a staggering 75 percent of the population dependent on some form of government handout.[18] The fruits of the sanctions were in sharp contrast to 1979, when flush with savings and financial resources, Iranians could afford prolonged strikes and business shutdowns without worrying about how to make ends meet. Not only did many Iranians have reason to worry about any disruptions to daily economic activities, but many of them relied on the government for their livelihood, which dampened their enthusiasm to rock the boat or find themselves in the crosshairs of the law.[19]

Some of the largest protests and bloodiest crackdowns came in the ethnic minority regions of Baluchistan in Iran's southeast and Kurdish provinces to the west. Although protesters across Iran did not distinguish between what was happening in major urban areas and the ethnic minority regions, the age-old Iranian fear of the disintegration of the country was too powerful to ignore and helped the Islamic Republic to argue that Iran's foreign enemies were encouraging secessionist forces, thereby dissuading larger numbers of people from joining the protests for fear of breaking up the country.

Khamenei early on decided not to make any concessions to the protesters—characterizing them as tools of foreign enemies. Even when acknowledging that the protests reflected genuine popular anger at the situation in the country, the deep state was convinced that there was a concerted effort afoot to weaken the Islamic Republic, force it to make deep concessions on nuclear, military, and strategic issues, and hasten its demise. The security forces and media associated with them claimed with increasing frequency that Iran was subject to "hybrid warfare."[20] This offensive, went the argument, involved economic sanctions, cyber tools, sabotage, and assassination campaigns, stoking ethnic tensions and funding dissident groups abroad, and the use of media and social media to foment an uprising in Iran while isolating the country internationally.

In a detailed address that predated the protests, Khamenei had commanded the country to counter hybrid warfare with hybrid resistance, employing similar tools to the ones used against Iran: media, social media, and cyber and military tools (such as supplying drones to Russia) to thwart outside pressure.[21] Khamenei pointed the finger of blame at the United States, European states, Israel, and Saudi Arabia. This meant that the response to the protests was not only a domestic political matter but also required mobilizing the country's defenses: doubling down on resistance and employing the kind of security strategies that the Islamic Republic had hitherto relied on.[22]

Still, there had been momentous change in the outlook and attitude of Iranians—one that opened a deep chasm between the leadership and the people, and would inevitably have ramifications for Iran's future. Many among the political class, across the spectrum, understood the legitimacy crisis that the protests had engendered. Even if Iran was under assault, the success of that campaign owed to popular unrest. Combating hybrid warfare demanded addressing discontent at home. Hard-liners, moderate conservatives, and reformists all criticized the political and social malaise ailing the country as well as the state of its faltering economy. The criticisms and calls for remedies did not endorse or discount hybrid warfare but instead leveled a significant challenge to Khamenei and ardent advocates of resistance. The critics argued that the reasons for popular anger were the mismanagement by the Raisi government, failure to sign the nuclear deal, steady collapse of the rial, total control of all levers of power by hard-liners, and dangerous narrowing of the political representation in the management of the country.

Even doyens of the conservative establishment—former speaker of Parliament Ali Larijani along with sitting minister of culture and tourism and former IRGC commander Ezatollah Zarghami—criticized the forcible enforcement of the veil. Larijani cited official statistics to say that the majority of women favored *voluntary* observation of the veil and the Islamic Republic should embrace that.[23] Zarghami asked facetiously in a tweet, "If people don't wish to be forcibly made to abide by religious tenets, who should they see?"[24] Even senior clerics in Qom, hearing concerns from their constituents and worried about the popular anger directed at them—which manifested in the killing of a senior cleric at a bank, and daily harassment of petty clerics and seminarians on the streets, the most visible manifestation of which was knocking turbans off the head of clerics—voiced their fears. They see daily the palpable decline in religious observance, especially among the disgruntled youths. The wages of resistance is being paid in growing secularism. Ayatollah Sistani broke his silence from his perch in Najaf to lament that his counsel had gone unheard.[25] Ayatollah Naser Makarem Shirazi, a senior cleric in Qom, said that the incompetent people responsible for the deteriorating economic conditions should be removed from power.[26] Even those counted in the resistance camp criticized the ruling establishment.[27] Hossein Qadayani, an influential hard-line columnist, stirred a controversy blaming the crisis facing the Islamic Republic on the incompetence of "super revolutionaries," a veiled reference to the cabal of hard-liners in Raisi's government.[28]

These criticisms reflected debates in the halls of power, within Khamenei's circle and the IRGC as well as between those running key institutions of the Islamic Republic. At issue was whether to blame the incompetence on the Raisi government, or that maximum pressure had finally succeeded in creating a chasm between the tired and angry population and the leadership still pursuing resistance. Was resistance even viable given the popular rejection of sacred defense and the Islamic Republic's vision of national security along with the free fall of the country's economy? Political dissent was growing, but equally alarming, so was secularism and a cultural sphere that sits astride and defies the one that the Islamic Republic stands for. Should the Islamic Republic crack down on its opposition and persevere? Or should it open the halls of power to a broader cross section of political opinion—in other words, abandon the idea of uniform control of the state by hard-liners in favor of inclusiveness and pragmatism, backing away from intransigeance on the nuclear issue and forward defense?

Moderate and reformist figures, former presidents Khatami and Rou-hani, scions of Khomeini and Rafsanjani families who have cast them-selves as advocates of pragmatic change as well as Ali Larijani, who represents the moderate wing of conservatives, have advocated pragma-tism and compromise. On the danger of the rift opening between pro-testers and state leaders, Khatami said, "We must not allow freedom to confront security, and as a result, freedom be trampled on in the name of security. . . . [Iran's history] is marked by a national movement against dictatorship, imperialism, backwardness, discrimination, corruption, and in tandem, demand for freedom, independence, development, jus-tice, and 'life' in keeping with human dignity."[29] Similar sentiments were echoed by influential voices within the ruling order. Former IRGC com-manders and war veterans, Vice President Mohsen Rezaie (commander of the IRGC during the war), Mohammad Baqer Qalibaf (speaker of Parliament), and Ali Shamkhani (secretary of the Supreme National Security Council) argued that the protests had shown that the Islamic Republic could not continue with unyielding resistance and under the leadership of hard-liners, and led the charge to compel pragmatic changes.[30] The three are influential in the IRGC (Rezaie is a former commander in chief, and Qalibaf enjoys broad respect and popularity in the force) as well as with the supreme leader and important constitu-encies in state institutions, the economy, and the clerical elite in Qom.

All of these voices—reformists, moderates, and IRGC pragmatists along with their like-minded politicians and bureaucrats—share a com-mon position on the need for change. They have looked to join hands to present the Islamic Republic with a viable way forward.

Resistance had reached its limit, protesters wanted it gone, and even critics within the ambit of the Islamic Republic wanted it tempered. The state that national security built had once again, as in 1979, found the population to be its Achilles' heel.

Zarif adroitly took to task Khamenei's grand strategy of resistance in its entirety, arguing in veiled terms that it was ill-conceived and failed to match Iran's goals to its resources as any good strategy should. "Throughout our history, we have defined our goals in terms of our as-pirations without regard for our capabilities and resources. . . . [The effects] are not only reflected in our foreign policy but in the long line of cars sitting in traffic before narrow tunnels [too]."[31] At question is not only whether Iran can continue to afford the cost of confronting and resisting the United States but also whether resistance could exist with or serve as the means for the realization of Iran's national goals of development. Zarif was echoing a growing sentiment among Iranians that in effect harked back to Amir Kabir, the Pahlavi era, and the Rafsanjani and Khatami periods—what the JCPOA was supposed to push Iran toward—to advocate a different grand strategy for Iran—one that anchored nationalism and security in returning to economic development and improved relations with the West, which would then garner greater popular support for the state.

This call for course correction has found greater poignancy as Iranians look to the examples of Saudi Arabia and United Arab Emirates' bold economic visions, and their investments in infrastructure, new technologies, and trade corridors. The kind of unity of purpose as well as the close bond between state and society that Iran experienced during its war with Iraq would be possible only under a different grand strategy, and by the same token, the current strategy of resistance is not sustainable absent popular support.

Khamenei, however, has remained defiant. He rather sees his conception of resistance as a continuation of sacred defense—itself successful in that it has ensured the survival of the Islamic Republic in its first decade.[32] That success continued to ensure Iran's independence from the United States in the following decades and then contributed to America's decision to leave the Middle East. Khamenei is convinced that Iran has contributed to curtailing US global hegemony and ending its unipolar moment, and as he has boasted, preventing another "engineering" of the map of the Middle East as happened after World War I.[33]

In private meetings, he alludes to Arab states' disappointment with America's decision to reduce its involvement in the Middle East—which in turn has opened the door to their rapprochement with Iran. That, he contends, was achieved by resistance. Furthermore, he asserts that China and Russia made the mistake of buying into the promise of globalization and the international liberal order. America soon turned against them. They too, he argues, will have to embrace resistance.[34] Similarly, he sees the war in Gaza, attesting to the power of resistance, as having inflicted a decisive blow to the United States. That strategic fiasco, thinks Khamenei, will weaken America's position in the Middle East and bring Iran closer to achieving its goals. He is not about to abandon the values that have made sacred defense possible and on which he based his grand strategy of resistance.

The protests too seem to have convinced him of his own wisdom: that the West is after regime change and an Iran that would be subservient to Western demands. The more a country is open to Western economic and cultural influence, the more vulnerable it is to Western machinations. Iran had allowed too much of Western ideas into its society and grown too lax in protecting itself—and even contemplated opening to the West with the JCPOA—and that accounted for the protests that it was facing. Khamenei saw a similar line of thinking in Putin's rants against the West and decision to invade Ukraine. Nor was he sufficiently rattled by the protests to countenance real change. The protests were serious, but never grew into a veritable mass movement. And soon after they abated, Iran normalized relations with Saudi Arabia, joined the international forums Shanghai Cooperation Organization and BRICS, and even achieved a temporary understanding with the United States to de-escalate tensions between the two countries. Still, the grand strategy of resistance no longer enjoys unwavering popular support, nor is its wisdom apparent to the political elite outside the ruling circle. And this trend is unlikely to be reversed.

. . .

In the aftermath of the protests, the Islamic Republic is no longer a state rooted in Khomeini's conception of velayat-e faqih (imperative of rule by the supreme jurisconsult or cleric), but in resistance. Khamenei no longer sees the power and legitimacy of the state in being ruled by the clerical hierarchy, with the supreme cleric at its apex. Instead, he understands the legitimacy of the state to be grounded in a security-minded system, dominated by the IRGC, and overseen by a unique leader with the right mix of knowledge of religion and modern statecraft.

Khamenei sees himself as a turbaned commander in chief: a political leader in a religious garb who commands a state dominated by security forces. In controversial comments in a meeting with Soleimani's family in January 2024, Khamenei reminisced about an intimate meeting with IRGC commanders, during which he spoke warmly to the commanders, feeling that it was God who was speaking to the officers with words that flowed from his mouth.[35] That he claimed that God spoke to him, showed that Khamenei does indeed see himself as a unique figure, above all other clerics or political actors. Nevertheless, that the time God spoke through him was when he was with IRGC commanders—as opposed to fellow clerics, for instance—demonstrated the unique way in which he sees himself as bonded with the IRGC, and as their supreme commander, and sees the IRGC as favored by God.

This view of his own role—and that of a future supreme leader—has led to widespread speculation that Khamenei could conceive of his son, Mojtaba, as his own successor. Mojtaba has completed his seminary education, is a war veteran, and has been deeply immersed in the affairs of the state as his father's principal aide. He has empowered the IRGC, thus opening the economy, politics, and all state institutions to its control.[36] Khamenei has, however, prevented the IRGC from developing independent of his own direct command. The force is omnipotent, but it lacks the kind of coherent leadership structure witnessed in the Egyptian or Pakistani militaries. Khamenei interacts with various IRGC commanders directly, and encourages competition among the force's various units and leaders.

In Iran's growing militarized politics, Khamenei is the commander of all commanders. In the summer before the protests, the Islamic Republic's public relations machine produced a jingoistic song titled "Salute to the Commander" ("Salaam Farmandeh"). The commander in the song is the Shia messiah, the hidden Twelfth Imam—whom the Islamic Republic views as Iran's true ruler, and on whose behalf the ruling order is governing—but in a veiled way, it was also a nod to earthly commanders, Soleimani, and more so, Khamenei. Children sang the song in schools and mosques as well as at religious gatherings, and in translation in several other countries. The choice of the title "commander" had clear military connotations, capturing the way in which Khamenei saw himself and his role in the state of resistance. When Iran was pondering its response to Israel's attack on its consulate in Damascus in April 2024, Khamenei emerged as the strongest advocate of a tough response; for him, in the words of one senior adviser, "The authority of the supreme leader was measured in defense of the homeland."[37] No longer did Khamenei see his own stature in religious authority, but in secular terms as the guardian of the country's security and interests. This vigilant defense seen through the prism of resistance has meant militarism and perpetual conflict with the West under the leadership of a cleric-statesman—one who is a sentinel of the messiah and one with the IRGC's troops in uniform, even if he no longer enjoys popular support for his vision of independence and resistance.

...

Still, the 2022 protests make it difficult, even for Khamenei, to altogether ignore the gulf that now separates state from society. Months of street protests ended, but the grievances that had inflamed them remained unabated and would thus shape the presidential election that followed Raisi's death in June 2024. The election campaign opened debate on the hard-liners' agenda and competence to govern—the quality of which had plummeted after Raisi replaced hundreds of bureaucrats with acolytes and loyalists—forcing hijab, and pursuing unending resistance and courting confrontation with the United States.[38]

The election came at a time when resistance was at a high point. Iran looked strong as the Axis of Resistance basked in its show of force in the Gaza war. But the run-up to the election was not a celebration of resistance; to the contrary, it showed that the state built to sustain resistance—through a unified hard-liner control of all levers of power, anchored in revolutionary values redefined by the Axis of Resistance—was failing at a basic level.[39] Khamenei had to seek a new balance between commitment to resistance and addressing the imperative of improving the state of the economy and ensuring political stability. He thus ascented to the reformist Massoud Pezeshkian entering the race.

Pezeshkian made improving the economy the cornerstone of his campaign, arguing that the economy would do better only if Iran engaged the United States and explored diplomatic options to reduce sanctions pressure on Iran. Zarif, the architect of the JCPOA, emerged as Pezeshkian's most influential adviser, making the case for dealmaking with the West, and forcefully rejecting the argument of hard-line candidates that the economy could grow at a rapid clip under maximal sanctions. Zarif's passionate pleas for engagement—at times questioning fundamental assumptions of resistance—struck a chord with the wary public. Even moderate conservatives broke with hard-liners to publicly endorse the call for diplomacy and engagement. Fatigue with resistance became a driving force in the election.

Khamenei remained committed to resistance, but by opening the door to the public criticism of hard-liners, he signaled that he was ready to follow a different course. Just as Hasan Rouhani's election had opened the door to nuclear negotiations and the signing of the JCPOA, so could Pezeshkian's presidency allow for new agreements whereby Iran would get sanctions relief in exchange for concessions on its nuclear and even regional policies.

Voters, however, remained unconvinced. The turnout in the first round was 39 percent, the lowest in a national vote since the beginning of the Islamic Republic. In the second round, Pezeshkian won with 53 percent of the vote, but only 49.8 percent of eligible voters cast their ballots. The anemic voter turnout, making clear the depth of public anger and apathy, has put the Islamic Republic on notice that its single-minded pursuit of resistance has opened a yawning chasm between state and society. That has in turn opened divisions in the ranks of the conservatives, the IRGC, and state leaders, hindering a consensus over how to chart a way forward.

Pezeshkian's election signals a tentative turn to pragmatism, but the shadow of resistance still looms large. On the day of his inauguration, Israel assassinated the political head of Hamas, Ismail Haniyeh, in Tehran, where he had traveled to attend the ceremonies. The audacious assassination was retribution for the October 7 attack and retaliation for Iran's support for Hamas. Then came Israel's attack on Hezbollah and

Iran's missile attack on Israel. All talk of moderation and engagement with the West was immediately overshadowed by fear of imminent escalation between Iran and Israel—which would in the least scuttle diplomacy between Iran and the United States.

• • •

As this book has shown, questions of security and stability have been ever present through Iran's modern history. Iranian political consciousness has been haunted by insecurity and chaos, shaping the rhythm of historical developments and the states ruling over the country. The echo of security in the state and society has grown louder under the Islamic Republic. That echo has shaped the state since 1979, and in turn, the state has increased security fears. The quickening tempo of threat perception and state building explains in good measure the trajectory of the development of the Islamic Republic.

Iran today is the state that national security has built. Its vision of development is anchored in resisting the United States as a necessary means to achieving national interests. The story of Iran is not just that of democracy and dictatorship, or struggle for or against revolution, religion, or ideology. Iran's modern history is also one of the interplay between the imperative of security and task of state building.

In his seminal book on grand strategy, historian John Lewis Gaddis wrote that in constructing a strategy, a country can act either as a fox or hedgehog.[40] "The fox knows many things, but the hedgehog knows one big thing."[41] The choice is between flexibility and adaptability versus steadfast commitment to one big idea. In his unwavering pursuit of resistance as the answer to Iran's security needs, Khamenei has acted as a hedgehog. Even so, in signing a nuclear deal in 2015 and normalizing ties with Saudi Arabia in 2023, he showed flashes of pragmatic suppleness. The future depends on whether those flashes grow more prominent, and whether the Islamic Republic understands that it must adopt the malleability of a fox, if it is to survive the contingencies to come.

NOTES

Introduction

1. Narges Bajoghli and Vali Nasr, "How the War in Gaza Revived the Axis of Resistance," *Foreign Affairs*, January 17, 2024, https://www.foreignaffairs.com/united-states/how-war-gaza -revived-axis-resistance.

2. Interview with Mohammad Javad Larijani, "Reaching the Peak Is the Start of Farther Horizons," *Khamenei.ir*, August 31, 2023, https://farsi.khamenei.ir/others-dialog?id=53729.

3. https://x.com/khamenei_ir/status/1701279442000339062?s=46&t=l2_DfjIc8MT8vjcBo Nkcog.

4. "Khamenei Refers to Resistance to Obligatory Hijab as 'Foreigner's Project,'" *BBC Persian*, April 3, 2024, https://www.bbc.com/persian/articles/cxezzz5j5zxo.

5. Khamenei's speech before Islamic Revolutionary Guard Corps (IRGC) commanders, "In Order to Reach the Peak," *Khamanei.ir*, August 19, 2023, https://farsi.khamenei.ir/video-content ?id=53604; interview with Larijani, "Reaching the Peak."

6. "The Vision for Islamic Republic of Iran in the Horizon of 2025," *Khamenei.ir*, February 27, 2004, https://farsi.khamenei.ir/message-content?id=9034.

7. "Comments during a Meeting with Pilgrims and Neighbors of the Shrine of Hazrat-e Ali ibn Musa Al-Reza," *Khamenei.ir*, March 21, 2009, https://farsi.khamenei.ir/speech-content?id=6082.

8. Robert Jervis, *How Statesmen Think: The Psychology of International Politics* (Princeton, NJ: Princeton University Press, 2017); Karen Yarhi-Milo, *Knowing the Adversary: Leaders, Intelligence, and Assessment of Intentions in International Relations* (Princeton, NJ: Princeton University Press, 2014).

9. Ayşe Zarakol, "States and Ontological Security: A Historical Rethinking," *Cooperation and Conflict* 52, no. 1 (2017): 48–68.

10. Anthony Giddens, *Modernity and Self-Identity* (Stanford, CA: Stanford University Press, 1991), 243; Jennifer Mitzen, "Ontological Security in World Politics: State Identity and the Security Dilemma," *European Journal of International Relations* 12, no. 3 (September 2006): 341–70.

11. Stephen Gaubard, "Lunch with FT: Henry Kissinger," *Financial Times*, May 23, 2008, https://www.ft.com/content/6d4b5fb8-285a-11dd-8f1e-000077b07658; Henry A. Kissinger, "Iran Must Be President Obama's Immediate Priority," *Washington Post*, November 16, 2012, https://www.washingtonpost.com/opinions/henry-kissinger-iran-must-be-president-obamas -immediate-priority/2012/11/16/2edf93e4-2dea-11e2-beb2-4b4cf5087636_story.html.

12. On this theme in international relations, see John Merscheimer and Sebastian Rosato, *How States Think: The Rationality of Foreign Policy* (New Haven, CT: Yale University Press, 2023).

13. On why states maximize power as means to protect themselves, see John Merscheimer, *The Tragedy of Great Power Politics* (New York: W. W. Norton, 2001).

Chapter 1: Loom of History

1. Mohammad Ali Eslami Nodoushan, *Iran and Its Lonliness* (Tehran: Sherkat Sahami Enteshar, 1997).

2. Mohiaddin Mesbahi, "Free and Confined: Iran in the International System," *Iranian Review of Foreign Affairs* 5, no. 2 (Spring 2011): 9–34; Arash Reisinezhad, "Iran's Geopolitical Strategy in West Asia: Containment of 'Geography' and 'History,'" *Iranian Review of Foreign Affairs* 11, no. 1 (Winter–Spring 2020): 59–88.

3. Said Amir Arjomand, *The Shadow of God and the Hidden Imam: Religion, Political Order, and Societal Change in Shi'ite Iran from the Beginning to 1890* (Chicago: University of Chicago Press, 1984), 210–12.

4. Abbas Amanat, *Iran: A Modern History* (New Haven, CT: Yale University Press, 2017), 33; Rula Abisaab, *Converting Persia: Religion and Power in the Safavid Empire* London: I. B. Tauris, 2004).

5. Said Amir Arjomand, "The Rise of Shah Esma'il as a Mahdist Revolution," in *Sociology of Shi'ite Islam: Collected Essays*, ed. Said Amir Arjomand (Leiden: E. J. Brill, 2016), 301–29; Roger M. Savory, *Iran under the Safavids* (New York: Cambridge University Press, 1980), 27–30.

6. Abbas Amanat, "Introduction: Iranian Identity Boundaries: A Historical Overview," in *Iran Facing Others*, ed. Abbas Amanat and Farzin Vejdani (New York: Palgrave Macmillan, 2012), 13–14; Said Amir Arjomand, *Turban for the Crown: The Islamic Revolution in Iran* (New York: Oxford University Press, 1988), 177–88; Vali Nasr, *The Shia Revival: How Conflicts within Islam Will Shape the Future* (New York: W. W. Norton, 2006), 74–75.

7. Ali Gheissari, "Unequal Treaties and the Question of Sovereignty in Qajar and Early Pahlavi Iran," Ann Lambton Memorial Lecture, Durham Middle East Papers 106, Institute for Middle Eastern and Islamic Studies, Durham University, 2023, 18–19; Ehsan Yarshater, "The Qajar Era in the Mirror of Time," *Iranian Studies* 34, nos. 1–4 (2001): 187–94.

8. Homa Katouzian, *The Persians: Ancient, Medieval and Modern Iran* (New Haven, CT: Yale University Press, 2010), 142–63.

9. Amanat, *Iran*, 212; Abbas Amanat, "'Russian Intrusion into the Guarded Domain': Reflections of a Qajar Statesman on European Expansion," *Journal of the American Oriental Society* 113, no. 1 (January–March 1993): 35–56; Maziar Behrooz, *Iran at War: Interactions with the Modern World and the Struggle with Imperial Russia* (London: I. B. Tauris, 2023), 49–102.

10. There is much scholarship on the various aspects of the Constitutional Revolution, including E. G. Browne, *The Persian Revolution of 1905–1909*, 2nd ed. (Washington, DC: Mage Publishers, 2006); Ahmad Kasravi, *History of Iran's Constitution* (Tehran: Negah, 1940); Janet Afary, *The Iranian Constitutional Revolution, 1906–1911* (New York: Columbia University Press, 1996); Fereydoun Adamiat, *Idea of Liberty and Beginnings of the Constitutional Movement of Iran* (Tehran, 1961); Fereydoun Adamiat, *Idea of Social Democracy and Iran's Constitutional Revolution* (Tehran, 1975).

11. "Why Didn't We Have a Raymond Aaron? Report of an Interview with Daryush Shayegan," *Andisheh-e Pouya* 18 (August 2016): 18.

12. Ahmad Ali Movarekh al-Dowleh Sepehr, *Iran in the Great War 1914–1918* (Tehran: Bank-e Melli, 1957).

13. Amanat, *Iran*, 396.

14. Cyrus Ghani, *Iran and the Rise of Reza Shah: From Qajar Collapse to Pahlavi Power* (London: I. B. Tauris, 1998), 21–63.

15. Homa Katouzian, "The Campaign against the Anglo-Iranian Agreement of 1919," *British Journal of Middle Eastern Studies* 25, no. 1 (1998): 5–46.

16. Eugene Weber, *Peasants into Frenchmen: The Modernization of Rural France, 1870–1914* (Stanford, CA: Stanford University Press, 1976); Afshin Matin-Asgari, *Both Eastern and Western: An Intellectual History of Iranian Modernity* (New York: Cambridge University Press, 2018), 79.

17. Reza Niazmand, *Reza Shah: From Birth to Monarchy* (Washington, DC: Foundation for Iranian Studies, 1996); Donald N. Wilbur, *Riza Shah Pahlavi: The Resurrection and Reconstruction of Iran* (New York: Exposition Press, 1975).

18. Niazmand, *Reza Shah*, 5.

19. Baqer Aqeli, *Reza Shah and the Unified Military* (Tehran: Namak, 1999), 211–378; Amanat, *Iran*, 407–11.

20. Shahrough Akhavi, *Religion and Politics in Contemporary Iran: Clergy-State Relations in the Pahlavi Period* (Albany: SUNY Press, 1980), 25–32.

21. Ghani, *Iran*, 395–407.

22. Daron Acemoglu and James A. Robinson, *The Narrow Corridor; States, Societies, and the Fate of Liberty* (New York: Penguin Random House, 2019), 1–32.

23. Vanessa Martin, "Religion and State in Khumaini's *Kashf al-Asrar*," *Bulletin of the School of Oriental and African Studies* 56, no. 1 (1993): 34–35.

24. Cited in Ariane M. Tabatabai, *No Conquest, No Defeat: Iran's National Security Strategy* (New York: Oxford University Press, 2020), 91.

25. Richard A. Stewart, *Sunrise at Abadan: The British and Soviet Invasion of Iran, 1941* (New York: Praeger, 1988), 1.

26. Aqeli, *Reza Shah*, 433–676.

27. Amanat, *Iran*, 504; Hasan Arfa, *Under Five Shahs* (New York: Johns Murray, 1964), 309–30.

28. Ervand Abrahamian, *Iran between Two Revolutions* (Princeton, NJ: Princeton University Press, 1982), 281–415; Sepehr Zabih, *The Communist Movement in Iran* (Berkeley: University of California Press, 1966); "Interview with Baheri, Mohammad," December 1983, and February 1984, Oral History of Iran Collection of the Foundation for Iranian Studies; "Interview with Amirshahi, Mahshid," August 1983, Oral History of Iran Collection of the Foundation for Iranian Studies.

29. Louise Fawcett, *Iran and the Cold War: The Azerbaijan Crisis of 1946* (New York: Cambridge University Press, 1992).

30. Robert Rossow, "The Battle of Azerbaijan, 1946," *Middle East Journal* 10, no. 1 (Winter 1956): 17.

31. Amanat, *Iran*, 512–19; Fawcett, *Iran*, 53–82; John Lewis Gaddis, *The United States and the Origins of the Cold War, 1941–1947* (New York: Columbia University Press, 1972), 282–315.

32. Mohammad Reza Pahlavi, *Answer to History* (New York: Stein and Day, 1980), 12.

33. "The King: I, the Patriots and the Military Will Not Allow Iran Become 'Iranistan,'" *Rastakhiz*, August 19, 1978, 1.

34. Gholam Reza Afkhami, *The Life and Times of the Shah* (Berkeley: University of California Press, 2009), 110–36.

35. Ronald W. Ferrier, "The Anglo-Iranian Oil Dispute: A Triangular Relationship," in *Mussadiq, Iranian Nationalism, and Oil*, ed. James A. Bill and Wm. Roger Louis (Austin: University of Texas Press, 1988), 164–99.

36. Mostafa Elm, *Oil, Power, and Principle: Iran's Oil Nationalization and Its Aftermath* (Syracuse: Syracuse University Press, 1992), 88–89, 92.

37. Mary Ann Heiss, *Empire and Nationhood: The United States, Great Britain, and Iranian Oil, 1950–1954* (New York: Columbia University Press, 1997), 20.

38. David Painter and Gregory Brew, *The Struggle for Iran: Oil, Autocracy, and the Cold War, 1951–1954* (Chapel Hill: University of North Carolina Press, 2023), 148.

39. "The Ambassador to Iran (Henderson) to the State Department," 788.13/7–2852: Telegram, July 28, 1952, *Foreign Relations of the United States, 1952–1954, Iran, 1951–1954, Volume X*, https://history.state.gov/historicaldocuments/frus1952-54v10/d189.

40. Mary Ann Heiss, "The International Boycott of Iranian Oil and the Anti-Mossadeq Coup of 1953," in *Mohammad Mosaddeq and the 1953 Coup in Iran*, ed. Mark J. Gasiorowski and Malcolm Byrne (Syracuse, NY: Syracuse University Press, 2004), 178–200.

41. Alireza Attari, "Dr. Mossadegh's Negative Balance and Its External Implications," *Tarikh-nameh-e Kharazmi* 3, no. 11 (Spring 2017): 45–75.

42. Rouhollah K. Ramazani, *Iran's Foreign Policy, 1941–1973* (Charlottesville: University of Virginia Press, 1975), 182.

43. "Memorandum Prepared in the Directorate of Plans, Central Intelligence Agency," March 3, 1953; Central Intelligence Agency, DDI Files, Job 80R01443R, box 1, folder 7, *Foreign Relations of the United States, 1952–1954, Iran, 1951–1954*, https://history.state.gov/historicaldocuments/frus1951-54Iran/d170.

44. *Memoirs of Noureddin Kianouri* (Tehran: Didgah, 1993), 217–26.

45. *Ardeshir Zahedi's Memoirs* (Bethesda, MD: Ibex Publishers, 2006), 1:188, 265–66, 273, 280; Ayatollah [Hossein Ali] Montazeri, *Reminiscences*, 2nd ed. (Essen, Germany: Ettehadieh Nasherin Irani dar Oroupa, 2001), 1:161–62; "Telegram from the Station in Iran to Central Intelligence Agency," August 17, 1953; *Foreign Relations of the United States, 1952–1954, Iran, 1951–1954*, documents 272, https://history.state.gov/historicaldocuments/frus1951-54Iran/d272; "Telegram from the Station in Iran to Central Intelligence Agency," August 17, 1953; *Foreign Relations of the United States, 1952–1954, Iran, 1951–1954*, documents 273, https://history.state.gov/historicaldocuments/frus1951-54Iran/d273.

46. For a comprehensive account of the events leading up to the coup, see Ervand Abrahamian, *The Coup: 1953, the CIA, and the Roots of Modern U.S.–Iranian Relations* (New York: New Press, 2013); Mark J. Gasiorowski, "The 1953 Coup D'Etat in Iran," *International Journal of Middle East Studies* 19, no. 3 (August 1987): 261–86; Ali Gheissari, "The U.S. Coup of 1953 in Iran, Sixty Years On," *Passport* (September 2013): 23–24.

47. Ray Takeyh, *The Last Shah: America, Iran, and the Fall of the Pahlavi Dynasty* (New Haven, CT: Yale University Press, 2021), 87–116; Ray Takeyh, "What Really Happened in Iran:

The CIA, the Ouster of Mossadegh and Restoration of the Shah," *Foreign Affairs* 93, no. 4 (July–August 2014): 2–12; Darioush Bayandor, "Don't Just Blame Washington for the 1953 Iran Coup," *Foreign Policy*, November 21, 2019, https://foreignpolicy.com/2019/11/21/dont-blame-washington-1953-iran-coup-mosaddeq/.

48. "Information Report Prepared in the Central Intelligence Agency," March 31, 1953, *Foreign Relations of the United States, 1952–1954, Iran, 1951–1954*, https://history.state.gov/historicaldocuments/frus1951-54Iran/d182.

49. See, for instance, Afkhami, *Life and Times of the Shah*; Abbas Milani, *The Shah* (New York: Palgrave Macmillan, 2011); Fakhreddin Azimi, *The Quest for Democracy in Iran: A Century of Struggle against Authoritarian Rule* (Cambridge, MA: Harvard University Press, 2008); Abrahamian, *Iran between Two Revolutions*; Homa Katouzian, *The Political Economy of Iran, 1926–1979* (New York: NYU Press, 1981); Mark J. Gasiorowski, *U.S. Foreign Policy and the Shah: Building a Client State in Iran* (Ithaca, NY: Cornell University Press, 1991); Arjomand, *Turban for the Crown*; Takeyh, *The Last Shah*.

50. Muhammad Reza Pahlavi, *Towards the Great Civilization* (1976–77; repr., Los Angeles: Pars, 2007).

51. Ali Rahnema, *The Rise of Modern Despotism in Iran: The Shah, the Opposition, and the United States 1953–1968* (London: Oneworld Academic, 2021).

52. Hossain Fardoust, *Memoirs of the Retired Full General Hossein Fardoust: Rise and Fall of Pahlavi Monarchy* (Tehran: Moasesseh-e Etela'at va Pajouhesha-ye Siyasi, 1991), 381–83; Siavosh Bashiri, *The Story of SAVAK* (Paris: Parang, 1987), 128–36; "Interview with Alavi Kiya, General Hasan," May 1983, Oral History of Iran Collection of the Foundation for Iranian Studies.

53. Sergey Radchencko, *To Run the World: The Kremlin's Cold War Bid for Global Power* (New York: Cambridge University Press, 2024), 484–85.

54. Katouzian, *The Political Economy*, 202–7.

55. Cited in Milani, *The Shah*, 202.

56. Milani, *The Shah*, 208–12; David Collier, "To Prevent a Revolution: John F. Kennedy and Promotion of Democracy in Iran," *Diplomacy and Statecraft* 24, no. 3 (September 2003): 456–75.

57. Muhammad Reza Pahlavi, *White Revolution* (Tehran: Bank-e Melli, 1965); Ali M. Ansari, "The Myth of the Iranian Revolution: Mohammad Reza Shah, 'Modernization' and Consolidation of Power," *Middle Eastern Studies* 37, no. 3 (July 2001): 1–24; Rouhollah K. Ramazani, "Iran's 'White Revolution': A Study in Political Development," *International Journal of Middle East Studies* 5, no. 2 (April 1974): 124–39.

58. Baqer Moin, *Khomeini: The Life of the Ayatollah* (London: I. B. Tauris, 1999), 92–106; Fakhreddin Azimi, "Khomeini and the White Revolution," in *A Critical Introduction to Khomeini*, ed. Arshin Adib-Moghaddam (New York: Cambridge University Press, 2014), 19–42.

59. Vali Nasr, "Politics in the Late-Pahlavi State: The Ministry of Economy and Industrial Policy, 1963–69," *International Journal of Middle East Studies* 32, no. 1 (February 2000): 97–122; Ramin Nassehi, "Domesticating Cold War Economic Ideas: The Rise of Iranian Developmentalism in the 1950s and 1960s," in *The Age of Arya Mehr: Late Pahlavi Iran and Its Global Entanglements*, ed. Roham Alvandi (London: Gingko Library, 2018), 35–69; Charles Issawi, "The Iranian Economy 1925–1975: Fifty Years of Economic Development," in *Iran under the Pahlavis*, ed. George Lenczowski (Stanford, CA: Hoover Institution Press, 1978), 129–66.

60. M. H. Pesaran, "Economy IX: In the Pahlavi Period," *Encyclopedia Iranica*, December 15, 1997, fasc. 2, 8:143–56.

61. Pahlavi, *Towards the Great Civilization*.

62. Trita Parsi, *Treacherous Alliance: The Secret Dealings of Israel, Iran, and the U.S.* (New Haven, CT: Yale University Press, 2007), 36.

63. John Lewis Gaddis, *Strategies of Containment: A Critical Appraisal of American National Security Policy during the Cold War* (New York: Oxford University Press, 2005), 302.

64. Roham Alvandi, *Nixon, Kissinger and the Shah: The United States and Iran in the Cold War* (New York: Oxford University Press, 2014), 65–84.

65. "UK Policy in Persian Gulf: Military Withdrawal by 1971 and Its Consequences," January 1–December 31, 1968, Foreign Office Papers, National Archive of Great Britain, FO 1016/754-759; Roham Alvandi, "Muhammad Reza Shah and the Bahrain Question, 1968–70," *British Journal of Middle East Studies* 37, no. 2 (2010): 159.

66. Alvandi, *Nixon, Kissinger and the Shah*, 63.

67. Afkhami, *The Life and Times of the Shah*, 302–3.

68. Arash Reisinezhad, *The Shah of Iran, the Iraqi Kurds, and the Lebanese Shia* (New York: Palgrave Macmillan, 2019), 22; Amir Asadollah Alam, *The Alam Diaries*, ed. Alinaqi Alikhani (Bethesda, MD: Iranbooks, 1995), 3:222; "Telegram from the Embassy in Iraq to the Department of State," December 16, 1964, National Archives and Records Administration, RG 59, central files 1964–66, POL 23–9 IRAQ, https://history.state.gov/historicaldocuments/frus1964 -68v21/d171; "Memorandum from the President's Assistant for National Security Affairs (Kissinger) to President Nixon," April 11, 1974, National Security Council, Nixon Intelligence Files, Subject Files, Iraqi Kurds, box 8, April 7, 1969–June 12, 1974, https://history.state.gov /historicaldocuments/frus1969-76v27/d246; "Interview with Ramsbotham, Sir Peter," January 1986, Oral History of Iran Collection of the Foundation for Iranian Studies; "Interview with Helms, Richard," July 1985, Oral History of Iran Collection of the Foundation for Iranian Studies.

69. Erfan Qaneifard, *Storm of Events: Conversation with Isa Pejman, the Shah's Special Envoy and SAVAK's Representative in Iraq's Kurdistan* (Tehran: Nashr-e Elm, 2011), 35–206.

70. Reisinezhad, *The Shah of Iran*, 229.

71. James F. Goode, "Assisting Our Brothers, Defending Ourselves: The Iranian Intervention in Oman, 1972–75," *Iranian Studies* 47, no. 3 (2014): 455; Calvin H. Allen and W. Lynn Rigsbee, *Oman under Qaboos, from Coup to Constitution 1970–1996* (London: Frank Cass, 2000), 72–73.

72. Cited in Marc Pellas, "Oman: How the Shah of Iran Saved the Regime," *Orient XXI*, March 5, 2020, https://orientxxi.info/magazine/oman-how-the-shah-of-iran-saved-the-regime,3681.

73. Cited in Goode, "Assisting Our Brothers," 443.

74. Pellas, "Oman."

75. J. E. Peterson, *Oman's Insurgencies: The Sultanate's Struggle for Supremacy* (London: Saqi, 2008), 294–395.

76. Reisinezhad, *The Shah of Iran*.

77. "Memorandum Prepared in the Office of Current Intelligence, Central Intelligence Agency," May 29, 1975, Central Intelligence Agency, DI/OCI Files, Job 85T00353R, box 1, folder 17, https://history.state.gov/historicaldocuments/frus1969-76v27/d131.

78. "Memorandum from the President's Assistant for National Security Affairs (Kissinger) to President Nixon," May 26, 1971, National Archives, Nixon Presidential Materials, NSC Files, box 755, Presidential Correspondence, Iran, M. R. Pahlavi, Shah of Iran Correspondence, https://history.state.gov/historicaldocuments/frus1969-76ve04/d128.

79. The Soviet overflights would lead to a formal protest by US ambassador Helms to the Shah. Private conversations with Ardeshir Zahedi, 2004.

80. "Editorial Note," Foreign Relations of the United States, 1969–1976, vol. XXVII, Iran, Iraq, 1973–76, https://history.state.gov/historicaldocuments/frus1969-76v27/d95.

81. Mohammad Homayounvash, *Iran and the Nuclear Question: History and Evolutionary Trajectory* (New York: Routledge, 2017), 15–16.

82. Reisinezhad, *The Shah of Iran*, 325; Parsi, *Treacherous Alliance*, 80.

83. Memorandum from Harold H. Saunders of the National Security Council Staff to the President's Assistant for National Security Affairs (Kissinger), May 11, 1973, National Archives, Nixon Presidential Materials, NSC Files, box 603, Country Files—Middle East, Iran, vol. V, May 1973–December 1973, https://history.state.gov/historicaldocuments/frus1969-76v27/d15.

84. "Memorandum from the Director of Central Intelligence (Helms) to the President's Assistant for National Security Affairs (Kissinger)," May 8, 1972, Central Intelligence Agency, Executive Registry Files, Job 80B01086A, box 1, Executive Registry Subject Files, I–13, Iran, https://history.state.gov/historicaldocuments/frus1969-76ve04/d190.

85. "Backchannel Message from the President's Assistant for National Security Affairs (Kissinger) to the Former Secretary of the Treasury (Connally)," June 29, 1972, National Archives, Nixon Presidential Materials, NSC Files, box 425, Backchannel Messages, Middle East, 1972, https://history.state.gov/historicaldocuments/frus1969-76ve04/d209.

86. Ray Takeyh, "The Shah, the Mullahs, and Iran's Longstanding Nuclear Ambitions," *Wall Street Journal*, December 10, 2020, https://www.wsj.com/articles/the-shah-the-mullahs-and-irans-longstanding-nuclear-ambitions-11607624794; Alvandi, *Nixon, Kissinger and the Shah*, 133; Homayounvash, *Iran and the Nuclear Question*, 24–40; "Interview with E'temad, Akbar," November 1982, Oral History of Iran Collection of the Foundation for Iranian Studies; *Iran's Atomic Energy Program: Mission, Structure, Politics, Interview with Akbar Etemad, the First President of the Atomic Energy Organization of Iran (1974–1978)* (Bethesda, MD: Foundation for Iranian Studies, 1997).

87. Cited in Samuel Huntington, *Order in Changing Societies* (New Haven, CT: Yale University Press, 1968), 179.

Chapter 2: Seeking Revolutionary Independence

1. "Interview with Sanjabi, Karim," October 15, 1983, Iranian Oral History Project, Harvard University.

2. Personal conversation with Mushahid Hussain, Islamabad, October 1997. At the time of the revolution, Hussain was a leading Pakistani journalist.

3. Religious revolutionaries who also rued Reza Shah's Kemalist reforms dated back Iran's loss of independence to his rise to power in the 1920s, which they attributed to British machinations. The British, writes Manuchehr Mohammadi, an influential foreign policy theorist of the

Islamic Republic, continued to dominate Iran's foreign policy and decision-making throughout the Pahlavi era. Whatever the Pahlavis did in the foreign policy arena was for Britain's benefit and not for the good of Iran. Manuchehr Mohammadi, *Survey of Iran's Foreign Policy during the Pahlavi Period, or Decision-Making in a State under Domination* (Tehran: Dadgostar, 1999), 133–35. Sadeq Zibakalam chronicles the panoply of anti–Reza Shah narratives extant in the Islamic Republic in his book *Reza Shah* (Tehran: Rouzaneh, 2019), especially 19–33. Also, important to note is that many of the oft-repeated innuendos against Reza Shah can be traced back to a concerted British campaign to besmirch his reputation. Abbas Amanat, *Iran: A Modern History* (New Haven, CT: Yale University Press, 2017), 496.

4. Assal Rad, *The State of Resistance: Politics, Culture, and Identity in Modern Iran* (New York: Cambridge University Press, 2022), 59–64.

5. Lucien George, "Les dernières émeutes sont les prémices d'une gigantesque explosion nous déclare l'ayatollah Khomeiny, chef spirituel des chiites," *Le Monde*, May 6, 1978, https://www.lemonde.fr/archives/article/1978/05/06/les-dernieres-emeutes-sont-les-premices-d-une-gigantesque-explosion-nous-declare-l-ayatollah-khomeiny-chef-spirituel-des-chiites_2978256_1819218.html.

6. Rasoul Ja'farian, *Iran's Religopolitical Trends and Institutions, 1941–1979* (Tehran: Elm, 2011), 146.]

7. Ali Bagheri Kani on Twitter, June 3, 2022, https://twitter.com/Bagheri_Kani/status/1532745324854497280?s=20.

8. Ervand Abrahamian, *Khomeinism* (Berkeley: University of California Press, 1993), 13–38.

9. Ali Gheissari and Vali Nasr, *Democracy in Iran: History and the Quest for Liberty* (New York: Oxford University Press, 2006), 87; "Melons for Everyone," *Economist*, October 30, 2014, https://www.economist.com/special-report/2014/10/30/melons-for-everyone.

10. Seyyed Ruhollah Khomeini, *Islamic Government or Rule by the Jurisconsult* (Tehran, 1970), 6.

11. Khomeini, *Islamic Government or Rule by the Jurisconsult*, 10–15.

12. Mohammad Ataie, "Exporting the 1978–79 Revolution: Pan-Islamic or Sectarian" (PhD diss., University of Massachusetts at Amherst, 2020), chap. 1, 2–3.

13. "Fourteen Recommendations about the Revolution and National Issues," in *The Writ of the Imam: Collection of Imam Khomeini's Works* (Tehran: Markaz Tanzim va Nashr Asar Imam Khomeini, 2000), 6:261–62.

14. Farideh Farhi and Saideh Lotfian, "Iran's Post-Revolution Foreign Policy Puzzle," in *World of Aspiring Powers: Domestic Foreign Policy Debates in China, India, Iran, Japan and Russia*, ed. Henry R. Nau and Deepa M. Ollapally (New York: Oxford University Press, 2012), 114–40.

15. In addition to the memoirs of American officials, there are a few books that detail the unfolding of the hostage crisis, such as Mark Bowden, *Guests of the Ayatollah: The First Battle in America's War with Militant Islam* (New York: Atlantic Monthly Press, 2006); Pierre Salinger, *America Held Hostage: The Secret Negotiations* (New York: Doubleday, 1981).

16. Abbas Amanat, *Apocalyptic Islam and Iranian Shi'ism* (London: I. B. Tauris, 2009), 212–19.

17. The religious revolutionary cadres were well-versed in the Islamist discourse and had read the works of its doyens, Mawlana Abu'l-Ala Mawdudi of Pakistan (d. 1979) or Sayyid Qutb of Egypt (d. 1966). Many encountered these texts in Afghanistan or Shia centers in the Arab world.

18. David Patrick Houghton, "Explaining the Origins of the Iran Hostage Crisis: A Cognitive Approach," *Terrorism and Political Violence* 18, no. 2 (2006): 259–79.

19. Christian Emery, "United States Iran Policy 1979–1980: The Anatomy and Legacy of American Diplomacy," *Diplomacy and Statecraft* 24, no. 4 (2013): 619–39.

20. Narges Bajoghli et al., *How Sanctions Work: Iran and the Impact of Economic Warfare* (Stanford, CA: Stanford University Press, 2024), 56–57.

21. Ray Takeyh, "The Other Carter Doctrine," *Foreign Affairs*, February 26, 2021, https://www.foreignaffairs.com/articles/united-states/2021-02-26/other-carter-doctrine.

22. William H. Sullivan, *Mission to Iran* (New York: W. W. Norton, 1981), 248–68; "Interview with Metrinko, Michael," May 23, June 14, August 29, October 27, 1988, and March 2, 1989, Oral History of Iran Collection of the Foundation for Iranian Studies; "Interview with Naas, Charles," May 13 and 31, and July 26, 1988, Oral History of Iran Collection of the Foundation for Iranian Studies.

23. Seyed Hossein Mousavian and Shahir Shahidsaless, *Iran and the United States: An Insider's View on the Failed Past and the Road to Peace* (New York: Bloomsbury, 2014), 55.

24. Ali Akbar Hashemi Rafsanjani, *Revolution and Victory, Record and Memoirs, 1979–1980*, ed. Abbas Bashiri (Tehran: Daftar-e Nashr-e Manabe-e Enqelab, 2004), 360–63.

25. Mohammad Ayatollahi Tabaar, "Causes of the U.S. Hostage Crisis in Iran: The Untold Account of the Communist Threat," *Security Studies* 26, no. 4 (2017): 665–97; Mohammad Ayatollahi Tabaar, *Religious Statecraft: The Politics of Islam in Iran* (New York: Columbia University Press, 2019), 111–46.

26. Sergey Radchencko, *To Run the World: The Kremlin's Cold War Bid for Global Power* (New York: Cambridge University Press, 2024), 488.

27. Gary Sick, *All Fall Down: America's Tragic Encounter with Iran* (New York: Random House, 1985), 181–86.

28. Seyyed Jalal Dehqani Firouzabadi, *The Foreign Policy of the Islamic Republic of Iran* (Tehran: Samt, 1990), 305–7.

29. Dehqani Firouzabadi, *The Foreign Policy*, 308–16.

30. On Bazargan and his views on politics, see H. E. Chehabi, *Iranian Politics and Religious Modernism: The Liberation Movement of Iran under the Shah and Khomeini* (Ithaca, NY: Cornell University Press, 1990).

31. "Memorandum from Gary Sick of the National Security Council Staff to the President's Assistant for National Security Affairs (Brzezinski)," November 5, 1979, Carter Library, National Security Affairs, Staff Material, Middle East File, box 30, Subject File, Iran 11/1/79–11/10/79, https://history.state.gov/historicaldocuments/frus1977-80v11p1/d4.

32. Mark J. Gasiorowski, "US Covert Operations toward Iran, February–November 1979: Was the CIA Trying to Overthrow the Islamic Regime," *Middle Eastern Studies* 51, no. 1 (2015): 115–35.

33. Mark J. Gasiorowski, "US Intelligence Assistance to Iran, May–October 1979," *Middle East Journal* 66, no. 4 (Autumn 2012): 613–27.

34. Sick, *All Fall Down*, 189.

35. Radchencko, *To Run the World*, 488.

36. I am grateful to Sergey Radchencko for sharing this quotation from his research in Soviet archives.

37. Rafsanjani, *Revolution and Victory*, 292–93, 368.

38. "Memorandum from Gary Sick."

39. Dehqani Firouzabadi, *The Foreign Policy*, 315–16.

40. "Mohsen Mirdamadi's Defence of the Actions of the Students following Imam's Line on November 4 [1979]," Markaz-e Daerotolma'ref-e Bozorg-e Eslami, November 3, 2015, https://www.cgie.org.ir/fa/news/83073/دفاعیه-محسن-میردامادی-از-اقدام-دانشجویان-پیرو-خط-امام-در-۱۳-آبان.

41. "America's Plots against Iran," in *The Writ of the Imam: Collection of Imam Khomeini's Works* (Tehran: Markaz Tanzim va Nashr Asar Imam Khomeini, 2000), 10:489–97; interview with Ibrahim Asgharzadeh, a key leader of the students who took the hostages, *Etemad Online*, November 16, 2018, https://www.etemadonline.com/آقای-شد-افراط-ها-افشاگری-در-245154/7-تاریخ-بخش.

42. One example is Khomeini's lieutenant and senior cleric, Ayatollah Mohammad Reza Mahdavi Kani. See Naser Ghazanfari, "We Pleaded That the Hostages Should Be Handed Over," *Ensaf*, October 23, 2020, http://www.ensafnews.com/264641/می-التماس-کنی-مهدوی%E2%80%8Cها/;E2%80%8Cکردیم-گروگان; "Ayatollah Mahdavi Kani Was Opposed to Capturing the American Embassy," *Didar News*, November 4, 2019, https://www.didarnews.ir/fa/news/39933/آمریکا- سفارت-تسخیر-مخالف-کنی-مهدوی-الله-آیت.

43. Personal conversations, June 2023.

44. Mousavian and Shahidsaless, *Iran and the United States*, 54.

45. Mousavian and Shahidsaless, *Iran and the United States*, 54–55; interview with Asgharzadeh. Baqer Moin argues that Khomeini took his time to gauge the impact of the hostage taking and whether it was advantageous before publicly supporting it. See Baqer Moin, *Khomeini: Life of the Ayatollah* (London: I. B. Tauris, 1999), 226–27.

46. Interview with Asgharzadeh.

47. Interview with Mohsen Rafiqdoust, later minister of the IRGC, *Abdi Media*, August 15, 2023, https://www.youtube.com/watch?v=gglNb1BlpMg.

48. Interview with Javad Mansouri (commander in chief of the IRGC in 1979–80), *Etemad Online*, July 3, 2017, https://www.etemadonline.com/اشغال-به-چمران-شهید-تند-واکنش-144298/9-سیاسی-بخش.

49. Interview with Mohsen Rafiqdoust.

50. For a discussion of the various explanations in Western academic sources for why the hostage crisis happened, see David Patrick Houghton, *U.S. Foreign Policy and the Iran Hostage Crisis* (New York: Cambridge University Press, 2001), 46–74.

51. Jimmy Carter, *Keeping Faith: Memoirs of a President* (New York: Bantam Books, 1982), 468.

52. Interview with Mohsen Rafiqdoust.

53. Zbigniew Brzezinski, *Power and Principle: Memoirs of a National Security Advisor, 1977–1981* (New York: Farrar, Straus and Giroux, 1983), 471.

54. Rouhollah K. Ramazani, "Iran's Export of the Revolution: Politics, Ends, and Means," in *The Iranian Revolution: Its Global Impact*, ed. John L. Esposito (Gainesville: Florida International University Press, 1990), 43–45.

55. Rafsanjani, *Revolution and Victory*, 292–300.

56. Rafsanjani, *Revolution and Victory*, 360–63.

57. Toby Matthiesen, "The Iranian Revolution and Sunni Political Islam," *New Analysis of Shia Politics, POEMPS Studies* 28 (December 2017), http://pomeps.org/the-iranian-revolution-and-sunni-political-islam#_ftnref12; Ataie, "Exporting the 1978–79 Revolution," chap. 1, 10–12, and chap. 2, 1–18.

58. Ataie, "Exporting the 1978–79 Revolution," chap. 1, 24–28.

59. Ataie, "Exporting the 1978–79 Revolution," chap. 2, 1–18; Mohammad Ataie, "Brothers, Comrades, and the Quest for the Islamist International: The First Generation of Liberation Movements in Revolutionary Iran," in *The Fate of Third Worldism in the Middle East*, ed. Rasmus Elling and Sune Haugbrolle (London: Oneworld, 2024), 121–44.

60. Ataie, "Exporting the 1978–79 Revolution," chap. 2, 16.

61. I owe this insight to Mohammad Ataie.

62. Laurence Louer, *Transnational Shiite Politics: Religious and Political Networks in the Gulf* (New York: Columbia University Press, 2008).

63. Vali Nasr, *The Shia Revival: How Conflicts within Islam Will Shape the Future* (New York: W. W. Norton, 2006), 119–68; Ataie, "Exporting the 1978–79 Revolution," chap. 3, 10.

64. Ataie, "Exporting the 1978–79 Revolution," chap. 3, 23–26. There are many references to training camps in Syria before the revolution in the memoirs of early founders of the IRGC. See, for instance, Mohsen Kazemi, *Memoirs of Marzieh Hadidchi* (Tehran: Soureh Mehr, 2014): 113–16; Seyyed Rahim-Safavi, *From South Lebanon to South Iran* (Tehran: Markaz Asnad Enqelab, 2009): 90–98. Hadidchi was the only woman commander of the IRGC, and Safavi would become the force's commander in chief.

65. "Interview with Sanjabi, Karim."

66. Vali Nasr, "Sectarianism and Shia Politics in Pakistan, 1979–Present," *Cahiers d'Etudes sur la Mediterranee Orientale et le Monde Turco-Iranien* 28 (1999): 311–23; Vali Nasr, "The Rise of Sunni Militancy in Pakistan: The Changing Role of Islamism and the Ulama in Society and Politics," *Modern Asian Studies* 34, no. 1 (January 2000): 139–80.

67. Vali Nasr, "International Politics, Domestic Imperatives, and the Rise of Politics of Identity: Sectarianism in Pakistan, 1979–1997," *Comparative Politics* 32, no. 2 (January 2000): 171–90.

68. Mohsen Rafiqdoust, *I Tell It for History: Memoirs of Mohsen Rafiqdoust (1979–80)*, ed. Saeed Alamiyan (Tehran: Soureh-e Mehr, 2013), 267–68.

69. Mohammad Ataie, "Exporting the Iranian Revolution: Ecumenical Clerics in Lebanon," *International Journal of Middle East Studies* 53, no. 4 (2021): 672–90.

70. Laurence Louer, "The Transformation of Shia Politics in the Gulf Monarchies," *New Analysis of Shia Politics, POEMPS Studies* 28 (December 2017), http://pomeps.org/new-analysis-of-shia-politics; Toby Matthiesen, "Hizbullah Al-Hijaz: A History of the Most Radical Saudi Shi'a Opposition Group," *Middle East Journal* 64, no. 2 (Spring 2010): 179–97.

71. Nasr, *The Shia Revival*, 147–68.

72. Rafsanjani, *Revolution and Victory*, 398–401.

73. Dehqani Firouzabadi, *The Foreign Policy*, 327.

74. Homeira Moshirzadeh, "Examination of the Islamic Republic's Foreign Policy from the Constructive Point of View," in *A Look at the Foreign Policy of the Islamic Republic of Iran*, ed. Nasrin Mosaffa (Tehran: Daftar Motale'at-e Siyasi va Beinollmealli, 2007).

75. Rafsanjani, *Revolution and Victory*, 273.

76. Jalil Roshandel, "Islamic Republic's Foreign Policy, Part I, from Revolution until Fall of 1982," *Radio Farda*, February 9, 2019, https://www.radiofarda.com/a/Islamic-republic-foreign -policy-part-1/29764251.html.

77. Ahmad Naqibzadeh, *Foreign Policy Process in Iran: Challenges, Costs and Alternatives* (Tehran: Moavenat-e Pajuheshi Daneshgah-e Azad-e Eslami, 2010); Mohammad Reza Tajik, *Foreign Policy: The Arena of Lack of Decision and Wisdom* (Tehran: Farhang Gofteman, 2004).

78. Article 11 of the Constitution. See *The Constitution of the Islamic Republic of Iran: Part 1, General Principles* (Tehran: Majles Shora-e Eslami), https://rc.majlis.ir/fa/law/show /133613.

79. Seyyed Javad Taha'ie, *An Account of the Foreign Policy of the Islamic Republic of Iran* (Tehran: Entesharat Markez Estratejik, 2009).

80. Rafsanjani, *Revolution and Victory*, 292–93, 398–401.

81. Nikolay Kozhanov, *Iran's Strategic Thinking: The Evolution of Iran's Foreign Policy, 1979–2018* (Berlin: Gerlach Press, 2018), 49.

82. John W. Parker, *Persian Dreams: Moscow and Tehran since the Fall of the Shah* (Dulles, VA: Potomac Books, 2009), 9.

83. Elahe Kulaie, Ebrahim Mottaqi, and Seyyed Davud Aqa-ie, eds., *Neither Eastern nor Western* (Tehran: Mizan, 2009). See also Mark J. Gasiorowski and Nikki Keddie, eds., *Neither East nor West: The Soviet Union, the United States and Iran* (New Haven, CT: Yale University Press, 1990).

84. Dehqani Firouzabadi, *The Foreign Policy*, 303.

85. Manuchehr Mohammadi, *A Survey of Iran's Foreign Policy during the Pahlavi Period, or, Decision-Making a State under Domination* (Tehran: Dadgostar, 1999), 135.

86. Nikolay Kozhanov, "Iran: Quest for Foreign Policy Identity," in *The Middle East: Politics and Identity*, ed. Irina Zvyagelskaya (Moscow: IMEMO, 2022), 293–94.

87. Dehqani Firouzabadi, *The Foreign Policy*, 301–4.

88. "The Necessity of Resistance Economy with Emphasis on Dr. Mossadegh's Approach during Oil Nationalization," *Proceedings of the National Conference on the History of Resistance Economics in Iran*, 2012, https://civilica.com/doc/213636/; "Resistance Economy, Mossadegh's Solution for Confronting Oil Sanctions," *Paydari-e Melli*, June 11, 2015, https://paydarymelli.ir/fa /news/14457/اقتصاد-مقاومتی-مقابله-با-تحریم های-نفتی-وقتی-مصدق-هم-نفت-را-از%C8%80%E2%مصدق-راهکار-مقاومتی-برای; اقتصاد-دولتش-کنار-گذاشت- Reza Ansari Bardeh and Mehdi Javanimoqaddam, "The Meaning of the Concept of Active Resistance in the Foreign Policy of the Islamic Republic of Iran," *Rahbord* 30, no. 98 (Spring 2022): 102–27.

89. Jack L. Snyder, *The Soviet Strategic Culture: Implications for Limited Nuclear Operations* (Santa Monica, CA: Rand, 1977), 8.

Chapter 3: The Struggle to Win the Revolution

1. On the events that unfolded over those two years, see Charles Kurzman, *The Unthinkable Revolution in Iran* (Cambridge, MA: Harvard University Press, 2004); Shaul Bakhash, *The Reign of Ayatollahs: Iran and the Islamic Revolution* (New York: Basic Books, 1984); Abbas Milani, *The Shah* (New York: Palgrave Macmillan, 2011), 360–430.

2. Gholam Reza Afkhami, *The Life and Times of the Shah* (Berkeley: University of California Press, 2009), 442.

3. Afkhami, *The Life and Times of the Shah*, 440; James A. Bill, *The Eagle and the Lion: The Tragedy of American-Iranian Relations* (New Haven, CT: Yale University Press, 1988), 219–26.

4. "Interview with Lahiji, Abdol-Karim," January 5 and 26, 1985, Oral History of Iran Collection of the Foundation for Iranian Studies.

5. Bakhash, *The Reign of Ayatollahs*, 14; "Interview with Homayoun, Daryush," September 11, 1982, Oral History of Iran Collection of the Foundation for Iranian Studies.

6. Charles Kurzman, "The Qum Protests and the Coming of the Iranian Revolution, 1975 and 1978," *Social Science History* 27, no. 3 (Fall 2003): 287–325.

7. Ali Gheissari and Vali Nasr, *Democracy in Iran: History and the Quest for Liberty* (New York: Oxford University Press, 2006), 78.

8. Nazanin Shahrokhi, *Women in Place: Politics of Gender Segregation in Iran* (Berkeley: University of California Press, 2019); Arzoo Osanloo, *The Politics of Women's Rights in Iran* (Princeton, NJ: Princeton University Press, 2009); Manouchehr Parvin and Mostafa Vaziri, "Islamic Man and Society in the Islamic Republic of Iran," in *Iran: Political Culture in the Islamic Republic*, ed. Samih Farsoun and Mehrdad Mashayekhi (New York: Routledge, 1992), 80–91.

9. Jahangir Amuzegar, *Iran's Economy under the Islamic Republic* (London: I. B. Tauris, 1993), 26–40; Suzanne Maloney, *Iran's Political Economy since the Revolution* (New York: Cambridge University Press, 2015), 107–39; Shaul Bakhash, "The Politics of Land, Law, and Social Justice in Iran," *Middle East Journal* 43, no. 2 (Spring 1989): 186–201.

10. Muhammad Baqir As-Sadr, *Our Economics* (Tehran: World Organization for Islamic Services, 1984).

11. Kevan Harris, "Social Welfare Policies and Dynamics of Elite and Popular Contentions," in *Power and Change in Iran: Politics of Contention and Conciliation*, ed. Daniel Brumberg and Farideh Farhi (Bloomington: Indiana University Press, 2016), 70–100.

12. Suzanne Maloney, "Agents or Obstacles? Parastatal Foundations and Challenges for Iranian Development," in *The Economy of Iran: The Dilemmas of an Islamic State*, ed. Parvin Alizadeh (London: I. B. Tauris, 2000), 145–76.

13. Maloney, *Iran's Political Economy*, 107–39; Bakhash, "The Politics of Land," 186–201; Hooshang Amirahmadi, *Revolution and Economic Transition: The Iranian Experience* (Albany: SUNY Press, 1990), 21–28; Arang Keshavarzian, "Regime Loyalty and *Bazari* Representation under the Islamic Republic of Iran: Dilemmas of the Society of Islamic Coalition," *International Journal of Middle East Studies* 41 (2009): 225–46.

14. Arang Keshavarzian, *Bazaar and State in Iran: The Politics of the Tehran Marketplace* (New York: Cambridge University Press, 2007), 1–29, 228–69; Keshavarzian, "Regime Loyalty," 225–46; Ahmad Ashraf, "Bazaar in the Iranian Revolution," *MERIP Reports* 113 (March–April 1983), https://meriorg/1983/03/bazaar-and-mosque-in-irans-revolution/.

15. Ali Akbar Hashemi Rafsanjani, *Revolution and Victory, Record and Memoirs, 1979–1980*, ed. Abbas Bashiri (Tehran: Daftar-e Nashr-e Manabe-e Enqelab, 2004), 181.

16. Seyyed Jalal Dehqani Firouzabadi, *The Foreign Policy of the Islamic Republic of Iran* (Tehran: Samt, 1990), 309; Rafsanjani, *Revolution and Victory*, 207–9; "Interview with Sanjabi, Karim," October 15, 1983, Iranian Oral History Project, Harvard University.

17. Cited in Ariane M. Tabatabai, *No Conquest, No Defeat: Iran's National Security Strategy* (New York: Oxford University Press, 2020), 188. See also Sepehr Zabih, *The Iranian Military in Revolution and War* (New York: Routledge, 1988), 115–35.

18. Rafsanjani, *Revolution and Victory*, 207–9.

19. Gregory F. Rose, "The Post-Revolutionary Purge of Iran's Armed Forces: A Revisionist Assessment," *Iranian Studies* 17, nos. 2–3 (Spring–Summer 1984): 154–57.

20. Fazlollah Farrokh, "Imam Khomeini's Reaction to the Slogan of Dismantling the Military in the Days Leading to the Revolution's Victory," Center for Documents of the Islamic Revolution, https://t.me/markazasnad/5869; interview with Captain Houshang Samadi, YouTube, August 18, 2020, https://www.youtube.com/watch?v=O4ntjRebtpA; "Interview with Captain Samadi," *Khabaronline*, September 25, 2019, https://www.khabaronline.ir/news/1303513 ناخدا-صمدی-وقتی-می-گویند-ارتش-در-جنگ-غافلگیر-شد-دیوانه-می-شوم/.

21. "Lecture to Graduates of Officer's Academy," in *The Writ of the Imam: Collection of Imam Khomeini's Works* (Tehran: Markaz Tanzim va Nashr Asar Imam Khomeini, 2000), 13:345–55.

22. Hossein Ardestani, *The Path: Oral History of Dr. Mohsen Rezaie, Volume 1: The Era of Fighting, the Crisis of Political Groups* (Tehran: Markaz-e Asnad va Tahqiqat-e Defa'e Moqaddas, 2016), 427-48; interview with General Yahya Rahim-Safavi, *Mehr News*, June 8, 2019, https://www.mehrnews.com/news/4635379/مخالفان-و-موافقان-ادغام-ارتش-و-سپاه-دلیل-اصرار-هاشمی-چه-بود.

23. Gholam Ali Rajaie, *Impressions from Imam Khomeini's Life* (Tehran: Moassesseh-e Tanzim va Nashr Asar Imam Khomeini, 2013), 1:115.

24. Rafsanjani, *Revolution and Victory*, 268; Mostafa Chamran, *Kurdistan* (Tehran: Bonyad-e Shahid, 1985).

25. Rafsanjani, *Revolution and Victory*, 232–33; "Interview with Sanjabi, Karim."

26. Rafsanjani, *Revolution and Victory*, 267–69.

27. "Ethnic and Regional Conflicts in the Early Years of the Revolution according to Ayatollah Hashemi Rafsanjani," https://rafsanjani.ir/records/مناز عات-قومی-و-منطقه-ای-در-سالهای-اول-اقلاب به-روایت-ایت-الله-هاشمی-رفسنجانی-. The chief of the Iranian military at the time, General Naser Farbod, was opposed to using the military to quell ethnic uprisings—preferring that the government reach a political settlement. It was his religious superiors who wanted the military to suppress turmoil in the Kurdish region. See his interviews in *Ayandegan*, July 22, 1979, 1; *Bamdad*, June 23, 1979, 1, 3; *Khalq-e Musalman*, October 7, 1979, 1–2.

28. "Ethnic and Regional Conflicts," in *The Writ of the Imam: Collection of Imam Khomeini's Works* (Tehran: Markaz Tanzim va Nashr Asar Imam Khomeini, 2000), 9:280–84; Chris de Krester, "Khomeini as Military Chief, Orders Kurdish Revolt Crushed," *Washington Post*, August 9, 1979, https://www.washingtonpost.com/archive/politics/1979/08/19/khomeini-as-military-chief-orders-kurdish-revolt-crushed/7ef59251-2429-44fd-ba41-b6117603506d/.

29. Ardestani, *Path*, 365–66; Mohsen Rafiqdoust, *I Tell It for History: Memoirs of Mohsen Rafiqdoust (1979–80)*, ed. Saeed Alamiyan (Tehran: Soureh-e Mehr, 2013), 76; Rafsanjani, *Revolution and Victory*, 306, 342–43; Ali Alfoneh, *Iran Unveiled: How the Revolutionary Guards Is Turning Theocracy into Military Dictatorship* (Washington, DC: AEI Press, 2013), 10–12; Mohammad Ataie, "Exporting the 1978–79 Revolution: Pan-Islamic or Sectarian" (PhD diss., University of Massachusetts at Amherst, 2020, chap. 1, 1; Maryam Alemzadeh, "The Attraction of Direct

Action: The Making of the Islamic Revolutionary Guards Corps in the Iranian Kurdish Conflict," *British Journal of Middle East Studies* (2021): 1–20.

30. Manouchehr Najafdari, *Behind the Gates of the City: The Memoirs of Brigidier Manouchehr Najafdari*, ed. Hossein Kavoshi (Tehran: Markaz Assad-e Enqelab-e Eslami, 2017), 423–25; "Lt. General Naser Farbod: From Collaboration with Fardust to Bazargan," *Tarikh-e Irani*, April 9, 2020, http://tarikhirani.ir/fa/news/8399/سرلشکر-ناصر-فرید-از-همکاری-با-فردوست-تا-بازرگان.

31. Rafsanjani, *Revolution and Victory*, 232–33.

32. Nader Entessar, "The Kurdish Factor in Iran-Iraq Relations," Middle East Institute, June 29, 2009, https://www.mei.edu/publications/kurdish-factor-iran-iraq-relations; Steven R. Ward, *Immortal: A Military History of Iran and Its Armed Forces* (Washington, DC: Georgetown University Press, 2009), 231–33.

33. Ahsan Butt, *Secession and Security: Explaining State Strategy against Separatists* (Ithaca, NY: Cornell University Press, 2017), 1–17.

34. Bakhash, *Reign of the Ayatollahs*, 52–165; Said Amir Arjomand, *Turban for the Crown: The Islamic Revolution in Iran* (New York: Oxford University Press, 1988), 154–63.

35. Twitter, March 16, 1979, https://twitter.com/AliHamid27/status/1544392071758446594/video/1.

36. Bakhash, *The Reign of Ayatollahs*, 71–91

37. Asghar Schirazi, *The Constitution of the Islamic Republic of Iran: Politics and the State in the Islamic Republic*, trans. John O'Kane (London: I. B. Tauris, 1997); Mohsen Milani, "Shi'ism and the State in the Constitution of the Islamic Republic of Iran," in *Iran: Political Culture in the Islamic Republic*, ed. Samih Farsoun and Mehrdad Mashayekhi (New York: Routledge, 1992), 92–109.

38. Vanessa Martin, *Creating an Islamic State: Khomeini and the Making of a New Iran* (London: I. B. Tauris, 2000), 159–65.

39. Said Amir Arjomand writes that the idea of Caesaropapism was embedded in the Safavid conception of the Shia monarchy in the sixteenth century. See Said Amir Arjomand, *The Shadow of God and Hidden Imam: Religion, Political Order, and Societal Change in Shi'ite in Iran from the Beginning to 1890* (Chicago: University of Chicago Press, 1984), 22, 98.

40. Gol Ali Babaie, *The Message of the Fish: Life Story [Interviews] of [General] Haj Hossein Hamedani* (Tehran: Soureh-e Mehr, 2016), 23–24.

41. Shahrzad Mojab, "The State and University: The 'Islamic Cultural Revolution' in the Institutions of Higher Education of Iran, 1980–87" (PhD diss., University of Illinois at Urbana-Champaign, 1991).

42. Ervand Abrahamian, *Tortured Confessions: Prisons and Public Recantations in Modern Iran* (Berkeley: University of California Press, 1999), 209–28; Ervand Abrahamian, *The Iranian Mojahedin* (New Haven, CT: Yale University Press, 1989), 206–23; Maziar Behrooz, *Rebels with a Cause: The Failure of the Left in Iran* (London: I. B. Tauris, 1999), 95–134.

43. Seyed Hossein Mousavian and Shahir Shahidsaless, *Iran and the United States: An Insider's View on the Failed Past and the Road to Peace* (New York: Bloomsbury, 2014), 53–74.

44. Mohammad Ayatollahi Tabaar, "Causes of the U.S. Hostage Crisis in Iran: The Untold Account of the Communist Threat," *Security Studies* 26, no. 4 (2017): 665–97.

45. "Hostage Taking Hastened the Resignation of the Interim Government: Interview with Ibrahim Yazdi [Bazargan's Foreign Minister]," *Tarikh-e Irani*, November 4, 2015, http://tarikhirani.ir/fa/news/5230/ابراهیم-یزدی-گروگانگیری-استعفای-دولت-موقت-را-جلو-انداخت.

46. Reza Alijani, "Reminiscences of the Commander of IRGC," *Radio Farda*, November 7, 2019, https://www.radiofarda.com/a/commentary-on-hostage-crisis-back-scene/30258568.html.

47. Mousavian and Shahidsaless, *Iran and the United States*, 53–74.

48. Sadeq Zibakalam and Hesam Basrouyehnejad Karimi, *Occupation: The Second Revolution and Birth of Anti-Americanism* (Tehran: Rouzaneh, 2021).

49. Mark J. Gasiorowski, "The Nuzhih Plot and Iranian Politics," *International Journal of Middle East Studies* 34 (2002): 645–66; Rafsanjani, *Revolution and Victory*, 407–9.

50. Hal Brands, "Saddam Hussein, the United States, and the Invasion of Iran: Was There a Green Light?," *Cold War History* 12, no. 2 (May 2012): 319–43.

51. Rouhollah K. Ramazani, "Iran's Export of the Revolution: Politics, Ends, and Means," in *The Iranian Revolution: Its Global Impact*, ed. John L. Esposito (Gainesville: Florida International University Press, 1990), 43.

52. Jeremy Friedman, "The Enemy of My Enemy: The Soviet Union, East Germany, and the Iranian Tudeh Party's Support for Ayatollah Khomeini," *Journal of Cold War Studies* 20, no. 2 (2018): 3–37.

53. Mohsen Milani, "Harvest of Shame: Tudeh and the Bazargan Government," *Middle Eastern Studies* 29, no. 2 (April 1993): 307–20.

54. Behrooz, *Rebels with a Cause*, 95–134; Ja'far Shiralinia, *History of Iran-Iraq War* (Tehran: Sayan, 2014) , 290.

55. Seyyed Abdol-Karim Mousavi Ardebili, *The Episode of March 5, 1981: The Rise and Fall of Counter-Revolution* (Tehran: Moassesseh Maktab-e Amir Al-Mo'menin, 1988), 640.

56. Mohammad Sadeq Kooshaki, "The Fate of Mohammad Reza Saadati's Strange File," Islamic Revolution's Document Center, July 27, 2020, https://irdc.ir/fa/news/6013/سرانجام-پرونده-مرموز-محمدرضا-سعادتی-.

57. Mohammad Hasan Rouzitalab, *Thunder in a Cloudless Sky: Oral History of Security Struggle with Mojahedin-e Khalq (1979–1989)* (Tehran: Nashr-e Iran, 2022).

58. Efraim Karsh, *The Iran-Iraq War, 1980–1988* (Oxford: Osprey Publishing, 2002), 73.

59. Ataie, "Exporting the 1978–79 Revolution," chap. 3, 6, 16.

60. "Interview with Nasr, Seyyed Hossein," October 1982 and January 1983, Oral History of Iran Collection of the Foundation for Iranian Studies.

61. Hamid Dabashi, "Ali Shari'ati's Islam: Revolutionary Uses of Faith in a Post-Traditional Society," *Islamic Quarterly* 27, no. 4 (January 1983): 203–22; "Interview with Nasr, Seyyed Hossein."

62. Abrahamian, *Tortured Confessions*, 209–28.

63. Gholam Reza Behdarvand Yani, *History of Iran after the Islamic Revolution, Volume 7, Great Victories* (Tehran: Markaz Asnad Jomhouri Eslami, 2022), 20–95.

64. Sick, *All Fall Down*, 280.

65. Richard Cottam, *Iran and the United States: A Cold War Case Study* (Pittsburgh: University of Pittsburgh Press, 1988), 220–21.

66. David Patrick Houghton, *U.S. Foreign Policy and the Iran Hostage Crisis* (New York: Cambridge University Press, 2001), 108.

67. Abol-Hasan Bani Sadr, *My Turn to Speak: Iran, the Revolution and Secret Deals with the U.S.* (Washington, DC: Potomac Books, 1991).

68. Zbigniew Brzezinski, "The Failed Mission: The Inside Account of the Attempt to Free the Hostages in Iran," *New York Times Magazine*, April 18, 1982, 4.

69. Mark Bowden, "The Desert One Debacle," *The Atlantic*, May 2006, https://www .theatlantic.com/magazine/archive/2006/05/the-desert-one-debacle/304803/; Houghton, *U.S. Foreign Policy and the Iran Hostage Crisis*, 113–36.

70. Bani Sadr, *My Turn to Speak*; Gary Sick, *October Surprise: America's Hostages in Iran and the Election of Ronald Reagan* (New York: Crown, 1991); Peter Baker, "A Four-Decade Secret: One Man's Story of Sabotaging Carter's Re-election," *New York Times*, March 18, 2023, https:// www.nytimes.com/2023/03/18/us/politics/jimmy-carter-october-surprise-iran-hostages .html.

71. Dehqani Firouzabadi, *The Foreign Policy*, 325–27.

72. "Imam Khomeini: America Can't Do a Damn Thing," *Keyhan*, September 30, 2015, 6.

Chapter 4: Sacred Defense: How the War Transformed Iran's Strategy

1. Steven R. Ward, *Immortal: A Military History of Iran and Its Armed Forces* (Washington, DC: Georgetown University Press, 2009), 297.

2. Ward, *Immortal*.

3. Suzanne Maloney, *Iran's Political Economy since the Revolution* (New York: Cambridge University Press, 2015), 169–72.

4. Cited in Ariane M. Tabatabai and Annie Tracy Samuel, "What the Iran-Iraq War Tells Us about the Future of Iran Nuclear Deal," *International Security* 41, no. 1 (Summer 2017): 154.

5. "Imam Khamenei: Defending the Country Needs Resistance, Not Surrender, This Is a Fact," *Tasnim*, September 21, 2022, https://www.tasnimnews.com/fa/news/1401/06/30 /2777229/امام-خامنه-ای-صیانت-از-کشور-با-مقاومت-به-دست-می-آید-نه-تسلیم-این-یک-اصل-است.am.

6. Seyyed Jalal Dehqani Firouzabadi, *The Foreign Policy of the Islamic Republic of Iran* (Tehran: Samt, 1990), 346–47.

7. Charles Kurzman, "Death Tolls of the Iran-Iraq War," October 31, 2013, https://kurzman.unc .edu/death-tolls-of-the-iran-iraq-war/.

8. For comprehensive accounts of this war, see Pierre Rizoux, *The Iran-Iraq War*, trans. Nicholas Elliott (Cambridge, MA: Harvard University Press, 2015); Williamson Murray and Kevin Woods, *The Iran-Iraq War: A Military and Strategic History* (New York: Cambridge University Press, 2014); Ja'far Shiralinia, *History of Iran-Iraq War* (Tehran: Sayan, 2014); Hossein Ala'i, *Analytical History of Iran-Iraq War* (Tehran: Marz va Boom, 2022).

9. Vali Nasr, *The Shia Revival: How Conflicts within Islam Will Shape the Future* (New York: W. W. Norton, 2006), 140.

10. Mohammad Ataie, "Exporting the 1978–79 Revolution: Pan-Islamic or Sectarian" (PhD diss., University of Massachusetts at Amherst, 2020), chap. 3, 2.

11. Falih A. Jabar, *The Shi'ite Movement in Iraq* (London: Al Saqi, 2005), 232; Lisa Blaydes, *The State of Repression: Iraq under Saddam Hussein* (Princeton, NJ: Princeton University Press, 2018), 247–48.

12. "Intelligence Cable Prepared in the Central Intelligence Agency," April 19, 1980, *Foreign Relations of the United States, 1977–1980, Volume XI, Part I, Iran: Hostage Crisis, November 1979–September 1980*, Carter Library, National Security Affairs, Brzezinski Material, Cables File, box 93, Iran, 4/18/80, Secret, Specat [handling restriction not declassified], exclusive. Sent to the Department of State, JCS/DIA, White House Situation Room, NSC Staff, and CIA Office of Current Operations, https://history.state.gov/historicaldocuments/frus1977-80v11p1/d260.

13. Ariane M. Tabatabai, *No Conquest, No Defeat: Iran's National Security Strategy* (New York: Oxford University Press, 2020), 188.

14. Accordingly, Saddam had paid $21 million to General Oveisi and promised more if his military preparations bore fruit. See "Paper Prepared in the Central Intelligence Agency," undated, *Foreign Relations of the United States, 1977–1980, Volume XI, Part I, Iran: Hostage Crisis, November 1979–September 1980*, National Security Council, Carter Intelligence Files, box 1031, Carter Intelligence Files September–December 1980, Secret [name not declassified]. The paper was sent to Saunders and Hunter of the NSC Staff under an August 15 covering memorandum, https://history.state.gov/historicaldocuments/frus1977-80v11p1/d343. See also "Interview with Heshmati, Kambiz," November 1983, Oral History of Iran Collection of the Foundation for Iranian Studies; "Interview with Mohaqqeqi, General Ahmad Ali," June 26, 1989, Oral History of Iran Collection of the Foundation for Iranian Studies; Majid Khadduri, *The Gulf War: The Origins and Implications of the Iran-Iraq Conflict* (New York: Oxford University Press, 1988), 84.

15. Khadduri, *The Gulf War*, 85–103.

16. Ebrahim Anvari Tehrani, "Iraqi Leadership's Preparations for Aggression against Iranian Territory," in *Review of the Various Aspects of Aggression and Defense* (Tehran: Dabirkhaneh Konferans Beinolmellali Tajavoz va Defa', 1989), 2:9–62.

17. Shiralinia, *History of Iran-Iraq War*, 15; Seyyed Yaqub Hosseini, *Military History of the Imposed War* (Tehran: Hey'at-e Ma'aref-e Jang, 2008), 1:113–14.

18. Arshin Adib-Moghaddam, "Inventions of the Iran-Iraq War," in *Debating the Iran-Iraq War in Contemporary Iran*, ed. Narges Bajoghli and Amir Moosavi (New York: Routledge, 2018), 76–95.

19. Will D. Sweringen, "Geo-Political Origins of the Iran-Iraq War," *Geographical Review* 78, no. 4 (October 1988): 405–16; Efraim Karsh, "Geopolitical Determinism: The Origins of the Iran-Iraq War," *Middle East Journal* 44, no. 2 (Spring 1990): 256–68.

20. Arash Reisinezhad, *The Shah of Iran, the Iraqi Kurds, and the Lebanese Shia* (New York: Palgrave Macmillan, 2019), 284–85.

21. Seyyed Mahmoud Do'aie, *A Sample of Reminiscences* (Tehran: Arouj, 2008), 174–77.

22. One official historian of the war, Mohammad Doroudian, writes that Iraq's attack on Iran came just seventy-five days after the ill-fated coup attempt at the Nojeh Airbase in western Iran, which was instigated by royalist officers still in uniform along with exiled activists. That had prompted another purge of the officer corps and thrown the Iranian military into turmoil.

Mohammad Doroudian, *Beginning to End of the War* (Tehran: Markaz Motale'at va Tahqiqat-e Jang, 2000), 24.

23. "Full Text of Shamkhani's Unsaid Recollections of the War," *Isna*, September 27, 2005, https://www.isna.ir/news/8407-01892/توانستیم-می-ایسنا-با-وگو-کفت-در-جنگ-از-شمخانی-های-ناگفته-کامل-متن; Shiralinia, *History of Iran-Iraq War*, 52.

24. Rizoux, *The Iran-Iraq War*, 68.

25. "The Return of Iraq's Government to the Arab Dark Ages," in *The Writ of the Imam: Collection of Imam Khomeini's Works* (Tehran: Markaz Tanzim va Nashr Asar Imam Khomeini, 2000), 12:246.

26. Ayatollah [Hossein Ali] Montazeri, *Reminiscences*, 2nd ed. (Essen, Germany: Ettehadieh Nasherin Irani dar Oroupa, 2001), 1:566–67.

27. "I Gave Saddam's Message for Negotiations to the Imam in a Private Meeting," *Etemad*, September 28, 2015; https://www.etemadnewspaper.ir/fa/main/detail/26417.

28. Hamid Ahmadi, *Lesson of Experience: The Reminiscences of Abol-Hasan Bani Sadr* (Berlin: Anjoman Motale'at va Tahqiqat-e Tarikh Shafahi Iran, 2001), 265–66.

29. Jabar, *The Shi'ite Movement*, 11–12; "Recollections of Do'aie [Former Iran Ambassador in Iraq] of His Meeting with Saddam," *Sharq*, December 6, 2015, https://www.sharghdaily.com صدام-با-از-دعا-80244/100-روزنامه-بخش./

30. Eric Davis, *Memories of State: Politics, History and Collective Identity in Modern Iraq* (Berkeley: University of California Press, 2005), 190–94; Rizoux, *The Iran-Iraq War*, 21.

31. Rizoux, *The Iran-Iraq War*, 135–50; Murray and Woods, *The Iran-Iraq War*, 138–70.

32. "The Policy of America and Its Allies: Sowing Division between Muslim Nations," in *The Writ of the Imam: Collection of Imam Khomeini's Works* (Tehran: Markaz Tanzim va Nashr Asar Imam Khomeini, 2000), 13:212, 222; Shiralinia, *History of Iran-Iraq War*, 69.

33. "Emphasis on Resilience and Sacrifice of the Nation in Defense of Islam," in *The Writ of Imam: Collection of Imam Khomeini's Works* (Tehran: Markaz Tanzim va Nashr Asar Imam Khomeini, 2000), 13:251; "The Powerful Resistance of the Iranian Nation before Iraq's Aggression," in *The Writ of Imam: Collection of Imam Khomeini's Works* (Tehran: Markaz Tanzim va Nashr Asar Imam Khomeini, 2000), 13:315.

34. Cited in Assal Rad, *The State of Resistance: Politics, Culture, and Identity in Modern Iran* (New York: Cambridge University Press, 2022), 67.

35. Ayatollah Khamenei's speech during the commemoration of sacred defense, *Telewebion*, September 20, 2023, https://telewebion.com/episode/0x8b1dofi.

36. "Imam Khamenei: Defending the Country."

37. Annie Tracy Samuel, "Guarding the Nation: The Iranian Revolutionary Guards, Nationalism and the Iran-Iraq War," in *Constructing Nationalism in Iran: From the Qajars to the Islamic Republic*, ed. Meir Litvak (New York: Routledge, 2017), 252–53.

38. Ward, *Immortal*, 289–96.

39. Tabatabai and Samuel, "What the Iran-Iraq War Tells Us," 156.

40. Rizoux, *The Iran-Iraq War*, 290–301.

41. Tabatabai and Samuel, "What the Iran-Iraq War Tells Us," 155–57; Annie Tracy Samuel, *The Unfinished History of the Iran-Iraq War: Faith, Firepower, and Iran's Revolutionary Guards* (New York: Cambridge University Press, 2022), 212.

42. Bahram Mostaghimi and Masoud Taromsari, "Double Standard: The Security Council and the Two Wars," in *Iranian Perspectives on the Iran-Iraq War*, ed. Farhang Rajaee (Gainesville: University Press of Florida, 1997), 62–70.

43. "Diplomatic Weakness for Ending Iran-Iraq War," *Roydad24*, September 26, 2020, https://www.rouydad24.ir/fa/news/231976/ضعف-دیپلماتیک-برای-پایان-دادن-به-جنگ-ایران-و-عراق.

44. Shiralinia, *History of Iran-Iraq War*, 220–21, 227; Mohammad Hasan Ostadi Moqaddam, *Understanding Sacred Defense* (Tehran: Khadem al-Reza, 2021), 130.

45. Shirzad Khazaie, *Chemical Warfare against Iran: A Military and Legal Analysis* (Tehran: Markaz Asnad Jomhouri Eslami, 2021); Mohammad Baqer Nikkhah, *War Crimes: Iraq's Chemical Attacks in War with Iran* (Tehran: Markaz Asnad va Tahqiqat-e Defa'e Moqaddas, 2012); "The Silence of International Organizations in the Face of Saddam's Chemical Crimes against Iran," Center for Documents of the Islamic Revolution, August 9, 2022, https://www.irdc.ir/fa/news/7962/%E2%80%8Cسکوت-مجامع-بین-المللی-در-قبال-جنایات-شیمیایی-صدام-علیه-ایران.

46. Steve Coll, *The Achilles Trap: Saddam Hussein, the C.I.A., and the Origins of America's Invasion of Iraq* (New York: Penguin Press, 2024), 115.

47. Efraim Karsh, *The Iran-Iraq War, 1980–1988* (Oxford: Osprey Publishing, 2002), 76–78.

48. Shane Harris and Matthew Aid, "CIA Files Prove America Helped Saddam as He Gassed Iran," *Foreign Policy*, August 26, 2013, https://foreignpolicy.com/2013/08/26/exclusive-cia-files-prove-america-helped-saddam-as-he-gassed-iran/.

49. Narges Bajoghli et al., *How Sanctions Work: Iran and the Impact of Economic Warfare* (Stanford, CA: Stanford University Press, 2024), 45.

50. Montazeri, *Reminiscences*, 1:568.

51. Afshon Ostovar, *Vanguard of the Imam: Religion, Politics, and Iran's Revolutionary Guards* (New York: Oxford University Press, 2016), 64–65.

52. Rizoux, *The Iran-Iraq War*, 157–65.

53. Maryam Alemzadeh, "The Attraction of Direct Action: The Making of the Islamic Revolutionary Guards Corps in the Iranian Kurdish Conflict," *British Journal of Middle East Studies* (2021): 1–20.

54. Mohammad Doroudian, *The War's Fundamental Issues* (Tehran: Entesharat-e Markaz-e Asnad Defa'e Moqaddas, 2018).

55. Shiralinia, *History of Iran-Iraq War*, 167–68.

56. Mohsen Milani, "Power Shifts in Revolutionary Iran," *Iranian Studies* 26, nos. 3–4 (Summer–Autumn 1993): 364–67.

57. Tabatabai, *No Conquest*, 199.

58. Milad Karimi, "Hovizeh and Bani Sadr's Sin," *Keyhan*, January 10, 2022, https://www.magiran.com/article/4256956; Shiralinia, *History of Iran-Iraq War*, 129.

59. "[Khamenei's] Letter to Commander of Ahvaz's 92nd Armored Division for the Operation to Free Sousangerd," *Khamenei.ir*, November 17, 1980, https://farsi.khamenei.ir/message-content?id=27379

60. "Imam's Harsh Encounter with Bani Sadr; Actions That Smelled of Treason," *Khabar Online*, March 27, 2017; https://www.khabaronline.ir/news/649316/ماجرای-برخورد-تند-امام-با-بنی-صدر-اقداماتی-که-بوی-خیانت-می-دادند.

61. Shiralinia, *History of Iran-Iraq War*, 133; Farhad Darvishi, *The Iran-Iraq War: Questions and Answers* (Tehran: Markaz Motale'at va Tahqiqat-e Jang, 2007), 103–4.

62. Seyyed Abdol-Karim Mousavi Ardebili, *The Episode of March 5, 1981: The Rise and Fall of Counter-Revolution* (Tehran: Moassesseh Maktab-e Amir Al-Mo'menin, 1988), 640; Shiralinia, *History of Iran-Iraq War*, 135.

63. "Definitive Answer to the Dissenters against Truth [Mojahedin-e Khalq]," in *The Writ of Imam: Collection of Imam Khomeini's Works* (Tehran: Markaz Tanzim va Nashr Asar Imam Khomeini, 2000), 14:342; "National Front's Call to Rebellion against the Quran," in *The Writ of Imam: Collection of Imam Khomeini's Works* (Tehran: Markaz Tanzim va Nashr Asar Imam Khomeini, 2000), 14:451.

64. Abdol-Razzaq Ahvazi, *Imam Khomeini According to Ayatollah Hashemi Rafsanjani* (Tehran: Moassesseh-e Tanzim va Nashr Asar Imam Khomeini, 1981), 124.

65. Ali Akbar Hashemi Rafsanjani, *Stability and Struggle: Hashemi's Memoirs, 1984*, ed. Mehdi Hashemi (Tehran: Nashr-e Ma'aref-e Enqelab, 2003), 514.

66. Sepehr Zabih, *The Iranian Military in Revolution and War* (New York: Routledge, 1988), 21.

67. Interview with Mohsen Rezaie in "The Story of Imam's Historic Saying: The Path to Jerusalem Passes through Karbala," *Entekhab*, September 26, 2014, https://www.entekhab.ir/fa/news /182333/با-آقای-هاشمی-و-میرحسین-در-مورد-جنگ-مصاحبه-کنید-ماجرای-این-سخن-تاریخی-امام-ره-راه-قدس-از-کربلا-می-گذرد.

68. Chronicles of the war are replete with stories of units formed by local people and led by local commanders into battle. One such example is General Qasem Soleimani's reminiscences about leading a unit of volunteers from his native Kerman in the deadly Karbala-5 offensive. "Karbala-5 in the Telling of Martyr Qasem Soleimani," *Khabargozari Daneshjou*, January 9, 2022, https://snn.ir /fa/news/988870/کربلای-5-به-روایت-شهید-قاسم-سلیمانی-کربلایی-در-جوار-کربلای-حسین-ع-به-وقوع-پیوست..

69. Murray and Woods, *The Iran-Iraq War*, 185

70. Maryam Alemzadeh, "The Islamic Revolutionary Guards Corps in the Iran-Iraq War: An Unconventional Military Survival," *British Journal of Middle East Studies* (2018): 1–18; Hossein Ardestani, "Formation of IRGC's Military Structure during the Fath Al-Mobin Operations, Oral History of Dr. Mohsen Rezaie," *Negin-e Iran* 50 (Fall 2015): 5–28.

71. Shiralinia, *History of Iran-Iraq War*, 167–68, 181.

72. Ja'far Shiralinia, "Shocking Letter of Some IRGC Operational Commanders," *Dideban-e Iran*, July 24, 2020, http://www.didbaniran.ir/87814نامه-تکان-دهنده-تعدادی-از-فرماندهان/3-بخش-سیاسی; "The Recording of the Session between Mohsen Rezaie and His Opponents عملیاتی-سپاه-متن-نامه-in 1984," *Hamshahri*, September 23, 2020, https://www.hamshahrionline.ir/news/551700 /بشنوید-صوت-کامل-جلسه-محسن-رضایی-با-معترضان-در-سال-63-چه-کسانی.

73. "An Article by Martyr Chamran Published in America," *Mashreq*, June 24, 2014, https://www.mashreghnews.ir/news/320997/مقاله-چاپ-شده-از-شهید-چمران-در-آمریکا.

74. Ward, *Immortal*, 259–61; Kaveh Farrokh, *Iran at War: 1500–1988* (Oxford: Osprey Publishing, 2011), 370.

75. Ostovar, *Vanguard of the Imam*, 75, 83–84; Rob Johnson, *The Iran-Iraq War* (New York: Palgrave Macmillan, 2011), 71–79; Razoux, *The Iran-Iraq War*, 345–61.

76. Coll, *The Achilles Trap*, 31–40, 74, 72.

77. Ward, *Immortal*, 261–79.

78. "I Wish I Too Was a Pasdar," in *The Writ of Imam: Collection of Imam Khomeini's Works* (Tehran: Markaz Tanzim va Nashr Asar Imam Khomeini, 2000), 15:496–97.

79. Shiralinia, *History of Iran-Iraq War*, 318.

80. Mohammad Doroudian, *From Beginning to End: A Review of the Iran-Iraq War* (Tehran: Markaz Asnad va Tahqiqat Dafa'e Moqaddas, 2012), 8.

81. Akbar Ganji, "Iran-Iraq War: Instrument for Power and Wealth," https://news.gooya.com /politics/pdf/AG09202013.pdf.

82. Ganji, "Iran-Iraq War." See also Samuel, *The Unfinished History*, 191–209.

83. Hamid Davoudabadi, *From Heavenly Ascendance of the Returnees* (Tehran: Nashr-e Yousef, 2010), 429; Shiralinia, *History of Iran-Iraq War*, 302–3.

84. Mohsen Rezaie, *Analysis of Al-Fajr Operation in Eight Conversations with Narrators of Imposed War, August 1986* (Tehran: Markaz Asnad va Tahqiqat-e Defa'e Moqaddas, 2011), 69–70; "Conversation with Ali Akbar Hashemi Rafsanjani," *Negin Iran* 23 (Winter 2007–2008): 11.

85. Rezaie, *Analysis of Al-Fajr Operation*, 42–44; Ali Akbar Hashemi Rafsanjani, *Hope and Worry: The Record and Recollections of Hashemi Rafsanjani, Year 1985*, ed. Sara Lahouti (Tehran: Daftar-e Nashr-e Ma'aref-e Eslami, 2008), 89–94.

86. "What We Should Know about Operation Kheybar," excerpts from Mohsen Rezaie's blog, *Paygah-e Etela'resani Mohsen Rezaie, Mashreq News*, March 2, 2015, https://www .mashreghnews.ir/news/394086/نقشه-و-عکس-بدانیم-خیر-درباره-عملیات-باید-آنچه; "The Recording of the Session between Mohsen Rezaie and His Opponents in 1984."

87. Ali Akbar Hashemi Rafsanjani, *Towards Destiny: The Record and Memoirs of Hashemi, Year 1984*, ed. Mohsen Hashemi (Tehran: Daftar Nashr-e Ma'aref-e Enqelab, 2006), 94; Montazeri, *Reminiscences*, 2:1056–59.

88. Rafsanjani, *Towards Destiny*, 383–434.

89. "Why Do We Call the War Sacred Defense," *Tasnim*, September 23, 2019, https://www .tasnimnews.com/fa/news/1398/07/01/2101739/نامیم-می-مقدس-دفاع-را-جنگ-چرا-گزارش.

90. "Order," in *The Writ of Imam: Collection of Imam Khomeini's Works* (Tehran: Markaz Tanzim va Nashr Asar Imam Khomeini, 2000), 19:386.

91. Rizoux, *The Iran-Iraq War*, 210–19; Samuel, *The Unfinished History*, 110–27.

92. Hadi Nakhaie, Mehdi Ansari, and Mohammad Doroudian, *Khorramshahr in the Long War* (Tehran: Markaz-e Sepah-e Pasdaran-e Enqelab-e Eslami, 2010).

93. Tabatabai, *No Conquest*, 215; Mohammad Doroudian, *Reasons for the Continuation of the War* (Tehran: Entesharat-e Markaz-e Asnad Defa'e Moqaddas, 2004), 140–51.

94. Mohammad Doroudian, *The Fundamental Questions of the War* (Tehran: Moassesseh-e Motale'at-e Siyasi Farhangi Andisheh-e Nab, 2001), 208–13; Hossein Ala'i, "Reasons for Continuation of the War after Capture of Khorramshahr and Process of Ending It," *Pajouheshnameh Defa'e Moqaddas* 1, no. 4 (2013): 63–97; Shiralinia, *History of Iran-Iraq War*, 205–12.

95. Doroudian, *The Fundamental Questions*, 210.

96. Ala'ie, *Analytical History of Iran-Iraq War*, 1:518–22; interview with Mohsen Rezaie in "The Story of Imam's Historic Saying."

97. See, for instance, "Continuation of the War after Capture of Khorramshahr," *Andisheh-e Qom*, n.d., https://www.pasokh.org/fa/telegram/View/951781/-خرمشهر-فتح-از-پس-جنگ-ادامه; "Capture of Khorramshahr and Why the War Continued," *Hawzah* 21 (May 2004), https://hawzah

.net/fa/Magazine/View/4892/4936/42295/جنگ-ادامه-چرایی-و-خرمشهر-فتح‏!; Doroudian, *Reasons for Continuation of the War.*

98. Ali Akbar Velayati, *Political History of Iraq's Imposed War on Iran* (Tehran: Daftar Nashr-e Farhang Eslami, 1997), 104.

99. Manuchehr Mohammadi, *The Imposed War: Collection of Articles* (Tehran: Basij Manteqeh-e 3, 1995), 51, 232.

100. Cited in Tabatabai, *No Conquest*, 207.

101. "Imam Khamenei: Defending the Country."

102. Seyyed Ahmad Khomeini, *Reason for the Sun: Recollections of Imam's Memento* (Tehran: Moaseseh-e Tanzim va Nashr-e Asar-e Imam Khomeini, 2005), 125.

103. Seyyed Ruhollah Khomeini, "This Class Was Deprived So It Advanced the Movement," in *The Book of Light: Collection of Imam Khomeini's Works* (Tehran: Moassesseh-e Tanzim va Nashr Asar Emam, 1980), 6:183–84.

104. Christopher Blattman, *Why We Fight: The Roots of War and the Paths to Peace* (New York: Viking, 2022), 269–70.

105. Doroudian, *Reasons for the Continuation of the War*, 140–51.

106. Shiralinia, *History of Iran-Iraq War*, 219; Ali Akbar Hashemi Rafsanjani, *After the Crisis: Memoirs of Hashemi Rafsanjani 1982*, ed. Fatemeh Hashemi (Tehran: Daftar-e Nashr-e Ma'aref-e Eslami, 2001), 376; "General Ala'i Account of the Meeting with Imam [Khomeini] about Continuing the War after Capture of Khorramshahr," *Tasnim*, April 28, 2020, https://www.iranchamber.com/calendar/converter/iranian_calendar_converter.ph.

107. Samuel, *The Unfinished History*, 128–48.

108. Velayati, *Political History*, 141.

109. Ali Reza Lotfollahzadegan, *Daily Account of Iran-Iraq War, Volume 20, Crossing the Border* (Tehran: Markaz Tahqiqat va Motale'at-e Jang Sepah Pasdaran Enqelab, 2000), 18–19.

110. Velayati, *Political History*, 137; Mohammad Hasan Mohaqqeqi, *Hidden Secrets: Unknowns of the Eight Year Defense According to the State and Military Leaders of War Years* (Tehran: Markaz Motale'at Pajoheshi 27 Be'sat, 2014), 317–19; Doroudian, *The Fundamental Questions*, 204; Shiralinia, *History of Iran-Iraq War*, 222.

111. "Mohsen Arabi's Conversation with Mohammad Doroudian about the Continuation of the War after Capture of Khorramshahr," *Asr-e Eslam*, July 14, 2021, http://www.asrislam.com/fa/news/26077/خرمشهر-فتح-از-بعد-جنگ-ادامه-درباره-درودیان-محمد-با-عربی-محسن-گفتگوی.

112. Mohammad Ayatollahi-Tabaar, "Factional Politics in the Iran-Iraq War," *Strategic Studies* 42, nos. 3–4 (2019): 480–506.

113. Shiralinia, *History of Iran-Iraq War*, 141–47.

114. Mohammad Ayatollahi Tabaar, *Religious Statecraft: The Politics of Islam in Iran* (New York: Columbia University Press, 2019), 147–85.

115. Karsh, *The Iran-Iraq War*, 84–85.

116. Nasr, *The Shia Revival*, 119–20.

117. Cited in Tabatabai, *No Conquest*, 206–7.

118. Davis, *Memories of State*, 192–93; Mohammad R. Kalantari, "The Media Contest during the Iran-Iraq War: The Failure of Mediatized Shi'ism," *Media, War and Conflict* 15, no. 3 (2022): 378–98.

119. "Untold Accounts of Karbala-5 According to [General] Rahim-Safavai," *Mashreq*, January 14, 2011, https://www.mashreghnews.ir/amp/24223.

120. Bernard Trainor, "Iraq Said to Gain Upper Hand at Basra," *New York Times*, February 7, 1987, 3.

121. Cited in Shiralinia, *History of Iran-Iraq War*, 224.

122. Rafsanjani, *Stability and Struggle*, 502, 525.

123. Rafsanjani, *Towards Destiny*, 11.

124. Rafsanjani, *Stability and Struggle*, 504, 517; "Conversation with Ali Akbar Hashemi Rafsanjani," 10–11.

125. Mohammad Doroudian, *Process of Ending the War* (Tehran: Sepah Pasdaran Enqelab-e Eslami, 2005), 180, 182–83.

126. Rafsanjani, *After the Crisis*, 238, 371, 374.

127. Rafsanjani, *After the Crisis*, 247–49; Rezaie, *Analysis of Al-Fajr Operation*, 59–60.

128. Dehqani Firouzabadi, *The Foreign Policy*, 332–86.

129. Seyyed Davoud Aqaie, "Islamic Republic of Iran's Foreign Policy during the Eight-Year War," *Majelleh-e Daneshkadeh-e Hoquq va Oloum-e Siyasi* 73 (Winter 2002): 1–34; Hossein Ardestani, "Iran: Interaction of War and Foreign Policy," *Negin-e Iran* 3 (Winter 2003): 21–33.

130. Seyyed Mohsen Kharrazi, "Varieties and Types of Sacred Defense in Islam," in *Review of Aspects of Aggression and Defense* 1 (1991): 98–106.

131. Reza Ra'iss Tousi, "Containment and Animosity: The United States and the War," in *Iranian Perspectives on the Iran-Iraq War*, ed. Farhang Rajaee (Gainesville: University Press of Florida, 1997), 49–70 .

132. Dilip Hiro, *The Longest War: The Iran-Iraq Military Conflict* (New York: Routledge, 1990), 71.

133. Shiralinia, *History of Iran-Iraq War*, 415.

134. Ward, *Immortal*, 269–72.

135. Murray and Woods, *The Iran-Iraq War*, 239.

136. Seyed Hossein Mousavian and Shahir Shahidsaless, *Iran and the United States: An Insider's View on the Failed Past and the Road to Peace* (New York: Bloomsbury, 2014), 96.

137. H. E. Chehabi, "Iran and Lebanon in the Revolutionary Decade," in *Distant Relations: Iran and Lebanon in the Last 500 Years*, ed. H. E. Chehabi (London: I. B. Tauris, 2006), 201–30; Mohammad Ataie, "Revolutionary Iran's 1979 Endeavor in Lebanon," *Middle East Policy* 20, no. 2 (June 2013): 137–52.

138. Mohammad Ataie, "Becoming Hezbollah: The Party's Evolution and Changing Roles," Crown Center for Middle East Studies, Brandeis University, January 27, 2023, https://www.brandeis.edu/crown/publications/crown-conversations/cc-16.html.

139. Masoud Asadollahi, *From Resistance to Victory: A History of Hezbollah* (Tehran: Zekr, 1999), 63; "Israel's Attack on Lebanon: America's Trap for Iran," in *The Writ of Imam: Collection of Imam Khomeini's Works* (Tehran: Markaz Tanzim va Nashr Asar Imam Khomeini, 2000), 16:354.

140. Velayati, *Political History*, 142–43; Hossein Ardestani, *Analysis of Iran-Iraq War, Volume 3, Punishing the Aggressor* (Tehran: Markaz Asnad va Tahqiqat-e Defa'e Moqaddas, 2016), 32–33.

141. Ataie, "Becoming Hezbollah."

142. Rizoux, *The Iran-Iraq War*, 271–89.

143. Bajoghli et al., *How Sanctions Work*, 57.

144. I am grateful to Narges Bajoghli for this insight.

145. James A. Bill, "The U.S. Overture to Iran, 1985–1986: An Analysis," in *Neither East nor West: The Soviet Union, the United States and Iran*, ed. Mark Gasiorowski and Nikki Keddie (New Haven, CT: Yale University Press, 1990), 166–79.

146. Fox Butterfield, "Arms for Hostages—Plain and Simple," *New York Times*, November 27, 1988, sec. 7, 10.

147. Hossein Ardestani, *Punishing the Aggressor* (Tehran: Markaz-e Motale'at va Tahqiqat-e Jang, 2000), 149.

148. Ja'far Shiralinia and Majid Tafreshi, "What Was the McFarlane Story? Conversation with Mohsen Hashemi, Hossein Ala'ie and Abbas Salimi Namin," *Iran*, November 2, 2020, https://www.irannewspaper.ir/newspaper/item/559059; Fereydoun Verdinejad, "The Untold Parts of McFarlane Affair," *Dr. Fereydoun Verdinejad* (blog), n.d., http://verdinejad.com/?page_id=1080.

149. Ali Akbar Hashemi Rafsanjani, "Islamic Revolution in the Third Decade," *Ketab-e Naqd Quarterly* 22 (Spring 2003): 10–11.

150. Mousavian and Shahidsaless, *Iran and the United States*, 97–98.

151. Shiralinia, *History of Iran-Iraq War*, 355.

152. Mousavian and Shahidsaless, *Iran and the United States*, 92–96; Velayati, *Political History*, 208; Ali Akbar Hashemi Rafsanjani, *Height of Defense: Memoirs of Hashemi Rafsanjani, Year 1986*, ed. Emad Hashemi (Tehran: Daftar-e Nashr-e Ma'aref-e Enqelab, 2009), 330–38.

153. Verdinejad, "The Untold Parts of McFarlane Affair"; Shiralinia, *History of Iran-Iraq War*, 595.

154. Rafsanjani, *Height of Defense*, 24; "The Unsaid from One of the Intelligence Officials of the Time about Ayatollah Montazeri," *Fars News*, December 21, 2021, https://www.farsnews.ir/news/14000930000053/ناگفته‎%8C%80%E2آیت‌-از‌-اطلاعات‌-وزارت‌-وقت‌-مقامات‌-از‌-یکی‌-های‌%8C%80%E2منتظری‌-الله‎; "The 'Liberation Movements' Unit, a Group under Montazeri's Protection That Served the Enemy," *Tasnim*, May 18, 2020, https://www.tasnimnews.com/fa/news/1399/02/24 بود‌-دشمن‌-خدمت‌-در‌-که‌-منتظری‌-حمایت‌-مورد‌-گروهی‌-آزادیبخش‌-های‌-نهضت‌-واحد‌-گزارش‎/2265312.

155. Emadeddin Baghi, *Truths and Judgments* (Tehran, 1999).

156. Bryan R. Gibson, *Covert Relationship: American Foreign Policy, Intelligence, and the Iran Iraq War, 1980–1988* (Westport, CT: Praeger, 2010), 78.

157. Ali Akbar Hashemi Rafsanjani, *End of Defense, Start of Reconstruction: Memoirs of Hashemi Rafsanjani, Year 1988*, ed. Ali Reza Hashemi (Tehran: Daftar Nashr-e Ma'aref-e Enqelab, 2011), 102.

158. Farrokh, *Iran at War*, 406–8.

159. Mousavian and Shahidsaless, *Iran and the United States*, 98.

160. Dehqani Firouzabadi, *The Foreign Policy*, 344.

161. Cited in Mousavian and Shahidsaless, *Iran and the United States*, 98.

162. "A Look at Iraqi Regime's Use of Chemical Weapons during the Imposed War," in *Review of the Various Aspects of Aggression and Defense* (Tehran: Dabirkhaneh Konferans Beinolmellali Tajavoz va Defa', 1989), 2:358–71.

163. Mousavian and Shahidsaless, *Iran and the United States*, 447–62; Hossein Bastani, "Why Did Ayatollah Khomeini Demand the Execution of Commanders Responsible for Iran's 'Defeat' in the War?," *BBC Persian*, September 23, 2014, https://www.bbc.com/persian/iran/2014/09 /140923_l39_file_iran_iraq_war.

164. Hashemi, *End of Defense*, 102; Shiralinia, *History of Iran-Iraq War*, 458.

165. Shiralinia, *History of Iran-Iraq War*, 462–64.

166. "Conversation with Ali Akbar Hashemi Rafsanjani," 10.

167. Shiralinia, *History of Iran-Iraq War*, 470.

168. Shiralinia, *History of Iran-Iraq War*, 471.

169. "Full Text of Imam Khomeini's Letter about Reasons for Accepting Resolution 598 and End to the War," *Mehr News*, September 29, 2006, https://www.mehrnews.com/news/386966 /متن-کامل-نامه-امام-خمینی-درباره-علل-پذیرش-قطعنامه-598-و-پایان.

170. "Conversation with Ali Akbar Hashemi Rafsanjani," 13.

171. Vahid Abedini, "The New Generation of Political Elites in Iran: Genealogy, Evolution, and Trajectory" (PhD diss., Florida International University, 2023), 181.

172. Ali Alfoneh, *Iran Unveiled: How the Revolutionary Guards Is Turning Theocracy into Military Dictatorship* (Washington, DC: AEI Press, 2013), 152–56.

173. Rad, *The State of Resistance*, 64–68.

174. "Imam Khamenei: Defending the Country."

175. Cited in Ray Takeyh, *Guardians of the Revolution: Iran and the World in the Age of the Ayatollahs* (New York: Oxford University Press, 2009), 90.

176. Takeyh, *Guardians of the Revolution*, 90.

177. Rad, *The State of Resistance*, 65.

178. Ostovar, *Vanguard of the Imam*, 133–40.

179. Karsh, *The Iran-Iraq War*, 62–65.

180. Mohammad Azizi, "Analysis of Participation of Various Social Strata in the Sacred Defense," *Pajouheshnameh Defa'e Moqaddas* 1, no. 2 (2012): 97–119; Ian Brown, *Khomeini's Forgotten Sons: The Story of Iran's Boy Soldiers* (London: Grey Seal, 1990).

181. Fariba Adelkhah, *Being Modern in Iran* (New York: Columbia University Press, 2000), 144.

Chapter 5: How the War Made the Islamic Republic

1. Gholam Ali Rajaie, "A Memory of Imam Khomeini's Nationalism," *Asr-e Iran*, June 18, 2007, https://www.asriran.com/fa/news/19682/خاطره%E2%80%8Cاي-از-ملي%E2%80%8Cامام-گرایي-خمینره.

2. Trita Parsi, *Treacherous Alliance: The Secret Dealings of Israel, Iran, and the U.S.* (New Haven, CT: Yale University Press, 2007), 106–9; Seymour M. Hersh, "The Iran Pipeline: A Hidden Chapter / Special Report; U.S. Is Said to Have Allowed Israel to Sell Arms to Iran," *New York Times*, December 8, 1991, 1.

3. Nate Jones, "Document Friday: When Iran Bombed Iraq's Nuclear Reactor," *Unredacted*, March 12, 2012, https://unredacted.com/2012/03/09/document-friday-when-iran-bombed -iraqs-nuclear-reactor/.

4. "Interview with Farhang, Mansour," October 21, 1989; February 25, and December 20, 1990, Oral History of Iran Collection of the Foundation for Iranian Studies.

5. Annie Tracy Samuel, *The Unfinished History of the Iran-Iraq War: Faith, Firepower, and Iran's Revolutionary Guards* (New York: Cambridge University Press, 2022), 195–96.

6. Mateo Mohammad Farzaneh, *Iranian Women and Gender in the Iran-Iraq War* (Syracuse, NY: Syracuse University Press, 2021).

7. Kaveh Ehsani, "War and Resentment: Critical Reflections on the Legacies of the Iran-Iraq War," in *Debating the Iran-Iraq War in Contemporary Iran*, ed. Narges Bajoghli and Amir Moosavi (New York: Routledge, 2018), 9–11.

8. Orkideh Behrouzan, "Medicalization as a Way of Life: The Iran-Iraq War and Considerations for Psychiatry and Anthropology," *Medicine Anthropology Theory* 2, no. 3 (2016): 40–60; Narges Bajoghli, "Learning to Play by Ear in Iran," *New York Times*, April 8, 2016, https://www.nytimes.com/2016/04/10/magazine/learning-to-play-by-ear-in-iran.html?searchResult Position=2.

9. Kamran Scot Aghaie, *The Martyrs of Karbala: Shi'i Symbols and Rituals in Modern Iran* (Seattle: University of Washington Press, 2004), 136–38.

10. Williamson Murray and Kevin Woods, *The Iran-Iraq War: A Military and Strategic History* (New York: Cambridge University Press, 2014), 235–36, 257–58.

11. Ali Khaji, Shoaoddin Fallahdoost, and Mohammad Reza Soroush, "Civilian Casualties of Iranian Cities by Ballistic Missile Attacks during the Iraq-Iran War (1980–1988)," *Chinese Journal of Traumatology* 1, no. 13 (April 2010): 87–90.

12. Murray and Woods, *The Iran-Iraq War*, 235–36, 257–58.

13. Steve Coll, *The Achilles Trap: Saddam Hussein, the C.I.A., and the Origins of America's Invasion of Iraq* (New York: Penguin Press, 2024), 114.

14. Cited in Assal Rad, *The State of Resistance: Politics, Culture, and Identity in Modern Iran* (New York: Cambridge University Press, 2022), 65.

15. Javad Mansouri, *The Oral History of Formation of Iran's Islamic Revolutionary Guards Corps* (Tehran: Markaz Assad-e Enqelab-e Eslami, 2014), 68–89.

16. Gol Ali Babaie, *The Message of the Fish: Life Story [Interviews] of [General] Haj Hossein Hamedani* (Tehran: Soureh-e Mehr, 2016), 26–29, 78–79.

17. "Javad Zarif's Three-Hour Interview," *Radio Farda*, April 26, 2021, https://www.radiofarda.com/a/31223108.html; Mohammad Javad Zarif, *Enduring Patience: Takeaways from Eight Years of Ministry* (Tehran: Etela'at, 2024): 114–52.

18. Mohammad Doroudian, *The Fundamental Questions of the War* (Tehran: Moassesseh-e Motale'at-e Siyasi Farhangi Andisheh-e Nab, 2001), 205.

19. Efraim Karsh, *The Iran-Iraq War, 1980–1988* (Oxford: Osprey Publishing, 2002), 79–83.

20. "Imam Khomeini's Last Will and Testament," n.d., https://www.al-islam.org/imam-khomeinis-last-will-and-testament/testament.

21. Philip Selznik, *The Organizational Weapon: A Study of Bolshevik Strategy and Tactics* (New York: Free Press, 1960).

22. Maziar Behrooz, "Factionalism in Iran under Khomeini," *Middle Easters Studies* 27, no. 4 (October 1994): 597–614.

23. Said Amir Arjomand, *After Khomeini: Iran under His Successors* (New York: Oxford University Press, 2009), 16–35.

24. Cited in "Meeting of a Group of Veterans and Commanders of Sacred Defense with the Supreme Leader," *Khamenei.ir*, July 21, 2022, https://farsi.khamenei.ir/print-content?id=50980.

25. Seyyed Jalal Dehqani Firouzabadi and Reza Zabihi, "The Impact of Islamic-Revolutionary Identity on the Behavior of the Islamic Republic on the Nuclear Issue," *Oloum Siyasi* 15, no. 59 (Fall 2012): 80.

26. Kevan Harris, *A Social Revolution: Politics and the Welfare State in Iran* (Berkeley: University of California Press, 2017), 80–115.

27. Mohammad Doroudian, *Beginning to End of the War* (Tehran: Markaz Motale'at va Tahqiqat-e Jang, 2000), 63.

28. Eric Lob, "Development, Mobilization and War: The Iranian Construction Jihad, Construction Mobilization, and Trench Builders Association (1979–2013)," in *Debating the Iran-Iraq War in Contemporary Iran*, ed. Narges Bajoghli and Amir Moosavi (New York: Routledge, 2018), 24.

29. Hossein Ardestani, "Construction Jihad in the Imposed War," *Negin-e Iran* 51 (Winter 2015): 5–8.

30. Vahid Abedini, "The New Generation of Political Elites in Iran: Genealogy, Evolution, and Trajectory" (PhD diss., Florida International University, 2023), 182.

31. Eric Lob, *Iran's Reconstruction Jihad: Rural Development and Regime Consolidation after 1979* (New York: Cambridge University Press, 2020), 125–70.

32. Mehdi Moslem, *Factional Politics in Post-Khomeini Iran* (Syracuse: Syracuse University Press, 2002), 47–81; Arang Keshavarzian, *Bazaar and State in Iran: The Politics of the Tehran Marketplace* (New York: Cambridge University Press, 2007), 228–69.

33. Harris, *A Social Revolution*, 80–115.

34. Harris, *A Social Revolution*, 137–40.

35. Suzanne Maloney, "Agents or Obstacles? Parastatal Foundations and Challenges for Iranian Development," in *The Economy of Iran: The Dilemmas of an Islamic State*, ed. Parvin Alizadeh (London: I. B. Tauris, 2000), 145–76.

36. Abedini, "The New Generation," 175–207.

37. Gholam Reza Behdarvand Yani, *History of Iran after the Islamic Revolution, Volume 7, Great Victories* (Tehran: Markaz Asnad Jomhouri Eslami, 2022), 3–10; Hesam Foruzan, *The Military in Post-Revolutionary Iran: The Evolution and Roles of the Revolutionary Guards* (New York: Routledge, 2016), 105–40.

38. Cited in Abedini, "The New Generation," 176.

39. Saeid Golkar, *Captive Society: The Basij Militia and Social Control in Iran* (New York: Columbia University Press, 2015); Afshon Ostovar, "Iran's Baseej: Membership in a Militant Islamist Organization," *Middle East Journal* 67, no. 3 (Summer 2013): 345–61.

40. Gol Ali Babaie, *The Operational Report Card of Habib Ibn Mazaher Battalion's Unit 27, Muhammad Rasul Allah from the Start to Finish of Sacred Defense* (Tehran: Markaz Pajouheshi-e 27 Besat, 2015).

41. Morad Veisi, "The Ringleader of Habib; Mojtaba Khamenei's Team," *Radio Farda*, August 19, 2019, https://www.radiofarda.com/a/30119166.html.

42. Ariane M. Tabatabai and Annie Tracy Samuel, "What the Iran-Iraq War Tells Us about the Future of Iran Nuclear Deal," *International Security* 41, no. 1 (Summer 2017): 156.

43. Hadi Ajili and Mahsa Rouhi, "Iran's Military Strategy," *Survival* 61, no. 6 (2019): 14; Ali Alfoneh, "What Iran's Military Journals Reveal about the Role of Missiles in Strategic Deterrence," Arab Gulf States Institute in Washington, June 25, 2020, https://agsiw.org/what-irans-military-journals-reveal-about-the-role-of-missiles-in-strategic-deterrence/.

44. "Javad Zarif's Three-Hour Interview"; Zarif, *Enduring Patience*, 461–65.

45. Cited in Dan Lamothe, "Animosity between David Petraeus and Iranian Commander, Qassem Soleimani, Still on Display," *Washington Post*, March 20, 2015, https://www.washington post.com/news/checkpoint/wp/2015/03/20/animosity-between-david-petraeus-and-iranian-commander-qassem-soleimani-still-on-display/; personal conversations with General Petraeus, September 2010.

46. Farideh Farhi, "The Antinomies of Iran's War Generation," in *Iran, Iraq and the Legacies of War*, ed. Gary Sick and Lawrence Potter (New York: Palgrave Macmillan, 2004), 101–20.

47. Seyyed Jalal Dehqani Firouzabadi, "Ontological Security in the Foreign Policy of the Islamic Republic of Iran," *Faslnameh-e Beinolmellai Ravabet-e Khareji* 1, no. 1 (Spring 2008): 42–76.

48. "Meeting of a Group of Veterans and Commanders of Sacred Defense with the Supreme Leader."

49. The education system has been an important vehicle for disseminating state views on history, culture, and national security with the aim of inculcating a uniform outlook among the population. Sussan Siavoshi, "Regime Legitimacy and Highschool Textbooks," in *Iran after the Revolution: Crisis of an Islamic State*, ed. Saeed Rahnema and Sohrab Behdad (London: I. B. Tauris, 1995), 203–17; Shervin Malekzadeh, "Education as Public Good or Private Resource: Accommodation and Demobilization in Iran's University System," in *Power and Change in Iran: Politics of Contention and Conciliation*, ed. Daniel Brumberg and Farideh Farhi (Bloomington: Indiana University Press, 2016), 101–34.

50. Roxanne Vaziri, *Warring Souls: Youth, Media, and Martyrdom in Post-Revolutionary Iran* (Durham, NC: Duke University Press, 2006).

51. See, for instance, Hossein Ardestani, "Oral History of Commander of Iran-Iraq War," *Negin-e Iran* 12, no. 24 (Fall 2013): 5–18; Mohammad Doroudian, *Probing the Lessons and Gains of the War* (Tehran: Markaz Asnad va Tahqiqat-e Defa'e Moqaddas, 2021); Mohammad Doroudian, *From Bloody City to Khorramshahr: Analysis of Political and Military Developments from Iraq's Preparations for Invasion to Liberation of Khorramshahr; From September 1980 to June 1982* (Tehran: Markaz Asnad va Tahqiqat-e Defa'e Moqaddas, 2021).

52. Amir Moosavi, "How to Write Death: Resignifying Martyrdom in Two Novels of the Iran-Iraq War," *Alif: Journal of Comparative Poetics* (August 15, 2015): 1–18; Amir Moosavi, "Stepping Back from the Front: A Glance at Home Front Narratives of the Iran-Iraq War in Persian and Arabic Fiction," in *Moments of Silence: Authenticity in Cultural Expressions of the Iran-Iraq War, 1980–1988*, ed. Arta Khakpour, Shouleh Vatanabadi, and Mohammad Mehdi Khorrami (New York: NYU Press, 2016), 120–36; Hamid Naficy, *A Social History of Iranian Cinema, Volume 4: The Globalizing Era, 1984–2010* (Durham, NC: Duke University Press, 2012), 1–92.

53. Narges Bajoghli, "*The Outcasts*: The Start of 'New Entertainment' in Pro-Regime Filmmaking in the Islamic Republic of Iran," in *Debating the Iran-Iraq War in Contemporary Iran*, ed. Narges Bajoghli and Amir Moosavi (New York: Routledge, 2018), 59–75; Amir Moosavi, "Dark Corners and the Limits of Ahmad Dehqan's War Fiction," in *Debating the Iran-Iraq War in Contemporary Iran*, ed. Narges Bajoghli and Amir Moosavi (New York: Routledge, 2018), 43–58.

54. I am indebted to Narges Bajoghli for her insights here.

55. Rad, *The State of Resistance*, 68–97.

56. Abdolreza Saleminejad, *Dezful: The Capital of Iran's Resistance* (Tehran: Niloufaran, 2014).

57. Annie Tracy Samuel, "Guarding the Nation: The Iranian Revolutionary Guards, Nationalism and the Iran-Iraq War," in *Constructing Nationalism in Iran: From the Qajars to the Islamic Republic*, ed. Meir Litvak (New York: Routledge, 2017), 248–50.

Chapter 6: After the War: Reform or Resistance

1. "Ayatollah Hashemi Rafsanjani's Interview with Members of the International Relations Quarterly," *Rafsanjani.ir*, March 21, 2013, https://rafsanjani.ir/records/مصاحبه-آیت-الله-هاشمی-رفسنجانی-با-اعضای-فصلنامه-مطالعات-بین-المللی.

2. Suzanne Maloney, *Iran's Political Economy since the Revolution* (New York: Cambridge University Press, 2015), 141–91; Hooshang Amirahmadi, *Revolution and Economic Transition: The Iranian Experience* (Albany: SUNY Press, 1990), 133–234.

3. Adel Hashemi, *The Making of Martyrdom in Modern Twelver Shi'ism: From Protesters and Revolutionaries to Shrine Defenders* (London: I. B. Tauris, 2022), 77.

4. Maqsoud Ranjbar, *Security Considerations in Iran's Foreign Policy* (Tehran: Pajouheshkadeh-e Motale'at-e Rahbordi, 2000).

5. Saeed Yaqubi, *The Foreign Policy of the Islamic Republic of Iran in the Development Era* (Tehran: Markaz-e Asnad-e Enqelab-e Eslami, 2000).

6. Ali Akbar Hashemi Rafsanjani, *Reconstruction and Development, Record and Memoirs, 1990*, ed. Ali Lahouti (Tehran: Daftar-e Nashr-e Ma'aref-e Enqelab-e Eslami, 2012), 8, 263.

7. Crane Brinton, *The Anatomy of Revolution* (New York: Prentice Hall, 1938), 205–36.

8. Cited in Said Amir Arjomand, *After Khomeini: Iran under His Successors* (New York: Oxford University Press, 2009), 34.

9. Mohammad Ayatollahi Tabaar, *Religious Statecraft: The Politics of Islam in Iran* (New York: Columbia University Press, 2019), 212–14; "A Look at the Negotiations of the Council for Reevaluation of the Constitution," *Hoqouq va Ejtema'* (blog), https://aalinaghi.blog.ir/1394/11/17/rfe37.

10. Ayatollahi Tabaar, *Religious Statecraft*, 198–204.

11. Seyed Hossein Mousavian and Shahir Shahidsaless, *Iran and the United States: An Insider's View on the Failed Past and the Road to Peace* (New York: Bloomsbury, 2014), 106.

12. Mohsen Milani, "The Transformation of the Velayat-i Faqih Institution from Khomeini to Khamenei," *Muslim World* 82, nos. 3–4 (July–October 1992): 175–90; Ahmad Kazemi-Moussavi, "A New Interpretation of the Theory of *Vilayat-i Faqih*," *Middle Eastern Studies* 28, no. 1 (January 1992): 101–7; Arjomand, *After Khomeini*, 38–41.

13. Wilfried Buchta, *Who Rules Iran? The Structure of Power in the Islamic Republic* (Washington, DC: Washington Institute for Near East Policy, 2002).

14. Mehrzad Boroujerdi and Kourosh Rahimkhani, "The Office of the Supreme Leader: The Epicenter of a Theocracy," in *Power and Change in Iran: Politics of Contention and Conciliation*, ed. Daniel Brumberg and Farideh Farhi (Bloomington: Indiana University Press, 2016), 135–65.

15. Alex Vatanka, *The Battle of the Ayatollahs in Iran: The United States, Foreign Policy, and Political Rivalry since 1979* (London: I. B. Tauris, 2021), 89–97.

16. Cited in Ja'far Shiralinia, *A Telling of the Life and Times of Ayatollah Ali Akbar Hashemi Rafsanjani* (Tehran: Sayan, 2017), 675.

17. Arjomand, *After Khomeini*, 172–91.

18. Sayyid Ali Khamenei, *Books and I* (Tehran: Mehr, 2001); Ali Reza Eshraghi and Yasaman Baji, "The Cleric Who Changed," Institute for War and Peace Reporting, June 3, 2010, https://www.refworld.org/docid/4c1091cf31.html.

19. Eshraghi and Baji, "The Cleric."

20. "Interview with Kazemiyyeh, Eslam," November 3, 1983, and May 8, 1984, Oral History of Iran Collection of the Foundation for Iranian Studies; "Comments in a Gathering of Young People," *Khamenei.ir*, April 27, 1998, https://farsi.khamenei.ir/newspart-index?tid=2444&npt=14.

21. I owe these insights to Mohammad Ataie.

22. Ali Akbar Hashemi Rafsanjani, *Patience and Victory, Memoirs and Record, 1995*, ed. Emad Hashemi (Tehran: Ma'aref-e Enqelab, 2018), 528–29, 548, 592, 606.

23. "Letter to Members of Parliament and Ministers [Reasons for Removal of Mr. Montazeri from Position of Deputy Leader]," in *The Writ of the Imam: Collection of Imam Khomeini's Works* (Tehran: Markaz Tanzim va Nashr-e Asar Imam Khomeini, 2000), 21:350.

24. Peyman Fathi, "We Should Not Wait for Anyone," *Khamenei.ir*, August 18, 2011, https://farsi.khamenei.ir/others-note?id=17025; Ali Aqa Mohammadi, "The Only Solution Is Resistance," *Khamenei.ir*, December 7, 2010, https://farsi.khamenei.ir/others-note?id=10558.

25. "Imam Khamenei Recollects the Details of His Own Experience with Terrorism," *Tasnim*, June 29, 2023, https://www.youtube.com/watch?v=oyTHajQ7MZg&t=27s.

26. "Mohsen Arabi's Conversation with Mohammad Doroudian about the Continuation of the War after Capture of Khorramshahr," *Asr-e Eslam*, July 14, 2021, http://www.asrislam.com /fa/news/26077/گفتگوی-محسن-عربی-با-محمد-درودیان-درباره-ادامه-جنگ-بعد-از-فتح-خرمشهر.

27. Ali Akbar Hashemi Rafsanjani, *Amir Kabir or the Hero of Struggle against Imperialism* (Tehran: Amir Kabir Publishing, 1968).

28. Hamidreza Esma'ili, *Political Thought of Ayatollah Hashemi Rafsanjani* (Tehran: Markaz-e Enqelab-e Eslami Iran, 2019), 43–51.

29. Rafsanjani, *Reconstruction and Development*, 595; Ali Akbar Hashemi Rafsanjani, *Moderation and Victory: Memoirs and Record of Hashemi Rafsanjani, 1991*, ed. Emad Hashemi Bahremani (Tehran: Daftar-e Nashr-e Ma'aref-e Enqelab, 2013), 437.

30. Rafsanjani, *Patience and Victory*; Rafsanjani *Reconstruction and Development*, 151–54; Mehdi Moslem, *Factional Politics in Post-Khomeini Iran* (Syracuse: Syracuse University Press, 2002), 142–51; "Recollections of Hashemi Rafsanjani about the Imam's Death and Choice of Ayatollah Khamenei to Become Leader of the Revolution," *Entekhab*, November 16, 2012,

https://www.entekhab.ir/fa/news/84010/ خاطرات-هاشمی-رفسنجانی-از-رحلت-امام-و-انتخاب-آیت
%E2%80%8Cخامنه‌الله%E2%80%8Cانقلاب-رهبری-به-ای.

31. Rafsanjani, *Reconstruction and Development*, 35–36.

32. Ali Akbar Hashemi Rafsanjani, *Hashemi Rafsanjani: Years of Struggle: Memories, Images, Chronology of Events* (Tehran: Daftar-e Nashr-e Ma'aref-e Enqelab, 1997), 1:269–90.

33. "The Historic 200-Page Interview with Ayatollah Hashemi Rafsanjani," *Ensafnews*, January 10, 2017, http://www.ensafnews.com/49370/.

34. Ali Baqeri Dolatabadi, *Unrealized Dreams: A Review of Ayatollah Hashemi Rafsanjani's Foreign Policy* (Tehran: Tisa, 2019), 113.

35. "A Look at the Doctrine of Omm Alqara and Its Place in Iran's Foreign Policy," *Resalat*, April 28, 2007, https://www.iranchamber.com/calendar/converter/iranian_calendar_converter.ph.

36. Baqeri Dolatabadi, *Unrealized Dreams*, 91.

37. "Interview with Ayatollah Hashemi Rafsanjani," https://rafsanjani.ir/records/آیت-مصاحبه
-الله-هاشمی-رفسنجانی-با-اعضای-فصلنامه-مطالعات-بین-المللی-.

38. Ali Akbar Hashemi Rafsanjani, "Islamic Revolution in the Third Decade," *Ketab-e Naqd Quarterly* 22 (Spring 2003): 10.

39. "[Mohsen] Rezaie: Hashemi Rafsanjani Stopped Export of Revolution," *Mashreq*, May 15, 2011, https://www.mashreghnews.ir/news/45990/هاشمي-رفسنجاني-صدور-انقلاب-را-متوقف-کرد;
"The Red Line in Policy of Tension Reducation . . . ," *Isna*, December 24, 2006, https://www
.isna.ir/news/8110-00644/اختصاصي-دکتر-محمد-رضا-تاجیک-خط-قرمز-در-سیاست-تنش-زدایي; Rafsanjani, *Reconstruction and Development*, 476; Seyyed Ruhollah Khomeini, *Export of Revolution from Imam Khomeini's View* (Tehran: Mo'assesseh-e Tanzim va Nashr-e Asar-e Imam Khomeini, 2008), 31–32.

40. Rafsanjani, *Moderation and Victory*, 20–21; Baqeri Dolatabadi, *Unrealized Dreams*, 637; Alireza Azqandi, "Tension Reduction in Foreign Policy: The Case of the Islamic Republic of Iran," *Majelleh-e Siyasat-e Khareji* 52 (2000): 1043; "Hashemi Rafsanjani: I Told the Imam to Solve the Issue of Relations with America during His Lifetime," *Isna*, September 22, 2013, https://www.iranchamber.com/calendar/converter/iranian_calendar_converter.ph.

41. Ali Baqeri Dolatabadi and Mohsen Shafi'i Seifabadi, *From Hashemi to Rouhani: A Review of Iran's Foreign Policy* (Tehran: Tisa, 2019).

42. On Rafsanjani'spresidency, see Arjomand, *After Khomeini*, 56–71; Maloney, *Iran's Political Economy*, 192–257; Amirahmadi, *Revolution and Economic Transition*, 235–90; Ali Gheissari and Vali Nasr, *Democracy in Iran: History and the Quest for Liberty* (New York: Oxford University Press, 2006), 105–26; Anoushiravan Ehteshami, *After Khomeini: The Iranian Second Republic* (New York: Routledge, 1995); Ray Takeyh, *Guardians of the Revolution: Iran and the World in the Age of the Ayatollahs* (New York: Oxford University Press, 2009), 111–28; Akbar Ganji, *The Red Eminence and the Grey Eminences: Pathology of Transition to the Developmental Democratic State* (Tehran: Tarh-e No, 1998).

43. Yaqubi, *The Foreign Policy of the Islamic Republic of Iran*, 75.

44. Baqeri Dolatabadi, *Unrealized Dreams*, 113.

45. Behrouz Hadizonouz, "Industrial Growth in the Context of the Economy's Framework: An Examination of the Economic and Industrial Situation of the Country," *Tadbir* 3 (July 1990):

26–29; Mas'oud Roughani Zanjani, "The Economic Situation, Industrial Production Capacity and Areas of Investment in Iran," *Tadbir* 3 (July 1990): 41–43.

46. Sohrab Behdad, "The Political Economy of Islamic Planning in Iran," in *Post-Revolutionary Iran*, ed. Hooshang Amirahmadi and Manouchehr Parvin (Boulder, CO: Westview Press, 1988), 107–25.

47. Fariba Adelkhah, *Being Modern in Iran* (New York: Columbia University Press, 2000), 13–18; Firouzeh Khalatbari, "The Tehran Stock-Exchange and Privatisation," in *The Economy of Islamic Iran*, ed. Thierry Coville (Paris: Peeters Publishers, 1994), 177–208.

48. Ayatollah [Hossein Ali] Montazeri, *Reminiscences*, 2nd ed. (Essen, Germany: Ettehadieh Nasherin Irani dar Oroupa, 2001), 1:650, 726–29; 2:1427–28, 1436–39.

49. Rafsanjani, *Reconstruction and Development*, 8.

50. "Rezaie's Letter to the Leader of the Revolution Criticizing Hashemi's [Rafsanjani] Actions," *Mashreq*, April 29, 2013, https://www.mashreghnews.ir/news/43672/هاشمی-عملکرد-از-انتقاد-در-نامه-رضايي-به-رهبر-انقلاب.

51. Mahmoud Safiri, *Truths and Expediencies: Conversation with Hashemi Rafsanjani* (Tehran: Ney, 2019), 136–37.

52. Kevan Harris, "Iran's Commanding Heights: Privatization and Conglomerate Ownership in the Islamic Republic," in *Crony Capitalism in the Middle East: Business and Politics from Liberalization to the Arab Spring*, ed. Ishac Diwan, Adeel Malik, and Izak Atiyas (Oxford: Oxford University Press, 2019), 363–99.

53. Nikolay Kozhanov, *Iran's Strategic Thinking: The Evolution of Iran's Foreign Policy, 1979–2018* (Berlin: Gerlach, 2018), 66–71.

54. Ayatollahi Tabaar, *Religious Statecraft*, 205–26.

55. Baqeri Dolatabadi, *Unrealized Dreams*, 279; Bahman Bakhtiari, *Parliamentary Politics in Revolutionary Iran: The Institutionalization of Factional Politics* (Gainesville: University Press of Florida, 1996), 185–234; Moslem, *Factional Politics in Post-Khomeini Iran*, 142–251; Gheissari and Nasr, *Democracy in Iran*, 108–9.

56. Ali Norouzi, *The Mirage of Development: A Critical Look at the Eight-Year Record of Hashemi Rafsanjani's Government* (Tehran: Zarrin, 1994).

57. Seyyed Davoud Aqaie, "The Place of the European Union in the Foreign Policy of the Development Period," *Faslnameh-e Siyasat* 3 (2008): 485–86.

58. "Ayatollah Rasanjani's Interview with the Keyhan Newspaper," *Rafsanjani.ir*, January 18, 2004, https://rafsanjani.ir/records/روزنامه-خبرنگار-کننده-مصاحبه-کیهان-روزنامه-با-رفسنجانی-هاشمی-آیت-ا-مصاحبه-کیهان-2/print; Sadeq Zibakalam, *Hashemi [Rafsanjani] without Retouching* (Tehran: Rouzaneh, 2009), 153.

59. Mousavian and Shahidsaless, *Iran and the United States*, 109–11.

60. "Ayatollah Hashemi Rafsanjani's Interview"; Rafsanjani, *Reconstruction and Development*, 586–88; Seyed Hossein Mousavian, *A New Structure for Security, Peace, and Cooperation in the Persian Gulf* (New York: Rowan and Littlefield, 2020), 63–98; Bahram Akhavan Kazemi, *A Review of Iran-Saudi Relations in the Last Two Decades* (Tehran: Markaz-e Chap va Nashr-e Sazman-e Tablighat-e Eslami, 1995).

61. "Ayatollah Hashemi Rafsanjani's Interview."

62. Rafsanjani, *Moderation and Victory*, 10; "Hashemi's [Rafsanjani] Account of 2009 Meeting with the Committee of Experts," *Mashreq*, April 29, 2013, https://www.magiran.com/article/2718749; Mahmoud Dehqan Tarazjani, *Foreign Relations with Neighbors in the Second Decade of the Islamic Revolution* (Tehran: Soroush, 2000), 91.

63. Rafsanjani, *Moderation and Victory*, 479.

64. Rafsanjani, *Moderation and Victory*, 15; Mohsen Milani, "Iran's Persian Gulf Policy in the Post-Saddam Era," in *Contemporary Iran: Economy, Society, Politics*, ed. Ali Gheissari (New York: Oxford University Press, 2009), 331–35.

65. Yaqubi, *The Foreign Policy of Islamic Republic of Iran*, 156.

66. For a book replete with accounts of diplomatic conversations, see Rafsanjani, *Moderation and Victory*.

67. Baqeri Dolatabadi, *Unrealized Dreams*, 127; Rafsanjani, *Moderation and Victory*, 1610.

68. Mousavian and Shahidsaless, *Iran and the United States*, 110.

69. Mousavian and Shahidsaless, *Iran and the United States*, 112–19; "Hashemi [Rafsanjani]: I Wrote to the Imam about Relations with America," *Mashreq*, August 21, 2013, https://www.magiran.com/article/2798462.

70. Giandomenico Pico, *Man without a Gun: One Diplomat's Secret Struggle to Free the Hostages, Fight Terrorism, and End a War* (New York: Crown, 1999), 3–4. Pico had served as the intermediary between Tehran and Washington in the negotiations. See also Rafsanjani, *Reconstruction and Development*, 219–46; Rafsanjani, *Moderation and Victory*, 93.

71. Rafsanjani, *Moderation and Victory*, 94.

72. Fouad Izadi, *U.S. Public Diplomacy toward Iran* (Tehran: Daneshgah Emam Sadeq, 2012).

73. Agis Salpukas, "Iran Signs Oil Deal with Conoco; First since 1980 Break with U.S.," *New York Times*, March 7, 1995, A1.

74. Paul Richter and Robin Wright, "Clinton Kills Pending Iran-Conoco Oil Deal: Policy Order Will Bar Development in Mideast Nation and Reassert Hard-Line Stance Taken since '79 Hostage Crisis," *Los Angeles Times*, March 15, 1995, https://www.latimes.com/archives/la-xpm-1995-03-15-fi-43080-story.html; Mousavian and Shahidsaless, *Iran and the United States*, 121–22.

75. Narges Bajoghli et al., *How Sanctions Work: Iran and the Impact of Economic Warfare* (Stanford, CA: Stanford University Press, 2024), 57–58.

76. Mahmoud Pargoo and Shahram Akbarzadeh, *Presidential Elections in Iran: Islamic Idealism since the Revolution* (Cambridge: Cambridge University Press, 2021), 82–86.

77. "Lecture at the Gathering of Pakistani Officers," in *The Writ of the Imam: Collection of Imam Khomeini's Works* (Tehran: Markaz Tanzim va Nashr Asar Imam Khomeini, 2000), 11:104.

78. Mousavian and Shahidsaless, *Iran and the United States*, 119.

79. Ayatollahi Tabaar, *Religious Statecraft*, 193–96.

80. James Piscatori, "The Rushdie Affair and the Politics of Ambiguity," *International Affairs* 66, no. 4 (October 1990): 767–89.

81. Rafsanjani, *Reconstruction and Development*, 529.

82. Rafsanjani, *Reconstruction and Development*, 17–18, 185–207; Ali Akbar Hashemi Rafsanjani, *Vitality of Development, Memoir and Record, 1993*, ed. Hasan Lahouti (Tehran: Ma'aref-e

Enqelab, 2023), 18; Ali Akbar Hashemi Rafsanjani, *Development and Rejuvenation, Record and Memoirs, 1992,* ed. Emad Hashemi (Tehran: Daftar-e Nashr-e Ma'aref-e Enqelab, 2022), 15.

83. Rafsanjani, *Moderation and Victory,* 442–44, 511–19.

84. Gheissari and Nasr, *Democracy in Iran,* 114–16.

85. Ali Rabi'i, *An Overview of Sociology of Transformation of Values* (Tehran: Farhang va Andisheh, 1997), 134–49.

86. Farhad Khosrokhavar, Shapur Etemad, and Masoud Mehrabi, "Report on Science in Post-Revolutionary Iran," parts 1 and 2: "Emergence of a Scientific Community?" and "The Scientific Community's Problem of Identity," *Critique: Critical Middle Eastern Studies* 13, nos. 2–3 (Summer–Fall 2004): 209–24, 363–82.

87. Aqaie, "The Place of the European Union," 486.

88. Kevan Harris, *A Social Revolution: Politics and the Welfare State in Iran* (Berkeley: University of California Press, 2017), 134–35.

89. Firouzeh Khalatbari, "Iran: A Unique Underground Economy," in *L'économie de l'Iran islamique, entre l'état et le marché,* ed. Thierry Coville (Tehran: Institut Français de Recherche en Iran, 1994), 113–131.

90. Ali M. Ansari, *Iran, Islam and Democracy: Politics of Managing Change* (London: Royal Institute of International Affairs, 2000), 52–81.

91. Vali Nasr, *Forces of Fortune: The Rise of the New Muslim Middle Class and What Will It Mean for Our World* (New York: Free Press, 2009), 50–84.

92. Mohammad Sadri and Ahmad Sadri, trans. and ed., *Reason, Freedom, and Democracy in Islam: The Essential Writings of Abdolkarim Soroush* (New York: Oxford University Press, 2000); Mehrzad Boroujerdi, *Iranian Intellectuals and the West: The Tormented Triumph of Nativism* (Syracuse: Syracuse University Press, 1996), 156–75; Arjomand, *After Khomeini,* 76–84; Eskandar Sadeghi-Boroujerdi, *Revolution and Its Discontents: Political Thought and Reform in Iran* (New York: Cambridge University Press, 2019), 136–86.

93. Arjomand, *After Khomeini,* 84–89.

94. Reza Davari Ardakani, *Philosophy in Crisis* (Tehran: Amir Kabir, 1994).

95. F. Gregory Gause III, "The Illogic of Dual Containment," *Foreign Affairs* 73, no. 2 (March–April 1994): 56–66.

96. Gheissari and Nasr, *Democracy in Iran,* 129.

97. Mohammad Khatami, *From the City's World to the World's City* (Tehran: Ney, 1997); Mohammad Khatami, *Islam, the Clergy, and the Islamic Revolution* (Tehran: Tar-e No, 2000).

98. Pargoo and Akbarzadeh, *Presidential Elections,* 86–100.

99. Kaveh Ehsani, "Prospects for Democracy in Iran" (paper delivered at Concordia University, Montreal, November 2004), 5.

100. Mohammad Reza Tajik, "What Are Our National Interests?," *Faslnameh Motale'at-e Rahbordi* 4, nos. 1–2 (Summer 2001): 48; Mohammad Reza Tajik and Seyyed Jalal Dehqani Firouzabadi, "Models for Exporting the Revolution in Iran's Foreign Policy Discourse," *Rahbord* 27 (Spring 2003): 73.

101. Arjomand, *After Khomeini,* 90–94.

102. Farhang Rajaee, "The 'Thermidor' of Islamic Yuppies: Conflict and Compromise in Iran's Politics," *Middle East Journal* 53, no. 2 (Spring 1999): 217–31; Bajoghli et al., *How Sanctions Work*, 36–37.

103. Kian Tajbakhsh, *Creating Local Democracy in Iran: State Building and the Politics of Decentralization* (New York: Cambridge University Press, 2022).

104. Reza Soleimani, *Khatami Government's Foreign Policy: De-Escalatory Diplomacy and Dialogue of Civilizations, 1997–2005* (Tehran: Entesharat-e Kavir, 2012).

105. "Words That Led to Montazeri's House Arrest," *Afkarnews*, June 17, 2011, https://www.afkarnews.com/بخش-سیاسی-3/35078-سخنانی-که-به-حصرخانگی-منتظری-انجامید.

106. Sadeghi-Boroujerdi, *Revolution*, 287–374.

107. Cited in Ali Alfoneh, *Iran Unveiled: How the Revolutionary Guards Is Turning Theocracy into Military Dictatorship* (Washington, DC: AEI Press, 2013), 28.

108. Douglas Jehl, "For Death of Its Diplomats Iran Vows Blood for Blood," *New York Times*, September 12, 1998, A4.

109. "Why Did Iran Decide against Attacking Afghanistan during the Reformist Government? A Few Reminiscences of the IRGC Commander of the Time for Attack on Herat," *Khabaronline*, July 30, 2019, https://www.khabaronline.ir/news/1284825/چرا-ایران-از-حمله-به-افغانستان-در-دوره-دولت-اصلاحات-منصرف-شد-.

110. Alfoneh, *Iran Unveiled*, 29.

111. "The Recording of the Session between Mohsen Rezaie and His Opponents in 1984," *Hamshahri*, September 23, 2020, https://www.hamshahrionline.ir/news/551700/کامل-صوت-بشنوید-جلسه-محسن-رضایی-با-معترضان-در-سال-۶۳-چه-کسانی-.

112. Raz Zimmt, "The Rise and Fall of the Crocodile Ayatollah," *IranSource*, January 6, 2021, https://www.atlanticcouncil.org/blogs/iransource/the-rise-and-fall-of-the-crocodile-ayatollah/.

113. Arjomand, *After Khomeini*, 180–81.

114. Akbar Ganji, "The Latter-Day Sultan: Power and Politics in Iran," *Foreign Affairs* 87, no. 6 (November–December 2008): 45–66.

115. Bahman Ahmadi Amouie, *The Political Economy of the Islamic Republic* (Tehran: Gam-e No, 2002); Bijan Khajepour, "Domestic Political Reforms and Private Sector Activity in Iran," *Social Research* 67, no. 2 (Summer 2000): 577–98.

116. Gheissari and Nasr, *Democracy in Iran*, 142–45.

117. Hesam Foruzan, *The Military in Post-Revolutionary Iran: The Evolution and Roles of the Revolutionary Guards* (New York: Routledge, 2016), 141–47; Afshon Ostovar, *Vanguard of the Imam: Religion, Politics, and Iran's Revolutionary Guards* (New York: Oxford University Press, 2016), 143–47; Alfoneh, *Iran Unvelied*, 165–91.

118. Stephane A. Dudoignon, *Les Gardiens de la Revolution Islamique d'Iran* (Paris: CNRS Editions, 2022), 167–86.

119. Misagh Parsa, *Democracy in Iran: Why It Failed and How It Might Succeed* (Cambridge, MA: Harvard University Press, 2016), 140–76.

120. Giorgia Perletta, *Political Radicalism and Ahmadinejad's Presidencies* (New York: Palgrave Macmillan, 2022), 85–90; Kasra Naji, *Ahmadinejad: The Secret History of Iran's Radical Leader* (London: I. B. Tauris, 2008), 1–56; Anoushiravan Ehteshami and Mahjoob Zweiri, *Iran and the*

Rise of the Neoconservatives: The Politics of Tehran's Silent Revolution (London: I. B. Tauris, 2007), 49–57.

121. Naji, *Ahmadinejad*, 57–90; Vali Nasr, "Iran's Peculiar Election: The Conservative Wave Rolls On," *Journal of Democracy* 16, no. 4 (October 2005): 9–22.

122. Nader Habibi, "How Ahmadinejad Changed Iran's Economy," *Journal of Developing Areas* 49, no. 1 (Winter 2015): 309–10; Ehteshami and Zweiri, *Iran*, 81–85.

123. Alfoneh, *Iran Unveiled*, 178–89.

124. Vali Nasr, "Showdown in Tehran," *Foreign Policy*, June 23, 2011, https://foreignpolicy.com /2011/06/23/showdown-in-tehran-2/.

125. Arjomand, *After Khomeini*, 149–71.

126. Saeed Jafari, "A Review of Foreign Policy of Iran 2005 to 2017: The Train Goes Off the Tracks," *Euronews*, November 2, 2019, https://per.euronews.com/2019/02/11/iran-foreign -policy-review-40-years-after-revolution-ahmadi-nejad-rouhani; Kozhanov, *Iran's Strategic Thinking*, 85–144.

127. David Menashri, "Iran's Regional Policy: Between Radicalism and Pragmatism," *Journal of International Affairs* 60, no. 2 (Spring–Summer 2007): 153–67.

Chapter 7: Forward Defense: Seeking Strategic Depth for Resistance

1. Mohsen Milani, "Iran's Policy towards Afghanistan," *Middle East Journal* 60, no. 2 (Spring 2006): 244–46.

2. Seyed Hossein Mousavian and Shahir Shahidsaless, *Iran and the United States: An Insider's View on the Failed Past and the Road to Peace* (New York: Bloomsbury, 2014), 165–74.

3. See "Shadow Commander: Iran's Military Mastermind," *BBC Two*, n.d., https://www.bbc .co.uk/programmes/p073601g.

4. Personal conversations, October 2021.

5. James Dobbins, "Negotiating with Iran: Reflections from Personal Experience," *Washington Quarterly* 33, no. 1 (2010): 149–62; Milani, "Iran's Policy," 247–48.

6. "Javad Zarif's First Interview after Foreign Ministry," YouTube, June 6, 2023, https://www .youtube.com/watch?v=3mXOsE2Yqho.

7. "Ayatollah Khamenei's Comments on the Thirty-Fourth Anniversary of Khomeini's Death," *Khamenei.ir*, June 4, 2023, https://farsi.khamenei.ir/speech-content?id=53057.

8. Qasem Eftekhari and Ali Baqeri Dolatabadi, "American Pressure and Iran's Growing Reliance on a Strategy of Deterrence," *Siyasat* 40, no. 4 (January 2011): 9.

9. Kayhan Barzegar, "Iran's Foreign Policy in Post-Invasion Iraq," *Middle East Policy* 15, no. 4 (Winter 2008): 53–54; Eftekhari and Baqeri Dolatabadi, "American Pressure," 2–7; Masoumeh Ansarifard and Amir Mohammad Hajiyousefi, "Deterrence as Islamic Republic of Iran's Security and Defense Strategy: Challenges, Requirements, and Strategic Model," *Faslnameh-e Elmi-e Ravabet-e Beinolmellal* 41, no. 3 (2021): 8–14.

10. David Remnick, "War without End," *New Yorker*, April 13, 2003, https://www.newyorker .com/magazine/2003/04/21/war-without-end.

11. Mohammad Baqer Qalibaf and Seyyed Mousa Pourmousavi, "The Middle East's New Geopolitics and Iran's Foreign Policy," *Pajouheshhaye Joqrafiyaie-Ensani* 41, no. 4 (Winter 2008):

53–69; "Interview with Hasan Kazemi Qomi [IRGC Commander and Iran's First Ambassador to Iraq after the US Invasion in 2003]: After Iraq It Was Iran's Turn," in *Oral History of the Foreign Policy of the Islamic Republic of Iran*, ed. Mohammad Hasan Rouztalab and Mohammad Rahmani (Tehran: Markaz-e Asnad Eslami, 2014), 408.

12. "Interview with Hasan Kazemi Qomi," 416–17.

13. Report of prominent hard-liner intellectual and activist Mehdi Mohammadi to the Basij Student Organization, Shahid Baqeri Base, "How Did the Nuclear Issue Reach That Point?," 23 (2013), https://t.me/Enghelaabioon_Javan/582. The report was intended to educate the rank and file of the Basij and IRGC along with their political acolytes.

14. Kamran Ghazanfari, *The Nuclear File and Its Open and Hidden Dimensions* (Tehran: Markaz Asnad Enqelab, 2015), 29–30.

15. Eftekhari and Dolatabadi, "American Pressure," 11–12.

16. "An Alleged Letter to Bush in 2003 Reignites Controversy in Iran," *Radio Farda*, May 27, 2020, https://en.radiofarda.com/a/an-alleged-letter-to-bush-in-2003-reignites-controversy-in -iran/30636870.html; personal conversations with both President Mohammad Khatami and Sadeq Kharrazi, ambassador to France at the time and his foreign policy adviser who had drafted the letter, Davos, Switzerland, January 2007.

17. Personal conversations with both President Mohammad Khatami and Sadeq Kharrazi, Davos.

18. Mousavian and Shahidsaless, *Iran and the United States*, 191–206.

19. Personal conversations with both President Mohammad Khatami and Sadeq Kharrazi.

20. Personal conversations, July 2017.

21. "Complete Text of Conversation with Seyyed Abbas Araghchi," *Ensaf News*, February 18, 2023, http://www.ensafnews.com/398044/متن-کامل-گفت-وگو-با-سیدعباس-عراقچی-صحE2%80%8C%.; Mohammad Javad Zarif et al., *Sealed Secret* (Tehran: Entesharat Etelaat, 2021): 255–56.

22. Cited in Annie Tracy Samuel, *The Unfinished History of the Iran-Iraq War: Faith, Firepower and Iran's Revolutionary Guards* (New York: Cambridge University Press, 2022), 217.

23. "[General] Zolqadr: All of America's Anti-Iranian Strategies Have Failed," *Mehr News*, June 24, 2007, https://www.mehrnews.com/news/506703/ذوالقدر-تمامی-راهبردهای-ضد-ایرانی-آمریکا ناکام-مانده-است-.

24. Farhad Qasemi, "A Theoretical Look at the Design of Deterrence in Iran's Foreign Policy," *Faslnameh-e Jeopolitik* 7 (2007): 119–21.

25. Vali Nasr, *The Shia Revival: How Conflicts within Islam Will Shape the Future* (New York: W. W. Norton, 2006); Yitzhak Nakash, *Reaching for Power: The Shi'i in the Modern Arab World* (Princeton, NJ: Princeton University Press, 2006).

26. Kayhan Barzegar, "Iran and the Shiite Crescent: Myths and Realities," *Brown Journal of World Affairs* 15, no. 1 (Fall–Winter 2008): 87–99.

27. Vali Nasr, "Regional Implications of Shi'a Revival in Iraq," *Washington Quarterly* 27, no. 3 (Summer 2004): 7–24.

28. Personal conversations with both President Mohammad Khatami and Sadeq Kharrazi.

29. I am grateful to Narges Bajoghli for this insight.

30. Assal Rad, *The State of Resistance: Politics, Culture, and Identity in Modern Iran* (New York: Cambridge University Press, 2022), 189–90.

31. Joby Warrick, *Black Flags: The Rise of ISIS* (New York: Doubleday, 2015), 101–221.

32. Vali Nasr, "Sects and Violence," *New York Times*, February 23, 2006, https://www.nytimes.com/2006/02/23/opinion/23iht-ednasr.html?searchResultPosition=17.

33. Patrick Cockburn, *Muqtada: Muqtada Al-Sadr, the Shia Revival, and the Future of Iraq* (New York: Scribner, 2008), 175–86.

34. Doron Zimmermann, "Calibrating Disorder: Iran's Role in Iraq and the Coalition Response, 2003–2006," *Civil Wars* 9, no. 1 (2007): 8–31.

35. Jeanne Godfroy et al., *The US Army in the Iraq War* (West Point, NY: West Point Books, 2019); Vali Nasr, "Who Wins in Iraq? Iran," *Foreign Policy* (March–April 2007): 40–41.

36. Documents that Khaddam took with him when he left Syria for Europe in 2005 have been serialized in the Arabic media outlet, *Al-Majalla*. His notes of Assad's meetings with Khatami and Khamenei in Tehran on March 6, 2003, have appeared in Ibrahim Hamidi, "Secret Minutes of Assad-Khamenei Meeting on the Eve of Invasion of Iraq," *Al-Majalla*, March 23, 2024, https://www.majalla.com/node/313361/لجنة-العراق-غزو-عشية-خامنئي-الأسد-للقاء-سري-محضر/ومذكرات-وثائق-لدعم-إيرانية-سورية-أمنية.

37. Hamidi, "Secret Minutes of Assad Khamenei Meeting."

38. Keyhan Barzegar, "Iran's Foreign Policy from the Viewpoint of Offensive and Defensive Realism," *Ravabet-e Khareji* 1, no. 1 (April 2009): 114–15.

39. Arash Reisinezhad, "Iran's Geopolitical Strategy in West Asia: Containment of 'Geography' and 'History,'" *Iranian Review of Foreign Affairs* 11, no. 1 (Winter–Spring 2020): 59–88; Mohammad Javad Fathi, Shohreh Pirani, and Akbar Ghafouri, "Strategic Loneliness and Iran's Strategic Policies in West Asia," *Iranian Research Letter of International Politics* 9, no. 2 (Spring–Summer 2021): 159–209; Barzegar, "Iran's Foreign Policy from the Viewpoint of Offensive and Defensive Realism," 143.

40. Arash Reisinezhad, *The Shah of Iran, the Iraqi Kurds, and the Lebanese Shia* (New York: Palgrave Macmillan, 2019), 1.

41. Ali Akbar Velayati, *Political History of Iraq's Imposed War on Iran* (Tehran: Daftar Nashr-e Farhang Eslami, 1997), 142.

42. Afshon Ostovar, "The Grand Strategy of Militant Clients: Iran's Way of War," *Security Studies* 28, no. 1 (January–March 2019): 150–88; Ariane Tabatabai, Jeffrey Martini, and Becca Wasser, *The Iran Threat Network* (Santa Monica, CA: Rand Corporation, 2021).

43. Behzad Qasemi, "The Geopolitics of Axis of Resistance and the National Security of the Islamic Republic of Iran on the Basis of the Discourse of the Islamic Revolution," *Faslnameh-e Afaq Amniyat* 11, no. 38 (Spring 2018): 5–33.

44. "Resistance Front / Axis of Resistance / Resistance Line in Southwest Asia," *Khamenei.ir*, https://farsi.khamenei.ir/newspart-index?tid=11101; "Imam Khamenei: Thanks to the Blessing of the Blood of Martyr Soleimani the Resistance Trend Is More Active and Hopeful Than Two Years Ago," *Tasnim*, January 1, 2022, https://www.tasnimnews.com/fa/news/1400/10/11/2636046/است-قبل-سال-دو-از-امیدوارتر-و-پررونق-مقاومت-جریان-سلیمانی-شهید-خون-برکت-به-ای-خامنه-امام.

45. Samuel, *The Unfinished History*, 212.

46. Barzegar, "Iran's Foreign Policy from the Viewpoint of Offensive and Defensive Realism," 123; Seyyed Hamzeh Safavi Homaie, *Deep Dive into Islamic Republic of Iran's Foreign Policy* (Tehran: Entesharat-e Daneshgah-e Emam Sadeq, 2008), 100; "Interview with Hasan Kazemi Qomi," 418.

47. Barzegar, "Iran's Foreign Policy from the Viewpoint of Offensive and Defensive Realism," 127–29.

48. Keyhan Barzegar and Masoud Rezaie, "Iran's Defense Strategy from Ayatollah Khamenei's Viewpoint," *Faslnameh Motale'at-e Rahbordi* 19, no. 4 (Winter 2016): 29–33.

49. Marzieh Esfahani, "Political Realism and Iran: Geopolitics and Defensive Realism," in *The Edinburgh Companion to Political Realism*, ed. Robert Schuett and Miles Hollingworth (Edinburgh: Edinburgh University Press, 2018), 437–39; Eskandar Sadeghi-Boroujerdi, "Strategic Depth, Counterinsurgency and the Logic of Sectarianization: The Islamic Republic of Iran's Security Doctrine and Its Regional Implications," in *Sectarianization: Mapping the New Politics of the Middle East*, ed. Nader Hashemi and Danny Postel (New York: Oxford University Press, 2016), 159–84.

50. Ansarifard and Hajiyousefi, "Deterrence," 14.

51. Ali Reza Golshani and Mohsen Baqeri, "The Place of Hezbollah of Lebanon in the Deterrence Strategy of the Islamic Republic of Iran," *Faslnameh-e Elmi Motale'at-e Ravabet-e Beinolmellali* 41, no. 3 (Fall 2021): 7–34.

52. Mehdi Khorramshad and Mohammad Baqer Beiki, *The Islamic Republic of Iran's Soft Power: A Study of the Case of Lebanon* (Tehran: Entesharat-e Daneshgah-e Emam Sadeq, 2008), 339.

53. "Who Dares to Attack Iran," *Entekhab*, November 11, 2011, https://www.entekhab.ir/fa /news/44086/دارد-را-ایران-به-حمله-جرات-کسی-چه-نصرالله-حسن-سید.

54. Hesam Forouzan, *The Military in Post-Revolutionary Iran: The Evolution and Roles of the Revolutionary Guards* (New York: Routledge, 2016), 183–200.

55. "Interview with Hasan Kazemi Qomi," 408.

56. Afshon Ostovar, "After Soleimani: Iran's Elite Commander Has Been Dead for a Year. The Machinery He Built Lives On," *Newlines Magazine*, January 3, 2021, https://newlinesmag .com/essays/after-soleimani/; Ali Hashem, "Iran Struggles to Fill Vacuum Left by Soleimani," *Navigator from CGP*, January 7, 2021, https://cgpolicy.org/articles/iran-struggles-to-fill-the -vacuum-left-by-soleimani/; Isaac Chotiner, "The Meaning of Qassem Suleimani's Death in the Middle East," *New Yorker*, January 3, 2020; https://www.newyorker.com/news/q-and-a/the -meaning-of-qassem-suleimanis-death-in-the-middle-east; Arash Azizi, *The Shadow Commander: Soleimani, the U.S. and Iran's Global Ambitions* (New York: Oneworld, 2020); *Commander of the Hearts: Biography and Memoirs of Martyred Lieutenant General Hajj Qasem Soleimani* (Tehran: Gorouh-e Farhangi Taqdir, 2020).

57. Michael Weiss, "Iran's Top Spy Is the Modern-Day Karla, John Le Carré's Villainous Mastermind," *Daily Beast*, January 3, 2020, https://www.thedailybeast.com/irans-top-spy-is-the -modern-day-karla-john-le-carres-villainous-mastermind; Dexter Filkins, "The Shadow Commander," *New Yorker*, September 30, 2013, https://www.newyorker.com/magazine/2013/09/30 /the-shadow-commander.

58. "How Was the Qods Force Formed," *ISNA*, January 5, 2020, https://www.isna.ir/news /98101511412/شد-تشکیل-چگونه-قدس-سپاه; "How Was IRGC's Qods Force Formed, and What Did It Do in the Region," *Tasnim*, May 3, 2021, https://www.tasnimnews.com/fa/news/1400/02/13 /2496067/کرد-چه-منطقه-در-و-شد-تشکیل-چگونه-سپاه-قدس-نیروی.

59. "The Qods Force from Formation to the Present," *IRNA*, February 7, 2022, https://www.irna.ir/news/84641777.

60. Liz Sly, "Petraeus: The Islamic State Isn't Our Biggest Problem in Iraq," *Washington Post*, March 20, 2015, https://www.washingtonpost.com/news/worldviews/wp/2015/03/20/petraeus-the-islamic-state-isnt-our-biggest-problem-in-iraq/?hpid=z2.

61. Eyal Zisser, "Iranian Involvement in Lebanon," *Military and Strategic Affairs* 3, no. 1 (May 2011): 11, 8–10.

62. "Full Interview of Commander Soleimani about the 33 Day War," *Aparat*, n.d., https://www.aparat.com/v/a7Xm.

63. Cited in Zisser, "Iranian Involvement," 10.

64. Mohammad Ayatollahi Tabaar, *Religious Statecraft: The Politics of Islam in Iran* (New York: Columbia University Press, 2019), 227–55.

65. Farideh Farhi, "The Tenth Presidential Elections and Their Aftermath," in *Iran: From Theocracy to the Green Movement*, ed. Negin Nabavi (New York: Palgrave Macmillan, 2012), 3–16.

66. Muhammad Sahimi, "The Political Evolution of Mousavi," *Tehran Bureau*, February 16, 2010, https://www.pbs.org/wgbh/pages/frontline/tehranbureau/2010/02/the-political-evolution-of-mousavi.html.

67. Fariba Adelkhah, "The Political Economy of the Green Movement: Contestation and Political Mobilization in Iran," in *Iran: From Theocracy to the Green Movement*, ed. Negin Nabavi (New York: Palgrave Macmillan, 2012), 17–38; Pouya Alimagham, *Contesting the Iranian Revolution: The Green Uprisings* (New York: Cambridge University Press, 2020), 33–51.

68. Misagh Parsa, *Democracy in Iran: Why It Failed and How It Might Succeed* (Cambridge, MA: Harvard University Press, 2016), 206–64.

69. Akbar Ganji, "Jonbesh Sabz 88 Ya Enqelab 89" ("The Green Movement of 2009 or the Revolution of 2010"), *Radio Farda*, December 3, 2014, https://www.radiofarda.com/a/f3-jalili-talk-green-movement/26723043.html.

70. Hasan Rouhani, *National Security and the Economic System* (Tehran: Markaz-e Tahqiqat-e Estratejic, 2012).

71. Narges Bajoghli, *Iran Reframed: Anxieties of Power in the Islamic Republic* (Stanford, CA: Stanford University Press, 2019).

72. Kim Zetter, *Countdown to Zero Day: Stuxnet and the Launch of the World's First Digital Weapon* (New York: Crown, 2014).

Chapter 8: The Rise of the Axis of Resistance

1. Toby Matthiesen, *Sectarian Gulf: Saudi Arabia and the Arab Spring That Wasn't* (Stanford, CA: Stanford Briefs, 2013); Madawi Al-Rashid, "Sectarianism as Counterrevolution," *Studies in Ethnicity and Nationalism* 11, no. 3 (December 2011): 513–26; Oliver Holmes, "Assad's Devious, Cruel Plan to Stay in Power by Dividing Syria—and Why It's Working," *New Republic*, August 15, 2011, https://newrepublic.com/article/93286/syria-assad-shabbiha-sectarianism.

2. Afshon Ostovar, *Vanguard of the Imam: Religion, Politics, and Iran's Revolutionary Guards* (New York: Oxford University Press, 2016), 192–203.

3. Ariane Tabatabai, "Syria Changed the Iranian Way of War," *Foreign Affairs*, August 16, 2019, https://www.foreignaffairs.com/articles/syria/2019-08-16/syria-changed-iranian-way -war.

4. Anoushiravan Ehteshami and Raymond A. Hinnebusch, *Syria and Iran: Middle Powers in a Penetrated Regional System* (New York: Routledge, 1997), 87–156.

5. Nadia von Maltzahn, *The Syria-Iran Axis: Cultural Diplomacy and International Relations in the Middle East* (London: I. B. Tauris, 2015), 174–207.

6. "Lieutenant General Safavi: Syria Is Iran's Bridge to Lebanon's Hezbollah; the Jihadists Are Zionists," *Khabar Online*, October 14, 2013, https://web.archive.org/web/20161013085536 /http://www.khabaronline.ir/(X(1)S(agmgmrptzlsncswisiwidpf2wb))/detail/317581/Politics /military.

7. Shamseddin Sadeghi and Kamran Lotfi, "Analysis of Iran's Position in the Syrian Crisis," *Jostarhaye Siyasi Moaser* 6, no. 1 (Spring 2015): 123–44.

8. "The Question of Why We Went to Syria and the Answer of the Martyred General Hossein Hamedani," *Aparat*, 2018, https://www.aparat.com/v/SyAhP/سؤال%D9%90_به_سوریه_چرا _حسین_شهید_سردار_پاسخ_و_رفتیم.

9. Vali Nasr, "Iran among the Ruins," *Foreign Affairs*, March–April 2018, 108–18.

10. Personal conversation with Foreign Minister Mohammad Javad Zarif, New York, September 2015.

11. "The Last Interview of the Martyred General Hossein Hamedani," *Tabnak*, October 6, 2015, https://www.tabnak.ir/fa/news/537873/همدانی-حسین-شهید-سردار-گفتگوی-آخرین.

12. "Hasan Nasrallah's Speech on Syria," *Jahan News*, May 14, 2020, https://www.iranchamber .com/calendar/converter/iranian_calendar_converter.ph.

13. "Say It Plain and Simple, What Is the Truth about the Syria Episod," *Aviny.com*, n.d., https://www.aviny.com/shobhe/siasi/121.aspx.

14. "The Last Interview of the Martyred General Hossein Hamedani."

15. Hassan Ahmadian and Payam Mohseni, "Iran's Syria Strategy: The Evolution of Deterrence," *International Affairs* 95, no. 2 (March 2019): 341–64.

16. "Why Must Iran Be Present in Syrian Crisis? Reasons for Protecting Iran's Missile Capability," *Basirat*, November 11, 2018, https://basirat.ir/fa/news/312847/.

17. Hamdrea Azizi, "Iran's New Naval Ambitions," *Foreign Affairs*, July 10, 2024, https://www .foreignaffairs.com/iran/irans-new-naval-ambitions.

18. "Iran's Strategic Depth Has Reached the Mediterranean," *Tasnim*, February 6, 2014, https://www.tasnimnews.com/fa/news/1392/11/17/274506/مدیترانه-دریای-به-ایران-استراتژیک-دفاع-عمق -سوری-در-عربی-غربی-توطئه-وجود-است-رسیده.

19. "General Safavi: We Have to Extend Our Strategic Depth by 5000 Kilometers," *Tasnim*, March 6, 2024, https://www.tasnimnews.com/fa/news/1402/12/16/3050867/باید-صفوی-سرلشکر -دهیم-افزایش-کیلومتر-هزار-5-را-خودمان-استراتژیک-عمق.

20. Raz Zimmt, "Iran's Support for Hamas and the Risk of Multi-Front Escalation," *War on the Rocks*, October 18, 2023, https://warontherocks.com/2023/10/irans-support-for-hamas-and -the-risk-of-multi-front-escalation/.

21. "Interview with Mahmoud Chaharbaghi, Commander of IRGC Artillery in Syria," YouTube, January 2, 2021, https://www.youtube.com/watch?v=k6dJzst_3k8.

22. Former foreign minister Kamal Kharrazi narrated this quote as part of a conversation he had with General Soleimani. Cited in "Interview with Mohammad Ataie," *Ravayatha-ye Asr-e Chaharshanbeh*, March 11, 2021, https://t.me/Wednesdaynarratives/211.

23. "A Look at the Last Published Interview with Commander Hossein Hamedani," *Ensaf News*, August 10, 2022, http://www.ensafnews.com/363091/نگاهی-به-آخرین-گفت%E2%80%8C وگوی-منتشرشده-با-س/.

24. See "Javad Zarif's Three-Hour Interview," *Radio Farda*, April 26, 2021, https://www.radiofarda.com/a/31223108.html.

25. Morad Veisi, "Sixteen Senior IRGC Commanders Who Led the Military Intervention in Syria," *Radio Farda*, July 10, 2020, https://www.radiofarda.com/a/IRGC-commanders-who-involved-in-Syrian-war/30717921.html.

26. Shahram Akbarzadeh, William Gourlay, and Anoushiravan Ehteshami, "Iranian Proxies in the Syrian Conflict: Tehran's 'Forward Defense' in Action," *Journal of Strategic Studies* (2022): 1–24.

27. "The Shaping of the Units of the International Brigade of Shias for Defense of the Shrine of Zeynab with the Name of Abolfazl," *Mehr News*, May 8, 2013, https://www.iranchamber.com/calendar/converter/iranian_calendar_converter.ph.

28. Ostovar, *Vanguard of the Imam*, 219; "How Was the Fatemiyoun Brigade Formed?," *Keyhan*, May 30, 2015, https://kayhan.ir/fa/news/46030/لشکر-فاطمیون-چگونه-شکل-گرفت.

29. Bita Bakhtiari and Behnam Qolipour, "The Fifteen Groups That Are Fighting in Iraq and Syria at 'Iran's Behest,'" *Radio Farda*, June 14, 2015, https://www.radiofarda.com/a/f8-shia-militia-in-iraq-and-syria/27071518.html.

30. *An Account of the Logic of Iran's Presence in Syria* (Tehran: Dar Masir Aftab, 2016).

31. Ibrahim Abbasi, "Reasons for Iran's Presence in Syria," *Motale'at-e Manafe'e Melli* (Spring 2016): 53–73.

32. Keyhan Barzegar, "Iran's Foreign Policy from the Viewpoint of Offensive and Defensive Realism," *Ravabet-e Khareji* 1, no. 1 (April 2009): 134–35; Kazem Zouqi Barani, "Unveiling the Strategy of the Islamic Republic of Iran in a Changing Geopolitics," in *International System and the Emerging Orders*, ed. Anahita Mo'tazedzadeh, Zohreh Poustinchi, and Ziaoddin Sabouri (Tehran: Abrar, 2021), 57–73.

33. Seyyed Hamzeh Safavi Homaie, *Deep Dive into Islamic Republic of Iran's Foreign Policy* (Tehran: Entesharat-e Daneshgah-e Emam Sadeq, 2008), 126.

34. Zouqi Barani, "Unveiling the Strategy," 57–73. Zouqi Barani is a prolific strategic analyst affiliated with the IRGC's Imam Hossein University.

35. "Moussavi's Advisor: Moussavi and Karoubi's [Leaders of 2009 Green Movement] Aim Is to Participate in Monday's Demonstrations [in Support of People of Tunisia and Egypt]," *BBC Persian*, February 13, 2011, https://www.bbc.com/persian/iran/2011/02/110213_l39_ardeshir_amirarjmand_bbc_25bahman.

36. "Ali Larijani: We Believe in Need for Reforms in Syria," *Diplomasi-e Irani*, November 23, 2012, http://www.irdiplomacy.ir/fa/news/1909501/علی-لاریجانی-معتقد-به-اصلاحات-در-سوریه-هستیم-.

37. "Karbaschi: I Don't Accept the Verdict, I Believe in What I Said," *Euronews*, July 20, 2018, https://parsi.euronews.com/2018/08/20/karbaschi-say-that-he-do-not-accept-the-verdict-but-he-believes-in-what-he-have-said.

38. Mohammad Reza Dehshiri and Seyyed Mohammad Hossein Hosseini, "Regional Geo-politics and Iran-Saudi Relations," *Ravabet-e Khareji* 8, no. 1 (Spring 2016): 111–43.

39. Ali Baqeri Dolatabadi and Mohsen Shafi'i Seifabadi, *From Rafsanjani to Rouhani: A Review of Iran's Foreign Policy from the Viewpoint of Constructivist Theory* (Tehran: Tisa, 2014), 283–87.

40. Adel Hashemi, *The Making of Martyrdom in Modern Twelver Shi'ism: From Protesters and Revolutionaries to Shrine Defenders* (London: I. B. Tauris, 2022), 113–36.

41. "The Qods Force from Formation to the Present," *IRNA*, February 7, 2022, https://www.irna.ir/news/84641777.

42. Stephane A. Dudoignon, *Les Gardiens de la Revolution Islamique d'Iran* (Paris: CNRS Editions, 2022), 211–35; "Who Are the Defenders of the Shrine?," *Neda-e Esfahan*, March 13, 2017, https://nedaesfahan.ir/66986.

43. Ostovar, *Vanguard of the Imam*, 204–29.

44. Shahram Akbarzadeh, "Iran and Daesh: The Case of a Reluctant Shia Power," *Middle East Policy* 22, no. 3 (September 2015): 44–54.

45. "Zarif: Iran Regards Iraq Security as Its Own," *Islamic Republic News Agency*, August 24, 2014, https://en.irna.ir/news/2735151/Zarif-Iran-regards-Iraq-security-as-its-own.

46. Dina Esfandiary and Ariane Tabatabai, "Iran's ISIS Policy," *International Affairs* 91, no. 1 (2015): 6–7.

47. Personal conversations, February 2020.

48. Cited in Esfandiary and Tabatabai, "Iran's ISIS Policy," 6.

49. "Iran's Leader: Iraq and Syria Were a Prelude to Sink Iran in a Quagmire," *Radio Farda*, June 26, 2016; https://www.radiofarda.com/a/f7-khamenei-over-Isis-operation-in-syria-and-iraq-and-against-iran/27820557.html.

50. Amir Pourdastan, "We Are Facing a New Form of Threat with the Name of 'Hybrid War,'" *Tasnim*, September 20, 2017, https://www.tasnimnews.com/fa/news/1396/06/20/1515412/امیر-پوردستان-با-چهره-ای-از-تهدید-به-نام-جنگ-ترکیبی-روبرو-هستیم.

51. Shahram Chubin, "Is Iran a Military Threat?," *Survival* 56, no. 2 (2014): 77–78.

52. "Hajj Qassem Soleimani and the Regional Security," *Khamenei.ir*, April 6, 2019, https://english.khamenei.ir/news/8217/Hajj-Qassem-Soleimani-and-the-regional-security-theory.

53. Mohsen Milani, "This Is What Détente Looks Like," *Foreign Affairs*, August 27, 2014, http://www.foreignaffairs.com/ articles/141937/mohsen-milani/this-is-what-detente-looks-like.

54. "Last Interview of General Hamedani"; "Interview with General Mahmoud Chaharbaghi: We Saw Everything Lost: The Story of the 18-Day Siege of Hajj Qasem [Soleimani] in Aleppo," *Tasnim News*, December 29, 2020, https://www.youtube.com/watch?v=L9KwYa8P8dA.

55. Hamidreza Azizi, "Iran and Russia in Syria: A Changing Alliance amid the War in Ukraine," in *Struggle for Alliance: Russia and Iran in the Era of the War in Ukraine*, ed. Abdolrasool Divsallar (New York: I. B. Tauris, 2024), 313–42.

56. Ali Ansari and Anise Bassiri Tabrizi, "The View from Tehran," in *Understanding Iran's Role in the Syrian Conflict*, ed. Anise Bassiri Tabrizi and Raffaello Pantucci (London: RUSI, 2016), 4–5.

57. "Javad Zarif's Three-Hour Interview."

58. Vali Nasr, "A Russian-Iranian Axis," *New York Times*, September 17, 2016, A17.

59. Abdolrasool Divsallar, "Authoritarian Alliance: The Systemic Factors That Bring Russia and Iran Together," in *Struggle for Alliance: Russia and Iran in the Era of the War in Ukraine*, ed. Abdolrasool Divsallar (New York: I. B. Tauris, 2024), 175–202.

60. "Javad Zarif's Three-Hour Interview."

61. Mohammad Ayatollahi Tabaar, "Iran's Russian Turn," *Foreign Affairs*, November 12, 2015, https://www.foreignaffairs.com/articles/iran/2015-11-12/irans-russian-turn.

62. Behrouz As'adi and Seyyed Ali Monavvari, "Analysis of Relations between Iran and Russia in the New Century: Strategic Alliance or Convergence of Interests," *Rahyaftaha-ye Siyasi va Beinolmellali* 12, no. 4 (August 2021): 181–210.

63. Personal conversations, October 2022.

64. Abdolrasool Divsallar, "Rising Interdependency: How Russo-Iranian Relations Have Evolved with the War in Ukraine," *Trends Research*, December 12, 2022, https://trendsresearch .org/insight/rising-interdependency-how-russo-iranian-relations-have-evolved-with-the-war -in-ukraine/.

65. Jonathan Tirone and Golnar Motevalli, "Russia and Iran Are Building a Trade Route That Defies Sanctions," *Bloomberg*, December 21, 2022, https://www.bloomberg.com/graphics /2022-russia-iran-trade-corridor/#xj4y7vzkg?leadSource=uverify%20wall?leadSource =uverify%20wall?leadSource=uverify%20wall?leadSource=uverify%20wall?leadSource =uverify%20wall.

66. Thomas de Waal, "Putin's Hidden Game in the South Caucasus," *Foreign Affairs*, June 3, 2024, https://www.foreignaffairs.com/azerbaijan/putins-hidden-game-south-caucasus.

67. "Velayati, the Leader's Advisor: What Does Logic Say? Should We Go to the West Who Has Always Acted as an Enemey or Russia Who Has Always Helped," *Khabar Online*, July 22, 2022, https://www.khabaronline.ir/news/1653867/ولایتی-مشاور-رهبری-عقل-چه-می-گوید-به-سمت-غرب که-همواره-برویم-.

68. Javad Heiran-Nia, "Drone Sale to Russia Spark a Debate in Iran," Atlantic Council, November 23, 2022, https://www.atlanticcouncil.org/blogs/iransource/drone-sales-to-russia -spark-a-debate-in-iran/.

69. Helen Lackner, *Yemen in Crisis: The Road to War* (London: Verso, 2019).

70. Mohsen Milani, "Iran's Game in Yemen," *Foreign Affairs*, April 19, 2015, https://www .foreignaffairs.com/articles/iran/2015-04-19/irans-game-yemen.

71. Farzad Rostami, Kamran Lotfi, and Saeed Pirmohammadi, "The War of Powers in Yemen and the Security of the Islamic Republic," *Faslnameh Motale'at-e Ravabet-e Beinolomellali* 11, no. 41 (Spring 2018): 9–35.

72. Thomas Juneau, "How War in Yemen Transformed the Iran-Houthi Partnership," *Studies in Conflict and Terrorism*, July 6, 2021, 1–23.

73. Michael Knights, "The Houthi War Machine: From Guerilla War to State Capture," *CTC Sentinel* 11, no. 8 (September 2018): 15–23.

74. Dehshiri and Hosseini, "Regional Geopolitics," 111–43.

75. Hossein Delirian, "Iran's Strategic Depth," *Tasnim*, May 3, 2014, https://www.tasnimnews .com/fa/news/1393/02/13/357643/عمق-استراتژیک-ایران.

76. "The Question of Why We Went to Syria."

77. Fred Kaplan, "Netanyahu's Deadly Gambit," *Slate*, March 3, 2015, https://slate.com/news-and-politics/2015/03/benjamin-netanyahu-speech-to-congress-the-israeli-prime-minister-wants-an-iranian-regime-change-or-outright-war.html.

78. Mamoon Alabbasi, "Iran Continues to Boast of Its Regional Reach," *Middle East Eye*, March 13, 2015, https://www.middleeasteye.net/news/iran-continues-boast-its-regional-reach.

79. Ali Akbar Hashemi Rafsanjani, *Development and Rejuvenation, Record and Memoirs, 1992*, ed. Emad Hashemi (Tehran: Daftar-e Nashr-e Ma'aref-e Enqelab, 2022); Ali Akbar Hashemi Rafsanjani, *Transfer of Power, Record and Memoir*, ed. Mohsen Hashemi Rafsanjani (Tehran: Ma'aref Enqelab, 2020), 220, 388–42.

80. Rafsanjani, *Transfer of Power*, 342.

81. Mohsen Rafiqdoust, *I Tell It for History: Memoirs of Mohsen Rafiqdoust (1979–80)*, ed. Saeed Alamiyan, (Tehran: Soureh-e Mehr, 2013), 327–76; Samuel, *The Unfinished History*, 218–20.

82. Personal conversations, September 2020.

83. Louisa Loveluck, "U.S. Commanders at Al-Asad Base Believe Iranian Missile Barrage Was Designed to Kill," *Washington Post*, January 13, 2020, https://www.washingtonpost.com/world/middle_east/al-asad-base-had-minutes-notice-before-the-iranian-rockets-came-crashing-down-in-an-hour-long-barrage/2020/01/13/50fc9dd6-33e2-11ea-971b-43bec3ff9860_story.html; David Martin and Mary Walsh, "Who Would Live and Who Would Die: The Inside Story of the Iranian Attack on Al-Asad Airbase," *60 Minutes*, August 8, 2021, https://www.cbsnews.com/news/iranian-attack-al-asad-air-base-60-minutes-2021-08-08/.

84. Tareq Baconi, "What Was Hamas Thinking?," *Foreign Policy*, November 22, 2023, https://foreignpolicy.com/2023/11/22/hamas-gaza-israel-netanyahu-palestine-apartheid-containment-resistance/?tpcc=recirc_trending062921.

85. Leila Seurat, "Hamas' Goal in Gaza," *Foreign Affairs*, December 11, 2023, https://www.foreignaffairs.com/israel/hamass-goal-gaza.

86. Toby Matthiesen, "How Gaza Reunited the Middle East," *Foreign Affairs*, February 9, 2024, https://www.foreignaffairs.com/middle-east/how-gaza-reunited-middle-east.

87. Narges Bajoghli and Vali Nasr, "How the War in Gaza Revived the Axis of Resistance," *Foreign Affairs*, January 17, 2024, https://www.foreignaffairs.com/united-states/how-war-gaza-revived-axis-resistance.

88. Henry Kissinger, "The Vietnam Negotiations," *Foreign Affairs* 47, no. 2 (January 1969): 214.

89. I owe this insight into the linkage between the demography and viability of a sustained conventional military campaign to Stephen Kotkin.

90. Cited in Saeid Golkar, *Captive Society: The Basij Militia and Social Control in Iran* (New York: Columbia University Press, 2015), 13.

Chapter 9: The Cost of Success

1. Annie Tracy Samuel, *The Unfinished History of the Iran-Iraq War: Faith, Firepower, and Iran's Revolutionary Guards* (New York: Cambridge University Press, 2022), 210–28.

2. Abdolrasool Divsallar, "Shifting Threats and Strategic Adjustment in Iran's Foreign Policy: The Case of Strait of Hormuz," *British Journal of Middle East Studies* 49, no. 5 (2022): 873–95.

3. Interview with Mohammad Javad Zarif, *Etemad*, January 23, 2021, https://etemadonline .com/content/460318/باید-هزینه-های-سیاست-خارجی-کم-شود-برای-اولین-بار-هزینه-گفت-وگو-با-آمریکا-را-پرداخت-کردم -اگر-مردم-بپذ-.

4. Jeffrey Goldberg, "How Iran Could Save the Middle East," *Atlantic*, July–August 2009, https://www.theatlantic.com/magazine/archive/2009/07/how-iran-could-save-the-middle -east/307502/.

5. Michael Singh, "Axis of Abraham: Arab Israeli Normalization Could Remake the Middle East," *Foreign Affairs* 101, no. 2 (March–April 2022): 40–50.

6. Maria Fantappie and Vali Nasr, "A New Order in the Middle East?," *Foreign Affairs*, March 22, 2023, https://www.foreignaffairs.com/china/iran-saudi-arabia-middle-east-relations.

7. "Iranian-Saudi Détente Remains Entangled in Bigger Games," *Amwaj*, August 14, 2023, https://amwaj.media/article/inside-story-iranian-saudi-detente-remains-entangled-in-bigger -games.

8. Daniel Lippman et al., "How Trump Decided to Kill Iran's Soleimani," *Politico*, January 3, 2020, https://www.politico.com/news/2020/01/03/donald-trump-iran-soleimani-093371.

9. Samuel, *The Unfinished History*, 215.

10. Azadeh Moaveni, "The Day after War Begins in Iran," *New York Times*, January 6, 2020, https://www.nytimes.com/2020/01/06/opinion/iran-soleimani-funeral.html.

11. "Commander Salami: A New Calculus Is Now in Play," *Entekhab*, April 15, 2024, https:// www.entekhab.ir/fa/news/775940/سردار-سلامی-معادله-جدیدی-رقم-خورده-اگر-اسرائیل-حمله-کند-از-مبدا-ایران -می-قرار-متقابل-تهاجم-مورد%E2%80%8Cکرد.

12. Hossein Harsij, Mojtaba Toyserkani and Leila Ja'fari, "Geopolitics of Iran's Soft Power," *Pajouheshnameh Oloum-e Siyasi* 4, no. 2 (2009): 225–69.

13. "Comments in Meeting with Members of the Leader's Council of Experts," *Khamenei.ir*, September 4, 2014, https://farsi.khamenei.ir/speech-content?id=27356.

14. Samuel, *The Unfinished History*, 195–99.

15. Mohammad Reza Tajik, "Unorganized Order: An Argument on Iran's National Security," *Faslnameh Motale'at-e Rahbordi* 1, no. 2 (1998): 117–28.

16. Cited in Samuel, *The Unfinished History*, 217–18.

17. Ali Motahhari, "We and America," *Etemad*, December 14, 2020, http://www.etemadnews paper.ir/fa/main/detail/160126/ما-و-آمریکا.

18. Seyyed Fazlollah Mirqaderi and Hossein Kiyani, "The Basis of Resistance Literature in the Quran," *Faslnameh-e Adabiyat-e Dini* 1, no. 1 (March–April 2012): 70.

19. Behzad Qasemi, "The Geopolitics of Axis of Resistance and the National Security of the Islamic Republic of Iran on the Basis of the Discourse of the Islamic Revolution," *Faslnameh-e Afaq Amniyat* 11, no. 38 (Spring 2018): 12–20.

20. Narges Bajoghli et al., *How Sanctions Work: Iran and the Impact of Economic Warfare* (Stanford, CA: Stanford University Press, 2024), 53–73.

21. Narges Bajoghli et al., *How Sanctions Work* (Stanford, CA: Stanford University Press, 2024), 53–73, 29–52.

22. Narges Bajoghli et al., *How Sanctions Work*, 74–110.

23. Narges Bajoghli et al., *How Sanctions Work*, 29–52.

24. Cited in "Every Day We Sink Further into the Quicksand of Syria," *Zeytoun*, February 19, 2017, https://www.zeitoons.com/26478.

25. "Mir Hossein Moussavi on the Fate of Hossein Hamedani: A Lesson for the Survivors," *Radio Farda*, August 9, 2022, https://www.radiofarda.com/a/mirhossein-musavi-hamadani /31980121.html.

26. "[General] Ja'fari [former head of IRGC]: Hamedani, Was the One Who 'Cleaned up the 2009 Insurgency' and 'Steadied the Syrian Military'," *Radio Farda*, October 17, 2015, https:// www.radiofarda.com/a/f16-iran-hamedani-jafari-88-syria/27311619.html.

27. "Seyyed Mohammad Khatami: We Should Not Let Freedom and Security Be Put against Each Other," *ISNA*, December 6, 2022, https://www.isna.ir/news/1401091509886/سید-محمد -خاتمی-نباید-گذاشت-تا-آزادی-و-امنیت-در-برابر-هم-قرار.

28. Samuel, *The Unfinished History*, 213.

29. Peter J. Katzenstein, "Introduction: Alternative Views on National Security," in *The Culture of National Security*, ed. Peter J. Katzenstein (New York: Columbia University Press, 1996), 2.

30. Narges Bajoghi, "Trump's Iran Strategy Will Fail. Here Is Why," *New York Times*, June 30, 2019, https://www.nytimes.com/2019/06/30/opinion/trump-iran-revolutionary-guards.html.

Chapter 10: The Nuclear Gambit

1. For a chronicle of the arguments of the resistance forces against the nuclear deal, see Kamran Ghazanfari, *The Nuclear File and Its Open and Hidden Dimensions* (Tehran: Markaz Asnad Enqelab, 2015).

2. Mohammad Homayounvash, *Iran and the Nuclear Question: History and Evolutionary Trajectory* (New York: Routledge, 2017), 48.

3. Ali Akbar Hashemi Rafsanjani, *Transfer of Power, Record and Memoir*, ed. Mohsen Hashemi Rafsanjani (Tehran: Ma'aref Enqelab, 2020), 342; Hasan Rouhani, *National Security and Nuclear Diplomacy* (Tehran: Markaz Tahqiqat-e Estratejik, 2012), 34.

4. Shahram Chubin, *Iran's Nuclear Ambitions* (Washington, DC: Carnegie Endowment for International Peace, 2006), 14–23.

5. Arash Reisinezhad, "Understanding Iran's Nuclear Goals," *National Interest*, January 17, 2014, https://nationalinterest.org/commentary/understanding-irans-nuclear-goals-9725.

6. Personal conversation with former Pakistani foreign minister Agha Shahi, Islamabad, May 1991.

7. "Ayatollah Hashemi Rafsanjani's Interview with Members of the International Relations Quarterly," *Rafsanjani.ir*, March 21, 2013, https://rafsanjani.ir/records/مصاحبه-آیت-الله-هاشمی -رفسنجانی-با-اعضای-فصلنامه-مطالعات-بین-المللی; Ali Akbar Hashemi Rafsanjani, *Vitality of Development, Memoir and Record, 1993*, ed. Hasan Lahouti (Tehran: Ma'aref-e Enqelab, 2023), 10.

8. Rouhani, *National Security*, 36–41.

9. Kenneth M. Pollock, *Unthinkable: Iran, the Bomb, and American Strategy* (New York: Simon and Schuster, 2013).

10. Report of prominent hard-liner intellectual and activist Mehdi Mohammadi to the Basij Student Organization, "How Did the Nuclear Issue Get to This Point?," *Enghelaabioun_Javan* 23 (2013), https://t.me/Enghelaabioon_Javan/582.

11. Rouhani, *National Security*, 58–80.

12. Mohammad Ayatollahi Tabaar, *Religious Statecraft: The Politics of Islam in Iran* (New York: Columbia University Press, 2019), 273–98.

13. Seyed Hossein Mousavian, *The Iranian Nuclear Crisis: A Memoir* (Washington, DC: Carnegie Endowment for International Peace, 2012), 97–184; Trita Parsi, *A Single Roll of the Dice: Obama's Diplomacy with Iran* (New Haven, CT: Yale University Press, 2012), 172–209.

14. Rouhani, *National Security*, 294–352.

15. Chubin, *Iran*, 24–43; Ayatollahi Tabaar, *Religious Statecraft*, 274–81.

16. "Text of Ayatollah Khamenei's Fatwa Issued on December 12, 2020 about Religious Prohibition of Nuclear Weapons," Embassy of Islamic Republic of Iran, Paris, https://france.mfa.ir /portal/newsview/543649/متن-فتوای-حضرت-آیت-الله-خامنه-ای-صادره-در-تاریخ-۲۱-آذر-۱۳۸۹-مبنی-بر-حرام-بودن -سلاح-هسته-ای.

17. Pollock, *Unthinkable*, 118–58.

18. Dana Allin and Steven Simon, *The Sixth Crisis: Iran, Israel, America and the Rumors of War* (New York: Oxford University Press, 2010), 45–74.

19. Parsi, *A Single Roll of the Dice*, 103–13.

20. Video of Rafsanjani's speech, Tarikh-e Moa'aser Telegram Channel, accessed January 1, 2023, https://t.me/c/1092725532/28442.

21. Golnaz Esfandiari, "Senior Iranian Official Reveals Details about Secret Talks with U.S.," *Radio Farda*, August 6, 2015, https://www.rferl.org/a/iran-secret-talks-salehi-nuclear-united -states/27174643.html.

22. Mousavian, *The Iranian Nuclear Crisis*, 460.

23. Seyyed Jalal Dehqani Firouzabadi and Mehdi Ataie, "Nuclear Discourse of the Eleventh Government," *Faslnameh-e Motale'at-e Rahbordi* 17, no. 1 (Spring 2014): 87–120; Rouhani, *National Security*, 633.

24. Jeffrey Goldberg, "The Obama Doctrine," *Atlantic*, April 2016, https://www.theatlantic .com/magazine/archive/2016/04/the-obama-doctrine/471525/.

25. William J. Burns, *The Back Channel: A Memoir of American Diplomacy and the Case of Renewal* (New York: Random House, 2019), 337–85.

26. Rouhani, *National Security*.

27. Ayatollahi Tabaar, *Religious Statecraft*, 281–82.

28. Mousavian, *The Iranian Nuclear Crisis*, 289–320.

29. Kelsey Davenport, "The Joint Comprehensive Plan of Action (JCPOA) at a Glance," Arms Control Association, March 2022, https://www.armscontrol.org/factsheets/JCPOA-at-a -glance.

30. Kenneth Katzman and Paul Kerr, "Iran Nuclear Agreement," *Congressional Research Service*, May 31, 2016, 18–19.

31. For an insider Iranian account of the talks, see Mohammad Javad Zarif et al., *Sealed Secret* (Tehran: Entesharat Etelaat, 2021).

32. Djavad Salehi-Esfahani, "Iran's Middle Class and the Nuclear Deal," Brookings Institution, April 8, 2021, https://www.brookings.edu/blog/future-development/2021/04/08/irans -middle-class-and-the-nuclear-deal/.

33. Annie Tracy Samuel, *The Unfinished History of the Iran-Iraq War: Faith, Firepower, and Iran's Revolutionary Guards* (New York: Cambridge University Press, 2022), 218–19.

34. "[Abbas] Abdi's Analysis of Reasons for Hardliners' Opposition to JCPOA," *Donia-e Eqtesad*, May 13, 2016; https://donya-e-eqtesad.com/خوان-سایت-بخش/62/3161534-دلایل-از-عبدی-تحلیل مخالفت-تندروها-با-برجام-.

35. "Comments during the Leader of the Revolution's Meeting with People of Azarbaijan," *Leader.ir*, February 16, 2013, https://www.leader.ir/fa/speech/10315/مردم-از-نفر-هزاران-شور-پر-دیدار آذربایجان-با-رهبر-معظم-انقلاب-.

36. "A Review of the Views of the Supreme Leader on JCPOA and the Nuclear Negotiating Team," *Imna.ir*, June 17, 2016, https://www.imna.ir/news/487035/معظم-رهبر-نظرات-بر-مروری های20%انقلاب8C%80%E2کننده20%مذاکره20%بچه20%مذاکره-در-مورد-برجام-و-تیم-مذاکره-کننده#تیم-.

37. "Today Is the Day for Everything; Negotiations as well as Missiles," *Entekhab.ir*, January 20, 2017, https://www.entekhab.ir/fa/news/260444/هم-مذاکره-هم-است-چیز-همه-روزگار موشک-جوری-باید-مذاکره-کرد-که-سرمان-کلاه-نرود-اینکه-روی-کاغذ-بنویسیم-ولی-تحریمها-برطرف-نمیشود-معلوم-میشود-اشکالی- هست-.

38. "Comments in the Gathering of Visitors to Imam Reza's Shrine," *Khamenei.ir*, March 21, 2007, https://farsi.khamenei.ir/speech-content?id=3378.

39. "Opposition to FATF Is Like Political Opposition to JCPOA," *Peyk-e Iran*, September 7, 2016, https://www.peykeiran.com/Content.aspx?ID=115970:; "Reaction to the Foreign Minister's Comments on Money Laundering," *Doniya-e Eqtesad*, November 14, 2018, https://donya -e-eqtesad.com/خبر-بخش/64/3463544-پولشویی-مورد-در-خارجه-امور-وزیر-سخنان-به-ها-واکنش-.

40. Personal conversation with a senior Arab leader present at the Camp David meeting, January 2016.

41. Cited in Goldberg, "The Obama Doctrine."

42. Trita Parsi, *Losing an Enemy: Obama, Iran, and the Triumph of Diplomacy* (New Haven, CT: Yale University Press, 2017), 318–51.

43. Ghazanfari, *The Nuclear File.*

44. The long of list of these accusations are discussed in Ghazanfari, *The Nuclear File*. See also Rouhani, *National Security*, 128–29.

45. Personal conversations, December 2015.

46. SIPRI Military Expenditures Data Base, n.d., https://www.sipri.org/databases/milex.

47. Hadi Kahalzadeh, "'Maximum Pressure' Hardened Iran against Compromise," *Foreign Affairs*, March 11, 2021, https://www.foreignaffairs.com/articles/iran/2021-03-11/maximum -pressure-hardened-iran-against-compromise.

48. Rouhani, *National Security*, 21.

49. Zarif outlined his arguments in the media, but also in his reports to the Iranian Parliament. For his last report and most comprehensive defense of the JCPOA, see "Twenty-Second Report on the Status of the JCPOA to the Islamic Assembly," Report 6428627, July 14, 2021; https://mfa.gov.ir/files/mfa/PDF/210711-MJZ-22nd%20Majlis%20Report-Full%20CD.pdf.

Zarif and his fellow neotiators laid out the various terms of the JCPOA and how they were negotiated in copious detail in six volumes too. See Zarif et al., *Sealed Secret*.

50. "Iran Sanctions under the Trump Administration," International Crisis Group, January 15, 2020, https://www.crisisgrouorg/middle-east-north-africa/gulf-and-arabian-peninsula/iran/iran-sanctions-under-trump-administration.

51. For the scale as well as the social and economic impact of these sanctions, see the Iran under Sanctions reports put out by the Rethinking Iran Project of Johns Hopkins University's School of Advanced International Studies, https://www.rethinkingiran.com/iran-under-sanctions.

52. Narrated by a senior European diplomat to Iran's foreign minister at the time, Mohammad Javad Zarif, from conversations with Zarif at the Munich Security Conference, February 2019.

53. Seyed Hossein Mousavian, "The Strategic Disaster of Leaving the Iran Deal," *Foreign Affairs*, May 10, 2018, https://www.foreignaffairs.com/articles/iran/2018-05-10/strategic-disaster-leaving-iran-deal.

54. "Mike Pompeo's Speech: What Are the Twelve Demands Given to Iran?," *Al Jazeera*, May 21, 2018, https://www.aljazeera.com/news/2018/5/21/mike-pompeo-speech-what-are-the-12-demands-given-to-iran.

55. Brenden Cole, "Mike Pompeo Says Iran Must Listen to the U.S. 'If They Want Their People to Eat,'" *Newsweek*, November 19, 2018, https://www.newsweek.com/mike-pompeo-says-iran-must-listen-us-if-they-want-their-people-eat-1208465.

56. Narges Bajoghli et al., *How Sanctions Work: Iran and the Impact of Economic Warfare* (Stanford, CA: Stanford University Press, 2024), 49.

57. Djavad Salehi-Isfahani, "The Dilemma of Iran's Resistance Economy," *Foreign Affairs*, March 17, 2021, https://www.foreignaffairs.com/articles/middle-east/2021-03-17/dilemma-irans-resistance-economy.

58. Agathe Demarais, "The End of the Age of Sanctions?," *Foreign Affairs*, December 27, 2022, https://www.foreignaffairs.com/united-states/end-age-sanctions.

59. See "China-Iran Trade Report (October 2020)," Bourse and Bazaar Foundation, https://www.bourseandbazaar.com/china-iran-trade-reports/october-2020?rq=China; "China-Iran Trade Report (March 2021)," Bourse and Bazaar Foundation, https://www.bourseandbazaar.com/china-iran-trade-reports/march-2021?rq=China; Esfandiar Batmanghelij and Bijan Khajepour, "Diplomatic and Economic Potential of Iran's New President Raisi," Rethinking Iran, YouTube, October 4, 2021, https://www.youtube.com/watch?v=CcZ4-enF-e4; Bijan Khajepour, "Three Scenarios for Iran's Economic Development," Middle East Institute, October 7, 2021, https://www.mei.edu/publications/three-scenarios-irans-economic-development.

60. Benoit Faucon, "Iranian Oil Exports Rise as Tehran Circumvents Sanctions, Finds New Buyers," *Wall Street Journal*, December 15, 2020, https://www.wsj.com/articles/iranian-oil-exports-rise-as-tehran-circumvents-sanctions-finds-new-buyers-11608052404.

61. Bijan Khajepour, "China's Emerging Role in Iran's Petroleum Sector," *Al-Monitor*, January 31, 2019, https://www.al-monitor.com/originals/2019/01/iran-china-energy-cooperation-nioc-sinopec-sanctions.html.

62. Jacopo Scita, "China-Iran Relations through the Prism of Sanctions," *Asian Affairs*, February 9, 2022, https://doi.org/10.1080/03068374.2022.2029060.

63. Bajoghli et al., *How Sanctions Work*, 43–44.

64. Liz Sly, "Two Saudi Oil Tankers, Norwegian Ship Apparently Attacked Near the Persian Gulf amid Rising Iran Tensions," *Washington Post*, May 13, 2019, https://www.washingtonpost.com/world/middle_east/two-saudi-oil-tankers-attacked-in-the-persian-gulf-amid-rising-iran-tensions/2019/05/13/c8907108-755e-11e9-bd25-c989555e7766_story.html.

65. David Axe, "Iran Knocked Out of the Sky a Very Special U.S. Drone (and Exposed a Key Weakness)," *National Interest*, June 20, 2019, https://nationalinterest.org/blog/buzz/iran-knocked-out-sky-very-special-us-drone-and-exposed-key-weakness-63577.

66. Michael D. Shear et al., "Strikes on Iran Approved by Trump, Then Abruptly Pulled Back," *New York Times*, June 10, 2019, https://www.nytimes.com/2019/06/20/world/middleeast/iran-us-drone.html.

67. Maziar Motamedi, "Khamenei Renews Revenge Vow as Soleimani Death Anniversary Nears," *Al Jazeera*, December 16, 2020, https://www.aljazeera.com/news/2020/12/16/khamenei-renews-revenge-vow-before-soleimani-killing-anniversary.

68. Ja'far Shiralinia, *A Telling of the Life and Times of Ayatollah Ali Akbar Hashemi Rafsanjani* (Tehran: Sayan, 2017), 917.

69. Personal conversations, May 2023.

70. Personal conversations, May 2023.

71. Personal conversations, February 2016.

72. Gareth Smyth, "Deciphering the Iranian Leader's Call for Resistance Economy," *Guardian*, April 19, 2016, https://www.theguardian.com/world/iran-blog/2016/apr/19/iran-resistance-economy-tehranbureau.

73. Bajoghli et al., *How Sanctions Work*, 49–57.

74. Seyyed Ali Khamenei, "The 'Second Phase of the Revolution' Statement Addressed to the Iranian Nation," *Khamenei.ir*, February 11, 2019, https://english.khamenei.ir/news/6415/The-Second-Phase-of-the-Revolution-Statement-addressed-to-the.

75. Hasan Rouhani, *National Security and the Economic System* (Tehran: Markaz-e Tahqiqat-e Estratejic, 2012).

76. "All Those 24 'Economists' Are Almost All Now in the Government [of Raisi], Parliament and Media," *Ensaf News*, December 20, 2022, http://www.ensafnews.com/388388/آن-۲۴-اقتصاددان-تقریبا-همگی-اکنون-در-/.

77. Djavad Salehi-Isfahani "No, Iranians Aren't Negotiating from a Weak Economic Position," *Responsible Statecraft*, August 30, 2022, https://responsiblestatecraft.org/2022/08/30/no-iranians-arent-negotiating-from-a-weak-economic-position/.

78. Vali Nasr, "Trump's Policies Have Convinced Iran to Build a More Advanced Nuclear Program before Negotiating," *Foreign Policy*, September 21, 2021, https://foreignpolicy.com/2020/09/21/trumps-policies-have-convinced-iran-to-build-a-more-advanced-nuclear-program-before-negotiating/.

79. Kahalzadeh, "Maximum Pressure."

80. Mahnaz Zahirnejad, "The Economic Effects of Sanctions and the Iranian Middle Class," in *Iran in the International System: Between Great Powers and Great Ideas*, ed. Heintz Gartner and Mitra Shahmoradi (New York: Routledge, 2020), 108–30.

81. Bajoghli et al., *How Sanctions Work*, 99.

82. Borzou Daragahi, "Middle Class Iranians Sought to Remake Their Nation. Here Is How They Were Betrayed," Atlantic Council, March 9, 2021, https://www.atlanticcouncil.org/blogs/iransource/middle-class-iranians-sought-to-remake-their-nation-heres-how-they-were-betrayed/; Mohammad Sadeghi Esfahlani and Jamal Abdi, "Sanctions Cripple Iran's Middle Class, Not the Regime," *Foreign Policy*, August 2, 2012, https://foreignpolicy.com/2012/08/02/sanctions-cripple-irans-middle-class-not-the-regime/.

83. Rick Gladstone, "Iran's Top Leader Faults Rouhani for Crisis, Says He Crossed 'Red Lines,'" *New York Times*, August 14, 2018, A4.

84. Djavad Salehi-Isfahani, "The Coronavirus Is Iran's Perfect Storm," *Foreign Affairs*, March 18, 2020, https://www.foreignaffairs.com/articles/iran/2020-03-18/coronavirus-irans-perfect-storm.

85. "How Merchants of Sanctions Shaped the Climate against JCPOA," *Qarn-e No*, August 12, 2022, https://www.iranchamber.com/calendar/converter/iranian_calendar_converter.php; Ramin Mostaghim and Nabih Bulos, "Imagine 'Homeland,' If All the Heroes Were Iranian. That's 'Gando,' Must-See TV in Iran," *Los Angeles Times*, July 19, 2019, https://www.latimes.com/world-nation/story/2019-07-19/iran-hit-tv-show-gando.

86. Mohammad Ayatollahi Tabaar, "Iran's War within: Ebrahim Raisi and the Triumph of Hardliners," *Foreign Affairs* 100, no. 5 (September–October 2021): 155–68.

87. Ali Reza Eshraghi and Amir Hossein Mahdavi, "The Revolutionary Guards Are Poised to Take over Iran," *Foreign Affairs*, August 27, 2020, https://www.foreignaffairs.com/articles/middle-east/2020-08-27/revolutionary-guards-are-poised-take-over-iran.

88. "Iran Nuclear Deal at Six: Now or Never," *International Crisis Group Middle East Report* 230 (January 17, 2022): 44.

89. Kelsey Davenport, "Iran Accelerates Highly Enriched Uranium Production," Arms Control Association, January–February 2024, https://www.armscontrol.org/act/2024-01/news/iran-accelerates-highly-enriched-uranium-production

90. "Iran Nuclear Deal at Six," 45.

91. David Albright, Sarah Burkhard, and Spencer Faragasso, "Updated Highlights of Comprehensive Survey of Iran's Advanced Centrifuges—March 2023," Institute for Science and International Security, March 21, 2023, https://isis-online.org/isis-reports/detail/updated-highlights-of-survey-of-irans-advanced-centrifuges-March2023#:~:text=Overall%2C%20Iran%20has%2012%2C994%20centrifuges,and%207231%20IR%2D1%20centrifuges.

92. "Iran Nuclear Deal at Six," 4–5.

93. Ronen Bergman and Farnaz Fassihi, "The Scientist and the A.I.-Assisted, Remote-Control Killing Machine," *New York Times*, September 19, 2021, 1.

94. Ronen Bergman, Rick Gladstone, and Farnaz Fassihi, "Blackout Hits Iran Nuclear Site in What Appears to Be Israeli Sabotage," *New York Times*, April 12, 2021, 1.

95. David Sanger et al., "As Hopes for Nuclear Deal Fade, Iran Rebuilds and Risks Grow," *New York Times*, November 22, 2021, 1; Francois Murphy, "Iran Adds Machines at Enrichment Plant Struck by Blast—IAEA," *Reuters*, April 21, 2021, https://www.reuters.com/world/middle-east/iran-adds-advanced-machines-underground-enrichment-plant-iaea-report-2021-04-21/.

96. Laurence Norman, "U.S. Sees Iran's Nuclear Program as Too Advanced to Restore Key Goal of 2015 Pact," *Wall Street Journal*, February 3, 2022, https://www.wsj.com/articles/u-s-sees

-irans-nuclear-program-as-too-advanced-to-restore-key-goal-of-2015-pact-11643882545?st
=ne9ed8ea4mkeiua&reflink=desktopwebshare_twitter.

97. "Ali Akbar Velayati: The First Priority of Raisi Government Must Be Cooperation with
China and Russia," *Payk-e Iran*, August 3, 2021, https://www.peykeiran.com/Content.aspx?ID
=23255:; Mehdi Sanaie, "Examination of Iran-Russie Relations", *Mahnameh-e Iras* 21 (2012):
http://ensani.ir/fa/article/80772/بررسی-روابط-ایران-و-روسیه.

98. Arash Reisinejad, *Iran and the New Silk Road* (Tehran: Tehran University Press, 2022);
Mohsen Shariatinia, "Decisive Factors in Iran-China Relations," *Faslnameh-e Ravabet-e Kharjei*
4, no. 2 (Summer 2012): 179–210; "Velayati: China Is Iran's Strategic Partner," *Barkhat News*,
August 16, 2022, https://www.barkhat.news/political/166067352387/velayati-china-is-a
-strategic-ally-of-iran.

99. Mohammad Ayatollahi Tabaar, "Iran's Russian Turn," *Foreign Affairs*, November 12, 2015,
https://www.foreignaffairs.com/articles/iran/2015-11-12/irans-russian-turn; Vali Nasr, "A
Russian-Iranian Axis," *New York Times*, September 17, 2016, A7.

100. Jamsheed Choksy and Carol Choksy, "China and Russia Have Iran's Back," *Foreign Affairs*, November 17, 2020, https://www.foreignaffairs.com/articles/united-states/2020-11-17
/china-and-russia-have-irans-back.

101. Behrouz As'adi va Seyyed Ali Monavvari, "Examination of Iran-Russia Relations in the
New Century: Strategic Alliance or Convergence of Interests," *Rahyaftha-ye Siyasi and Beinolmellali* 12, no. 4 (August 2021): 181–210.

102. "Iran, Russia, China Hold Joint Naval Drill amid Growing Ties," *Radio Free Europe*,
January 21, 2022, https://www.rferl.org/a/iran-russia-china-exercises/31663080.html.

103. Mohsen Shariatinia, "Iran-China Relations: From a Romantic Triangle to Lasting
Relations," *Faslnameh-e Elmi Rahyafthaye Siyasi va Beinolmellali* 11, no. 3 (Spring 2020):
95–114.

104. Valiollah Haami Kalvanaq, *Iran-China Relations before and after the Revolution* (Tehran:
Markaz Asnad-e Enqelab-e Eslami, 2011).

105. Daniel Markey, *China's Western Horizon: Beijing and the New Geopolitics of Eurasia* (New
York: Oxford University Press, 2020), Vali Nasr, *The Dispensable Nation: American Foreign Policy
in Retreat* (New York: Doubleday, 2013), 215–50.

106. "Full Text of Joint Statement on Comprehensive Strategic Partnership between I.R.
Iran, R. China," March 23, 2016, https://www.president.ir/EN/91435.

107. Personal conversation with Ali Khoshroo, former Iran ambassador to the United Nations, September 2019; *The 25-Year Plan for Iran-China Cooperation and the Outlook for Relations
between Iran and China in the Next Two Decades* (Tehran: Majma'-e Beinolmellali Asatid Mosalman Daneshgah-ha, 2020).

108. Personal conversations, October 2019.

109. Mohammad Ayatollahi Tabaar, "No Matter Who Is U.S. President, Iran Will Drive a
Harder Bargain Than Before," *Foreign Affairs*, October 20, 2020, https://www.foreignaffairs.com
/articles/iran/2020-10-20/no-matter-who-us-president-iran-will-drive-harder-bargain.

110. "Commander: Iran Likely to Revise Nuclear Policies in Case of Israel Attack," *Farsnews*,
April 18, 2024, https://farsnews.ir/Qaysar/1713447814430542974/Commander%3A-Iran-Likely
-to-Revise-Nuclear-Policies-in-Case-of-Israeli-Attack.

Chapter 11: The Price of Resistance

1. Narges Bajoghli et al., *How Sanctions Work: Iran and the Impact of Economic Warfare* (Stanford, CA: Stanford University Press, 2024).

2. Hadi Kahalzadeh, "'Maximum Pressure' Hardened Iran against Compromise," *Foreign Affairs*, March 11, 2021, https://www.foreignaffairs.com/articles/iran/2021-03-11/maximum -pressure-hardened-iran-against-compromise. I am grateful to Kahalzadeh for updating his figures through 2022–23 in private correspondences.

3. Esfandyar Batmanghelidj, "The Inflation Weapon: How American Sanctions Harm Iranian Households," Sanctions and Security Research Project, January 2022, https:// sanctionsandsecurity.org/publications/the-inflation-weapon-how-american-sanctions-harm -iranian-households/; Esfandyar Batmangelidj and Erica Moret, "The Hidden Toll of Sanctions," *Foreign Affairs*, January 17, 2022, https://www.foreignaffairs.com/articles/world/2022-01 -17/hidden-toll-sanctions.

4. Kahalzadeh, "Maximum Pressure"; "The Fall in the Middle Class by 5 Million," *Arman-e Emrouz*, October 24, 2023, https://www.armandaily.ir/طبقه-متوسط-نفری-میلیون-5-ریزش/.

5. See, for instance, Niloofar Adnani, "Irreparable Loss: Sanctions and the Disruptions of Children's Education in Baluchistan, Iran," Bourse and Bazaar Foundation, December 2021, https://www.bourseandbazaar.com/research-1/2021/12/16/irreperable-loss-sanctions-and -childrens-education-in-baluchistan.

6. Yousef Foroutan, *Memoirs of Commander Yousef Foroutan, Member of the First Commanders Council of the IRGC*, ed. Masoumeh Samavi (Tehran: Markaz Assad Enqelab Eslami, 2019), 273–304.

7. "Rafsanjani: Sanctions Have Hollowed the Bones of the Majority of the Population," *DW .com*, June 16, 2015, https://www.dw.com/fa-ir/است-یکانده-را-جامعه-اکثریت-استخوان-تحریم-رفسنجانی/a -18521077.

8. Vivian Lee and Farnaz Fassihi, "Lament in a Restive Iran, 'We Are Breaking under Financial Pressure,'" *New York Times*, October 2, 2022, A6.

9. Khamenei's speech before IRGC commanders, "In Order to Reach the Peak," *Khamenei. ir*, August 19, 2023, https://farsi.khamenei.ir/video-content?id=53604; "Reaching the Peak Is the Start of Further Horizons," *Khamenei.ir*, August 31, 2023, https://farsi.khamenei.ir/others -dialog?id=53729.

10. Azadeh Moaveni, "'It's Like War Out There.' Iran's Women Haven't Been This Angry in a Generation," *New York Times*, October 10, 2022, A20.

11. Azadeh Moaveni, "Two Weeks in Tehran," *London Review of Books* 44, no. 21 (November 2022), https://www.lrb.co.uk/the-paper/v44/n21/azadeh-moaveni/diary.

12. Narges Bajoghli, "'Woman, Life, Freedom': Iran's Protests Are a Rebellion for Bodily Autonomy," *Vanity Fair*, September 29, 2022, https://www.vanityfair.com/news/2022/09 /mahsa-amini-irans-protests-rebellion-bodily-autonomy.

13. "Alamolhoda: If Flaunting of Hijab Became Widespread," *Entekhab*, October 7, 2022, https://www.entekhab.ir/fa/news/697830/گرایش-و-اخلاقی-فساد-نتیجه-در-شد-رایج-حجابی-بی-اگر-الهدی-علم شود%E2%80%8Cبند-و-بار-می%E2%80%8Cشود-جوانی-که-باید-مجاهد-شود-بی%E2%80%8Cهای-جنسی-باعث-می%E2%80%8Cشود.

14. Adam Tooze, "Iran's Contested Demographic Revolution," Substack, October 15, 2022, https://adamtooze.substack.com/p/chartbook-161-irans-contested-demographic.

15. Mohammad Nadimi, "Syriafication of Iran," *Aparat*, December 2022, https://www.aparat .com/v/rVxNn; Elham Abedini, "Syriafication of Iran: Signs and Contexts," *IRNA*, October 9, 2022, https://www.irna.ir/news/84907177/سوریه-سازی-ایران-نشانه-ها-و-زمینه-ها; Mohammad Reza Farhadi, "Why Is America Pursuing Syriafication of Iran," *Basirat*, November 5, 2022, https://basirat.ir/fa/news/340900/چرا-آمریکا-به-دنبال-سوریه-سازی-ایران-است.

16. "Those Who Take Their Scarves Off in the Street," *Entekhab*, October 21, 2022, https://www.entekhab.ir/fa/news/699771/آنهایی-که-در-خیابان-روسری-از-سر-می-کنند-بدانند-با-چهار-تا-در%8C%80%2E%شود-به-انقلاب-وارد-نمی-آورند%8C%80%2E%ای-روسری-خدشه-.

17. "Message from a Wartime Commander: We Will Not Sell Our Honor for Your Susrvival," *Iran Wire*, November 4, 2022, https://iranwire.com/fa/news/109365-1/پیام-یکی-از-فرماندهان-ارشد-جنگ-شرفمان-را-برای-بقای-شما-نمیفروشیم-.

18. "Based on Reports, 75% of People Cannot Make Ends Meet without Government Handouts," *Entekhab*, December 20, 2022, https://www.entekhab.ir/fa/news/707623/ها %E2%80%8C% بر-75-درصد-مردم-بدون-اعانه-نمی C8%80%2E%توانند-زندگی-خود فرشاد-مومنی-طبق-گزارش % E 2 % 8 0 تواند-ادامه-داشته-باشد-ایرانC8%80%2E%را-بگذرانند-پرسش-اصلی-این-است-که-مداراای-نجیبانه-مردم-ایران-با-فقر-تا-کجا-می-دچار-حس-بی-آینده-بودن-شده-مرحله-بعد-از-بی-آینده-بودن-فروپاشی-است-.

19. Esfandyar Batmanghelidj, "How Sanctions Hurt Iran's Protesters," *Foreign Affairs*, April 4, 2023, https://www.foreignaffairs.com/middle-east/iran-sanctions-how-protesters.

20. "Imam Khamenei: Recent Events Were Hybrid Warfare," *Tasnim*, November 2, 2022; "The Enemy's Objective Is to Break Iran's Unity," *Khamenei.ir*, November 13, 2022, https://farsi .khamenei.ir/others-dialog?id=51314.

21. "Jihad to Put Forth the Truth and Hybrid Offensive," *Javan*, February 9, 2022, https:// www.javanonline.ir/fa/news/1078604/فرمان-جهاد-تبیین-و-تهاجم-ترکیبی.

22. "National Uprising against Hybrid Warfare," *Khamenei.ir*, November 13, 2022, https:// farsi.khamenei.ir/others-report?id=51310.

23. "Ali Larijani: Look at the Shah's Era," *Navid Torbat*, October 12, 2022, http://www .navidtorbat.ir/fa/News/19243/علی-لاریجانی-به-زمان-شاه-نگاه-کنید-مگر-ترویج-بی-حجابی-نمیE2%80%8C%شد-اما-چقدر-از-مردم-حجاب-داشتند؛-آن-زماC8%80%2E%.

24. "'If People Don't Want to Be 'Enjoined to Do Good,' Who Should They See?," *Fararou*, October 7, 2022, https://fararou.com/fa/news/579785/ضرغامی-مردم-اگر-نخوان-امر-به-معروف-بشن-باید-کیو-ببین.

25. "Report of Ayatollah Sistani's Worry over Recent Events in Iran," *Khabar Online*, December 7, 2022, https://www.khabaronline.ir/news/1704062/پیام-روایت-نگرانی-آیت-الله-سیستانی-از-خدادهای-اخیر-ایران-اشرفی-.

26. "Ayatollah Makrem Shirazi in Meeting with Qalibaf," *Khabar Online*, December 28, 2022, https://www.khabaronline.ir/news/1712327/آیت-الله-مکارم-شیرازی-در-دیدار-قالیباف-شرایط-اقتصادی-نه-تنها.

27. "Former Hardliners Turn into Formidable Critics of the Iranian State," *Amwaj Media*, September 27, 2023, https://amwaj.media/article/inside-story-former-hardliners-turn-into -formidable-critics-of-iranian-state.

28. "The Harsh Criticism of a Hard-liner Activist," *Ensaf News*, November 14, 2022, http:// www.ensafnews.com/380937/.

29. Cited in "We Mustn't Allow Freedom and Security to Confront One Another," *Iranian Students' News Agency*, December 6, 2022, https://www.isna.ir/news/1401091509886/سید-محمد-خاتمی-نباید-گذاشت-تا-آزادی-و-امنیت-در-برابر-هم-قرار-.

30. "Amid Protests, Talk of Reform Crosses Political Divide in Iran," *Amwaj Media*, December 28, 2022, https://amwaj.media/article/inside-story-amid-protests-talk-of-reform-crosses-political-divide-in-iran.

31. "We Chose This Ourselves: Why Is 'Compromising' a Negative and 'Uncompromising' a Positive?," *Rouz*, June 3, 2023, http://roozplus.com/fa/news/282244/محمد-جواد-ظریف-خودمان-کار-منفی-و-سازش-ناپذیر-مثبت-است-ما-در-طول-تاریخ-اهدافمان-را-بر-اساس C 8 % 8 0 % 2 E % انتخاب-کردیم-چرا-سازش-ایم.C%8 8 0%2E%آرزوهایمان-چیده-.

32. Ayatollah Khamenei's speech during the commemoration of sacred defense, *Telewebion*, September 20, 2023, https://telewebion.com/episode/0x8b1dof1.

33. See Khamenei's interview in *Entekhab.ir*, n.d., https://www.entekhab.ir/fa/amp/news/731364.

34. Private conversations.

35. "Khamenei: God Speaks to IRGC Commanders through Me," *Independent*, January 2, 2024, https://www.independentpersian.com/tv/خامنه%8C%80%2E%ایران-با-من-زبان-با-خدا-:ای-کند-t6YJUCfa.C%8 80%2E%فرماندهان-سپاه-صحبت-می-.

36. Ali Reza Eshraghi and Amir Hossein Mahdavi, "The Evolution of the Revolutionary Guards," in *The Sacred Republic: Power and Institutions in Iran*, ed. Mehran Kamrava (New York: Oxford University Press, 2023), 187–220.

37. Personal correspondences with senior adviser to Iranian government, April 2024.

38. Azadeh Moaveni, "Election in Iran," *London Review of Books*, 46, no. 13 (July 4, 2024), https://www.lrb.co.uk/the-paper/v46/n13/azadeh-moaveni/election-in-iran; interview with the conservative presidential candidate Mostafa Pourmohammadi, *Mehrnews*, June 12, 2024, https://donya-e-eqtesad.com/بخش-سایت-خوان-62/4079869-قول-پورمحمدی-به-زنان-لایحه-عفاف-حجاب-را-پی-می-گیرم-فیلم-.

39. Narges Bajoghli and Vali Nasr, "A More Normal Iran?," *Foreign Affairs*, July 29, 2024, https://www.foreignaffairs.com/iran/more-normal-iran-masoud-pezeshkian.

40. John Lewis Gaddis, *On Grand Strategy* (New York: Penguin Press, 2018), 1–29.

41. Gaddis, *On Grand Strategy*, 4.

BIBLIOGRAPHY

Abedini, Vahid. "The New Generation of Political Elites in Iran: Genealogy, Evolution, and Trajectory." PhD diss., Florida International University, 2023.

Abisaab, Rula. *Converting Persia: Religion and Power in the Safavid Empire*. London: I. B. Tauris, 2004.

Abrahamian, Ervand. *The Coup: 1953, the CIA, and the Roots of Modern U.S.–Iranian Relations*. New York: New Press, 2013.

———. *Iran between Two Revolutions*. Princeton, NJ: Princeton University Press, 1982.

———. *The Iranian Mojahedin*. New Haven, CT: Yale University Press, 1989.

———. *Khomeinism*. Berkeley: University of California Press, 1993.

———. *Tortured Confessions: Prisons and Public Recantations in Modern Iran*. Berkeley: University of California Press, 1999.

Acemoglu, Daron, and James A. Robinson. *The Narrow Corridor; States, Societies, and the Fate of Liberty*. New York: Penguin Random House, 2019.

Adelkhah, Fariba. *Being Modern in Iran*. New York: Columbia University Press, 2000.

———. "The Political Economy of the Green Movement: Contestation and Political Mobilization in Iran." In *Iran: From Theocracy to the Green Movement*, edited by Negin Nabavi, 17–38. New York: Palgrave Macmillan, 2012.

Adib-Moghaddam, Arshin. "Inventions of the Iran-Iraq War." In *Debating the Iran-Iraq War in Contemporary Iran*, edited by Narges Bajoghli and Amir Moosavi, 76–96. New York: Routledge, 2018.

Adnani, Niloofar. "Irreparable Loss: Sanctions and the Disruptions of Children's Education in Baluchistan, Iran." Bourse and Bazaar Foundation, December 2021. https://www.bourseandbazaar.com/research-1/2021/12/16/irreperable-loss-sanctions-and-childrens-education-in-baluchistan

Afary, Janet. *The Iranian Constitutional Revolution, 1906–1911*. New York: Columbia University Press, 1996.

Afkhami, Gholam Reza. *The Life and Times of the Shah*. Berkeley: University of California Press, 2009.

Aghaie, Kamran Scot. *The Martyrs of Karbala: Shi'i Symbols and Rituals in Modern Iran*. Seattle: University of Washington Press, 2004.

Ahmadian, Hassan, and Payam Mohseni. "Iran's Syria Strategy: The Evolution of Deterrence." *International Affairs* 95, no. 2 (March 2019): 341–64.

Ajili, Hadi, and Mahsa Rouhi. "Iran's Military Strategy." *Survival* 61, no. 6 (2019): 139–52.

Akbarzadeh, Shahram. "Iran and Daesh: The Case of a Reluctant Shia Power." *Middle East Policy* 22, no. 3 (September 2015): 44–54.

Akbarzadeh, Shahram, William Gourlay, and Anoushiravan Ehteshami. "Iranian Proxies in the Syrian Conflict: Tehran's 'Forward Defense' in Action." *Journal of Strategic Studies* (2022): 1–24.

Akhavi, Shahrough. *Religion and Politics in Contemporary Iran: Clergy-State Relations in the Pahlavi Period.* Albany: SUNY Press, 1980.

Alemzadeh, Maryam. "The Attraction of Direct Action: The Making of the Islamic Revolutionary Guards Corps in the Iranian Kurdish Conflict." *British Journal of Middle East Studies* (2021): 1–20.

———. "The Islamic Revolutionary Guards Corps in the Iran-Iraq War: An Unconventional Military Survival." *British Journal of Middle East Studies* (2018): 1–18.

Alfoneh, Ali. *Iran Unveiled: How the Revolutionary Guards Is Turning Theocracy into Military Dictatorship.* Washington, DC: AEI Press, 2013.

———. "What Iran's Military Journals Reveal about the Role of Missiles in Strategic Deterrence." Arab Gulf States Institute in Washington, June 25, 2020. https://agsiw.org/what-irans-military-journals-reveal-about-the-role-of-missiles-in-strategic-deterrence/.

Alimagham, Pouya. *Contesting the Iranian Revolution: The Green Uprisings.* New York: Cambridge University Press, 2020.

Allen, Calvin H., and W. Lynn Rigsbee. *Oman under Qaboos, from Coup to Constitution 1970–1996.* London: Frank Cass, 2000.

Allin, Dana, and Steven Simon. *The Sixth Crisis: Iran, Israel, America and the Rumors of War.* New York: Oxford University Press, 2010.

Al-Rashid, Madawi. "Sectarianism as Counterrevolution." *Studies in Ethnicity and Nationalism* 11, no. 3 (December 2011): 513–26.

Alvandi, Roham. "Muhammad Reza Shah and the Bahrain Question, 1968–70." *British Journal of Middle East Studies* 37, no. 2 (2010): 159–77.

———. *Nixon, Kissinger and the Shah: The United States and Iran in the Cold War.* New York: Oxford University Press, 2014.

Amanat, Abbas. *Apocalyptic Islam and Iranian Shi'ism.* London: I. B. Tauris, 2009.

———. "Introduction: Iranian Identity Boundaries: A Historical Overview." In *Iran Facing Others*, edited by Abbas Amanat and Farzin Vejdani, 1–37. New York: Palgrave Macmillan, 2012.

———. *Iran: A Modern History.* New Haven, CT: Yale University Press, 2017.

———. "'Russian Intrusion into the Guarded Domain': Reflections of a Qajar Statesman on European Expansion." *Journal of the American Oriental Society* 113, no. 1 (January–March 1993): 5–56.

Amirahmadi, Hooshang. *Revolution and Economic Transition: The Iranian Experience.* Albany: SUNY Press, 1990.

Amuzegar, Jahangir. *Iran's Economy under the Islamic Republic.* London: I. B. Tauris, 1993.

Ansari, Ali M. *Iran, Islam and Democracy: Politics of Managing Change.* London: Royal Institute of International Affairs, 2000.

———. "The Myth of the Iranian Revolution: Mohammad Reza Shah, 'Modernization' and Consolidation of Power." *Middle Eastern Studies* 37, no. 3 (July 2001): 1–24.

Ansari, Ali M., and Anise Bassiri Tabrizi. "The View from Tehran." In *Understanding Iran's Role in the Syrian Conflict*, edited by Anise Bassiri Tabrizi and Rafaello Pantucci. London: RUSI, 2016. https://rusi.org/explore-our-research/publications/occasional-papers/understanding-irans-role-syrian-conflict.

Arfa, Hasan. *Under Five Shahs*. New York: Johns Murray, 1964.

Arjomand, Said Amir. "Ideological Revolution in Shi'ism." In *Authority and Political Culture in Shi'ism*, edited by Said Amir Arjomand, 178–209. Albany: SUNY Press, 1988.

———. *After Khomeini: Iran under His Successors*. New York: Oxford University Press, 2009.

———. *From Nationalism to Revolutionary Islam*. Albany: SUNY Press, 1984.

———. "The Rise of Shah Esma'il as a Mahdist Revolution." In *Sociology of Shi'ite Islam: Collected Essays*, edited by Said Amir Arjomand, 301–29. Leiden: E. J. Brill, 2016.

———. *The Shadow of God and Hidden Imam: Religion, Political Order, and Societal Change in Shi'ite in Iran from the Beginning to 1890*. Chicago: University of Chicago Press, 1984.

———. "Shi'ite Jurists and Iran's Law and Constitutional Order in the Twentieth Century." In *Sociology of Shi'ite Islam*, edited by Said Amir Arjomand, 257–97. Leiden: E. J. Brill, 2016.

———. *Turban for the Crown: The Islamic Revolution in Iran*. New York: Oxford University Press, 1988.

Ashraf, Ahmad, "Bazaar in the Iranian Revolution." *MERIP Reports* 113 (March–April 1983). https://meriorg/1983/03/bazaar-and-mosque-in-irans-revolution/.

Ataie, Mohammad. "Becoming Hezbollah: The Party's Evolution and Changing Roles." Crown Center for Middle East Studies, Brandeis University, January 27, 2023. https://www.brandeis.edu/crown/publications/crown-conversations/cc-16.html.

———. "Brothers, Comrades, and the Quest for the Islamist International: The First Generation of Liberation Movements in Revolutionary Iran." In *The Fate of Third Worldism in the Middle East*, edited by Rasmus Elling and Sune Haugbrolle, 121–44. London: Oneworld, 2024.

———. "Exporting the Iranian Revolution: Ecumenical Clerics in Lebanon." *International Journal of Middle East Studies* 53, no. 4 (2021): 672–90.

———. "Exporting the 1978–79 Revolution: Pan-Islamic or Sectarian." PhD diss., University of Massachusetts at Amherst, 2020.

———. "Revolutionary Iran's 1979 Endeavor in Lebanon." *Middle East Policy* 20, no. 2 (June 2023): 137–52.

Axe, David. "Iran Knocked Out of the Sky a Very Special U.S. Drone (and Exposed a Key Weakness)." *National Interest*, June 20, 2019. https://nationalinterest.org/blog/buzz/iran-knocked-out-sky-very-special-us-drone-and-exposed-key-weakness-63577.

Ayatollahi Tabaar, Mohammad. "Causes of the U.S. Hostage Crisis in Iran: The Untold Account of the Communist Threat." *Security Studies* 26, no. 4 (2017): 665–97.

———. "Factional Politics in the Iran-Iraq War." *Strategic Studies* 42, nos. 3–4 (2019): 480–506.

———. "Iran's Russian Turn." *Foreign Affairs*, November 12, 2015. https://www.foreignaffairs.com/articles/iran/2015-11-12/irans-russian-turn.

———. "Iran's War within: Ebrahim Raisi and the Triumph of Hardliners." *Foreign Affairs* 100, no. 5 (September–October 2021): 155–68.

———. "No Matter Who Is U.S. President, Iran Will Drive a Harder Bargain Than Before." *Foreign Affairs*, October 20, 2020. https://www.foreignaffairs.com/articles/iran/2020-10-20/no-matter-who-us-president-iran-will-drive-harder-bargain.

———. *Religious Statecraft: The Politics of Islam in Iran*. New York: Columbia University Press, 2019.

Azimi, Fakhreddin. "Khomeini and the White Revolution." In *A Critical Introduction to Khomeini*, edited by Arshin Adib-Moghaddam, 19–42. New York: Cambridge University Press, 2014.

———. *The Quest for Democracy in Iran: A Century of Struggle against Authoritarian Rule*. Cambridge, MA: Harvard University Press, 2008.

Azizi, Arash. *The Shadow Commander: Soleimani, the U.S. and Iran's Global Ambitions*. New York: Oneworld, 2020.

Azizi, Hamidreza, "Iran's New Naval Ambitions." *Foreign Affairs*, July 10, 2024. https://www.foreignaffairs.com/iran/irans-new-naval-ambitions.

———. "Iran and Russia in Syria: A Changing Alliance amid the War in Ukraine." In *Struggle for Alliance: Russia and Iran in the Era of the War in Ukraine*, edited by Abdolrasool Divsallar, 313–42. New York: I. B. Tauris, 2024.

Baconi, Tareq. "What Was Hamas Thinking?" *Foreign Policy*, November 22, 2023. https://foreignpolicy.com/2023/11/22/hamas-gaza-israel-netanyahu-palestine-apartheid-containment-resistance/?tpcc=recirc_trending062921.

Bajoghli, Narges. *Iran Reframed: Anxieties of Power in the Islamic Republic*. Stanford, CA: Stanford University Press, 2019.

———. "*The Outcasts*: The Start of 'New Entertainment' in Pro-Regime Filmmaking in the Islamic Republic of Iran." In *Debating the Iran-Iraq War in Contemporary Iran*, edited by Narges Bajoghli and Amir Moosavi, 59–75. New York: Routledge, 2018.

———. "'Woman, Life, Freedom': Iran's Protests Are a Rebellion for Bodily Autonomy." *Vanity Fair*, September 29, 2022. https://www.vanityfair.com/news/2022/09/mahsa-amini-irans-protests-rebellion-bodily-autonomy.

Bajoghli, Narges, and Vali Nasr. "How the War in Gaza Revived the Axis of Resistance." *Foreign Affairs*, January 17, 2024. https://www.foreignaffairs.com/united-states/how-war-gaza-revived-axis-resistance.

———. "A More Normal Iran?" *Foreign Affairs*, July 29, 2024. https://www.foreignaffairs.com/iran/more-normal-iran-masoud-pezeshkian.

Bajoghli, Narges, Vali Nasr, Djavad Salehi-Isfahani, and Ali Vaez. *How Sanctions Work: Iran and the Impact of Economic Warfare*. Stanford, CA: Stanford University Press, 2024.

Bakhash, Shaul. "The Politics of Land, Law, and Social Justice in Iran." *Middle East Journal* 43, no. 2 (Spring 1989): 186–201.

———. *The Reign of Ayatollahs: Iran and the Islamic Revolution*. New York: Basic Books, 1984.

Bakhtiari, Bahman. *Parliamentary Politics in Revolutionary Iran: The Institutionalization of Factional Politics*. Gainesville: University Press of Florida, 1996.

Barzegar, Kayhan. "Iran and the Shiite Crescent: Myths and Realities." *Brown Journal of World Affairs* 15, no. 1 (Fall–Winter 2008): 87–99.

———. "Iran's Foreign Policy in Post-Invasion Iraq." *Middle East Policy* 15, no. 4 (Winter 2008): 47–58.

Batmanghelidj, Esfandyar. "How Sanctions Hurt Iran's Protesters." *Foreign Affairs*, April 4, 2023. https://www.foreignaffairs.com/middle-east/iran-sanctions-how-protesters.

———. "The Inflation Weapon: How American Sanctions Harm Iranian Households." Sanctions and Security Research Project, January 2022. https://sanctionsandsecurity.org/publications/the-inflation-weapon-how-american-sanctions-harm-iranian-households/.

Batmanghelidj, Esfandyar, and Erica Moret. "The Hidden Toll of Sanctions." *Foreign Affairs*, January 17, 2022. https://www.foreignaffairs.com/articles/world/2022-01-17/hidden-toll-sanctions.

Bayandor, Darioush. "Don't Just Blame Washington for the 1953 Iran Coup." *Foreign Policy*, November 21, 2019. https://foreignpolicy.com/2019/11/21/dont-blame-washington-1953-iran-coup-mosaddeq/.

Behdad, Sohrab. "The Political Economy of Islamic Planning in Iran." In *Post-Revolutionary Iran*, edited by Hooshang Amirahmadi and Manouchehr Parvin, 107–25. Boulder, CO: Westview Press, 1988.

Behrooz, Maziar. "Factionalism in Iran under Khomeini." *Middle Easters Studies* 27, no. 4 (October 1994): 597–614.

———. *Iran at War: Interactions with the Modern World and the Struggle with Imperial Russia*. London: I. B. Tauris, 2023.

———. *Rebels with a Cause: The Failure of the Left in Iran*. London: I. B. Tauris, 1999.

Behrouzan, Orkideh. "Medicalization as a Way of Life: The Iran-Iraq War and Considerations for Psychiatry and Anthropology." *Medicine Anthropology Theory* 2, no. 3 (2016): 40–60.

Bill, James A. *The Eagle and the Lion: The Tragedy of American-Iranian Relations*. New Haven, CT: Yale University Press, 1988.

———. "The U.S. Overture to Iran, 1985–1986: An Analysis." In *Neither East nor West: The Soviet Union, the United States and Iran*, edited by Mark J. Gasiorowski and Nikki Keddie, 166–79. New Haven, CT: Yale University Press, 1990.

Blattman, Christopher. *Why We Fight: The Roots of War and the Paths to Peace*. New York: Viking, 2022.

Blaydes, Lisa. *The State of Repression: Iraq under Saddam Hussein*. Princeton, NJ: Princeton University Press, 2018.

Boroujerdi, Mehrzad. *Iranian Intellectuals and the West: The Tormented Triumph of Nativism*. Syracuse: Syracuse University Press, 1996.

Boroujerdi, Mehrzad, and Rahimkhani, Kourosh. "The Office of the Supreme Leader: The Epicenter of a Theocracy." In *Power and Change in Iran: Politics of Contention and Conciliation*, edited by Daniel Brumberg and Farideh Farhi, 135–65. Bloomington: Indiana University Press, 2016.

Bowden, Mark, "The Desert One Debacle." *Atlantic*, May 2006. https://www.theatlantic.com/magazine/archive/2006/05/the-desert-one-debacle/304803/.

———. *Guests of the Ayatollah: The First Battle in America's War with Militant Islam*. New York: Atlantic Monthly Press, 2006.

Brands, Hal. "Saddam Hussein, the United States, and the Invasion of Iran: Was There a Green Light?" *Cold War History* 12, no. 2 (May 2012): 319–43.

Brinton, Crane. *The Anatomy of Revolution*. New York: Prentice Hall, 1938.

Brown, Ian. *Khomeini's Forgotten Sons: The Story of Iran's Boy Soldiers*. London: Grey Seal, 1990.

Browne, E. G. *The Persian Revolution of 1905–1909*. 2nd ed. Washington, DC: Mage Publishers, 2006.

Brzezinski, Zbigniew. "The Failed Mission: The Inside Account of the Attempt to Free the Hostages in Iran." *New York Times Magazine*, April 18, 1982, 4.

———. *Power and Principle: Memoirs of a National Security Advisor, 1977–1981*. New York: Farrar, Straus and Giroux, 1983.

Buchta, Wilfried. *Who Rules Iran? The Structure of Power in the Islamic Republic*. Washington, DC: Washington Institute for Near East Policy, 2002.

Burns, William J. *The Back Channel: A Memoir of American Diplomacy and the Case of Renewal*. New York: Random House, 2019.

Butt, Ahsan. *Secession and Security: Explaining State Strategy against Separatists*. Ithaca, NY: Cornell University Press, 2017.

Carter, Jimmy. *Keeping Faith: Memoirs of a President*. New York: Bantam Books, 1982.

Chehabi, H. E. "Iran and Lebanon in the Revolutionary Decade." In *Distant Relations: Iran and Lebanon in the Last 500 Years*, edited by H. E. Chehabi, 201–30. London: I. B. Tauris, 2006.

———. *Iranian Politics and Religious Modernism: The Liberation Movement of Iran under the Shah and Khomeini*. Ithaca, NY: Cornell University Press, 1990.

Choksy, Jamsheed, and Carol Choksy. "China and Russia Have Iran's Back." *Foreign Affairs*, November 17, 2020. https://www.foreignaffairs.com/articles/united-states/2020-11-17/china-and-russia-have-irans-back.

Chubin, Shahram. *Iran's Nuclear Ambitions*. Washington, DC: Carnegie Endowment for International Peace, 2006.

———. "Is Iran a Military Threat?" *Survival* 56, no. 2 (2014): 65–88.

Cockburn, Patrick. *Muqtada: Muqtada Al-Sadr, the Shia Revival, and the Future of Iraq*. New York: Scribner, 2008.

Coll, Steve. *The Achilles Trap: Saddam Hussein, the C.I.A., and the Origins of America's Invasion of Iraq*. New York: Penguin Press, 2024.

Collier, David R. "To Prevent a Revolution: John F. Kennedy and Promotion of Democracy in Iran." *Diplomacy and Statecraft* 24, no. 3 (September 2003): 456–75.

Cottam, Richard. *Iran and the United States: A Cold War Case Study*. Pittsburgh: University of Pittsburgh Press, 1988.

Dabashi, Hamid. "Ali Shari'ati's Islam: Revolutionary Uses of Faith in a Post-Traditional Society." *Islamic Quarterly* 27, no. 4 (January 1983): 203–22.

———. *Theology of Discontent: The Ideological Foundations of the Islamic Revolution in Iran*. New York: NYU Press, 1993.

Davenport, Kelsey. "The Joint Comprehensive Plan of Action (JCPOA) at a Glance." Arms Control Association, March 2022. https://www.armscontrol.org/factsheets/JCPOA-at-a-glance.

Davis, Eric. *Memories of State: Politics, History and Collective Identity in Modern Iraq*. Berkeley: University of California Press, 2005.

Demarais, Agathe. "The End of the Age of Sanctions?" *Foreign Affairs*, December 27, 2022. https://www.foreignaffairs.com/united-states/end-age-sanctions.

de Waal, Thomas. "Putin's Hidden Game in the South Caucasus." *Foreign Affairs*, June 3, 2024. https://www.foreignaffairs.com/azerbaijan/putins-hidden-game-south-caucasus.

Divsallar, Abdolrasool. "Shifting Threats and Strategic Adjustment in Iran's Foreign Policy: The Case of Strait of Hormuz." *British Journal of Middle East Studies* 49, no. 5 (2022): 873–95.

———. "Rising Interdependency: How Russo-Iranian Relations Have Evolved with the War in Ukraine." *Trends Research*, December 12, 2022. https://trendsresearch.org/insight/rising-interdependency-how-russo-iranian-relations-have-evolved-with-the-war-in-ukraine/.

———. "Authoritarian Alliance: The Systemic Factors That Bring Russia and Iran Together." In *Struggle for Alliance: Russia and Iran in the Era of the War in Ukraine*, edited by Abdolrasool Divsallar, 175–202. New York: I. B. Tauris, 2024.

Dobbins, James. "Negotiating with Iran: Reflections from Personal Experience." *Washington Quarterly* 33, no. 1 (2010): 149–62.

Dudoignon, Stephane A. *Les Gardiens de la Revolution Islamique d'Iran (The Guardians of the Islamic Revolution in Iran)*. Paris: CNRS Editions, 2022.

Ehsani, Kaveh. "Prospects for Democracy in Iran." Paper delivered at Concordia University, Montreal, November 2004.

———. "War and Resentment: Critical Reflections on the Legacies of the Iran-Iraq War." In *Debating the Iran-Iraq War in Contemporary Iran*, edited by Narges Bajoghli and Amir Moosavi, 3–22. New York: Routledge, 2018.

Ehteshami, Anoushiravan. *After Khomeini: The Iranian Second Republic*. New York: Routledge, 1995.

Ehteshami, Anoushiravan, and Raymond A. Hinnebusch. *Syria and Iran: Middle Powers in a Penetrated Regional System*. New York: Routledge, 1997.

Ehteshami, Anoushiravan, and Mahjoob Zweiri. *Iran and the Rise of the Neoconservatives: The Politics of Tehran's Silent Revolution*. London: I. B. Tauris, 2007.

Elm, Mostafa. *Oil, Power, and Principle: Iran's Oil Nationalization and Its Aftermath*. Syracuse: Syracuse University Press, 1992.

Emery, Christian. "United States Iran Policy 1979–1980: The Anatomy and Legacy of American Diplomacy." *Diplomacy and Statecraft* 24, no. 4 (2013): 619–39.

Entessar, Nader. "The Kurdish Factor in Iran-Iraq Relations." Middle East Institute, June 29, 2009. https://www.mei.edu/publications/kurdish-factor-iran-iraq-relations.

Esfahani, Marzieh. "Political Realism and Iran: Geopolitics and Defensive Realism." In *The Edinburgh Companion to Political Realism*, edited by Robert Schuett and Miles Hollingworth, 431–44. Edinburgh: Edinburgh University Press, 2018.

Esfandiary, Dina, and Ariane M. Tabatabai. "Iran's ISIS Policy." *International Affairs* 91, no. 1 (2015): 1–15.

Eshraghi, Ali Reza, and Yasaman Baji. "The Cleric Who Changed." Institute for War and Peace Reporting, June 3, 2010. https://www.refworld.org/docid/4c1091cf31.html.

Eshraghi, Ali Reza, and Amir Hossein Mahdavi. "The Evolution of the Revolutionary Guards." In *The Sacred Republic: Power and Institutions in Iran*, edited by Mehran Kamrava, 187–220. New York: Oxford University Press, 2023.

———. "The Revolutionary Guards Are Poised to Take over Iran." *Foreign Affairs*, August 27, 2020. https://www.foreignaffairs.com/articles/middle-east/2020-08-27/revolutionary-guards-are-poised-take-over-iran.

Fantappie, Maria, and Vali Nasr. "A New Order in the Middle East?" *Foreign Affairs*, March 22, 2023. https://www.foreignaffairs.com/china/iran-saudi-arabia-middle-east-relations.

Farhi, Farideh. "The Antinomies of Iran's War Generation." In *Iran, Iraq and the Legacies of War*, edited by Gary Sick Lawrence Potter, 101–20. New York: Palgrave Macmillan, 2004.

———. "The Tenth Presidential Elections and Their Aftermath." In *Iran: From Theocracy to the Green Movement*, edited by Negin Nabavi, 3–16. New York: Palgrave Macmillan, 2012.

Farhi, Farideh, and Saideh Lotfian. "Iran's Post-Revolution Foreign Policy Puzzle." In *World of Aspiring Powers: Domestic Foreign Policy Debates in China, India, Iran, Japan and Russia*, edited by Henry R. Nau and Deepa M. Ollapally, 114–40. New York: Oxford University Press, 2012.

Farrokh, Kaveh. *Iran at War: 1500–1988*. Oxford: Osprey Publishing, 2011.

Farzaneh, Mateo Mohammad. *Iranian Women and Gender in the Iran-Iraq War*. Syracuse, NY: Syracuse University Press, 2021.

Fawcett, Louise. *Iran and the Cold War: The Azerbaijan Crisis of 1946*. New York: Cambridge University Press, 1992.

Ferrier, Ronald W. "The Anglo-Iranian Oil Dispute: A Triangular Relationship." In *Mussadiq, Iranian Nationalism, and Oil*, edited by James A. Bill and Wm. Roger Louis, 164–99. Austin: University of Texas Press, 1988.

Filkins, Dexter. "The Shadow Commander." *New Yorker*, September 30, 2013. https://www.newyorker.com/magazine/2013/09/30/the-shadow-commander.

Forouzan, Hesam. *The Military in Post-Revolutionary Iran: The Evolution and Roles of the Revolutionary Guards*. New York: Routledge, 2016.

Friedman, Jeremy. "The Enemy of My Enemy: The Soviet Union, East Germany, and the Iranian Tudeh Party's Support for Ayatollah Khomeini." *Journal of Cold War Studies* 20, no. 2 (2018): 3–37.

Gaddis, John Lewis. *On Grand Strategy*. New York: Penguin Press, 2018.

———. *Strategies of Containment: A Critical Appraisal of American National Security Policy during the Cold War*. New York: Oxford University Press, 2005.

———. *The United States and the Origins of the Cold War, 1941–1947*. New York: Columbia University Press, 1972.

Ganji, Akbar. "The Latter-Day Sultan: Power and Politics in Iran." *Foreign Affairs* 87, no. 6 (November–December 2008): 45–66.

Gasiorowski, Mark J. "The 1953 *Coup D'Etat* in Iran." *International Journal of Middle East Studies* 19, no. 3 (August 1987): 261–86.

———. "The Nuzhih Plot and Iranian Politics." *International Journal of Middle East Studies* 34 (2002): 645–66.

———. "US Covert Operations toward Iran, February–November 1979: Was the CIA Trying to Overthrow the Islamic Regime." *Middle Eastern Studies* 51, no. 1 (2015): 115–35.

———. *U.S. Foreign Policy and the Shah: Building a Client State in Iran*. Ithaca, NY: Cornell University Press, 1991.

———. "US Intelligence Assistance to Iran, May–October 1979." *Middle East Journal* 66, no. 4 (Autumn 2012): 613–27.

Gasiorowski, Mark J., and Nikki Keddie, eds. *Neither East nor West: The Soviet Union, the United States and Iran*. New Haven, CT: Yale University Press, 1990.

Gause, F. Gregory, III. "The Illogic of Dual Containment." *Foreign Affairs* 73, no. 2 (March–April 1994): 56–66.

Ghani, Cyrus. *Iran and the Rise of Reza Shah: From Qajar Collapse to Pahlavi Power*. London: I.B. Tauris, 1998.

Gheissari, Ali. "Unequal Treaties and the Question of Sovereignty in Qajar and Early Pahlavi Iran." Ann Lambton Memorial Lecture, Durham Middle East Papers 106, Institute for Middle Eastern and Islamic Studies, Durham University, 2023, 8–41.

———. "The U.S. Coup of 1953 in Iran, Sixty Years On." *Passport* (September 2013): 23–24.

Gheissari, Ali, and Vali Nasr. *Democracy in Iran: History and the Quest for Liberty*. New York: Oxford University Press, 2006.

Gibson, Bryan R. *Covert Relationship: American Foreign Policy, Intelligence, and the Iran Iraq War, 1980–1988*. Westport, CT: Praeger, 2010.

Giddens, Anthony. *Modernity and Self-Identity*. Stanford, CA: Stanford University Press, 1991.

Godfroy, Jeanne, James S. Powell, Matthew D. Morton, and Matthew M. Zais. *The US Army in the Iraq War*. 2 vols. West Point, NY: West Point Books, 2019.

Golkar, Saeid. *Captive Society: The Basij Militia and Social Control in Iran*. New York: Columbia University Press, 2015.

Goode, James F. "Assisting Our Brothers, Defending Ourselves: The Iranian Intervention in Oman, 1972–75." *Iranian Studies* 47, no. 3 (2014): 441–62.

Habibi, Nader. "How Ahmadinejad Changed Iran's Economy." *Journal of Developing Areas* 49, no. 1 (Winter 2015): 305–12.

Harris, Kevan. "Iran's Commanding Heights: Privatization and Conglomerate Ownership in the Islamic Republic." In *Crony Capitalism in the Middle East: Business and Politics from Liberalization to the Arab Spring*, edited by Ishac Diwan, Adeel Malik, and Izak Atiyas, 363–99. Oxford: Oxford University Press, 2019.

———. *A Social Revolution: Politics and the Welfare State in Iran*. Berkeley: University of California Press, 2017.

———. "Social Welfare Policies and Dynamics of Elite and Popular Contentions." In *Power and Change in Iran: Politics of Contention and Conciliation*, edited by Daniel Brumberg and Farideh Farhi, 70–100. Bloomington: Indiana University Press, 2016.

Harris, Shane, and Matthew Aid. "CIA Files Prove America Helped Saddam as He Gassed Iran." *Foreign Policy*, August 26, 2013. https://foreignpolicy.com/2013/08/26/exclusive-cia-files-prove-america-helped-saddam-as-he-gassed-iran/.

Hashemi, Adel. *The Making of Martyrdom in Modern Twelver Shi'ism: From Protesters and Revolutionaries to Shrine Defenders*. London: I. B. Tauris, 2022.

Heiss, Mary Ann. *Empire and Nationhood: The United States, Great Britain, and Iranian Oil, 1950–1954*. New York: Columbia University Press, 1997.

———. "The International Boycott of Iranian Oil and the Anti-Mossadeq Coup of 1953." In *Mohammad Mosaddeq and the 1953 Coup in Iran*, edited by Mark J. Gasiorowski and Malcolm Byrne, 178–200. Syracuse, NY: Syracuse University Press, 2004.

Hiro, Dilip. *The Longest War: The Iran-Iraq Military Conflict*. New York: Routledge, 1990.

Homayounvash, Mohammad. *Iran and the Nuclear Question: History and Evolutionary Trajectory*. New York: Routledge, 2017.

Houghton, David Patrick. "Explaining the Origins of the Iran Hostage Crisis: A Cognitive Approach." *Terrorism and Political Violence* 18, no. 2 (2006): 259–79.

———. *U.S. Foreign Policy and the Iran Hostage Crisis.* New York: Cambridge University Press, 2001.

Huntington, Samuel. *Order in Changing Societies.* New Haven, CT: Yale University Press, 1968.

Issawi, Charles, "The Iranian Economy 1925–1975: Fifty Years of Economic Development." In *Iran under the Pahlavis,* edited by George Lenczowski, 129–66. Stanford, CA: Hoover Institution Press, 1978.

Jabar, Falih A. *The Shi'ite Movement in Iraq.* London: Al Saqi, 2005.

Jervis, Robert. *How Statesmen Think: The Psychology of International Politics.* Princeton, NJ: Princeton University Press, 2017.

Johnson, Rob. *The Iran-Iraq War.* New York: Palgrave Macmillan, 2011.

Juneau, Thomas. "How War in Yemen Transformed the Iran-Houthi Partnership." *Studies in Conflict and Terrorism,* July 6, 2021, 1–23.

Kahalzadeh, Hadi. "'Maximum Pressure' Hardened Iran against Compromise." *Foreign Affairs,* March 11, 2021. https://www.foreignaffairs.com/articles/iran/2021-03-11/maximum-pressure-hardened-iran-against-compromise.

Kalantari, Mohammad R. "The Media Contest during the Iran-Iraq War: The Failure of Mediatized Shi'ism." *Media, War and Conflict* 15, no. 3 (2022): 378–98.

Karsh, Efraim. "Geopolitical Determinism: The Origins of the Iran-Iraq War." *Middle East Journal* 44, no. 2 (Spring 1990): 256–68.

———. *The Iran-Iraq War, 1980–1988.* Oxford: Osprey Publishing, 2002.

Katouzian, Homa. "The Campaign against the Anglo-Iranian Agreement of 1919." *British Journal of Middle Eastern Studies* 25, no. 1 (1998): 5–46.

———. *Mussadiq and the Struggle for Power in Iran.* London: I. B. Tauris, 1999.

———. *The Persians: Ancient, Medieval and Modern Iran.* New Haven, CT: Yale University Press, 2010.

———. *The Political Economy of Iran, 1926–1979.* New York: NYU Press, 1981.

———. *State and Society in Iran: The Eclipse of the Qajars and the Emergence of the Pahlavis.* London: I. B. Tauris, 2006.

Katzenstein, Peter J. "Introduction: Alternative Views on National Security." In *The Culture of National Security,* edited by Peter J. Katzenstein, 1–32. New York: Columbia University Press, 1996.

Kazemi-Moussavi, Ahmad. "A New Interpretation of the Theory of *Vilayat-i Faqih.*" *Middle Eastern Studies* 28, no. 1 (January 1992): 101–7.

Keshavarzian, Arang. *Bazaar and State in Iran: The Politics of the Tehran Marketplace.* New York: Cambridge University Press, 2007.

———. "Regime Loyalty and *Bazari* Representation under the Islamic Republic of Iran: Dilemmas of the Society of Islamic Coalition." *International Journal of Middle East Studies* 41 (2009): 225–46.

Khadduri, Majid. *The Gulf War: The Origins and Implications of the Iran-Iraq Conflict.* New York: Oxford University Press, 1988.

Khajepour, Bijan. "Domestic Political Reforms and Private Sector Activity in Iran." *Social Research* 67, no. 2 (Summer 2000): 577–98.

Khaji, Ali, Shoaoddin Fallahdoost, and Mohammad Reza Soroush. "Civilian Casualties of Iranian Cities by Ballistic Missile Attacks during the Iraq-Iran War (1980–1988)." *Chinese Journal of Traumatology* 1, no. 13 (April 2010): 87–90.

Khalatbari, Firouzeh. "The Tehran Stock-Exchange and Privatisation." In *The Economy of Islamic Iran*, edited by Thierry Coville, 177–208. Paris: Peeters Publishers, 1994.

———. "Iran: A Unique Underground Economy." In *L'économie de l'Iran islamique, entre l'état et le marché*, edited by Thierry Coville, 113–31. Tehran: Institut Français de Recherche en Iran, 1994.

Khosrokhavar, Farhad, Shapur Etemad, and Masoud Mehrabi. "Report on Science in Post-Revolutionary Iran." Parts 1 and 2: "Emergence of a Scientific Community?" and "The Scientific Community's Problem of Identity." *Critique: Critical Middle Eastern Studies* 13, nos. 2–3 (Summer–Fall 2004): 209–24, 363–82.

Kinzer, Stephen. *All the Shah's Men: An American Coup and the Roots of Middle East Terror*. New York: Wiley and Sons, 2003.

Kissinger, Henry. "The Vietnam Negotiations." *Foreign Affairs* 47, no. 2 (January 1969): 212–34.

Knights, Michael. "The Houthi War Machine: From Guerilla War to State Capture." *CTC Sentinel* 11, no. 8 (September 2018): 15–23.

Kozhanov, Nikolay. "Iran: Quest for Foreign Policy Identity." In *The Middle East: Politics and Identity*, edited by Irina Zvyagelskaya, 290–300. Moscow: IMEMO, 2022.

———. *Iran's Strategic Thinking: The Evolution of Iran's Foreign Policy, 1979–2018*. Berlin: Gerlach Press, 2018.

Kurzman, Charles. "Death Tolls of the Iran-Iraq War." October 31, 2013. https://kurzman.unc.edu/death-tolls-of-the-iran-iraq-war/.

———. "The Qum Protests and the Coming of the Iranian Revolution, 1975 and 1978." *Social Science History* 27, no. 3 (Fall 2003): 287–325.

———. *The Unthinkable Revolution in Iran*. Cambridge, MA: Harvard University Press, 2004.

Lackner, Helen. *Yemen in Crisis: The Road to War*. London: Verso, 2019.

Lob, Eric. "Development, Mobilization and War: The Iranian Construction Jihad, Construction Mobilization, and Trench Builders Association (1979–2013)." In *Debating the Iran-Iraq War in Contemporary Iran*, edited by Narges Bajoghli and Amir Moosavi, 23–42. New York: Routledge, 2018.

———. *Iran's Reconstruction Jihad: Rural Development and Regime Consolidation after 1979*. New York: Cambridge University Press, 2020.

Louer, Laurence. "The Transformation of Shia Politics in the Gulf Monarchies." *New Analysis of Shia Politics, POEMPS Studies* 28 (December 2017). http://pomeps.org/new-analysis-of-shia-politics.

———. *Transnational Shiite Politics: Religious and Political Networks in the Gulf*. New York: Columbia University Press, 2008.

Malekzadeh, Shervin. "Education as Public Good or Private Resource: Accommodation and Demobilization in Iran's University System." In *Power and Change in Iran: Politics of Contention and Conciliation*, edited by Daniel Brumberg and Farideh Farhi, 101–34. Bloomington: Indiana University Press, 2016.

Maloney, Suzanne. "Agents or Obstacles? Parastatal Foundations and Challenges for Iranian Development." In *The Economy of Iran: The Dilemmas of an Islamic State*, edited by Parvin Alizadeh, 145–76. London: I. B. Tauris, 2000.

———. *Iran's Political Economy since the Revolution*. New York: Cambridge University Press, 2015.

Markey, Daniel. *China's Western Horizon: Beijing and the New Geopolitics of Eurasia*. New York: Oxford University Press, 2020.

Martin, Vanessa. *Creating an Islamic State: Khomeini and the Making of a New Iran*. London: I. B. Tauris, 2000.

———. "Religion and State in Khumaini's *Kashf al-Asrar*." *Bulletin of the School of Oriental and African Studies* 56, no. 1 (1993): 34–35.

Matin-Asgari, Afshin. *Both Eastern and Western: An Intellectual History of Iranian Modernity*. New York: Cambridge University Press, 2018.

Matthiesen, Toby. "Hizbullah Al-Hijaz: A History of the Most Radical Saudi Shi'a Opposition Group." *Middle East Journal* 64, no. 2 (Spring 2010): 179–97.

———. "How Gaza Reunited the Middle East." *Foreign Affairs*, February 9, 2024. https://www.foreignaffairs.com/middle-east/how-gaza-reunited-middle-east.

———. "The Iranian Revolution and Sunni Political Islam." *New Analysis of Shia Politics, POEMPS Studies* 28 (December 2017). http://pomeps.org/the-iranian-revolution-and-sunni-political-islam#_ftnref12.

———. *Sectarian Gulf: Saudi Arabia and the Arab Spring That Wasn't*. Stanford, CA: Stanford Briefs, 2013.

Menashri, David. "Iran's Regional Policy: Between Radicalism and Pragmatism." *Journal of International Affairs* 60, no. 2 (Spring–Summer 2007): 153–67.

Merscheimer, John. *The Tragedy of Great Power Politics*. New York: W. W. Norton, 2001.

Merscheimer, John, and Sebastian Rosato. *How States Think: The Rationality of Foreign Policy*. New Haven, CT: Yale University Press, 2023.

Mesbahi, Mohiaddin. "Free and Confined: Iran in the International System." *Iranian Review of Foreign Affairs* 5, no. 2 (Spring 2011): 9–34.

Milani, Abbas. *The Shah*. New York: Palgrave Macmillan, 2011.

Milani, Mohsen. "Harvest of Shame: Tudeh and the Bazargan Government." *Middle Eastern Studies* 29, no. 2 (April 1993): 307–20.

———. "Iran's Game in Yemen." *Foreign Affairs*, April 19, 2015. https://www.foreignaffairs.com/articles/iran/2015-04-19/irans-game-yemen.

———. "Iran's Persian Gulf Policy in the Post-Saddam Era." In *Contemporary Iran: Economy, Society, Politics*, edited by Ali Gheissari, 349–66. New York: Oxford University Press, 2009.

———. "Iran's Policy towards Afghanistan." *Middle East Journal* 60, no. 2 (Spring 2006): 235–56.

———. "Power Shifts in Revolutionary Iran." *Iranian Studies* 26, nos. 3–4 (Summer–Autumn 1993): 359–74.

———. "Shi'ism and the State in the Constitution of the Islamic Republic of Iran." In *Iran: Political Culture in the Islamic Republic*, edited by Samih Farsoun and Mehrdad Mashayekhi, 92–109. New York: Routledge, 1992.

———. "This Is What Détente Looks Like." *Foreign Affairs*, August 27, 2014. http://www
.foreignaffairs.com/ articles/141937/mohsen-milani/this-is-what-detente-looks-like.

———. "The Transformation of the Velayat-i Faqih Institution from Khomeini to Khamenei."
Muslim World 82, nos. 3–4 (July–October 1992): 175–90.

Mitzen, Jennifer. "Ontological Security in World Politics: State Identity and the Security Dilemma." *European Journal of International Relations* 12, no. 3 (September 2006): 341–70.

Moaveni, Azadeh. "Two Weeks in Tehran." *London Review of Books* 44, no. 21 (November 2022).
https://www.lrb.co.uk/the-paper/v44/n21/azadeh-moaveni/diary.

———. "Election in Iran." *London Review of Books* 46, no. 13 (July 4, 2024). https://www.lrb.co
.uk/the-paper/v46/n13/azadeh-moaveni/election-in-iran.

Moin, Baqer. *Khomeini: Life of the Ayatollah*. London: I. B. Tauris, 1999.

Mojab, Shahrzad. "The State and University: The 'Islamic Cultural Revolution' in the Institutions of Higher Education of Iran, 1980–87." PhD diss., University of Illinois at Urbana-
Champaign, 1991.

Moosavi, Amir. "Dark Corners and the Limits of Ahmad Dehqan's War Fiction." In *Debating the
Iran-Iraq War in Contemporary Iran*, edited by Narges Bajoghli and Amir Moosavi, 43–58.
New York: Routledge, 2018.

———. "How to Write Death: Resignifying Martyrdom in Two Novels of the Iran-Iraq War."
Alif: Journal of Comparative Poetics (August 15, 2015): 1–18.

———. "Stepping Back from the Front: A Glance at Home Front Narratives of the Iran-Iraq
War in Persian and Arabic Fiction." In *Moments of Silence: Authenticity in Cultural Expressions
of the Iran-Iraq War, 1980–1988*, edited by Arta Khakpour, Shouleh Vatanabadi, and Mohammad Mehdi Khorrami, 120–36. New York: NYU Press, 2016.

Moslem, Mehdi. *Factional Politics in Post-Khomeini Iran*. Syracuse: Syracuse University Press,
2002.

Mostaghimi, Bahram, and Masoud Taromsari. "Double Standard: The Security Council and
the Two Wars." In *Iranian Perspectives on the Iran-Iraq War*, edited by Farhang Rajaee, 62–70.
Gainesville: University Press of Florida, 1997.

Mousavian, Seyed Hossein. *The Iranian Nuclear Crisis: A Memoir*. Washington, DC: Carnegie
Endowment for International Peace, 2012.

———. *A New Structure for Security, Peace, and Cooperation in the Persian Gulf*. New York:
Rowan and Littlefield, 2020.

———. "The Strategic Disaster of Leaving the Iran Deal." *Foreign Affairs*, May 10, 2018. https://
www.foreignaffairs.com/articles/iran/2018-05-10/strategic-disaster-leaving-iran-deal.

Mousavian, Seyed Hossein, and Shahir Shahidsaless. *Iran and the United States: An Insider's View
on the Failed Past and the Road to Peace*. New York: Bloomsbury, 2014.

Murray, Williamson, and Kevin Woods. *The Iran-Iraq War: A Military and Strategic History*. New
York: Cambridge University Press, 2014.

Nabavi, Negin. *Intellectuals and the State in Iran: Politics, Discourse, and the Dilemma of Authenticity*. Gainesville: University Press of Florida, 2003.

Naficy, Hamid. *A Social History of Iranian Cinema, Volume 4: The Globalizing Era, 1984–2010*.
Durham, NC: Duke University Press, 2012.

Naji, Kasra. *Ahmadinejad: The Secret History of Iran's Radical Leader*. London: I. B. Tauris, 2008.

Nakash, Yitzhak. *Reaching for Power: The Shi'i in the Modern Arab World*. Princeton, NJ: Princeton University Press, 2006.

Nasr, Vali. *The Dispensable Nation: American Foreign Policy in Retreat*. New York: Doubleday, 2013.

———. *Forces of Fortune: The Rise of a New Middle Class and What It Will Mean for Our World*. New York: Free Press, 2009.

———. "International Politics, Domestic Imperatives, and the Rise of Politics of Identity: Sectarianism in Pakistan, 1979–1997." *Comparative Politics* 32, no. 2 (January 2000): 171–90.

———. "Iran among the Ruins." *Foreign Affairs*, March–April 2018, 108–118.

———. "Iran's Peculiar Election: The Conservative Wave Rolls On." *Journal of Democracy* 16, no. 4 (October 2005): 9–22.

———. "Politics in the Late-Pahlavi State: The Ministry of Economy and Industrial Policy, 1963–69." *International Journal of Middle East Studies* 32, no. 1 (February 2000): 97–122.

———. "Regional Implications of Shi'a Revival in Iraq." *Washington Quarterly* 27, no. 3 (Summer 2004): 7–24.

———. "The Rise of Sunni Militancy in Pakistan: The Changing Role of Islamism and the Ulama in Society and Politics." *Modern Asian Studies* 34, no. 1 (January 2000): 139–80.

———. "Sectarianism and Shia Politics in Pakistan, 1979–Present." *Cahiers d'Etudes sur la Mediterranee Orientale et le Monde Turco-Iranien* 28 (1999): 311–23.

———. *The Shia Revival: How Conflicts within Islam Will Shape the Future*. New York: W. W. Norton, 2006.

———. "Showdown in Tehran." *Foreign Policy*, June 23, 2011. https://foreignpolicy.com/2011/06/23/showdown-in-tehran-2/.

———. "Trump's Policies Have Convinced Iran to Build a More Advanced Nuclear Program before Negotiating." *Foreign Policy*, September 21, 2021. https://foreignpolicy.com/2020/09/21/trumps-policies-have-convinced-iran-to-build-a-more-advanced-nuclear-program-before-negotiating/.

———. "Who Wins in Iraq? Iran." *Foreign Policy* (March–April 2007): 40–41.

Nassehi, Ramin. "Domesticating Cold War Economic Ideas: The Rise of Iranian Developmentalism in the 1950s and 1960s." In *The Age of Arya Mehr: Late Pahlavi Iran and Its Global Entanglements*, edited by Roham Alvandi, 35–69. London: Gingko Library, 2018.

Osanloo, Arzoo. *The Politics of Women's Rights in Iran*. Princeton, NJ: Princeton University Press, 2009.

Ostovar, Afshon. "The Grand Strategy of Militant Clients: Iran's Way of War." *Security Studies* 28, no. 1 (January–March 2019): 150–88.

———. "Iran's Baseej: Membership in a Militant Islamist Organization." *Middle East Journal* 67, no. 3 (Summer 2013): 345–61.

———. "After Soleimani: Iran's Elite Commander Has Been Dead for a Year. The Machinery He Built Lives On." *Newlines Magazine*, January 3, 2021. https://newlinesmag.com/essays/after-soleimani/.

———. *Vanguard of the Imam: Religion, Politics, and Iran's Revolutionary Guards*. New York: Oxford University Press, 2016.

Painter, David, and Gregory Brew. *The Struggle for Iran: Oil, Autocracy, and the Cold War, 1951–1954*. Chapel Hill: University of North Carolina Press, 2023.

Pargoo, Mahmoud, and Shahram Akbarzadeh. *Presidential Elections in Iran: Islamic Idealism since the Revolution*. Cambridge: Cambridge University Press, 2021.

Parker, John W. *Persian Dreams: Moscow and Tehran since the Fall of the Shah*. Dulles, VA: Potomac Books, 2009.

Parsa, Misagh. *Democracy in Iran: Why It Failed and How It Might Succeed*. Cambridge, MA: Harvard University Press, 2016.

Parsi, Trita. *Losing an Enemy: Obama, Iran, and the Triumph of Diplomacy*. New Haven, CT: Yale University Press, 2017.

———. *A Single Roll of the Dice: Obama's Diplomacy with Iran*. New Haven, CT: Yale University Press, 2012.

———. *Treacherous Alliance: The Secret Dealings of Israel, Iran, and the U.S.* New Haven, CT: Yale University Press, 2007.

Parvin, Manouchehr, and Mostafa Vaziri. "Islamic Man and Society in the Islamic Republic of Iran." In *Iran: Political Culture in the Islamic Republic*, edited by Samih Farsoun and Mehrdad Mashayekhi, 80–91. New York: Routledge, 1992.

Pellas, Marc. "Oman: How the Shah of Iran Saved the Regime." *Orient XXI*, March 5, 2020. https://orientxxi.info/magazine/oman-how-the-shah-of-iran-saved-the-regime,3681.

Perletta, Giorgia. *Political Radicalism and Ahmadinejad's Presidencies*. New York: Palgrave Macmillan, 2022.

Pesaran, M. H. "Economy IX: In the Pahlavi Period." *Encyclopedia Iranica*, December 15, 1997, fasc. 2, 8:143–56.

Peterson, J. E. *Oman's Insurgencies: The Sultanate's Struggle for Supremacy*. London: Saqi, 2008.

Pico, Giandomenico. *Man without a Gun: One Diplomat's Secret Struggle to Free the Hostages, Fight Terrorism, and End a War*. New York: Crown, 1999.

Piscatori, James. "The Rushdie Affair and the Politics of Ambiguity." *International Affairs* 66, no. 4 (October 1990): 767–89.

Pollock, Kenneth M. *Unthinkable: Iran, the Bomb, and American Strategy*. New York: Simon and Schuster, 2013.

Rad, Assal. *The State of Resistance: Politics, Culture, and Identity in Modern Iran*. New York: Cambridge University Press, 2022.

Radchencko, Sergey. *To Run the World: The Kremlin's Cold War Bid for Global Power*. New York: Cambridge University Press, 2024.

Rahnema, Ali. *The Rise of Modern Despotism in Iran: The Shah, the Opposition, and the United States 1953–1968*. London: Oneworld Academic, 2021.

Ra'iss Tousi, Reza. "Containment and Animosity: The United States and the War." In *Iranian Perspectives on the Iran-Iraq War*, edited by Farhang Rajaee, 49–70. Gainesville: University Press of Florida, 1997.

Rajaee, Farhang. "The 'Thermidor' of Islamic Yuppies: Conflict and Compromise in Iran's Politics." *Middle East Journal* 53, no. 22 (Spring 1999): 217–31.

Ramazani, Rouhollah K. "Iran's Export of the Revolution: Politics, Ends, and Means." In *The Iranian Revolution: Its Global Impact*, edited by John L. Esposito, 43–45. Gainesville: Florida International University Press, 1990.

———. *Iran's Foreign Policy, 1941–1973*. Charlottesville: University of Virginia Press, 1975.

———. "Iran's 'White Revolution': A Study in Political Development." *International Journal of Middle East Studies* 5, no. 2 (April 1974): 124–39.

Reisinezhad, Arash. "Iran's Geopolitical Strategy in West Asia: Containment of 'Geography' and 'History.'" *Iranian Review of Foreign Affairs* 11, no. 1 (Winter–Spring 2020): 59–88.

———. *The Shah of Iran, the Iraqi Kurds, and the Lebanese Shia.* New York: Palgrave Macmillan, 2019.

———. "Understanding Iran's Nuclear Goals." *National Interest*, January 17, 2014. https://nationalinterest.org/commentary/understanding-irans-nuclear-goals-9725.

Remnick, David. "War without End." *New Yorker*, April 13, 2003. https://www.newyorker.com/magazine/2003/04/21/war-without-end.

Rizoux, Pierre. *The Iran-Iraq War.* Translated by Nicholas Elliott. Cambridge, MA: Harvard University Press, 2015.

Rose, Gregory F. "The Post-Revolutionary Purge of Iran's Armed Forces: A Revisionist Assessment." *Iranian Studies* 17, nos. 2–3 (Spring–Summer 1984): 153–94.

———. "*Velayat-e Faqih* and the Recovery of Islamic Identity in the Thought of Ayatollah Khomeini." In *Religion and Politics in Iran: Shi'ism from Quietism to Revolution*, edited by Nikki R. Keddie, 166–88. New Haven, CT: Yale University Press, 1983.

Rossow, Robert. "The Battle of Azerbaijan, 1946." *Middle East Journal* 10, no. 1 (Winter 1956): 17–32.

Sadeghi-Boroujerdi, Eskandar. *Revolution and Its Discontents: Political Thought and Reform in Iran.* New York: Cambridge University Press, 2019.

———. "Strategic Depth, Counterinsurgency and the Logic of Sectarianization: The Islamic Republic of Iran's Security Doctrine and Its Regional Implications." In *Sectarianization: Mapping the New Politics of the Middle East*, edited by Nader Hashemi and Danny Postel, 159–84. New York: Oxford University Press, 2016.

Sadeghi Esfahlani, Mohammad, and Jamal Abdi. "Sanctions Cripple Iran's Middle Class, Not the Regime." *Foreign Policy*, August 2, 2012. https://foreignpolicy.com/2012/08/02/sanctions-cripple-irans-middle-class-not-the-regime/.

Sadri, Mohammad, and Ahmad Sadri, trans. and eds. *Reason, Freedom, and Democracy in Islam: The Essential Writings of Abdolkarim Soroush.* New York: Oxford University Press, 2000.

Salehi-Isfahani, Djavad. "The Coronavirus Is Iran's Perfect Storm." *Foreign Affairs*, March 18, 2020. https://www.foreignaffairs.com/articles/iran/2020-03-18/coronavirus-irans-perfect-storm.

———. "The Dilemma of Iran's Resistance Economy." *Foreign Affairs*, March 17, 2021. https://www.foreignaffairs.com/articles/middle-east/2021-03-17/dilemma-irans-resistance-economy.

———. "Iran's Middle Class and the Nuclear Deal." Brookings Institution, April 8, 2021. https://www.brookings.edu/blog/future-development/2021/04/08/irans-middle-class-and-the-nuclear-deal/.

———. "No, Iranians Aren't Negotiating from a Weak Economic Position." *Responsible Statecraft*, August 30, 2022. https://responsiblestatecraft.org/2022/08/30/no-iranians-arent-negotiating-from-a-weak-economic-position/.

Salinger, Pierre. *America Held Hostage: The Secret Negotiations.* New York: Doubleday, 1981.

Samuel, Annie Tracy. "Guarding the Nation: The Iranian Revolutionary Guards, Nationalism and the Iran-Iraq War." In *Constructing Nationalism in Iran: From the Qajars to the Islamic Republic*, edited by Meir Litvak, 248–62. New York: Routledge, 2017.

———. *The Unfinished History of the Iran-Iraq War: Faith, Firepower, and Iran's Revolutionary Guards*. New York: Cambridge University Press, 2022.

Savory, Roger M. *Iran under the Safavids*. New York: Cambridge University Press, 1980.

Schirazi, Asghar. *The Constitution of the Islamic Republic of Iran: Politics and the State in the Islamic Republic*. Translated by John O'Kane. London: I. B. Tauris, 1997.

Seifzadeh, Hossein S. "Revolution, Ideology, and the War." In *Iranian Perspectives on the Iran-Iraq War*, edited by Farhang Rajaee, 90–96. Gainesville, FL: University Press of Florida, 1997.

Selznik, Philip. *The Organizational Weapon: A Study of Bolshevik Strategy and Tactics*. New York: Free Press, 1960.

Seurat, Leila. "Hamas' Goal in Gaza." *Foreign Affairs*, December 11, 2023. https://www.foreignaffairs.com/israel/hamass-goal-gaza.

Shahrokhi, Nazanin. *Women in Place: Politics of Gender Segregation in Iran*. Berkeley: University of California Press, 2019.

Siavoshi, Sussan. "Regime Legitimacy and Highschool Textbooks." In *Iran after the Revolution: Crisis of an Islamic State*, edited by Saeed Rahnema and Sohrab Behdad, 203–17. London: I. B. Tauris, 1995.

Sick, Gary. *All Fall Down: America's Tragic Encounter with Iran*. New York: Random House, 1985.

———. *October Surprise: America's Hostages in Iran and the Election of Ronald Reagan*. New York: Crown, 1991.

Singh, Michael. "Axis of Abraham: Arab Israeli Normalization Could Remake the Middle East." *Foreign Affairs* 101, no. 2 (March–April 2022): 40–50.

Snyder, Jack L. *The Soviet Strategic Culture: Implications for Limited Nuclear Operations*. Santa Monica, CA: Rand, 1977.

Stewart, Richard A. *Sunrise at Abadan: The British and Soviet Invasion of Iran, 1941*. New York: Praeger, 1988.

Sullivan, William H. *Mission to Iran*. New York: W. W. Norton, 1981.

Sweringen, Will D. "Geo-Political Origins of the Iran-Iraq War." *Geographical Review* 78, no. 4 (October 1988): 405–16.

Tabatabai, Ariane M. *No Conquest, No Defeat: Iran's National Security Strategy*. New York: Oxford University Press, 2020.

———. "Syria Changed the Iranian Way of War." *Foreign Affairs*, August 16, 2019. https://www.foreignaffairs.com/articles/syria/2019-08-16/syria-changed-iranian-way-war.

Tabatabai, Ariane M., Jeffrey Martini, and Becca Wasser. *The Iran Threat Network*. Santa Monica, CA: Rand Corporation, 2021.

Tabatabai, Ariane M., and Annie Tracy Samuel. "What the Iran-Iraq War Tells Us about the Future of Iran Nuclear Deal." *International Security* 41, no. 1 (Summer 2017): 152–85.

Tajbakhsh, Kian. *Creating Local Democracy in Iran: State Building and the Politics of Decentralization*. New York: Cambridge University Press, 2022.

Takeyh, Ray. "The Coup That Wasn't: Carter and Iran." *Survival* 64, no. 4 (2020): 137–50.

———. *Guardians of the Revolution: Iran and the World in the Age of the Ayatollahs*. New York: Oxford University Press, 2009.

———. *The Last Shah: America, Iran, and the Fall of the Pahlavi Dynasty*. New Haven, CT: Yale University Press, 2021.

———. "The Other Carter Doctrine." *Foreign Affairs*, February 26, 2021. https://www.foreignaffairs.com/articles/united-states/2021-02-26/other-carter-doctrine.

———. "What Really Happened in Iran: The CIA, the Ouster of Mossadegh and Restoration of the Shah." *Foreign Affairs* 93, no. 4 (July–August 2014): 2–12.

Vatanka, Alex. *The Battle of the Ayatollahs in Iran: The United States, Foreign Policy, and Political Rivalry since 1979*. London: I. B. Tauris, 2021.

Vaziri, Roxanne. *Warring Souls: Youth, Media, and Martyrdom in Post-Revolutionary Iran*. Durham, NC: Duke University Press, 2006.

von Maltzahn, Nadia. *The Syria-Iran Axis: Cultural Diplomacy and International Relations in the Middle East*. London: I. B. Tauris, 2015.

Ward, Steven R. *Immortal: A Military History of Iran and Its Armed Forces*. Washington, DC: Georgetown University Press, 2009.

Warrick, Joby. *Black Flags: The Rise of ISIS*. New York: Doubleday, 2015.

Weber, Eugene. *Peasants into Frenchmen: The Modernization of Rural France, 1870–1914*. Stanford, CA: Stanford University Press, 1976.

Wilbur, Donald N. *Riza Shah Pahlavi: The Resurrection and Reconstruction of Iran*. New York: Exposition Press, 1975.

Yarhi-Milo, Karen. *Knowing the Adversary: Leaders, Intelligence, and Assessment of Intentions in International Relations*. Princeton, NJ: Princeton University Press, 2014.

Yarshater, Ehsan. "The Qajar Era in the Mirror of Time." *Iranian Studies* 34, nos. 1–4 (2001): 187–94.

Zabih, Sepehr. *The Communist Movement in Iran*. Berkeley: University of California Press, 1966.

———. *The Iranian Military in Revolution and War*. New York: Routledge, 1988.

Zahirnejad, Mahnaz. "The Economic Effects of Sanctions and the Iranian Middle Class." In *Iran in the International System: Between Great Powers and Great Ideas*, edited by Heintz Gartner and Mitra Shahmoradi, 108–30. New York: Routledge, 2020.

Zarakol, Ayşe. "States and Ontological Security: A Historical Rethinking." *Cooperation and Conflict* 52, no. 1 (2017): 48–68.

Zetter, Kim. *Countdown to Zero Day: Stuxnet and the Launch of the World's First Digital Weapon*. New York: Crown, 2014.

Zimmermann, Doron. "Calibrating Disorder: Iran's Role in Iraq and the Coalition Response, 2003–2006." *Civil Wars* 9, no. 1 (2007): 8–31.

Zimmt, Raz. "Iran's Support for Hamas and the Risk of Multi-Front Escalation." *War on the Rocks*, October 18, 2023. https://warontherocks.com/2023/10/irans-support-for-hamas-and-the-risk-of-multi-front-escalation/.

———. "The Rise and Fall of the Crocodile Ayatollah." *IranSource*, January 6, 2021. https://www.atlanticcouncil.org/blogs/iransource/the-rise-and-fall-of-the-crocodile-ayatollah/.

Zisser, Eyal. "Iranian Involvement in Lebanon." *Military and Strategic Affairs* 3, no. 1 (May 2011): 3–16.

Persian Books and Articles

Adamiat, Fereydoun. فکر آزادی و مقدمه نهضت مشروطیت ایران (*Idea of Liberty and Beginnings of the Constitutional Movement of Iran*). Tehran, 1961.

———. فکر دموکراسی اجتماعی و نهضت مشروطه ایران (*Idea of Social Democracy and Iran's Constitutional Revolution*). Tehran: 1975.

———. ایدئولوژی نهضت مشروطه ایران (*The Ideology of Iran's Constitutional Movement*). Tehran: Payam, 1977.

Ahmadi Amouie, Bahman. اقتصاد سیاسی جمهوری اسلامی (*The Political Economy of the Islamic Republic*). Tehran: Gam-e No, 2002.

Ahvazi, Abdol-Razzaq. امام خمینی به روایت آیت الله هاشمی رفسنجانی (*Imam Khomeini According to Ayatollah Hashemi Rafsanjani*). Tehran: Moassesseh-e Tanzim va Nashr-e Asar Imam Khomeini, 1981.

Akhavan Kazemi, Bahram. مروری بر روابط ایران وعربستان در دو دهه اخیر (*A Review of Iran-Saudi Relations in the Last Two Decades*). Tehran: Markaz-e Chap va Nashr-e Sazman-e Tablighat-e Eslami, 1995.

"نگاهی به استفاده رژیم عراق از سلاح های شیمیایی در جنگ تحمیلی" ("A Look at Iraqi Regime's Use of Chemical Weapons during the Imposed War"). Documents prepared by the Documents Center of War Propaganda Secretariat. In بازشناسی جنبه های تجاوز و دفاع (*Review of the Various Aspects of Aggression and Defense*). Tehran: Dabirkhaneh Konferans Beinolmellali Tajavoz va Defa', 1989): 2:358.

روایتی از حضور ایران در سوریه (*An Account of the Logic of Iran's Presence in Syria*). Tehran: Dar Masir Aftab, 2016.

Ansari Bardeh, Reza, and Mehdi Javanimoqaddam. "مفهوم راهبرد مقاومت در سیاست خارجی جمهوری اسلامی" ("The Meaning of the Concept of Active Resistance in the Foreign Policy of the Islamic Republic of Iran"). *Rahbord* 30, no. 98 (Spring 2022): 102–27.

Ansarifard, Masoumeh, and Amir Mohammad Hajiyousefi.

"بازدارندگی به مثابه استراتژی امنیتی دفاعی جمهوری اسلامی ایران؛ چالشها، الزامات، و مدل راهبرد" ("Deterrence as Islamic Republic of Iran's Security and Defense Strategy: Challenges, Requirements, and Strategic Model"). *Faslnameh-e Elmi-e Ravabet-e Beinolmellal* 41, no. 3 (2021): 8–14.

Anvari Tehrani, Ebrahim. "تمحیدات رهبران عراق برای تجاوز به قلمرو ایران" ("Iraqi Leadership's Preparations for Aggression against Iranian Territory"). In بازشناسی جنبه های تجاوز و دفاع (*Review of the Various Aspects of Aggression and Defense*), 2:9–62. Tehran: Dabirkhaneh Konferans Beinolmellali Tajavoz va Defa', 1989.

Aqaie, Seyyed Davoud. "سیاست خارجی جمهوری اسلامی ایران در دوران جنگ هشت ساله" ("Islamic Republic of Iran's Foreign Policy during the Eight-Year War"). *Majelleh-e Daneshkadeh-e Hoquq va Oloum-e Siyasi* 73 (Winter 2002): 1–34.

———. "جایگاه اتحادیه اروپا در سیاست خارجی دوران سازندگی" ("The Place of the European Union in the Foreign Policy of the Development Period"). *Faslnameh-e Siyasat* 3 (2008): 485–86.

Aqeli, Baqer. رضا شاه و قشون متحد الشکل (*Reza Shah and the Unified Military*). Tehran: Namak, 1999.

Ardestani, Hossein. تجلی جنگ ایران وعراق، جلد ۳، تنبیه متجاوز (*Analysis of Iran-Iraq War, Volume 3, Punishing the Aggressor*). Tehran: Markaz Asnad va Tahqiqat-e Defa'e Moqaddas, 2016.

———. راه: تاریخ شفاهی دکتر محسن رضایی، جلد اول: دوران مبارزه، بحران گروه های سیاسی (*The Path: Oral History of Dr. Mohsen Rezaie, Volume 1: The Era of Fighting, the Crisis of Political Groups*) (Tehran: Markaz-e Asnad va Tahqiqat-e Defa'e Moqaddas, 2016).

———. "جهاد سازندگی در جنگ تحمیلی" ("Construction Jihad in the Imposed War"). *Negin-e Iran* 51 (Winter 2015): 5–8.

———. "شکل گیری سازمان رزم سپاه پاسداران در عملیات فتح المبین تاریخ شفاهی دکتر محسن رضایی" ("Formation of IRGC's Military Structure during the Manifest Victory Operations, Oral History of Dr. Mohsen Rezaie"). *Negin-e Iran* 50 (Fall 2015): 5–28.

———. "ایران؛ تعامل جنگ و سیاست خارجی" ("Iran: Interaction of War and Foreign Policy"). *Negin-e Iran* 3 (Winter 2003): 21–33.

———. "تاریخ شفاهی فرماندهان جنگ ایران و عراق" ("Oral History of Commander of Iran-Iraq War"). *Negin-e Iran* 12, no. 24 (Fall 2013): 5–18.

———. تنبیه متجاوز (*Punishing the Aggressor*). Tehran: Markaz-e Motale'at va Tahqiqat-e Jang, 2000.

As'adi, Behrouz, and Seyyed ali Monavvari. "بررسی روابط ایران و روسیه در قرن جدید: اتحاد استراتژیک یا هم گرایی منافع" ("Analysis of Relations between Iran and Russia in the New Century: Strategic Alliance or Convergence of Interests"). *Rahyaf-taha-ye Siyasi va Beinolmellali* 12, no. 4 (August 2021): 181–210.

Asadollahi, Masoud. از مقاومت تا پیروزی: تاریخچه حزب الله (*From Resistance to Victory: A History of Hezbollah*). Tehran: Zekr, 1999.

Attari, Alireza. "سیاست موازنه منفی دکتر مصدق و بازتاب های خارجی آن" ("Dr. Mossadegh's Negative Balance and Its External Implications"). *Tarikhnameh-e Kharazmi* 3, no. 11 (Spring 2017): 45–75.

Azizi, Mohammad. "تحلیل مشارکت اقشار مختلف در دفاع مقدس" ("Analysis of Participation of Various Social Strata in the Sacred Defense"). *Pajouheshnameh Defa'e Moqaddas* 1, no. 2 (2012): 97–119.

Azqandi, Alireza. "تنش زدایی در سیاست خارجی: مورد جمهوری اسلامی" ("Tension Reduction in Foreign Policy: The Case of the Islamic Republic of Iran"). *Majelleh-e Siyasat-e Khareji* 52 (2000): 1035–48.

Babaie, Gol Ali. کارنامه عملیاتی گردان حبیب ابن مظاهر لشکر ۲۷ محمد رسول الله از تاسیس تا پایان دفاع مقدس (*The Operational Report Card of Habib Ibn Mazaher Battalion's Unit 27, Muhammad Rasul Allah from the Start to Finish of Sacred Defense*). Tehran: Markaz Pajouheshi-e 27 Besat, 2015.

Baghi, Emadeddin. واقعیت ها و قضاوت ها (*Truths and Judgments*). Tehran, 1999.

Baqeri Dolatabadi, Ali. رویاهای ناتمام، بررسی سیاست خارجی آیت الله هاشمی رفسنجانی (*Unrealized Dreams: A Review of Ayatollah Hashemi Rafsanjani's Foreign Policy*). Tehran: Tisa, 2019.

Baqeri Dolatabadi, Ali, and Mohsen Shafi'i Seifabadi. از هاشمی تا روحانی: بررسی سیاست خارجی ایران (*From Hashemi to Rouhani: A Review of Iran's Foreign Policy*). Tehran: Tisa, 2019.

———. از هاشمی تا روحانی: بررسی سیاست خارجی ایران در پیرو نظریه سازندگی (*From Rafsanjani to Rouhani: A Review of Iran's Foreign Policy from the Viewpoint of Constructivist Theory*). Tehran: Tisa, 2014.

Barzegar, Keyhan. "سیاست خارجی ایران از نظر رئالیسم تهاجمی و دفاعی" ("Iran's Foreign Policy from the Viewpoint of Offensive and Defensive Realism"). *Ravabet-e Khareji* 1, no. 1 (April 2009): 114–53.

Barzegar, Keyhan, and Masoud Rezaie. "راهبرد دفاعی ایران از منظر آیت الله خامنه ای" ("Iran's Defense Strategy from Ayatollah Khamenei's Viewpoint"). *Faslnameh Motale'at-e Rahbordi* 19, no. 4 (Winter 2016): 7–34.

Bashiri, Siavosh. قصه ساواک (*The Story of SAVAK*). Paris: Parang, 1987.

Behdarvand Yani, Gholam Reza. تاریخ ایران پس از انقلاب اسلامی، جلد ۷، پیروزی های بزرگ (*History of Iran after the Islamic Revolution, Volume 7, Great Victories*). Tehran: Markaz Asnad Jomhouri Eslami, 2022.

Bigdeli, Ali, and Ibrahim Abbasi. "دلائل حضور ایران در سوریه" ("Reasons for Iran's Presence in Syria"). *Motale'at-e Manafe'e Melli* (Spring 2016): 53–73.

Chamran, Mostafa, کردستان (*Kurdistan*). Tehran: Bonyad-e Shahid, 1985.

سردار دلها: زندگینامه وخاطرات سپهبد شهید حاج قاسم سلیمانی (*Commander of the Hearts: Biography and Memoirs of Martyred Lieutenant General Hajj Qasem Soleimani*). Tehran: Gorouh-e Farhangi Taqdir, 2020.

Darvishi, Farhad. جنگ ایران وعراق؛ پرسش ها وپاسخ ها (*The Iran-Iraq War: Questions and Answers*). Tehran: Markaz Motale'at va Tahqiqat-e Jang, 2007.

Davari Ardakani, Reza. فلسفه در بحران (*Philosophy in Crisis*). Tehran: Amir Kabir, 1994.

Davoudabadi, Hamid. از معراج برگشتگان (*From Heavenly Ascendance of the Returnees*). Tehran: Nashr-e Yousef, 2010. Dehqan Tarazjani, Mahmoud. روابط خارجی ایران وهمسایگان در دهه دوم انقلاب اسلامی (*Foreign Relations with Neighbors in the Second Decade of the Islamic Revolution*). Tehran: Soroush, 2000.

Dehqani Firouzabadi, Seyyed Jalal. سیاست خارجی جمهوری اسلامی (*The Foreign Policy of the Islamic Republic of Iran*). Tehran: Samt, 1990.

———. "امنیت هستی شناختی در سیاست خارجی جمهوری اسلامی ایران" ("Ontological Security in the Foreign Policy of the Islamic Republic of Iran"). *Faslnameh-e Beinolmellai Ravabet-e Khareji* 1, no. 1 (Spring 2008): 42–76.

Dehqani Firouzabadi, Seyyed Jalal, and Mehdi Ataie. "گفتمان هسته ای دولت یازدهم" ("Nuclear Discourse of the Eleventh Government"). *Faslnameh-e Motale'at-e Rahbordi* 17, no. 1 (Spring 2014): 87–120.

Dehqani Firouzabadi, Seyyed Jalal, and Reza Zabihi. "تاثیر هویت اسلامی-انقلابی بر رفتار سیاست خارجی جمهوری اسلامی ایران در موضوع هسته ای" ("The Impact of Islamic-Revolutionary Identity on the Behavior of the Islamic Republic on the Nuclear Issue"). *Oloum Siyasi* 15, no. 59 (Fall 2012): 75–102.

Dehshiri, Mohammad Reza, and Seyyed Mohammad Hossein Hosseini. "ژئوپولیتیک منطقه و روابط ایران و عربستان" ("Regional Geopolitics and Iran-Saudi Relations"). *Ravabet-e Khareji* 8, no. 1 (Spring 2016): 111–43.

Do'aie, Seyyed Mahmoud. گوشه ای از خاطرات (*A Sample of Reminiscences*). Tehran: Arouj, 2008.

Doroudian, Mohammad. از آغاز تا پایان: سیری در جنگ ایران و عراق (*From Beginning to End: A Review of the Iran-Iraq War*). Tehran: Markaz Asnad va Tahqiqat Dafa'e Moqaddas, 2012.

———. آغاز تا پایان جنگ (*Beginning to End of the War*). Tehran: Markaz Motale'at va Tahqiqat-e Jang, 2000.

از خونین شهر تا خرمشهر: بررسی وقایع سیاسی-نظامی جنگ از زمینه سازی تهاجم عراق تا آزادسازی خرمشهر؛ از شهریور ۱۳۵۹ تا خرداد ۱۳۶۱ (*From Bloody City to Khorramshahr: Analysis of Political and Military Developments from Iraq's Preparations for Invasion to Liberation of Khorramshahr; From September 1980 to June 1982*). Tehran: Markaz Asnad va Tahqiqat-e Defa'e Moqaddas, 2021.

———. پرسش های اساسی جنگ (*The Fundamental Questions of the War*). Tehran: Moassesseh-e Motale'at-e Siyasi Farhangi Andisheh-e Nab, 2001.

————. نقبی بر درسها و دستاوردهای جنگ (*Probing the Lessons and Gains of the War*). Tehran: Markaz Asnad va Tahqiqat-e Defa'e Moqaddas, 2021.

————. روند پایان جنگ (*Process of Ending the War*). Tehran: Sepah Pasdaran Enqelab-e Eslami, 2005.

————. علل تداوم جنگ (*Reasons for the Continuation of the War*). Tehran: Entesharat-e Markaz-e Asnad Defa'e Moqaddas, 2004.

————. مسائل اصلی جنگ (*The War's Fundamental Issues*). Tehran: Entesharat-e Markaz-e Asnad Defa'e Moqaddas, 2018.

Eftekhari, Qasem, and Ali Baqeri Dolatabadi. "اعمال فشار آمریکا و تشدید گرایش ایران به استراتژی بازدارندگی" ("American Pressure and Iran's Growing Reliance on a Strategy of Deterrence"). *Siyasat* 40, no. 4 (January 2011): 1–20.

Eslami Nodoushan, Mohammad Ali. ایران وتنهایش (*Iran and Its Loneliness*). Tehran: Sherkat Sahami Enteshar, 1997.

Esma'ili, Hamidreza. اندیشه سیاسی آیت الله هاشمی رفسنجانی (*Political Thought of Ayatollah Hashemi Rafsanjani*). Tehran: Markaz-e Enqelab-e Eslami Iran, 2019.

Fathi, Mohammad Javad, Shohreh Pirani, and Akbar Ghafouri. "تنهائی استراتژیک و سیاستهای راهبردی ایران در غرب آسیا" ("Strategic Loneliness and Iran's Strategic Policies in West Asia"). *Iranian Research Letter of International Politics* 9, no. 2 (Spring–Summer 2021): 159–209.

Ganji, Akbar. عالیجناب سرخپوش وعالیجنابان خاکستری: آسیب شناسی گذر به دولت دموکراتیک توسعه گرا (*The Red Eminence and the Grey Eminences: Pathology of Transition to the Developmental Democratic State*). Tehran: Tarh-e No, 1998.

Ghazanfari, Kamran. پرونده هسته ای وابعاد پیدا وپنهان آن (*The Nuclear File and Its Open and Hidden Dimensions*). Tehran: Markaz Asnad Enqelab, 2015.

Golshani, Ali Reza, and Mohsen Baqeri. "جایگاه حزب الله لبنان در استراتژی بازدارنده جمهوری اسلامی ایران" ("The Place of Hezbollah of Lebanon in the Deterrence Strategy of the Islamic Republic of Iran"). *Faslnameh-e Elmi Motale'at-e Ravabet-e Beinolmellali* 41, no. 3 (Fall 2021): 7–34.

Haami Kalvanaq, Valiollah. روابط ایران وچین قبل وبعد از انقلاب (*Iran-China Relations before and after the Revolution*). Tehran: Markaz Asnad-e Enqelab-e Eslami, 2011.

Hadizonouz, Behrouz. "توسعه صنعتی در پیچ و خم ساختار اقتصادی، نگاهی به وضع اقتصادی و صنعتی کشور" ("Industrial Growth in the Context of the Economy's Framework: An Examination of the Economic and Industrial Situation of the Country"). *Tadbir* 3 (July 1990): 26–29.

Hamidi, Ibrahim. "محضر سري للقاء الأسد - خامنئي عشية غزو العراق" ("Secret Minutes of Assad-Khamenei Meeting on the Eve of Invasion of Iraq"). *Al-Majalla*, March 23, 2024. https://www.majalla.com /node/313361/وثائق-ومذكرات/محضر-سري-للقاء-الأسد-خامنئي-عشية-غزو-العراق-لجنة-أمنية-سورية-إيرانية-لدعم.

Harsij, Hossein, Mojtaba Toyserkani, and Leila Ja'fari. "ژئوپولیتیک قدرت نرم در ایران" ("Geopolitics of Iran's Soft Power"). *Pajouheshnameh Oloum-e Siyasi* 4, no. 2 (2009): 225–69.

Hosseini, Seyyed Yaqub. تاریخ نظامی جنگ تحمیلی (*Military History of the Imposed War*). 2 vols. Tehran: Hey'at-e Ma'aref-e Jang, 2008.

Izadi, Fouad. دیپلماسی عمومی آمریکا در قبال ایران (*U.S. Public Diplomacy toward Iran*). Tehran: Daneshgah Emam Sadeq, 2012.

Ja'farian, Rasoul. جریان ها وسازمان های مذهبی-سیاسی ایران، ۱۳۲۰-۱۳۵۷ (*Iran's Religopolitical Trends and Institutions, 1941–1979*). Tehran: Elm, 2011.

Kasra, Niloufar. "قیام تنباکو، نخستین استادگی در برابر شاه" ("The Tobacco Rebellion: The First Resistance to the Shah"). Tehran: Institute for Iranian Contemporary Historical Studies, n.d. http://www.iichs.ir/News-167/قیام-تنباکو،-نخستین-ایستادگی-در-برابر-شاه-/?id=167.

Kasravi, Ahmad. تاریخ مشروطه ایران (*History of Iran's Constitution*). Tehran: Negah, 1940.

Kharrazi, Seyyed Mohsen. In "اشکال و انواع دفاع مقدس از نظر اسلام" ("Varieties and Types of Sacred Defense in Islam"). بازشناسی جنبه های تجاوز ودفاع (*Review of Aspects of Aggression and Defense*) (1991): 1: 98–106. Tehran: Dabirkhaneh Konferans Beinolmellali Tajavoz va Defa', 1989.

Khazaie, Shirzad. جنگ شیمیایی عراق علیه ایران: بررسی نظامی وحقوقی (*Chemical Warfare against Iran: A Military and Legal Analysis*). Tehran: Markaz Asnad Jomhouri Eslami, 2021.

Khorramshad, Mehdi, and Mohammad Baqer Beiki. قدرت نرم جمهوری اسلامی؛ مطالعه مورد لبنان (*The Islamic Republic of Iran's Soft Power: A Study of the Case of Lebanon*). Tehran: Entesharat-e Daneshgah-e Emam Sadeq, 2008.

Kulaie, Elahe, Ebrahim Mottaqi, and Seyyed Davud Aqaie, eds. نه شرقی، نه غربی (*Neither Eastern nor Western*). Tehran: Mizan, 2009.

Lotfollahzadegan, Ali Reza. روز شمار جنگ ایران و عراق، جلد ۲۰، عبور از مرز (*Daily Account of Iran-Iraq War, Volume 20, Crossing the Border*). Tehran: Markaz Tahqiqat va Motale'at-e Jang Sepah Pasdaran Enqelab, 2000.

Mansouri, Javad. تاریخ شفاهی تاسیس سپاه پاسداران انقلاب اسلامی ایران (*The Oral History of Formation of Iran's Islamic Revolutionary Guards Corps*). Tehran: Markaz Assad-e Enqelab-e Eslami, 2014.

"دفاعیه محسن میردامادی از اقدام دانشجویان پیرو خط امام در ۱۳ آبان" ("Mohsen Mirdamadi's Defense of the Actions of the Students following Imam's Line on November 4 [1979]"). Markaz-e Daerotolma'ref-e Bozorg-e Eslami, November 3, 2015. https://www.cgie.org.ir/fa/news/دفاعیه-محسن-میردامادی-از-اقدام-دانشجویان-پیرو-خط-امام-در-۱۳-آبان/83073/.

Mirqaderi, Seyyed Fazlollah, and Hossein Kiyani. "بن مایه ادبیات مقاومت درقرآن" ("The Basis of Resistance Literature in the Quran"). *Faslnameh-e Adabiyat-e Dini* 1, no. 1 (March–April 2012): 69–95.

Mohammadi, Manuchehr. جنگ تحمیلی؛ مجموعه مقالات (*The Imposed War: Collection of Articles*). Tehran: Basij Manteqeh-e 3, 1995.

———. مروری بر سیاست خارجی ایران در دوران پهلوی، یا، تصمیم گیری در نظام تحت سلطه (*A Survey of Iran's Foreign Policy during the Pahlavi Period, or, Decision-Making a State under Domination*). Tehran: Dadgostar, 1999.

Mohammadi, Mehdi. "هسته ای چگونه به آنجا رسید" *Shahid Baqeri Base* 23 (2013). https://t.me/Enghelaabioon_Javan/582.

Mohaqqeqi, Mohammad Hasan. اسرار مکتوم، ناگفته های دفاع هشت ساله از زبان مسئولان کشوری و لشکری (*Hidden Secrets: Unknowns of the Eight Year Defense According to the State and Military Leaders of War Years*). Tehran: Markaz Motale'at Pajoheshi 27 Be'sat, 2014.

Moshirzadeh, Homeira. "تحلیل سیاست خارجی جمهوری اسلامی از منظر سازندگی" ("Examination of the Islamic Republic's Foreign Policy from the Constructive Point of View"). In نگاهی به سیاست خارجی جمهوری اسلامی ایران (*A Look at the Foreign Policy of the Islamic Republic of Iran*), edited by Nasrin Mosaffa. Tehran: Daftar Motale'at-e Siyasi va Beinollmealli, 2007.

Nakhaie, Hadi, Mehdi Ansari, and Mohammad Doroudian. خرمشهر در جنگ طولانی (*Khorramshahr in the Long War*). Tehran: Markaz-e Sepah-e Pasdaran-e Enqelab-e Eslami, 2010.

Naqibzadeh, Ahmad. فرایند تصمیم گیری در سیاست خارجی ایران: چالش ها، آسیب ها و راه کارها (*Foreign Policy Process in Iran: Challenges, Costs and Alternatives*). Tehran: Moavenat-e Pajuheshi Danesh-gah-e Azad-e Eslami, 2010.

Niazmand, Reza. رضا شاه: از تولد تا سلطنت (*Reza Shah: From Birth to Monarchy*). Washington, DC: Foundation for Iranian Studies, 1996.

Nikkhah, Mohammad Baqer. جنایات جنگ: حمله شیمیایی در جنگ عراق با ایران (*War Crimes: Iraq's Chemical Attacks in War with Iran*). Tehran: Markaz Asnad va Tahqiqat-e Defa'e Moqaddas, 2012.

Norouzi, Ali. سراب سازندگی: دیدگاه انتقادی درباره عملکرد هشت ساله دولت هاشمی رفسنجانی (*The Mirage of Development: A Critical Look at the Eight-Year Record of Hashemi Rafsanjani's Government*). Tehran: Zarrin, 1994.

Ostadi Moqaddam, Mohammad Hasan. آشنایی با دفاع مقدس (*Understanding Sacred Defense*). Tehran: Khadem al-Reza, 2021.

Qalibaf, Mohammad Baqer, and Seyyed Mousa Pourmousavi. "ژئوپولیتیک نوین خاورمیانه و سیاست خارجی ایران" ("The Middle East's New Geopolitics and Iran's Foreign Policy"). *Pajouheshhaye Joqrafiyaie-Ensani* 41, no. 4 (Winter 2008): 53–69.

Qasemi, Behzad. "ژئوپولیتیک محور مقاومت وامنیت ملی جمهوری اسلامی ایران بر اساس گفتمان انقلاب اسلامی" ("The Geopolitics of Axis of Resistance and the National Security of the Islamic Republic of Iran on the Basis of the Discourse of the Islamic Revolution"). *Faslnameh-e Afaq Amniyat* 11, no. 38 (Spring 2018): 5–33.

Qasemi, Farhad. "نگاهی تئوریک بر طراحی مدل بازدارندگی سیاست خارجی ایران" ("A Theoretical Look at the Design of Deterrence in Iran's Foreign Policy"). *Faslnameh-e Jeopolitik* 7 (2007): 119–21.

Rabi'i, Ali. نگاه به جامعه شناسی تحولات ارزشی (*An Overview of Sociology of Transformation of Values*). Tehran: Farhang va Andisheh, 1997.

Reisinejad, Arash. ایران و راه ابریشم نوین (*Iran and the New Silk Road*). Tehran: Tehran University Press, 2022.

Rajaie, Gholam Ali. برداشت های سیره امام خمینی (*Impressions from Imam Khomeini's Life*). Tehran: Moassesseh-e Tanzim va Nashr-e Asar Imam Khomeini, 2013.

Ranjbar, Maqsoud. ملاحظات امنیتی جمهوری اسلامی در سیاست خارجی (*Security Considerations in Iran's Foreign Policy*). Tehran: Pajouheshkadeh-e Motale'at-e Rahbordi, 2000.

Roshandel, Jalil. "ملاحظات امنیتی جمهوری اسلامی در سیاست خارجی۰" ("Islamic Republic's Foreign Policy, Part I, from Revolution until Fall of 1982"). *Radio Farda*, February 9, 2019. https://www.radiofarda.com/a/Islamic-republic-foreign-policy-part-1/29764251.html.

Rostami, Farzad, Kamran Lotfi, and Saeed Pirmohammadi. "جنگ قدرتها در یمن و امنیت جمهوری اسلامی" ("The War of Powers in Yemen and the Security of the Islamic Republic"). *Faslnameh Motale'at-e Ravabet-e Beinolomellali* 11, no. 41 (Spring 2018): 9–35.

Roughani Zanjani, Mas'oud. "وضعیت اقتصادی، ظرفیتهای تولیدی و زمینه های سرمایه گذاری در ایران" ("The Economic Situation, Industrial Production Capacity and Areas of Investment in Iran"). *Tadbir* 3 (July 1990): 41–43.

Sadeghi, Shamseddin, and Lotfi, Kamran. "تحلیل موازعه جمهوری اسلامی در قبال بحران سوریه" ("Analysis of Iran's Position in the Syrian Crisis"). *Jostarhaye Siyasi Moaser* 6, no. 1 (Spring 2015): 123–44.

Safavi Homaie, Seyyed Hamzeh. کالبدشکافی سیاست خارجی جمهوری اسلامی ایران (*Deep Dive into Islamic Republic of Iran's Foreign Policy*). Tehran: Entesharat-e Daneshgah-e Emam Sadeq, 2008.

Safiri, Mahmoud. حقیقت ها و مصلحت ها: گفتگو با هاشمی رفسنجانی (*Truths and Expediencies: Conversation with Hashemi Rafsanjani*). Tehran: Ney, 2019.

Sepehr, Ahmad Ali Movarekh al-Dowleh. ۱۹۱۴-۱۹۱۸ ایران در جنگ بزرگ، (*Iran in the Great War 1914–1918*). Tehran: Bank-e Melli, 1957.

Shariatinia, Mohsen. "عوامل تائین کننده روابط ایران و چین" ("Decisive Factors in Iran-China Relations"). *Faslnameh-e Ravabet-e Kharjei* 4, no. 2 (Summer 2012): 179–210.

———. "روابط ایران و چین: گذر از مثلث رمانتیک به پیوند پایدار" ("Iran-China Relations: From a Romantic Triangle to Lasting Relations"). *Faslnameh-e Elmi Rahyafthaye Siyasi va Beinolmellali*, 11, no. 3 (Spring 2020): 95–114.

Shiralinia, Ja'far. تاریخ جنگ ایران و عراق (*History of Iran-Iraq War*). Tehran: Sayan, 2014.

———. روایتی از زندگی زمانه آیت الله علی اکبر هاشمی رفسنجانی (*A Telling of the Life and Times of Ayatollah Ali Akbar Hashemi Rafsanjani*). Tehran: Sayan, 2017.

Soleimani, Reza. سیاست خارجی دولت خاتمی: دیپلماسی تنش زدایی و گفتگو تمدن ها؛ ۱۳۷۶-۱۳۸۴ (*Khatami Government's Foreign Policy: De-Escalatory Diplomacy and Dialogue of Civilizations, 1997–2005*). Tehran: Entesharat-e Kavir, 2012.

Taha'ie, Seyyed Javad. درآمدی بر مبانی سیاست خارجی جمهوری اسلامی ایران (*An Account of the Foreign Policy of the Islamic Republic of Iran*). Tehran: Entesharat Markez Estratejik, 2009.

Tajik, Mohammad Reza. سیاست خارجی: عرصه فقدان تصمیم و تدبیر (*Foreign Policy: The Arena of Lack of Decision and Wisdom*). Tehran: Farhang Gofteman, 2004.

———. "انتظام در پراکندگی، بحثی در امنیت ملی ایران" ("Unorganized Order: An Argument on Iran's National Security"). *Faslnameh Motale'at-e Rahbordi* 1, no. 2 (1998): 117–28.

———. "منافع ملی ما کدامند؟" ("What Are Our National Interests?"). *Faslnameh Motale'at-e Rahbordi* 4, nos. 1–2 (Summer 2001): 47–65.

Tajik, Mohammad Reza, and Seyyed Jalal Dehqani Firouzabadi. "الگوهای صدور انقلاب در گفتمانهای سیاست خارجی ایران" ("Models for Exporting the Revolution in Iran's Foreign Policy Discourse"). *Rahbord* 27 (Spring 2003): 61–80.

———. "چرا ما رمون آرون نداشتیم؟ گزارش یک نشست و گفت و گو با داریوش شایگان" ("Why Didn't We Have a Raymond Aaron? Report of an Interview with Daryush Shayegan"). *Andisheh-e Pouya* 18 (August 2016): 17–18.

Yaqubi, Saeed. سیاست خارجی جمهوری اسلامی ایران در عصر سازندگی (*The Foreign Policy of the Islamic Republic of Iran in the Development Era*). Tehran: Markaz-e Asnad-e Enqelab-e Eslami, 2000.

Zibakalam, Sadeq. هاشمی بدون روتوش (*Hashemi [Rafsanjani] without Retouching*). Tehran: Rouzaneh, 2009.

———. رضا شاه (*Reza Shah*). Tehran: Rouzbeh, 2019.

Zibakalam, Sadeq, and Hesam Basrouyehnejad Karimi. اشغال: انقلاب دوم، تولد آمریکا ستیزی (*Occupation: The Second Revolution and Birth of Anti-Americanism*). Tehran: Rouzaneh, 2021.

Zouqi Barani, Kazem. "تبیین راهبرد سیاست منطقه ای جمهوری اسلامی ایران در گذر ژئوپولیتیک" ("Unveiling the Strategy of the Islamic Republic of Iran in a Changing Geopolitics"). In نظام بین المللی و نظم های در حال ظهور (*International System and the Emerging Orders*), edited by Anahita Mo'tazedzadeh, Zohreh Poustinchi, and Ziaoddin Sabouri, 57–73. Tehran: Abrar, 2021.

Original Sources and Memoirs

Ahmadi, Hamid. درس تجربه: خاطرات ابوالحسن بنی صدر (*Lesson of Experience: The Reminiscences of Abol-Hasan Bani Sadr*). Berlin: Anjoman Motale'at va Tahqiqat-e Tarikh Shafahi Iran, 2001.

Ala'ie, Hossein. تاریخ تحلیلی جنگ ایران وعراق (*Analytical History of Iran-Iraq War*). 3rd ed. 2 vols. Tehran: Marz va Boom, 2022.

———. "چگونگی تداوم جنگ پس از فتح خرمشهر و روند پایان جنگ" ("Reasons for Continuation of War after Captue of Khorramshahr and Process of Ending It"). *Pajouheshnameh Defa'e Moqaddas* 1, no. 4 (2013): 63–97.

Alam, Amir Asadollah. یادداشت های علم (*The Alam Diaries*). Edited by Alinaqi Alikhani. Bethesda, MD: Iranbooks, 1995.

Algar, Hamid, trans. *Islam and Revolution: Writings and Declarations of Imam Khomeini*. Berkeley, CA: Mizan Press, 1981.

"مصاحبه آیت الله هاشمی رفسنجانی با اعضاء فصلنامه مطالعات بین المللی" ("Ayatollah Hashemi Rafsanjani's Interview with Members of the International Relations Quarterly"). *Rafsanjani.ir*, March 21, 2013. https://rafsanjani.ir/records/مصاحبه-آیت-الله-هاشمی-رفسنجانی-با-اعضای-فصلنامه-مطالعات-بین-المللی.

Babaie, Gol Ali. پیغام ماهی ها: سرگذشت حاج حسین همدانی (*The Message of the Fish: Life Story [Interviews] of [General] Haj Hossein Hamedani*). Tehran: Soureh-e Mehr, 2016.

Bani Sadr, Abol-Hasan. *My Turn to Speak: Iran, the Revolution and Secret Deals with the U.S.* Washington, DC: Potomac Books, 1991.

قانون اساسی جمهوری اسلامی؛ فصل اول، اصول کلی (*The Constitution of the Islamic Republic of Iran: Part 1, General Principles*). Tehran: Majles Shora-e Eslami. https://rc.majlis.ir/fa/law/show/133613.

"منازعه قومی و منطقه ای در سالهای اول انقلاب به روایت آیت الله هاشمی رفسنجانی" ("Ethnic and Regional Conflicts in the Early Years of the Revolution according to Ayatollah Hashemi Rafsanjani"). https://rafsanjani.ir/records/منازعات-قومی-و-منطقه-ای-در-سالهای-اول-اقلاب-به-روایت-ایت-الله-هاشمی-رفسنجانی.

Fardoust, Hossein. خاطرات ارتشبد بازنشسته حسین فردوست: ظهور وسقوط سلطنت پهلوی (*Memoirs of the Retired Full General Hossein Fardoust: Rise and Fall of Pahlavi Monarchy*). Tehran: Moassesseh-e Etela'at va Pajouhesha-ye Siyasi, 1991.

Foroutan, Yousef. خاطرات سردار یوسف فروتن، عضو اولین شورای فرماندهی سپاه پاسداران (*Memoirs of Commander Yousef Foroutan, Member of the First Commanders Council of the IRGC*). Edited by Masoumeh Samavi. Tehran: Markaz Assad Enqelab Eslami, 2019.

"متن کامل ناگفته های شمخانی از جنگ" ("Full Text of Shamkhani's Unsaid Recollections of the War"). *Isna*, September 27, 2005. https://www.isna.ir/news/8407-01892/متن-کامل-ناگفته-های-شمخانی-از-جنگ-در-گفت-وگو-با-ایسنا-می-توانستیم-.

"متن کامل مصاحبه سردار سلیمانی در مورد جنگ ۳۳ روزه" ("Full Interview of Commander Soleimani about the 33 Day War"). *Aparat*, n.d. https://www.aparat.com/v/a7Xm.

"همه چیز را از دست رفته میدیدیم: ماجرای ۱۸ روز محاصره حاج قاسم در حلب" ("Interview with General Mahmoud Chaharbaghi: We Saw Everything Lost: The Story of the 18-Day Siege of Hajj Qasem [Soleimani] in Aleppo"). *Tasnim News*, December 29, 2020. https://www.youtube.com/watch?v=L9KwYa8P8dA.

برنامه انرژی اتمی ایران: تلاش ها وتنش ها (*Iran's Atomic Energy Program: Mission, Structure, Politics: Interview with Akbar Etemad, the First President of the Atomic Energy Organization of Iran [1974–1978]*). Bethesda, MD: Foundation for Iranian Studies, 1997.

Iran Oral History Project, Harvard University, interview with Karim Sanjabi.

"گفتگو با حسن کاظمی قمی: بعد از عراق نوبت ایران بود" ("Interview with Hasan Kazemi Qomi [IRGC Commander and Iran's First Ambassador to Iraq after the US Invasion in 2003]: After Iraq It Was Iran's Turn." In تاریخ شفاهی سیاست خارجی جمهوری اسلامی (*Oral History of the Foreign Policy of the Islamic Republic of Iran*), edited by Mohammad Hasan Rouztalab and Mohammad Rahmani, 408–18. Tehran: Markaz-e Asnad Eslami, 2014.

"Interview with Mahmoud Chaharbaghi, Commander of IRGC Artillery in Syria." YouTube, January 2, 2021. https://www.youtube.com/watch?v=k6dJzst_3k8.

"مصاحبه سه ساعته جواد ظریف" ("Javad Zarif's Three-Hour Interview"). *Radio Farda*, April 26, 2021. https://www.radiofarda.com/a/31223108.html.

"اولین گفتگوی جواد ظریف پس از وزارت" ("Javad Zarif's First Interview After Foreign Ministry"). YouTube, June 6, 2023. https://www.youtube.com/watch?v=3mXOsE2Yqho.

Kazemi, Mohsen. خاطرات مرضیه حدیدچی (*Memoirs of Marzieh Hadidchi*). Tehran: Soureh Mehr, 2014.

Khamenei, Sayyid Ali. من و کتاب (*Books and I*). Tehran: Mehr, 2001.

Khatami, Mohammad. از دنیا شهر تا شهر دنیا (*From the City's World to the World's City*). Tehran: Ney, 1997.

———. اسلام، روحانیت و انقلاب اسلامی (*Islam, the Clergy, and the Islamic Revolution*). Tehran: Tar-e No, 2000.

Khomeini, Seyyed Ahmad. دلیل آفتاب: خاطرات یادگار امام (*Reason for the Sun: Recollections of Imam's Memento*). Tehran: Moaseseh-e Tanzim va Nashr-e Asar-e Imam Khomeini, 2005.

Khomeini, Seyyed Ruhollah. صحیفه نور، مجموعه آثار امام خمینی (*The Book of Light: Collection of Imam Khomeini's Works*). 22 vols. Tehran: Moaseseh-e Tanzim va Nashr-e Asar Emam, 1980.

———. صدور انقلاب از دیدگاه امام خمینی (*Export of Revolution from Imam Khomeini's View*). Tehran: Mo'assesseh-e Tanzim va Nashr-e Asar-e Imam Khomeini, 2008.

———. حکومت اسلامی (*Islamic Government*). N.p., 1971.

———. حکومت اسلامی یا ولایت فقیه (*Islamic Government or Rule by the Jurisconsult*). Tehran, 1970.

Kooshaki, Mohammad Sadeq. "سرانجام پرونده مرموز محمد رضا سعادتی" Markaz Ansand Enqelab-e Eslami: Islamic Revolution's Document Center, July 27, 2020. https://irdc.ir/fa/news/6013 /سرانجام-پرونده-مرموز-محمدرضا-سعادتی.

خاطرات نورالدین کیانوری (*Memoirs of Noureddin Kianouri*). Tehran: Didgah, 1993.

Montazeri, Ayatollah [Hossein Ali]. خاطرات (*Reminiscences*). 2nd ed. 2 vols. Essen, Germany: Ettehadieh Nasherin Irani dar Oroupa, 2001.

Mousavi Ardebili, Seyyed Abdol-Karim. غائله ۱۴ اسفند ۱۳۵۹: ظهور و سقوط ضد انقلاب (*The Episode of March 5, 1981: The Rise and Fall of Counter-Revolution*). Tehran: Moassesseh Maktab-e Amir Al-Mo'menin, 1988.

Najafdari, Manouchehr. پشت دروازه های شهر؛ خاطرات سرتیپ منوچهر نجفدری (*Behind the Gates of the City: The Memoirs of Brigidier Manouchehr Najafdari*). Edited by Hossein Kavoshi. Tehran: Markaz Assad-e Enqelab-e Eslami, 2017.

National Archives of the United States, National Security and Diplomatic History Archives.

Oral History of Iran Collection of the Foundation for Iranian Studies, interviews with:

General Hasan Alavi Kia

Mahshid Amirshahi

Mohammad Baheri

William Burr

Akbar E'temad

Mansour Farhang

Richard Helms

Kambiz Heshmati

Daryush Homayoun

Eslam Kazemiyyeh

Abdol-Karim Lahiji

Michael Metrinko

Hamid Mohamedi

General Ahmad Ali Mohaqqeqi

Charles Naas

Seyyed Hossein Nasr

Reza Niazmand

Sir Peter Ramsbotham

Pahlavi, Mohammad Reza. *Answer to History*. New York: Stein and Day, 1980.

———. به سوی تمدن بزرگ (*Towards the Great Civilization*). Los Angeles: Pars, 2007. First published 1976–77.

———. انقلاب سفید (*White Revolution*). Tehran: Bank-e Melli, 1965.

Qaneifard, Erfan. تند باد حوادث گفتگو با عیسی پژمان: مأمور ویژه شاه و نماینده ساواک در کردستان عراق (*Storm of Events: Conversation with Isa Pejman, the Shah's Special Envoy and SAVAK's Representative in Iraq's Kurdistan*). Tehran: Nashr-e Elm, 2011.

"سؤال چرا به سوریه رفتیم و پاسخ شهید حسین همدانی" ("The Question of Why We Went to Syria and the Answer of the Martyred General Hossein Hamedani"). *Aparat*, 2018. https://www.aparat.com/v/SyAhP/سؤال_چرا_به_سوریه_رفتیم_و_پاسخ_سردار_شهید_حسین_%D9%90.

Rafiqdoust, Mohsen. (۱۳۵۸-۱۳۵۷) برای تاریخ میگویم: خاطرات محسن رفیقدوست (*I Tell It for History: Memoirs of Mohsen Rafiqdoust [1979–80]*). Edited by Saeed Alamiyan. Tehran: Soureh-e Mehr, 2013.

Rafsanjani, Ali Akbar Hashemi. امیر کبیر یا قهرمان ملی مبارزه با استعمار (*Amir Kabir or the Hero of Struggle against Imperialism*). Tehran: Amir Kabir Publishing, 1968.

———. پس از بحران: خاطرات هاشمی رفسنجانی سال ۱۳۶۱ (*After the Crisis: Memoirs of Hashemi Rafsanjani 1982*). Edited by Fatemeh-e Hashemi. Tehran: Daftar-e Nashr-e Ma'aref-e Eslami, 2001.

———. پایان دفاع، آغاز بازسازی: خاطرات هاشمی رفسنجانی، سال ۱۳۶۷ (*End of Defense, Start of Reconstruction: Memoirs of Hashemi Rafsanjani, Year 1988*). Edited by Ali Reza Hashemi. Tehran: Daftar Nashr-e Ma'aref-e Enqelab, 2011.

———. سازندگی و شکوفایی، کارنامه وخاطرات، ۱۳۷۰ (*Development and Rejuvenation, Record and Memoirs, 1992*). Edited by Emad Hashemi. Tehran: Daftar-e Nashr-e Ma'aref-e Enqelab, 2022.

———. هاشمی رفسنجانی: دوران مبارزه: خاطرات، تصویرها، گاه شمار (*Hashemi Rafsanjani: Years of Struggle: Memories, Images, Chronology of Events*). 2 vols. Tehran: Daftar-e Nashr-e Ma'aref-e Enqelab, 1997.

———. اوج دفاع: خاطرات هاشمی رفسنجانی سال ۱۳۶۵ (*Height of Defense: Memoirs of Hashemi Rafsanjani, Year 1986*). Edited by Emad Hashemi. Tehran: Daftar-e Nashr-e Ma'aref-e Enqelab, 2009.

———. امید ودلواپسی؛ کارنامه وخاطرات هاشمی رفسنجانی سال ۱۳۶۴ (*Hope and Worry: The Record and Recollections of Hashemi Rafsanjani, Year 1985*). Edited by Sara Lahouti. Tehran: Daftar-e Nashr-e Ma'aref-e Eslami, 2008.

————. "انقلاب اسلامی در دهه سوم." ("Islamic Revolution in the Third Decade"). *Ketab-e Naqd Quarterly* 22 (Spring 2003): 8–15.

————. اعتدال وپیروزی: کارنامه وخاطرات هاشمی رفسنجانی، ۱۳۶۹ (*Moderation and Victory: Memoirs and Record of Hashemi Rafsanjani, 1991*). Edited by Emad Hashemi Bahremani. Tehran: Daftar-e Nashr-e Ma'aref-e Enqelab, 2013.

————. صبر وپیروزی، خاطرات و کارنامه ۱۳۷۴ (*Patience and Victory, Memoirs and Record, 1995*). Edited by Emad Hashemi. Tehran: Ma'aref-e Enqelab, 2018.

————. بازسازی و سازندگی، کارنامه وخاطرات ۱۳۶۸ (*Reconstruction and Development, Record and Memoirs, 1990*). Edited by Ali Lahouti. Tehran: Daftar-e Nashr-e Ma'aref-e Enqelab-e Eslami, 2012.

————. انقلاب و پیروزی: کارنامه وخاطرات ۱۳۵۷-۱۳۵۸ (*Revolution and Victory, Record and Memoirs, 1979–1980*). Edited by Abbas Bashiri. Tehran: Daftar-e Nashr-e Manabe-e Enqelab, 2004.

————. آرامش و چالش: خاطرات هاشمی ۱۳۶۲ (*Stability and Struggle: Hashemi's Memoirs, 1984*). Edited by Mehdi Hashemi. Tehran: Nashr-e Ma'aref-e Enqelab, 2003.

————. به سوی سرنشت؛ کارنامه و خاطرات هاشمی، سال ۱۳۶۲. (*Towards Destiny: The Record and Memoirs of Hashemi, Year 1984*). Edited by Mohsen Hashemi. Tehran: Daftar Nashr-e Ma'aref Enqelab, 2006).

————. انتقال قدرت، کارنامه و خاطرات ۱۳۷۶ (*Transfer of Power, Record and Memoir*). Edited by Mohsen Hashemi Rafsanjani. Tehran: Ma'aref Enqelab, 2020.

————. رونق سازندگی، خاطرات و کارنامه، ۱۳۷۱ (*Vitality of Development, Memoir and Record, 1993*). Edited by Hasan Lahouti. Tehran: Ma'aref-e Enqelab, 2023.

Rahim-Safavi, Seyyed Yahya, از جنوب لبنان تا جنوب ایران (*From South Lebanon to South Iran*). Tehran: Markaz Asnad Enqelab, 2009.

Rezaie, Mohsen. بررسی عملیات الفجر در هشت گفتگو با راویان جنگ تحمیلی، مرداد ۱۳۶۵ (*Analysis of Al-Fajr Operation in Eight Conversations with Narrators of Imposed War, August 1986*). Tehran: Markaz Asnad va Tahqiqat-e Defa'e Moqaddas, 2011.

Rouhani, Hasan. امنیت ملی و دیپلماسی هسته ای (*National Security and Nuclear Diplomacy*). Tehran: Markaz Tahqiqat-e Estratejik, 2012.

————. امنیت ملی و نظام اقتصادی (*National Security and the Economic System*). Tehran: Markaz-e Tahqiqat-e Estratejic, 2012.

Rouzitalab, Mohammad Hasan. رعد در آسمان بی ابر: تاریخ شفاهی مبارزه امنیتی با سازمان مجاهدین خلق (۱۳۵۷-۱۳۶۷) (*Thunder in a Cloudless Sky: Oral History of Security Struggle with Mojahedin-e Khalq [1979–1989]*). Tehran: Nashr-e Iran, 2022.

Saleminejad, Abdolreza. دزفول: پایتخت مقاومت ایران (*Dezful: The Capital of Iran's Resistance*). Tehran: Niloufaran, 2014.

برنامه ۲۵ ساله همکاری های تهران و پکن و چشم انداز مناسبات ایران و چین در دو دهه آینده (*The Twenty-Five-Year Plan for Iran-China Cooperation and the Outlook for Relations between Iran and China in the Next Two Decades*). Tehran: Majma'-e Beinolmellali Asatid Mosalman Daneshgah-ha, 2020.

بیست و دومین گزارش سه ماهه اجرای برنامه جامع اقدام مشترک (برجام) به مجلس شورای اسلامی ("Twenty-Second Report on the Status of the JCPOA to the Islamic Assembly"). Report 6428627, July 14, 2021. https://mfa.gov.ir/files/mfa/PDF/210711-MJZ-22nd%20Majlis%20Report-Full%20CD.pdf.

Velayati, Ali Akbar. تاریخ سیاسی جنگ تحمیلی (*Political History of Iraq's Imposed War on Iran*). Tehran: Daftar Nashr-e Farhang Eslami, 1997.

"چشم انداز جمهوری اسلامی در افق ۱۴۰۴" ("*The Vision for Islamic Republic of Iran in the Horizon of 2025*"). *Khamenei.ir*, February 27, 2004. https://farsi.khamenei.ir/message-content?id=9034.

صحیفه امام: مجموعه آثار امام خمینی (*The Writ of the Imam: Collection of Imam Khomeini's Works*). Tehran: Markaz Tanzim va Nashr-e Asar Imam Khomeini, 2000.

خاطرات اردشیر زاهدی (*Ardeshir Zahedi's Memoirs*). 2 vols. Bethesda, MD: Ibex Publishers, 2006.

Zarif, Mohammad Javad. پایاب شکیبایی: برداشتهای هشت سال وزارت (*Enduring Patience: Takeaways from Eight Years of Ministry*). Tehran: Etela'at, 2024.

Zarif, Mohammad Javad, Ali Akbar Salehi, Seyyed Abbas Araghchi, and Majid Takht Ravanchi. راز سر به مهر (*Sealed Secret*). 6 vols. Tehran: Entesharat Etelaat, 2021.

INDEX

Page numbers in *italics* denote maps.